DATE DUE

NEGOTIATING AT THE MARGINS

NEGOTIATING AT THE MARGINS

The Gendered Discourses of Power and Resistance

Edited by Sue Fisher
and Kathy Davis

RUTGERS UNIVERSITY PRESS
New Brunswick, New Jersey

Library of Congress Cataloging-in-Publication Data

Fisher, Sue, 1936–
    Negotiating at the margins : the gendered discourses of power and
resistance / Sue Fisher, Kathy Davis.
        p.   cm.
    Includes bibliographical references.
    ISBN 0-8135-1970-5 (cloth) — ISBN 0-8135-1971-3 (pbk)
    1. Feminisim. 2. Power (Social sciences) 3. Passive resistance.
4. Control (Psychology)   I. Davis, Kathy.   II. Title.
HQ1154.F56   1993
303.3—dc20
                                                        92-35965
                                                        CIP

British Cataloging-in-Publication information available

CONTENTS

NEGOTIATING THROUGH CULTURAL DISCOURSES

ACKNOWLEDGMENTS

Our thanks and appreciation go to the many colleagues and students with whom we have discussed the issues of power and resistance during the past decade. We especially thank Mary Ann Clawson, Willem de Haan, and Joe Rouse as well as two anonymous reviewers for their thoughtful and constructive comments on the introduction and the overall organization of the book.

The book was made possible in part by the Pew Trust Funds of Wesleyan University and the Anna Maria van Schuurman Center, Graduate School for Advanced Research in Women's Studies of the University of Utrecht, which enabled us to work together "in person" for several months.

Last but not least, we thank one another for the enjoyable and productive experience of working together on this book. Several chapters have been previously published as journal articles. We thank the appropriate journals for permission to reprint the material.

Susan Bordo's "'Material Girl': The Effacements of Postmodern Culture" appeared in *Michigan Quarterly Review* (Fall 1990):653–677.

Kathy Davis's "Cultural Dopes and She-Devils: Cosmetic Surgery as Ideological Dilemma" is an expanded version of "Remaking the She-Devil: A Critical Look at Feminist Approaches to Beauty," which appeared in *Hypatia* 6(Summer 1991):21–43.

Sue Fisher's "Gender, Power, and Resistance: Is Care the Remedy?" is a revised version of "A Discourse of the Social: Medical Talk/Power Talk\Oppositional Talk?" which appeared in *Discourse and Society* 2(April 1991):157–182.

INTRODUCTION

POWER AND THE
FEMALE SUBJECT

Kathy Davis and Sue Fisher

This book takes shape against the backdrop of a venerable tradition of feminist scholarship concerning how power and resistance work in everyday life. As categories of analysis, power, resistance, and women's everyday experiences were introduced by feminist scholars in an attempt to understand women's subordination. Although each category has been central to exploring women's social practices and locating them in a gendered social order, their use has not gone uncontested.

The notion that women's everyday lives provide a site for understanding their subordination has raised questions about the generalizability of women's lived experiences. Both the ways these experiences are generated as well as the similarities and differences in women's everyday lives have become topics for feminist analysis. Similarly the longstanding assumption in feminist scholarship that a relationship exists between power and resistance has raised questions about how we simultaneously can hold onto the view that women construct their own lives *and* that they do so within determinant conditions.

These questions have been both dilemmatic and difficult to investigate. If the analytic starting place is the relationship between structured forms of constraint and women's agency, how do we investigate the ways women's activities are limited through asymmetrical power structures and at the same time treat women as active and knowledgeable participants in the constitution of social life? Or conversely, how do we focus on women's resistance without losing sight of the structural constraints that make it difficult for them to resist at all?

Although as feminist scholars we do not want to be forced into choosing between analyses that focus on structure to the exclusion of agency or agency to the exclusion of structure, in practice this is an all too common result. On the one hand, if we focus on asymmetrical social structures, we tend to lose sight of how women produce and reproduce but also resist and undermine these structures. We then run the risk of treating women as if they are passive victims of repressive systems. On the other hand, if we focus on women's agency, we often fail to locate this agency within a social and/or political context. Here if women resist but are not successful, we run the risk of blaming the victim—of attributing responsibility to women for conditions over which they often have little control.

This dilemma is at the heart of the work we both do. We each deal with it differently, however, and these differences are the source of an ongoing discussion between us. These conversations have not been easy and on occasion even frustrating, but they have always been challenging and inevitably fruitful. It is this debate about how to conceptualize and investigate power and resistance in women's everyday social practices which provides the theme of this collection—a theme that has its roots in the history of feminist scholarship.

CONTEMPORARY FEMINIST SCHOLARSHIP

Although power and resistance have been central concerns within contemporary feminist scholarship, they have not always been discussed explicitly. In the early days of second-wave feminism, the relationship between the sexes was discussed as if it was abundantly clear that gender made a difference. Men and women were socialized differently and had different educational and occupational opportunities. Men were socialized into rational and assertive roles; women into roles that were emotional and passive. These differences provided the explanation for the myriad distributive injustices found in both the home and the workplace. Consciousness-raising made these inequities visible, ultimately transforming the idiosyncratic problems of individual women into that shared and by now infamous "problem with no name" (Friedan 1963). The hope was that with political consciousness and group solidarity, women would become active players in plurality politics and thereby have an impact on the legislative process. Emancipation was finally just around the corner, or so many of us thought.

Some who came to feminism with a Marxist background readily thought in terms of male domination and female subordination, but for others the transition was not quite so obvious. However, it was not long before the "problem with no name" was more generally recast in explicitly political terms. In the struggle between the sexes, power became the name and sexual politics the game—and a very serious game it was. As Kate Millett (1970:24) noted in her plea for a more radical approach toward understanding women's social situation,

> It is opportune, perhaps today even mandatory, that we develop a more relevant psychology and philosophy of power relationships beyond the simple conceptual framework provided by our traditional formal politics. Indeed, it may be imperative that we give some attention to defining a theory of politics which treats power relationships on grounds less conventional than those to which we are accustomed.

Thus from the earliest days of second-wave feminism onward, one of our recurrent struggles has been about the centrality of power in our analyses of relations between the sexes. Explanations of sexual difference from a sex-roles perspective had a biological intonation that was hopelessly inadequate. In order to come to terms with women's subordinate position, we have had to recast gender in terms of power. This emphasis shifts our understanding of sexual difference from biology and socialization to include social, cultural, and psychological dimensions. Gender becomes a cultural given, which organizes all levels of social life and, using the language of power, converts men and women into the dominant and the subordinate.

Although the concepts of gender and power offer an idiom for talking about relations between the sexes, the move from sex roles to sexual politics also brings to center stage a problem that has occupied feminist theory for more than two decades: how to understand male domination and female subordination. This problem contains a call to search for origins and, ultimately, explanations of women's subordinate position—a search that takes several different theoretical paths (see Tong 1989).

On the one hand, Marxist feminists look to the emergence of capitalism in the Western world for the roots of gender inequality (Hartsock 1983a, 1983b; Rubin 1975; Mitchell 1966, 1971). Their explanations locate women's oppression in their exclusion from wage labor. Women, by virtue of this exclusion, are subjected to a special form of oppression. In the division of labor, they are relegated to the private, domestic sphere and are materially dependent on husbands or fathers.

On the other hand, radical feminists identify patriarchy as the source of the problem. Whether in the private or public sphere, women are the victims of male supremacy (MacKinnon 1982; Daly 1978). Individual men have control over women, their bodies, their labor, their children, and their lives—control that is upheld collectively by the male sex (Brown 1981).

In an attempt to bridge the gap between radical and Marxist feminists, socialist feminists combine both origin stories into one explanation (Jaggar 1983; Sargent 1981; Eisenstein 1979). Patriarchy and capitalism are wed in a theoretical attempt to provide a more comprehensive account of female subordination and male domination (Hartmann 1981). Although ultimately this is an unhappy marriage, it marks the culmination of a long line of theorizing.[1]

Although these perspectives do not exclude the theoretical possibility of resistance, all too frequently their primary focus is on the ways power oppresses. These attempts to theorize women's subordination by posing capitalism and patriarchy as origin and explanation have since come under criticism (Rosaldo 1980). Albeit unintentionally, they run the risk of victimizing women by representing them as the passive objects of monolithic systems of oppression. From this perspective, women are presented as the victims of either economic domination, patriarchal oppression, or a combination of both. This presentation leaves little conceptual or political space for uncovering the subtle and ambivalent ways women may be negotiating at the margins of power, sometimes constrained by but also resisting and even undermining asymmetrical power structures.

At this point postmodern feminists enter the debate. They take the assumptions of their predecessors' analyses to task (Haraway 1991; Butler 1989; Riley 1988; Scott 1988). At the heart of their argument is rejection of the possibility that there exists only one feminist story replete with origin and explanation for women's subordinate social position. To sustain an origin story requires an epistemological stance that is becoming increasingly suspect. It presupposes an objective reality and an independent observer with privileged access to The Real and The True. Gender is treated as a self-explanatory and universalistic category of analysis, and women are essentialized in the process. This position rests on the notion that power moves in one direction, from the top to the bottom, dividing society into discrete social groups—those who by virtue of their location have power and those who do not.

While postmodern feminists work out these ideas in predictably diverse ways, their core assumptions are similar. There is general agreement that the philosophical tradition in which the Real is understood to be "an external or universal subject or substance, existing 'out there' independent of the knower" (Flax 1990:34) and in which Truth is understood to correspond directly to it has to be rejected out of hand. The position of the knower and the status of reality and truth are redefined, and in the process their foundational underpinnings are weakened.[2] Both empiricist and standpoint feminism fall under this critique (Harding 1986). Gone is the privileged knower—the feminist theorist who by virtue of her material position or lived experience as a woman has a "better" view of reality, scientifically or morally. Both the theorist and her object of knowledge are reconceptualized as historically and culturally variable, as firmly situated within and helping to construct the context of inquiry itself. The truth can thus be little more than a discursive effect produced through local, heterogeneous, and contextual cultural discourses.

Although in earlier feminisms gender is taken for granted as an unproblematic category of analysis, postmodern feminists argue that this leaves Woman as an essential identity untouched (Butler 1989; Riley 1988; Scott 1988). They invite the deconstruction of the category woman, claiming that while earlier formulations construct their interpretations differently, they share a reliance on universal explanations— explanations that obscure differences among women and similarities between women and men. Postmodern feminists generally agree that the call for sisterhood rests on the foundation of a shared system of sexual difference and therefore relies on the assumption that the categories men and women are coherent (Scott 1988). This coherence obliterates the specific historical conditions of the production and reproduction of the binary opposition—man/woman. In so doing, cross-cultural antagonisms between men and women are eclipsed and heterosexual coherence along with feminist racism are reproduced and recirculated (Butler 1989). They argue that woman is not an already fully constituted category, a homogeneous group to be dragged through the transformations of history (Riley 1988). Like all other categories, woman is a fictive device—a device that is socially, historically, and discursively constructed in relationship to other categories (i.e., women/men, white women/black women). Despite their apparent link to the natural, these categories and their positions in relationship to one another are both constructed and given meaning through repeated discursive practices. By refusing master theories of gender, we can see the category woman in all its alterity and difference. Feminist scholars can, then, direct their attention to the ways femininity is negotiated in the various contexts of everyday life.[3]

In a similar vein, postmodern feminists undertake a reconceptualization of power. Following Foucault, they argue that power cannot be treated as essentially repressive or prohibitive (cf. Fraser 1989). It does not emanate in the state or from the economic and political elite. Nor is power imposed in a top-down fashion from the structures of capitalist-patriarchal domination only to emerge as the oppression women experience in their everyday lives. Power does not rely on violence and suppression for its enforcement, but must, instead, be recast as continuous, subtle, and productive. It creates possibilities for knowledge in and through the production of discourses. Thus modern power operates continuously in a subtle but penetrating manner. It is a "capillary" circulating through the social body and exerting its authority through self-surveillance and everyday, disciplinary micropractices—practices more fundamental than beliefs (ideology). These practices insinuate themselves within gestures, habits, bodies, and desires. Power exercised in this way seems to be everywhere and nowhere. It depends for its very existence on the multiplicity of points of resistance. With power dispersed in this way, resistance cannot be reduced to a single locus of rebellion or revolt.

Part of the appeal of postmodernism is that it offers a powerful way to critique and discredit the essentializing tendencies of radical feminism, where women are seen as universally oppressed by men as men and universally privileged by a kind of biological or spiritual superiority. Similarly, it provides a more powerful way to understand differences among women and between men and women than is possible within the frameworks of Marxist or socialist feminism. Finally, postmodernism proposes a remedy for what has become a disheartening project for many. As long as women's subordination is viewed as the result of systemic forms of repression, that is, capitalism and patriarchy, the only solution is a massive collective movement and a total overhaul of these systems. If this political project seems overwhelming, the more modest course of political action suggested by the postmodern focus on knowledge and power—on how power is discursively constructed and how politics are about contestations over meaning—seems appealing.[4]

This very appeal, however, becomes another source of contestation. Despite Foucault's (1980b) claim that where there is power, resistance is soon to follow, it is not always easy to target points of resistance. As Nancy Hartsock (1990) points out, resistance often seems to disappear in postmodern analyses of power into a welter of disorganized and fragmentary counterdiscourses. For many feminist scholars, the focus on discourse and counterdiscourse provides little hope for an effective feminist politics (see Hartsock 1990). Moreover, without a feminist subject with some shared collective interests, it is difficult to envision social transformations.

These theoretical debates about the most appropriate way to understand domination and subordination, power and resistance, are at the very heart of the dilemma we are taking as the topic of this collection.

THE DILEMMA: GENDERED STRUCTURES AND WOMEN'S AGENCY

Each position in our theoretical debates takes a very different stand on the nature of power and resistance as well as on the meaning of gender and the character of women's agency. Taken together, they seem to offer little possibility for a productive dialogue about the relationship between structured forms of constraint and women's agency.

On the one hand, some theories accept gender as an unproblematic category of analysis and portray power as emanating predominately from above—from the state, patriarchy, the economy, or hegemonic ideologies. They focus primarily on the cause of women's subordination.[5] From this perspective, all women suffer from forces which are taken in advance as the root of the problem. The oppressive features of power are the analytical focus, and thus the agenda for feminist struggle is well established. The theory provides the normative criteria for social change along feminist lines. Feminist research involves looking for instances of women's oppression as well as exploring how women actually engage, either individually or collectively, against the joint forces of patriarchal violence and capitalist exploitation.

The postmodern perspective, on the other hand, turns the story around. Since modern power is everywhere and nowhere, operating at the lowest level of the social body and through the most minute social practices, it makes little sense to talk the language of liberation, that is, to talk about freeing women from the capitalistic and patriarchal chains that bind them. Given the centrality of micropractices rather than ideology to understanding the workings of power, it also makes little sense to talk about finding ways to reverse the effects of false consciousness by demystifying distorted ideological beliefs. By linking power to knowledge and arguing that it circulates in and through the production of discourses, the focus shifts from the repressive to the productive features of power. Power produces all social categories, including women, constituting them as both objects and subjects of knowledge.

The origin story—one single explanation for the oppression of all women—undergoes an epistemological shift to interpreting how difference and sameness are produced in discourses of femininity. Analytically, the focus is on how to connect power to the production of femininities,

9

and the agenda for feminist struggle is different. Postmodern feminist theory provides a view of reality as historically contingent and culturally variable. Feminist research now involves interpreting how power/knowledge/resistance work in the local, heterogenous context of discursive production.

Power and resistance are integral to both traditions in feminist theory. The first yields a convincing picture of how power oppresses women, showing how gender inequality is produced in various social contexts. However, while resistance is called for, an unintended consequence of this focus on the magnitude of the power and the activities of the powerful ironically tends to obscure differences and renders women powerless and their resistance invisible. The second tradition relocates power. Here the inadequacies of top-down, repressive analyses of power are pointed out and what counts as political is redefined, thereby opening up multiple sites for resistance. From this perspective, it is possible to investigate how power and resistance work in even the most routine micropractices—micropractices described as political. Women continue to reproduce, but they also confront and discursively penetrate the practices of which they are a part. Although this focus on what Nancy Fraser (1989) calls a "politics of everyday life" offers advantages for feminist analysis, it also presents some serious limitations.

As Stuart Hall (1986) points out, without a structural conception of society it is impossible to assess how strong the power is, the extent of the resistance, or the changing balance between them. In addition, without a normative standard, there is no way to take a position, to justify a feminist course of action (Fraser 1989). Moreover, if men and women are discursive constructions, the focus is not on what they are actually doing but rather on how masculinity and femininity are produced and function within a system of signs. Interaction disappears, absorbed in a symbolic order which determines the form in which our thoughts may be expressed. Although resistance is an ever-present possibility, this perspective leaves us without a way to theorize women's agency other than discursively. And finally, there is a real danger that postmodern feminism's attempts to decenter the female subject may have silenced the voices of women who had only just begun to see themselves as political subjects (Hartsock 1990). By focusing on the discursive micropractices of power, we may lose sight of the necessity for a collective feminist struggle against women's persistent location at the margins of power—their subordination and exclusion.

Although these traditions of feminist thought may seem hopelessly at odds, many feminist scholars, relying on different theoretical vantage

10

points, are attempting to bridge the gap. On the one hand, this means maintaining a commitment to structural constraint while highlighting the ways women actually, if not always successfully, resist. To this end, theories as diverse as those of Marx and, more recently, Giddens (1984), Bourdieu (1977), and Habermas (1984, 1987) are drawn upon. On the other hand, this means maintaining a commitment to discursive production as locus of cultural control, while emphasizing the ways discourses intersect with women's concrete material lives and become a site of struggle. The theories of Foucault (1980a, 1980b) and Derrida (1981) are helpful for this project.

Attempts to bridge these theoretical gaps are, at the same time, attempts to reintegrate feminist politics and feminist epistemology. The first steps toward this reintegration were taken from a firm location in one camp or another. As the rethinking of this relationship matures, the emphasis shifts.

RETHINKING FEMINIST POLITICS AND EPISTEMOLOGY

In an early paper, Biddy Martin (1982) documents a kind of analytic symmetry between postmodern and feminist thinking. However, she also warns that the notion that discourse provides a total understanding of how individual and collective differences are constructed, how hierarchy and inequality are produced as discursive effects constructed in particular contexts and through a range of available discourses, leaves an important issue unaddressed. This formulation does not question the structure of the communicative relationship or how it operates as an instrument for the exercise of power.

While Martin both sees the appeal of postmodern theories and issues a warning about their limitations, she does not attempt to reformulate the relationship between feminist politics and feminist epistemology. Sandra Harding (1986) does. She suggests that we learn to live with and theorize tensions and contradictions in feminist theories. In *The Science Question in Feminism* she applauds both feminist empiricist and feminist standpoint traditions, claiming that each successfully undermines the masculinist biases of science. In addition, she embraces the postmodern stand against totalizing theories, including feminist ones, while at the same time arguing that we need both totalizing and partial theories, critical theories and epistemological critiques. Although she recognizes the inherent contradictions involved in this undertaking, still she urges femi-

11

nists to synthesize what we already know and learn to live creatively with tensions.

Nancy Fraser (1989) approaches the relationship between politics and epistemology in a somewhat different way. In a series of essays in which she conducts a critical and constructive feminist rereading of several notable thinkers in avant-garde social theory—Foucault, Derrida, Habemas and Rorty—she makes a convincing case for joining feminist politics with contemporary epistemological critiques. She argues, that "you can't get a politics straight out of epistemology, even when the epistemology is a radical anti-epistemology like historicism, pragmatism or deconstruction." Yet she advocates redefining feminist politics to include struggle over cultural meanings and social identities, that is, the struggle to construct "authoritative definitions of social situations and legitimate interpretations of social needs" (Fraser 1989:6). She encourages us to take up a position "in between"—between the feminist movement and professional discourses (including, parenthetically, those of academia). As critical intellectuals, our task becomes creating bridges between these discourses, thereby—as she hopes—opening up new arenas for struggle.

In our opinion, it is this struggle to join feminist politics with a radical rethinking of its epistemological foundations that is at the forefront of contemporary feminist scholarship. A dual approach to feminist theory as represented by Harding and Fraser shares a normative commitment to transform gender asymmetries. At the same time, these theories are oriented toward exploring and deconstructing the discursive character of both social life and social identities, including what constitutes "the political." From this perspective some feminist scholars embrace tensions as something to explore rather than avoid in the name of theoretical or political purity (cf. Code 1991; Flax 1990; Hirsch and Keller 1990; Nicholson 1990; Young 1990; Jaggar and Bordo 1986). Although much of this discussion has been carried out at the theoretical level, there have also been attempts to link this theoretical enterprise to the analysis of the gendered micropractices of everyday life (Fisher 1991; Bordo 1988; Davis 1988; Gordon 1988; Probyn 1987; Wilson 1985). It is in this struggle to rethink the relationship between politics and episteomology that the present volume is situated.

NEGOTIATING AT THE MARGINS

Taking the dual approach to feminist theory as our starting point, we have collected essays aimed at the empirical exploration of the tensions between structured forms of constraint and women's agency. While the essays draw on a variety of theoretical standpoints and use an array of methodological strategies, discourse, defined broadly, provides a central theme in each analysis. In each essay close attention is paid to the discursive micropractices though which power and resistance are negotiated by women who are all too frequently situated at the margins of the social and symbolic orders. These margins provide fertile sites for feminist theorizing as well as for delineating women's power practices. It is here that women routinely engage in struggles ranging from the most mundane to the most heroic.

Not coincidently the book begins and ends with the subject of women's bodies and the discourses of feminine beauty. These essays set the theoretical parameters of the collection as a whole. From Kathy Davis's call for reinstating women as agents who knowledgeably negotiate their bodies within the limitations and possibilities of their lives to Susan Bordo's timely warning that even women's most heartfelt "choices" are caught up in intersecting and repressive discourses of feminine inferiority, the margins for women's power practices are established. The remaining essays move within these boundaries. Some focus more on the cultural and structural constraints of femininity and others on women's agency and potential for resistance. However, each essay addresses the ways women negotiate at but also within the margins of power.

The collection is organized into three sections. In the first, the authors address the body and its adornments. The authors in the second section focus on the ways in which structural tensions are made visible and mediated in local sites. Cultural discourses are the topic of the third section. Here the authors use popular culture as the location from which to explore the negotiation of conflicting and contested gendered discourses.

Each section provides a crosscut of methodological, theoretical, and substantive concerns within the theoretical line set out by the collection as a whole. The book is arranged so it can be used in different ways by different readers. Essays can be grouped together or contrasted in terms of their location, the methodologies used for analyzing discourse, or their theoretical stance concerning power and resistance. Our arrangement reflects the current state of the art in feminist theory, which more than ever before is oriented toward opening up discussion rather than shoring up divisions.

In part one, "Negotiating the Body and Its Adornments," the body provides a rich analytic text through which power struggles can be explored. In the first article, Kathy Davis takes the body as a site at which culture inscribes gendered discourses and women resist them. She argues that while there is both a beauty industry and dominant discourses about female beauty, women are not passive victims of hegemonic systems. In her study, women provide accounts of why they "chose" to have their body or some part of it remade surgically. In and through these accounts women construct themselves as rational and their choices as reasonable under the circumstances. In so doing, they actively negotiate the boundaries of normalcy and present their decisions as a matter of justice, a social opportunity to right a biological wrong.

Elizabeth Wilson takes fashion as a discourse, showing how lesbians construct their sexual identity through clothing. Appearance becomes the site for the creation of gendered sexual identities which do not correspond to and therefore resist cultural notions of masculinity and femininity. By actively transgressing sartorial codes for gender-appropriate dress, both lesbians and gay men often succeed in "messing up" prevailing gender identities and playfully opening up new spaces for themselves on the margins of prevailing gender norms. Wilson discusses the possibilities fashion can offer for rebellion, for resisting prevailing hegemonic assumptions, while at the same time she takes into account how such resistance may be defused into mere style, producing assimilation rather than subversion.

In her essay, Linda Boynton Arthur shows, once again, how clothing can function as a discourse—in this case providing a way to exercise control over women as well as a way for women to undermine the male-defined constraints of their community. Her analysis is focused on the Mennonite community, where female dress conventions are so tightly controlled by the church fathers that the smallest infraction can lead to expulsion. Nevertheless, the women manage, usually with each others' aid and abettance, to negotiate the boundaries of appropriate dress, resisting patriarchal control. Functioning in their social groups—age-sets—they both reinforce the dress code and resist it. In either case they wrest power away from the men whose task it is to supervise the maintenance of the symbolic order.

Part two, "Negotiating Discourses at Local Sites," explores the ways the gendered discourses of power and resistance work in institutional contexts. Each author addresses how specific institutions—health care, social work, the legal system, education, and housing—provide a site for negotiating conflicting discourses. While the institutions and the historical periods discussed vary, these essays all focus on how institutions and dominant discourses intersect with the situated practices of women.

Sue Fisher takes nurse practitioners' relatively recent emergence as medical professionals as a site for investigating the production of gendered discourses, identities, and professional statuses. Drawing on a Foucauldian perspective, she provides an in-depth analysis of the discursive practices of both male physicians and female nurse practitioners. She argues that while doctors persistently recirculate both their professional authority and hegemonic assumptions about women, work, and the nuclear family, nurse practitioners do not. They reproduce and undermine their medical authority while primarily circulating an alternative discourse of femininity. In so doing, they open up for their patients the possibility of exploring the oppressive contingencies of their lives.

Linda Gordon examines how family violence is constructed as a social problem in the dossiers of Boston social service agencies at the end of the nineteenth century. Starting from a critique of theories of social control, she defines gender as a power system in which women are subordinated through relations that are contradictory, ambiguous, and conflictual. In the face of this system, women make choices and take action, displaying remarkable perseverance, courage, and inventiveness. Although their tactics generally failed, they nevertheless demanded and sometimes got help from agencies. Moreover, in providing narratives about domestic violence, they encouraged the identification of new problems. Gordon clearly dispels the notion that women, however poor and oppressed, are best viewed as victims. Instead she suggests an approach that places women's agency at the forefront of any historical analysis of patriarchal forms of social control.

In her analysis of criminal stories in fin-de-siècle Paris, Ann-Louise Shapiro shows how female criminals draw upon the prevailing cultural discourses on gender and deviancy, while at the same time turning them around to their own advantage. She analyzes these acts of resistance in a broader context of social upheaval, where traditional notions of dependent femininity and fallen womanhood were making room for more egalitarian notions of the free but potentially unruly female. The context of nineteenth-century pretrial investigations and courtroom hearings provides a site at which female defendants and their accusers negotiated both the possibility for and the limits of resistance. In so doing, they managed to create some degree of freedom within the gendered margins of normative expectations and culturally prevalent explanations for feminine conduct.

When in the early 1980s a union of technical and clerical workers went on strike against Yale University, some of the clerical workers joined the strike and others did not. Nina Gregg investigates how female clerical workers justified their decision to join or not join the strikers. Placing the

15

decision to support the union or remain loyal to the university in the context of multiple identities—identities based in class, race, and gender—she shows how both decisions were reasonable. The issues of power and resistance get played off against women's lived experiences and their complex subject positions. Whatever the outcome, the process entails a "rational" weighing of alternatives and negotiating between the Scylla of identity politics and the Charybdis of contested loyalties.

While Rob Rosenthal acknowledges the major structural influences that contributed to the explosion in the numbers of homeless people in recent years, he does not present these people as passive victims of structural forces. Instead he focuses on the ways individuals cope. He demonstrates how homeless women, a subpopulation of the "Skidders," struggle to make a life for themselves and their children. Taking advantage of the discourses of gender and motherhood, these Skidders manage to build up their own social support networks. Using their accounts as a starting point, he shows how gender contributes to both their homelessness and the ways they resist.

"Negotiating through Cultural Discourse" is the topic of the last section. Rather than presupposing a monolithic symbolic order, each of the essays treats dominant discourses as multilayered, complex, and contested. As such they are subject to continual disruptions that open up possibilities for not only insidious forms of control but equally insidious forms of resistance.

In the context of dominant discourses that inscribe different gendered realities for boys and girls, Mary Ann Clawson shows how young women construct a place for themselves in a male-gendered activity. Using interviews with two women vocalists in college rock bands, she argues that each draws on different gender discourses to negotiate a space for herself, to authorize herself as a musician in the male-dominated world of rock-and-roll bands.

Norma Claire Moruzzi's essay looks at how the social construction of both the body and the feminine functions as discourses which constrain and offer possibilities for women in their struggle as gendered subjects and political beings. Taking the film *The Battle of Algiers* as a focus for her analysis, she discusses the women guerrillas of the Algerian Revolution who resisted French authority by removing their veils in order to pass through military checkpoints without being searched for bombs. Moruzzi explores how cultural meanings attached to the veil are strategically subverted and a different gendered subject is produced when women (literally) disguise themselves as women in order to engage in radical political actions. Whereas the veil enables symbolic action (as symbol of Arab femininity and the Algerian national resistance), the strategic removal of the veil allows a woman agency. She becomes a political subject, a revolutionary, actively fighting against those in power.

Taking the cultural discourses of new traditionalism and postfeminism as a starting point, Elspeth Probyn shows how they converge in contemporary television programs around the issue of choice. She explores how choices are negotiated in the arena of prime time, paying particular attention to how cultural discourses of women's choices are recirculated in the gendered images of women choosing the security of love, children, and heterosexual marriage. Cultural choices also open up the possibility for resistance. This notion is demonstrated by analyzing the infamous kiss between two female protagonists in the television series *L.A. Law*.

The issue of choice is picked up again in the final essay as Susan Bordo tackles gender, race, and the problem of plasticity in postmodern culture. She critically explores some of the contemporary images in which women can remake themselves, moving from the "scalpel slaves" who seek cosmetic surgery to Madonna as the postmodern feminist heroine who is purportedly "in control of her image, not trapped by it." Bordo warns us to remember the limits of agency, keeping in mind that it remains embedded in a nexus of normalizing power and the social realities of domination and subordination.

These essays share both a detailed examination of discourse and a commitment to the notion that women's location at the margins of the structural and symbolic orders provides an ideal site from which to explore the relationship between structured forms of constraint and women's agency. In each essay, close attention is paid to the ways power and resistance are negotiated. From this common base, each of the articles addresses a struggle over contested meanings and social identities and does so differently. Some authors demonstrate women's agency against the backdrop of explicit structural constraints. Structure/agency, power/resistance, and gender are discussed in terms of women's lived social practices and the concrete, material contingencies of their lives. Other authors, by contrast, emphasize interpretation—the realm of the symbolic. Power/knowledge/resistance and gender are presented as tied to the ways femininity is produced or reproduced in the historically contingent and culturally variable symbolic practices of women. Some essays cross theoretical boundaries as they move between structural and cultural definitions of power and control.

As a group these essays show us how power and resistance can be analyzed in ways that account for both structural and cultural forms of domination while, at the same time, taking women's agency seriously. In so doing they provide a convincing case for how the dilemmas in feminist theory—dilemmas between structure and agency, power and resistance, for example—can be put to productive use. It is our hope that these essays contribute to the ongoing development of feminist theorizing which embraces rather than avoids dilemmas and tensions as a welcome opportunity for further inquiry.

NOTES

1. The exclusion of major branches of feminist theory, the psychoanalytic, for example, is intentional. They are not immediately and directly related to the story we are in the process of telling.

2. Some postmodern feminists are moving away from an unsituated and unreflexive epistemological position to one that is partially situated. See Harding's (1991) discussion of "strong objectivity" and Haraway's (1988) discussion of "situated knowledges."

3. It is this position that provides a point of contact between some postmodern feminists and feminists working in other traditions. The focus on how femininity is negotiated in the context of everyday life and at the level of micropractices provides a foundation for a continued commitment to political engagement (cf. Fraser and Nicholson 1990).

4. This paragraph is informed by the thoughtful comments provided by Mary Ann Clawson.

5. Marxist theory does contain a notion of power that is relational and the theoretical underpinnings for an analysis of domination and resistance. To paraphrase Marx, people make their own history, but not always as they wish. The implication here is that while people resist, and this resistance at times even shapes a given social system, the dominant have systematic access to certain types of power—power that is often determinative.

REFERENCES

Bordo, Susan. 1988. "Anorexia Nervosa: Psychopathology as the Crystallization of Culture." In *Feminism and Foucault: Reflections on Resistance,* ed. Irene Diamond and Lee Quinby. Boston: Northeastern University Press.

Bourdieu, Pierre. 1977. *Towards a Theory of Practice.* Oxford: Oxford University Press.

Brown, Carol. 1981. "Mothers, Fathers and Children: From Private to Public Patriarchy." In *Women and Revolution,* ed. Lydia Sargent. Boston: South End.

Butler, Judith. 1989. *Gender Trouble: Feminism and the Subversion of Identity.* New York: Routledge.

18

Code, Lorraine. 1991. *What Can She Know? Feminist Theory and the Construction of Knowledge*. Ithaca. N.Y.: Cornell University Press.

Daly, Mary. 1978. *Gyn/Ecoloyg*. London: Women's Press.

Davis, Kathy. 1988. *Power under the Microscope: Toward a Grounded Theory of Gender Relations in Medical Encounters*. Dordrecht: Foris Publishing.

Derrida, Jacques. 1981. *Positions*. Trans. Alan Bass. Chicago: University of Chicago Press.

Eisenstein, Zillah R., ed. 1979. *Capitalist Patriarchy and the Case for Socialist Feminism*. New York: Monthly Review Press.

Fisher, Sue. 1991. "A Discourse of the Social: Medical Talk/Power Talk/Oppositional Talk." *Discourse and Society* 2(2):157–182.

Flax, Jane. 1990. *Thinking Fragments: Psychoanalysis, Feminism, and Postmodernism in the Contemporary West*. Berkeley: University of California Press.

Foucault, Michel. 1980a. *The History of Sexuality*. Vol. 1. Trans. Robert Hurley. New York: Vintage/Random House.

———. 1980b. "Two Lectures." in *Power/Knowledge*. Trans. Colin Gordon. New York: Pantheon.

Fraser, Nancy. 1989. *Unruly Practices: Power, Discourse and Gender in Contemporary Social Theory*. Minneapolis: University of Minnesota Press.

Fraser, Nancy, and Linda Nicholson. 1990. "Social Criticism without Philosophy: An Encounter between Feminism and Postmodernism." In *Feminism/Postmodernisms*, ed. Linda Nicholson. New York: Routledge.

Friedan, Betty. 1963. *The Feminine Mystique*. New York: Dell Publishing.

Giddens, Anthony. 1984. *The Constitution of Society*. Cambridge, England: Polity Press.

Gordon, Linda. 1988. *Heroes of Their Own Lives: The Politics and History of Family Violence*. New York: Penguin Books.

Habermas, Jürgen. 1984. *The Theory of Communicative Action*. Vol. 1. Trans. Thomas McCarthy. Boston: Beacon Press.

———. 1987. *The Theory of Communicative Action*. Trans. Vol. 2. Thomas McCarthy. Boston: Beacon Press.

Hall, Stuart. 1986. "The Problem of Ideology: Marxism without Guarantees." *Journal of Communications Inquiry* 10(2):28–44.

Haraway, Donna J. 1988. "Situated Knowledges: The Science Question in Feminism as a Site of Discourse on the Privilege of Partial Perspectives. *Feminist Studies* 14(3):535–599.

———. 1991. *Simians, Cyborgs, and Women: The Reinvention of Nature*. London: Free Association Books.

Harding, Sandra. 1986. *The Science Question in Feminism*. Ithaca, N.Y.: Cornell University Press.

———. 1991. *Whose Science; Whose Knowledge: Thinking from Women's Lives*. Ithaca, N.Y.: Cornell University Press.

Hartmann, Heidi. 1981. "The Unhappy Marriage of Marxism and Feminism." In *Women and Revolution*, ed. Lydia Sargent. Boston: South End.

Hartsock, Nancy. 1983a. "The Feminist Standpoint: Developing the Ground for a Specific Feminist Historical Materialism." In *Discovery Reality: Feminist*

19

Perspectives on Epistemology, Metaphysics, Methodology and the Philosophy of Science, ed. Sandra Harding and Merill Hintikka. Dordrecht: Reidel.

———. 1983b. *Money, Sex and Power*. New York: Longman.

———. 1990. "Foucault on Power." In *Feminism/Postmodernism*, ed. Linda J. Nicholson. New York: Routledge.

Hirsch, Marianne, and Evelyn Fox Keller, eds. 1990. *Conflicts in Feminism*. New York: Routledge.

Jaggar, Alison M. 1983. *Feminist Politics and Human Nature*. Totowa, N.Y.: Rowman and Allanheld.

Jaggar, Alison M., and Susan R. Bordo, eds. 1986. *Gender/Body/Knowledge: Feminist Reconstructions of Being and Knowing*. New Brunswick, N.J.: Rutgers University Press.

MacKinnon, Catherine. 1982. "Feminism, Marxism, Method and the State: An Agenda for Theory." *Signs* 7(3):515–544.

Martin, Biddy. 1982. "Feminism, Criticism, and Foucault." *New German Critique* 27 (Fall):3–30.

Millett, Kate. 1970. *Sexual Politics*. Garden City, N.Y.: Doubleday.

Mitchell, Juliet. 1966. "Women: the Longest Revolution." *New Left Review* 40:11–37.

———. 1971. *Women's Estate*. New York: Pantheon.

Nicholson, Linda, ed. 1990. *Feminism/Postmodernism*. New York: Routledge.

Probyn, Elspeth. 1987. "The Anorexic Body." In *Body Invaders: Panicsex in America*, ed. A. Krober and M. Krober. New York: St. Martin's Press.

Riley, Denise. 1988. *'Am I That Name?' Feminism and the Category of 'Women' in History*. Basingstroke and London: Macmillan.

Rosaldo, Michelle Z. 1980. "The Use and Abuse of Anthropology: Reflections on Feminism and Cross-Cultural Understanding." *Signs* 5(3):389–417.

Rubin, Gayle. 1975. "The Traffic in Women: Notes on the Political Economy of Sex." In *Toward an Anthropology of Women*, ed. Rayna Rapp Reiter. New York: Monthly Review.

Sargent, Lydia, ed. 1981. *Women and Revolution*. Boston: South End.

Scott, Joan. 1988. *Gender and the Politics of History*. New York: Columbia University Press.

Tong, Rosemarie. 1989. *Feminist Thought*. Boulder, Colo.: Westview Press.

Wilson, Elizabeth. 1985. *Adorned in Dreams: Fashion and Modernity*. London: Virago Press.

Young, Iris. 1990. *Justice and the Politics of Difference*. Princeton: Princeton University Press.

NEGOTIATING THE BODY AND ITS ADORNMENTS

CULTURAL DOPES AND SHE-DEVILS: COSMETIC SURGERY AS IDEOLOGICAL DILEMMA

Kathy Davis

> I do not put my trust in fate, nor my faith in God. I will be what I want, not what He ordained. I will mould a new image for myself out of the earth of my creation. I will defy my Maker and remake myself.
>
> —Fay Weldon, *The Life and Loves of a She-Devil*

From the constraining corsets of the nineteenth century to Cher's celebrated removal of her bottom rib to achieve a slender waist, women have a tradition of suffering for beauty. In order to meet cultural requirements of femininity, they have gone to great pains to improve and transform their bodies (Banner 1983; Lakoff and Scherr 1984; Perrot 1984). Although the aesthetic ideals of feminine shape and countenance have varied greatly from culture to culture and shifted dramatically over the years, the underlying assumption always seems to be that beauty is worth time, money, pain, and sometimes even life itself.

Feminists have tended to cast a critical eye on women's preoccupation with their appearance. The quest for beauty is generally described in terms of suffering and oppression. Women are presented as the victims of both beauty and the ideologies of feminine inferiority which beauty practices produce and maintain. Originally the culprit was sought in the system of cultural beauty norms which demanded eternal youth and impossible beauty from women: slender but voluptuous shapes, faces unmarked by the passage of time, and, most of all, an appearance in keeping with the conventions of upper-class, Western femininity (Perutz 1970; Henley 1977; Millman 1980; Baker 1984; Brownmiller 1985; Chapkis 1986; Wolf 1991). By linking the beauty practices of individual women

23

to the structural constraints of the beauty system, a convincing case was made for treating beauty as an essential ingredient of the social subordination of women—an ideal way to keep women in line by lulling them into believing that they could gain control over their lives through continued vigilance over their bodies.

In recent years, feminist discourses on beauty as oppression have begun to make way for postmodern perspectives which deal with beauty in terms of cultural discourses (Davis 1991b). The body remains a central concern, but this time as a text through which culture writes its meanings (Suleiman 1985; Probyn 1987; Haug et al. 1987; Diamond and Quinby 1988; Jaggar and Bordo 1989; Jacobus, Keller, and Shuttleworth 1990; Spitzack 1991). Following Foucault, the female body is portrayed as an imaginary site, always available to be inscribed. It is here that femininity in all her diversity can be constructed—through scientific discourses, medical technologies, the popular media, and everyday common-sense. In this framework, routine beauty practices belong to the disciplinary and normalizing regime of body improvement and transformation, part and parcel of the production of "docile bodies" (Foucault 1980). The postmodern shift in feminist theory enables a sensitivity to the multiplicity of meanings surrounding the female body as well as the insidious workings of power in and through cultural discourses on beauty and femininity.

Although the theoretical frameworks for understanding women's beauty practices differ in their emphasis on beauty as oppression or as cultural discourse, the focus remains on how these practices work to control or discipline women. Whether blinded by consumer capitalism, oppressed by patriarchal ideologies, or inscribed within the discourses of femininity, the woman who wants to improve her appearance marches to the beat of a hegemonic "feminine beauty system"—a system that polices, constrains, and inferiorizes her (MacCannell and MacCannell 1987:208). If she plays the beauty game, she can only do so as "cultural dope"[1]—as duped victim of false consciousness or normalized object of disciplinary regimes. Resisting the beauty system entails turning our backs on its enticements—either by looking for our authentic selves lying dormant under all the layers of makeup (Freedman 1986) or by discovering subtle ways to undermine or transform the system through alternative cultural discourses and practices (Bordo 1989).

Within contemporary feminist discourse on beauty, cosmetic surgery tends to be regarded as a particularly dramatic illustration of the oppressive nature of the feminine beauty system. It is part of the continuum of restrictive and painful beauty practices—of a kind with leg waxing, eyebrow plucking, and the wearing of girdles. At the same time, however, it

24

goes beyond the usual maintenance work in that it often involves excessive pain, serious side effects, and even the possibility of permanent maiming should the operation fail to achieve the desired result. With its expanding arsenal of techniques for reshaping and remaking the body, cosmetic surgery would seem to be the site par excellence for disciplining and normalizing the female body. Thus, if feminists have had reason to be skeptical of the more mundane practices of the beauty system, it is not surprising that they are even more critical of cosmetic surgery as oppressive to women and implicated in the reproduction of a discourse of feminine inferiority. For feminists it is difficult to imagine how a woman might willingly or knowledgeably embark on a course of action like reshaping her body through cosmetic surgery. It is difficult to view her as agent, that is, as someone who chooses the operation as the best possible course of action under the circumstances. Since cosmetic surgery seems to be a practice that is, almost by definition, disempowering for women, it can only be the problem, never a solution.

COSMETIC SURGERY: A FEMINIST DILEMMA

Feminist skepticism of cosmetic surgery stands in shrill contrast to its growing popularity among women of all ages and walks of life. Cosmetic surgery has become a multi-million-dollar industry. It is estimated that more than a half a million operations are performed annually in the United States to improve facial and bodily features (Wolf 1991), and the rate of surgery increases by 10 percent every year. This trend is by no means limited to the United States; in Britain cosmetic surgery doubles every decade. Even in the Netherlands, where a Calvinist tradition cautions against frivolity and hedonistic excess, statistics show that every type of cosmetic operation has doubled in frequency since 1981 (Starmans 1988). Women—and more than 90 percent of the recipients of cosmetic surgery are women—continue to flock to the surgeon's office, often facing waiting lists of up to two years.[2]

Despite its popularity, cosmetic surgery is always painful, sometimes requiring hospitalization for several weeks and even intensive care. In addition to the pain involved in any major operation, cosmetic surgery patients may be treated as complainers by the staff. Their suffering is viewed as self-induced and therefore not taken as seriously as the suffering of patients with cancer or heart disease. Once home, the patient waits excitedly to see how the surgery turned out. The results, however, are often disappointing. Face-lifts "fall" after several years and have to be

25

redone. Liposuctions often leave unsightly hollows and bumps on thighs and buttocks. Breast reductions are reputed to leave massive scarring. Silicone implants for breast augmentations can feel unpleasantly cold, become "encapsulated" by fibroid tissue, or "leak" and cause irreparable damage to the autoimmune system. And, last but not least, the patient may simply find that the surgery does not bring the relief she had expected and she is confronted with the same unhappiness she had before the surgery.

Cosmetic surgery is invariably expensive. In the United States where a fee-for-services health care system prevails, operations either strain individual budgets or raise the cost of experience-rated insurance policies. In countries with socialized medicine, the state picks up the bill for the surgery, thereby draining increasingly scarce financial resources. In the Netherlands, where health care is paid for by the state, the patient has to run a humiliating gamut of medical experts who decide whether she is eligible for surgery. She not only has to convince medical experts that she is in need of surgery, but she often has to justify her decision to others as well. Families may see the operation as an affront ("That's the family nose you're changing"). Lovers and husbands wonder why it is necessary ("You're married, so why do you need to have your breasts changed?"). Cosmetic surgery is regarded as slightly frivolous, something for Michael Jackson, perhaps, but not for the rest of us. Not surprisingly, many women opt for secrecy and prefer to go through the ordeal alone.

The contradiction between the myriad dangers and discomforts and the enormous popularity of cosmetic surgery among women makes it easy to understand why it might present something of a stumbling block for feminist analysis. As a longtime feminist, I too viewed cosmetic surgery critically, wondering how any woman of sound mind, let alone correct principles, could possibly consider taking such a step. This stance was rudely shaken, however, by a disturbing experience I had several years ago. While on a luncheon date with a friend who is an attractive, self-confident, successful professional woman and a feminist, she confided over coffee that she was about to have cosmetic surgery. Somewhat defensively, she explained that she was tired of putting up with being flat-chested. She had tried everything (therapy, feminism, talks with friends), but no matter what she did, she simply could not accept it. There was no other solution; she would just have to "do" something about it. She had decided to have her breasts enlarged. Finally, she was going to "take her life into her own hands." My friend knew all about the risks of cosmetic surgery. Moreover, she was highly critical of the suffering women have to endure because their bodies do not match the normative requirements of feminine beauty. And yet she felt compelled to have cosmetic surgery. In other words, here was a feminist who actively and knowledgeably opted for the surgical fix. How was I to make sense of this?

I found it unsatisfactory to reject my friend's explanation as the deluded imaginings of a "cultural dope." Nor did I feel comfortable with the view that cosmetic surgery is inevitably disempowering in the face of my friend's claim that it was in her case the only way she could exert control over her life. Confronted with my friend's experience, several questions emerged which cast doubt on the adequacy of my own beliefs as well as current feminist frameworks for coming to terms with women's involvement in cosmetic surgery. How can we criticize the oppressive dimensions of cosmetic surgery without identifying the women who desire it as somehow more duped, socially determined, or culturally enmeshed in the discourses of femininity and beauty than their more enlightened sisters? How can we explore the ambivalencies in women's desire for cosmetic surgery? How can we uncover the ways women maintain or reinforce discourses of feminine inferiority in their decisions to undergo cosmetic surgery, without losing sight of how women may be simultaneously resisting these very same discourses? In other words, how can women who embark on cosmetic surgery be reinstated as agents who negotiate their bodies within the limitations and constraints of the contexts in which they live?

In this chapter, I attempt to tackle these questions. I propose an approach that treats cosmetic surgery as an ideological dilemma,[3] that is, as a dilemmatic situation where women grapple actively and knowledgeably with opposing cultural discourse of femininity, beauty, and what should or should not be done about the female body. In order to grasp what might be at stake in the decision to have cosmetic surgery, I begin with a brief foray into the realm of feminist fiction. Using Fay Weldon's *The Lives and Loves of a She-Devil* (1983) as a source of inspiration, I put forth as remedy to the problem of the "cultural dope" a theoretical framework for understanding women's involvement in cosmetic surgery. This is followed by a closer look at how women justify their decisions to have their bodies altered surgically.

THE DEMISE OF THE CULTURAL DOPE

Fay Weldon's (1983) *The Life and Loves of a She-Devil* is a bitterly humorous account of a wife's revenge against an unfaithful husband. The heroine of the story, Ruth, is a fat, ugly, middle-aged housewife, mother,

27

and drudge whose husband, Bobo, leaves her for Mary Fisher—rich, beautiful, successful, and, of course, thin. Initially devastated, Ruth gathers together her courage and decides to get even. Her revenge involves, among other things, a series of cosmetic surgeries. Over a period of several years she has her entire body remade surgically and is transformed into a beautiful woman, enabling her to vanquish her rival and win her husband back, this time, however, as a broken man who is firmly and irrevocably under her thumb.

Weldon's novel leaves us with several puzzles. It is a feminist novel about sexual politics, replete with shocking examples of female oppression and male treachery. However, it is also a tale with a surprising twist—a female protagonist who wins, that is, who comes out on top in the battle of the sexes. It is the story of a woman who suffers to such an extent under cultural norms of feminine beauty that she is willing to undergo the pain and expense of cosmetic surgery to alter every part of her body. Ironically, the heroine also uses cosmetic surgery as a source of empowerment, as a way to regain control over her life. Ruth is both a victim of the feminine beauty system and one of its most devastating critics. Her decision to undergo cosmetic surgery supports the status quo of feminine inferiority while at the same time it shifts the power balance—temporarily, at least—in her own relationships.

We could, of course, discard Ruth as merely a fictional character, hardy representative of women who really undergo cosmetic surgery. Her quest for power and beauty then becomes just another instance of feminist (science) fiction, to be enjoyed but otherwise ignored. However, before we leave the make-believe world of Weldon's heroine, let us take the imaginary more seriously. It is my contention that her book contains some important lessons about why women might insist upon altering their bodies surgically, even at great cost to themselves—lessons that need to be incorporated in feminist accounts of femininity and beauty.

To begin with, Weldon's tale can be interpreted as a bitter commentary on the constraints of femininity as well as the institution of heterosexual love. Discussing her plans to have cosmetic surgery, Ruth compares herself to Hans Christian Andersen's little mermaid: "I am paying with physical pain. Hans Andersen's little mermaid wanted legs instead of a tail, so that she could be properly loved by her Prince. She was given legs, and by inference the gap where they join at the top, and after that, every step she took was like stepping on knives" (Weldon 1983:148).

This fairy tale links, as no other, women's subordination in heterosexual relationships with beauty. It is about women's compliance with

28

the beauty system and their willingness to undergo terrible suffering for the love of a man. The tale has a subtext, however. It is also a story about feminine wiles and subterfuge—the woman who applies deceit knowledgeably and with forethought in order to get her way. The little mermaid knows the rules of the game and plays by them. So too does Ruth: "'Of course it hurts,' she said. 'It's meant to hurt. Anything that's worth achieving has its price. And, by corollary, if you are prepared to pay that price you can achieve almost anything'" (Weldon 1983:148).

This is no "cultural dope," blinded by social forces beyond her control or comprehension. She does not see cosmetic surgery as the perfect solution, and she is well aware of its enormous price for women who undertake it. Under the circumstances, however, it is the best she can do. For she knows only too well that the context of structured gender inequality makes this solution—as perhaps any solution—at best a temporary one. In other words, she plays the game, assessing the situation with its structured constraints and limited possibilities. She knows what she wants, but at the same time she knows how limited her choices are. Within the context in which she lives, Ruth makes her choices—perhaps not freely, but at least knowledgeably.

Cosmetic surgery thus becomes a resource of sorts in the power struggle between the sexes. Whereas no one (including Ruth herself) particularly *likes* the means to the end, it cannot be denied that, by the time the book comes to a close, Ruth has a better bargaining position than she had earlier. She not only has more control over her immediate circumstances, but she has gained a different perspective on her future. As she notes at the end of the book, it was, after all, just a matter of power: "I have all, and he has none. As I was, so he is now" (Weldon 1983:240). In this way, Weldon's novel offers a scathing portrayal of the feminine beauty norms without reducing women to the position of deluded victim. Her protagonist is a "she-devil," and if we might wish her a better life, the matter of her agency cannot be ignored.

Caught off guard by a literary ploy, Weldon's readers begin, perhaps in spite of themselves, to entertain issues that tend to be skipped over in the more straightforward rhetoric of academic feminism. Previously held notions of the docile female, trapped by the constraints of beauty, are forgotten—at least for the moment—in favor of a vision where women as knowledgeable agents and cosmetic surgery can fit together. By putting the contradictory and disturbing dimensions of cosmetic surgery together with a feminist critique of the power relations between the sexes, Weldon shows how ambivalencies can be embraced rather than dismissed or avoided.

29

I contend that it is at the precise point of discomfort—either our own or other women's—that a feminist analysis of cosmetic surgery needs to begin. We need to find ways to explore cosmetic surgery as a complex and dilemmatic situation for women: problem and solution, oppression and liberation, all in one.

GROUNDING FEMINIST APPROACHES TO BEAUTY

Cosmetic surgery is not imposed upon women, who, blinded by the promise of a new body, meekly place their bodies under the surgeon's knife. Nor is it strictly a matter of individual choice, independent of the cultural and social practices of the beauty system. The decision to undergo cosmetic surgery is a problematic one, requiring ongoing deliberation and justification. To understand why women decide to alter their bodies surgically, we must not smooth out the difficulties they face while making the decision. We must use an approach that allows us to explore how the decision is deliberated, debated, and struggled over. Feminist theory on beauty requires grounding, that is, it must take the ambiguous, contradictory, everyday social practices of women as its starting point. To understand how cosmetic surgery might be constructed as a welcome option within a context of limited possibilities, we must reconceptualize the notions of structural constraint and individual choice.

When we talk of beauty as structural constraint, we need to abandon simplified oppression models once and for all. Women are not merely the victims of the terrors visited upon them by the beauty system. On the contrary, they partake in its delights as well. The link between beauty and femininity cannot be described strictly in terms of repression. The gratifying, positive, and even exciting dimensions of beauty need to be taken into account as well. Cultural discourses on beauty and femininity, like the social practices of body improvement, inevitably open up possibilities for action, just as they limit them. This implies that understanding cosmetic surgery requires sorting out its constraining and enabling features. Even the most critical feminist analysis of cosmetic surgery must take both dimensions into account.

In order to talk about beauty and individual choice, we need a more sophisticated conceptualization of agency. Contemporary social theory provides some guidelines for how women might be reinstated as active and knowledgeable actors within a context of structured limitations (Davis 1991a). Theoretical frameworks are required which link social practices of actors with structured forms of domination and subordination.

This entails showing how structures of hierarchy are continually being reproduced but also undermined and transformed by the everyday social practices of individuals. Along these lines, a feminist conception of agency would render women as active participants in the constitution of social life. Despite being limited by conditions over which they have no or merely partial control, women will always have some degree of awareness about their situation as well as the consequences of their actions. Applied to cosmetic surgery, this concept enables us to treat women who have willingly chosen and later defend cosmetic surgery for themselves as knowing what they have done. Their decision may have been knowledgeable and rational, even as it reproduced a complex of power structures which construct the female body as inferior and in need of change.

The reconceptualization I am suggesting here opens at least three new avenues of inquiry unavailable as long as the "cultural dope" approach to women's relationship to beauty and beauty practices is maintained. These three avenues of approach are the problem of agency or the remaking of one's body and life, the problem of normalcy or just being ordinary, and the problem of justice or refusing to suffer beyond what is fair. In exploring these themes, I draw on my research into how women account for their decision to have their bodies altered surgically.[4]

REMAKING THE BODY

Since I cannot change the world, I will change myself.
—Fay Weldon, *The Life and Loves of a She-Devil*

In view of the discomfort, expense, and potential side effects of cosmetic surgery, the decision to have it requires careful deliberation. The women I talked to had generally gone to great lengths to familiarize themselves with the pros and cons of the surgery, including discussing it with medical experts, contacting other women who had undergone similar operations, and gathering information from the media. They had to assemble their case, often against considerable opposition from medical professionals, family, and friends.

Betty,[5] a thirty-one-year-old housewife who is married to a construction worker, describes the long and painful trajectory she followed before obtaining a breast augmentation. She asserts that she has suffered all her life from having small breasts. However, she never actually considered doing anything about it until she saw a program on television about breast implants. After talking to a sympathetic aunt, she began to enter-

31

tain the possibility of cosmetic surgery: "So, I went to my general practitioner. But at first I didn't mention it, I just couldn't bring myself to say
it. I was so ashamed. Finally, I did and the doctor said: 'It's not like
you've got *nothing* there now, is it?' '*No*, I don't have *any*thing,' I said.
'Oh, *yeah*. Come on. You do too.'"

It is not unusual that physicians must be convinced a woman has a
valid reason for wanting cosmetic surgery. In countries with national
health insurance, general practitioners perform a gatekeeping function
and are often reluctant to refer a patient to a medical specialist for what
is seen as an unnecessary medical intervention. A common response is to
belittle the problem, trying to talk the patient out of it. Betty—like many
of the women I interviewed—had already passed that stage where she
could be cajoled into believing that nothing was wrong. She stuck to her
guns and finally managed to get a referral to a plastic surgeon. The surgeon was willing to do the surgery, but explained that she should be
aware of the side effects. Silicone implants can calcify, become overgrown
with fibrous tissue, or even worse, migrate and have to be surgically removed. The odds were 50/50 that she would have some side effects. She
should think about it carefully.[6]

Although Betty was apprehensive about the surgery, she reasoned:

It can't possibly be worse than what I have now. (Interviewer:
Even with all the risks, the implants getting hard?) I'd still do it.
He [the surgeon] warned me at the beginning about all the things
that could go wrong, that they might have to be taken out and
that we couldn't do anything more if that happened. He said,
"And then you would have to face the possibility of being left
with less than what you have now." I said: "Well, I don't have
anything now, so that doesn't matter." At least I will have tried
to do something about it myself, at least there's that.

Betty is not unaware of the risks of surgery. She defends her decision,
weighing these risks against what she sees as a situation where she had
nothing to lose. It couldn't get worse than it already was. However, there
is more to her account than a rational assessment of the odds. She presents the very fact that she was able to take the decision at all as a positive
step, even if the surgery didn't work out. It is better to have tried and
failed than never to have tried at all.

Potential side effects and reluctant physicians are not the only hur-
dles to overcome. Although Betty managed to still her own anxieties

about the surgery, her family and friends were anything but enthusiastic. Her husband wondered why she felt she had to do this ("Is this *really* necessary?"). Family and friends were also skeptical, and she found herself having to defend her decision against their criticisms:

A lot of people just can't understand it. They say, "You're married, you have a husband, children, why do you want something like that now? You don't *have* to look good anymore." Well, I think that's ridiculous. I mean, I want it for myself, for my own feeling that I look good. . . . It's important for me because I'm the one who has to see it [her breasts] every day, and I don't like the way it looks and I hate myself when I look at it. I don't want to live like that—I don't feel that old—I'm just thirty-one and I'm the one who has to spend the rest of my life looking at it. Well, that's how I see it. . . . I guess I think you have to think of yourself sometimes. I have thought about other people often enough. I thought it was really brave of me to take this step. Now I'm glad.

Portraying cosmetic surgery as a courageous act is not unusual. Women who undergo cosmetic surgery initiate a dramatic change, becoming agents in the transformation and remaking of their lives as well as their bodies. The decision to undergo cosmetic surgery is framed within a discourse of opposition—as a moment when a woman overcomes her own shame and anxieties in the face of opposition from family, friends, and even physicians. Acting against the dictates of others in order to do something for herself, the constraints of feminine docility where others' wishes and opinions are always more important than her own are pushed aside. The decision to have cosmetic surgery is described in terms of great relief and even exhilaration. This is true, surprisingly, even when the results of the surgery are not as satisfactory, medically or aesthetically, as the woman had hoped.[7]

A critique of the oppressive features of femininity and the beauty system need not be abandoned, however. In fact, the women I talked to were often experts, knowing better than anyone just how oppressive norms for feminine beauty can be. The following example shows how cultural discourses of beauty and femininity can be reproduced in an account of cosmetic surgery, while at the same time the woman displays a critical awareness of the oppressiveness of these very same discourses.

Joanne is a successful businesswoman in her early forties who is

33

anticipating a face-lift. She justifies the surgery with a tirade against management jobs and the gendered norms which work against middle-aged women.

> I've worked in several organizations and I've seen what happens to older women—they end up in some out-of-the-way place in the organization. I've seen how they are driven crazy—not to the extent that they have to be committed, but just completely shoved into the background. That kind of process—and it definitely has to do with whether you are seen as someone who is attractive, who still counts—and if you refuse to play the game, well, it's a game, the whole damn thing is a game.

She is now in the middle of her own career, with a child to support, and she can't afford to "let that happen to her." She presents a face-lift as a way of postponing the inevitable, of being able to play the game as long as possible. Although Joanne's account displays compliance with a double standard that makes aging acceptable in men but sanctionable in women, she is, at the same time, highly critical. She reiterates that a face-lift does not change structural constraints on women in the labor force ("You can't eliminate the problem with a new face, but . . ."). She is also familiar with feminist discussions about the gendered inequities of feminine beauty norms ("We are not here to please men—if women want to fix themselves up, it should be because we want to for ourselves, for our own pleasure"). She is critical of a society that has turned women's bodies into consumer goods ("All the myths—like you have to market yourself if you want to get anywhere . . . life has become one big advertising campaign").

Although she displays an ongoing discursive penetration[8] of how women's quest for beauty is embedded in the broader discourses of feminine inferiority and consumer capitalism, Joanne still decides to have a face-lift: "It's just a rational thing—you don't want any extra handicaps in the race. It's hard enough, so why should you put up with things that you can do something about with relatively little effort and if they don't make that much difference anyway—well, why shouldn't you?"

Thus she acknowledged that the scale is tipped against career women, while at the same time she displays determination to make the best of a bad situation. Her decision is presented as a rational weighing of factors, and she emerges as an agent, exercising control over her life within a situation that is not entirely of her own making.

Joanne's notion of freedom is not without a certain irony, however, as her final, somewhat rueful concluding remark shows: "Yeah, well, look, at a certain point, you're just old. But by then, you don't have to earn a living anymore and that gives you some freedom. Then you can look ugly, let it all hang out—then you *can* break the norms. And, let me tell you, that's what I plan to do, too. When I'm old, I am really going to take advantage of the situation."

This account is complex. It draws on individualistic discourses of body control with its attendant fantasies of getting one's life in hand. At the same time, it displays Joanne's awareness that this is not the *real* solution or maybe not a solution at all. Freedom is a matter of degree for her, to be negotiated with a mixture of rational assessment of her possibilities, a large dose of self-irony, and a thinly veiled critique of the constraints on women within the ageist world of big business.

These examples show how women's concern with their appearance is part of an ongoing skirmish within gendered structures of hierarchy and difference where women continually and routinely take stock of their possibilities and act accordingly. Although they may not oversee all the implications of their behavior or be able to assess the conditions under which decisions are taken in their entirety, they generally have some knowledge of the conditions under which their activities take place. Cosmetic surgery is undertaken with the intent of improving the present state of affairs. Remembering the inventiveness of Weldon's she-devil, it is perhaps not surprising after all that women are able to turn even an oppressive practice like cosmetic surgery on its head, transforming it into a moment of personal courage and triumph. The decision is inextricably connected to women's sense of themselves as agents. Understanding cosmetic surgery, therefore, requires, among other things, taking this agency seriously.

TOWARD NORMALCY

Just to be ordinary must be wonderful. . . . all she has ever wanted is to be like other women.
—Fay Weldon, *The Life and Loves of a She-Devil*

The boundaries between beauty and ugliness as well as between the ordinary and the deviant are collectively reproduced within the everyday "maintenance" work of femininity. The existence of a practice such as cosmetic surgery is predicated on the assumption that some bodies are in need of surgical correction in order to meet the norms of acceptable femininity. However, the actual line between the ordinary and the extraordinary turns out to be quite difficult to delineate. Beauty is, as the saying goes, in the eye of the beholder.

In the course of my research, I was invariably asked whether the women I interviewed really *needed* cosmetic surgery. The implication was clearly that a woman would have to be seriously deformed or obviously hideous to consider altering her body so drastically. My struggles to come up with an answer to this question are instructive as they reflect the ambivalence surrounding the subject of beauty and the female body. My first inclination is to give a resounding no. After all, I have never actually encountered a woman whose appearance seemed deficient enough to me to require surgical alteration. In fact, in the course of my fieldwork where I observed numerous consultations with applicants for cosmetic surgery, I was often hard pressed to know what the offending feature was, let alone be convinced that cosmetic surgery was necessary.[9] Does this mean, then, that the answer to the question should be no? Or does it merely indicate that appearance is normative and that my assessment does not necessarily have to coincide with the person's own? I soon discovered that an applicant for cosmetic surgery could be perfectly attractive to me (as well as to other people in her life) and still experience some part of her body as irredeemably ugly—so ugly that it cast a shadow over her life, negatively influencing how she felt about herself, her relationships, her sexuality, and her work. In her perception, her body had crossed a subjectively defined boundary between the ordinary and the extraordinary, going beyond what she or, for that matter any woman, should normally be expected to bear.

The following account poignantly illustrates the difficulties inherent in normative assessments of women's bodies. Julie, an attractive social worker in her early thirties, describes her extensive cosmetic surgery requiring hospitalization for the removal of moles on her back and face. As a young child she experienced these moles as a source of great shame and self-revulsion. Shaking her head sadly, she recalls: "And everyone saw them—I mean, I didn't know anyone else who had that and naturally everyone saw that I had these strange things on my face. And they always made a big point of telling me that I was worth a whole lot, you know, and that I was really a nice person and that it didn't make any difference how you looked on the outside. But I just never could feel that way. Never."

For Julie, the moles on her face marked her, setting her apart from the rest of the children and subjecting her to extreme visibility. She describes the torment she experienced, caught between her inability to accept her body and the well-meaning reassurances of her family and friends who insisted that it didn't matter and that they loved her the way she was. Although she acknowledges the good intentions behind such remarks, she did not find them helpful. In fact, they often backfired, confirming her sense that she wasn't "normal" ("Why else would someone need to say something like that?"). In her account, suffering over her appearance is a private matter: she is, ultimately, the only one who can really judge her body and how she should feel about it.

It took years, however, before she began to consider having cosmetic surgery: "I just needed a lot of time before I could admit openly to myself that I just really hated them. And that I just really wanted to have them taken off. But that was . . . something I had always felt, but I just never could admit it. And that whole business about how you are fine the way you are—that was like a big, heavy blanket, covering up how I really felt.

Julie's perception of the seriousness of the problem as well as the necessity of a surgical solution differs from the perception of her family and friends. This confirms the normativity involved in beauty; it does not, however, diminish her suffering. Forced to separate her body from her feelings, she describes her sense of being disembodied, a mind without a body. In her account, the decision to undergo cosmetic surgery paradoxically reinstates her in an active and lived relationship to her body; she becomes, once again, an embodied subject.

At this point it might seem that if a woman is unhappy with her appearance, then the answer to the question of whether she needs cosmetic surgery should be an unqualified yes. This is not my contention, however. Julie's account suggests that being able to understand why women might want to alter their bodies by surgical means entails being able to take the complexities of their embodied subjectivity into account.[10] Beauty is not a matter of fixed standards, but rather a matter of active negotiation along the boundaries of normalcy, that is, women's ongoing interaction with their bodies and the cultural and social constraints of the beauty system. Understanding cosmetic surgery entails an analysis of subjectively experienced boundaries, that is, how women decide what is normal (and therefore to be borne with the help of the usual beauty maintenance practices) and what goes beyond the limits of normal appearance (and therefore requires unusual measures).

Cosmetic surgery remains, however, an extraordinary solution for an extraordinary problem. Most of the women I interviewed described their decision as the only possible solution, a kind of last resort. Cosmetic surgery is an exception to the rule—the rule being that beauty problems are ordinary and should be endured as part and parcel of the feminine condition.

The simultaneous acknowledgment of the ordinary and extraordinary features of women's involvement in beauty practices can be seen in the following account. Geraldine, a thirty-six-year-old saleswoman, is contemplating having her breasts lifted after a second pregnancy. As if to counter possible objections that she might be taking this step too lightly, she explains: "It's not that I think it's so important to have big breasts. . . . I don't have to be a Vanessa[11] or anything, but I just want to have it like it was before I had two children."

Two pregnancies have taken their toll on Geraldine's body, leaving her with sagging breasts. She justifies her desire to have a breast augmentation with the argument that she just wants to have her body the way it was: the body of a preparturient adolescent. The conflation of normal femininity with eternal youth has been cited as one of the more devastating effects of the contemporary beauty craze, and Geraldine's defense seems to be just one more instance of it. However, things are not quite so simple, as the following remark attests. Here she displays a decidedly critical stance toward cosmetic surgery in general and face-lifts in particular: "I've always had the feeling about face-lifts—well, I probably don't really even take it seriously when people say they want to have their wrinkles removed. That just belongs to getting older. You know, your eyelids start to droop a little. That's just part of the whole process. I have all that too."

Geraldine uses the same kind of argumentative strategy to attack the phenomenon of face-lifts that she used just a few minutes before to defend a breast augmentation for herself. Wrinkles are part of the normal aging process, something to be accepted as "the way things are." Sagging breasts, on the other hand, are quite a different kettle of fish. Here the "normal aging process" proves not so acceptable after all and indeed provides grounds for deciding to turn the tables on nature and have cosmetic surgery.

> And, it's really awful when, for example, the insurance company tells you that it's [breast augmentation] strictly a cosmetic operation. I have a lot of problems with that because I would never do that. I would never have my wrinkles removed or anything like that. As long as you don't have psychological problems with it, then in my opinion you shouldn't have anything done about it. But this is really getting to be a psychological problem, and

that's why I finally decided that I had to do something about it after all.

Geraldine constructs her case as special, setting it apart from the run-of-the-mill cosmetic surgery. She establishes herself as someone who generally opposes cosmetic surgery because it is something done only for beauty and therefore not to be taken seriously. Although she too wants cosmetic surgery, she presents her problem as unusual—the exception to the rule and therefore legitimate. In her case—but only in her case—cosmetic surgery is warranted.

Beauty is not just a matter of straightforward standards, and in many cases the standards have nothing to do with aesthetics. Julie's and Geraldine's accounts show how women's suffering over their appearance is connected to their sense of themselves in their bodies. The two women attest convincingly that embodiment is actively negotiated along the normative boundaries of femininity. Cosmetic surgery becomes in their accounts a way to break through an impasse. In order to become ordinary, an extraordinary step may be, paradoxically, the only course of action.

RIGHTING THE WRONG

We are here in this world to improve upon His original idea. To create justice, truth and beauty where He so obviously and lamentably failed.
—Fay Weldon, *The Life and Loves of a She-Devil*

Too much suffering "for beauty's sake" tips the scales, raising the question of fairness. Although women are prepared to endure considerable hardship to meet cultural beauty norms, a time comes when they may begin to feel there are limits. It is at this point that cosmetic surgery may seem the only fair course of action. Having become a matter of justice, it is defended in the moral discourse of rights—the right to a normal appearance:

Geraldine: I don't have to look like—oh, you know—Vanessa. It's just that in my case— I look at my body and I just feel like this doesn't belong. It looks like, well, I can imagine that this is the way a woman of seventy would look. Why should I have to put up with that?

39

the right to happiness and well-being:

> Julie: And, then, at a certain point, I just felt like—if it would make me feel better not to have these things [the moles], why shouldn't I try to do something about it. If you really just can't live with it, then you really should be able to do something about it.

the right to services available through medical technology:

> Joanne: I was already feeling that I looked a whole lot older than the other women [in the company] and I didn't want to look out of place. So I was already thinking about having it (a face-lift) and finally I decided why shouldn't I profit from all that technology anyway—it's available so why shouldn't I be allowed to take advantage of it?

The women I interviewed tended to justify their decision to have cosmetic surgery as an entitlement, as something they deserved and therefore should be allowed to have. In the examples above, each woman has already established that her suffering has reached the limit of what is reasonable within the usual normative and practical constraints of femininity. With this as a background, she can now frame her decision to undergo cosmetic surgery as a morally acceptable step. It is even something she should do in order to alleviate her pain. Given that cosmetic surgery is becoming increasingly available to women as an option for limiting their suffering over their bodies, it is not surprising that it might come to be viewed as a right: the right not to suffer that which can be corrected, the right to a reasonable level of well-being in a society that promises not only health but also happiness to its citizens, or the right to the goods and services offered by a rapidly expanding medical technology.[12]

Cosmetic surgery may be a newly discovered right, but as most of my respondents indicated, it is by no means an unlimited right. Where cosmetic surgery is concerned, moderation is clearly in order. Thus Geraldine is quick to explain that she does not demand the impossible (to look like Vanessa); she just wants to look her age. Julie doesn't have to be ecstatic about her appearance; she just wants to be able to live with herself. Even Joanne, who takes the pragmatic view and wants to take advantage of technology's advances, is not demanding a complete overhaul; she just wants an equal chance to compete in the rat race for a little while longer. The case for cosmetic surgery is presented in terms of justice: a woman's right to her fair share—no more, but also no less.

Although cosmetic surgery is presented as a right, it is still a right requiring some justification. Even those who have a vested interest in the practice may find they have some explaining to do. For example, plastic surgeons have to account for their willingness to transgress medical mandates and perform elective surgery on otherwise healthy bodies (Dull and West 1991).[13] In this context, the recipients also need to justify their decision to have cosmetic surgery, accomplishing it within a dynamic context of opposing or contradictory cultural discourses about femininity, bodies, individual freedom, and more. With a remarkable degree of flexibility, women draw on these discourses to explain and defend, but also to criticize and qualify their decision. The same individual may find herself arguing her case within a discourse of equal rights ("Every person has a right to be happy," "Why her and not me?"), only to make an abrupt about-face in the next moment to worry about the sanctity of the human body ("My father says: These are the ears that God gave you"), priorities and values ("I know that it's the inside that counts"), or the community of females ("Sure, every woman has something wrong with her").

In order to see how this flexibility works, let us return to Julie. On the one hand she uses a distinctly feminist discourse of gender solidarity to criticize feminine beauty practices: "I think it's just idiotic to make such a fuss about appearance, you know what I mean? That it can become such a big deal. Every woman has something wrong—I mean, we are all dissatisfied with something, our breasts or hips or whatever. I think that women should be valued as they are and shouldn't be ashamed about how they look."

On the other hand she takes another stance when defending her decision to have cosmetic surgery. Here she draws on a discourse of individualism and personal autonomy: "I just had the feeling that I could never talk to anyone about my problem—that I found myself so ugly—I always had the feeling that I was on my own. . . . And so I have always tried to remember that something can be very insignificant in someone else's eyes, but for yourself, it can influence everything."

Julie's condemnation of what she calls "making a fuss about appearance" is linked to cultural discourses which devalue women, making them feel ashamed of their bodies. She is not only critical of the cultural devaluation of women's bodies, but she implicitly advocates resisting this devaluation by refusing to go along with it. This position could lead to obvious difficulties as she explains her own preoccupation with appear-

41

ance. In that case, however, she is able to draw upon a different discourse—a discourse that enables her to take a counterstand. Here the discourse of solidarity ("We are all in this together") makes room for a more individualistic stance: only you can know what you need and do something about it. This argument too may be found in feminist discourse—this time, however, a liberal-feminist discourse that advocates individual autonomy and self-fulfillment.[14]

One could argue that Julie is taking opposing positions in a rather short space of time—something that might be construed as a sign of confusion or perhaps even hypocrisy. However, as Billig (1987) notes, arguments are inevitably embedded in broader discursive contexts of controversy. Positions taken in a debate or discussion are rarely internally consistent, requiring the actor to draw upon appropriate contradictory discourses, depending on the target at which they are directed. Thus Julie can display her alignment with a feminist critique of oppressive beauty norms at one moment, while in the next defending her own right to alter her body surgically to meet these very norms in another discourse—a discourse which in turn draws, albeit implicitly, on the equally feminist notion of autonomy.

Justifying cosmetic surgery is a complicated business, requiring a series of complex and interrelated argumentative moves. On the one hand, cosmetic surgery has to be taken out of the sphere of feminine caprice and the triviality of beauty and established as a matter of justice, deserved on the basis that there are limits to how much anyone should have to suffer. This argument requires drawing on the notion of generalized rights, one of them being that there are just limits to pain.[15] In the course of defending their decision to have cosmetic surgery, my respondents applied generalized notions of a just measure of pain to a new social field—the beauty system—and in so doing undermined the notion that beauty inevitably requires suffering. In short, they argued that there are limits to how much they should have to suffer even for beauty.

On the other hand, the limitations of this right are given due acknowledgment. As we have seen, women can also display considerable awareness of arguments that might be made against cosmetic surgery, and they often express agreement with these arguments. In fact, I have not encountered a single case where the respondent argued that cosmetic surgery is something every woman should have. Nor was it presented as the ultimate solution to women's beauty problems. Instead, cosmetic surgery was presented as a limited solution, chosen for the time being and with the restrictions well in mind.

This twofold strategy is well illustrated by Geraldine, who defends her decision to have surgery as follows: "I just don't want people to think of me as a body—as though that were the only important thing. I want them to think I am important for myself, for the person I am and not all the other things. . . . It's ridiculous. You're what's important. And, well, I know all that. I think so, too—that it's true. Except when it comes to my breasts."

Cosmetic surgery is both a generalized matter of entitlement and a special case, applicable to this particular instance. The two arguments work together to provide a case for refusing suffering and righting a wrong.

CONCLUSION

Cosmetic surgery remains a problematic solution in a dilemmatic situation, that is, it involves a choice between at least two more or less unacceptable courses of action. Each decision has to be explained and justified, often to a disapproving audience of family, friends, medical representatives, and others. In order to account for their decision, women have to make their way through an ideological obstacle course of conflicting and contradictory themes about what should (and should not) be done to the female body. Listening to their justificatory practices helps shed light on the troubling question of why women might willingly and even exuberantly choose to have their bodies altered surgically at great risk and cost to themselves. In so doing, they can help us understand the complex relationship between the cultural discourses of femininity, beauty, and women's involvement in the beauty system. This beauty system is not a closed system, but a set of contradictory themes and practices which give rise to ongoing discussion, deliberation, and argumentation. A good starting point for further inquiry would be to explore women's justificatory practices in order to understand their involvement in cosmetic surgery as well as the dilemmatic features of the discourse and practices of feminine beauty. By looking at how women defend, legitimate, but also criticize their decision to undergo cosmetic surgery, we can understand why they are willing to take on the risks and hardships of surgery, yet we do not reduce them to the position of "cultural dope." Cosmetic surgery becomes an ideological dilemma, to be negotiated within the constraints of a gendered order where the female body is devalued and women are excluded from the domain of justice.

Feminists have demonstrated convincingly that beauty is a political issue. My research suggests that it is a moral issue as well. It touches on the complex normativity of embodiment as well as on the necessity of expanding conceptions of justice to include the problem of beauty and women's bodies. Women need to be viewed as moral actors who negotiate what should or should not be done to alleviate their pain. In a context where women suffer too much and too long for beauty, cosmetic surgery may be the only way to take action.

NOTES

An earlier version of this chapter appeared in *Hypatia* 6(2) (Summer 1991): 21–43. Whereas that paper focused on the theoretical problems posed by cosmetic surgery for contemporary feminist theory on beauty and the female body, this chapter draws on my empirical research into women's reasons for undergoing cosmetic surgery. I thank Lorraine Code, Willem de Haan, Sue Fisher, Ine Gremmen, Lena Inowlocki, and Selma Sevenhuijsen for their helpful and provocative comments.

1. This term was coined by Garfinkel (1967) to criticize functionalist or Parsonian conceptions of agency where the human actor has so completely internalized the norms and values of her society that her activities become limited to acting out a predetermined script.

2. Although men are also recipients of cosmetic surgery, they engage in it to a much lesser extent and for somewhat different reasons. For example, all breast corrections (with the exception of transsexuals), 96 percent of all face-lifts, and 88 percent of all eyelid corrections are performed on women (Finkelstein 1991). It is estimated that more men will start approaching the plastic surgeon as the demands of competitive employment bring about an increased emphasis on youthful and energetic appearance in men.

3. The term *ideological dilemma* was coined by Billig et al. (1988) and belongs to a rhetorical approach to ideology—an approach that has informed the present chapter as well. The assumption is that ideologies are not closed systems of thought, to be dutifully accepted or internalized and automatically followed. The discourses of everyday life contain shared but also opposing ideological themes that give rise to dilemmatic situations requiring ongoing argument and debate. Analyzing ideology means showing how people deliberate about their social worlds, that is, ideology-in-action. For a good introduction to ideological dilemmas, see Billig et al. 1988.

4. I interviewed women in clinical and nonclinical settings who had undergone or were about to undergo various cosmetic surgeries (face-lifts, breast corrections, liposuctions, " tummy tucks," etc.). I was interested in how they decided to have the surgery, how they justified their decision, and how they felt about the outcome. In addition to talking to plastic surgeons and medical experts about

cosmetic surgery, for two years I observed consultations between medical representatives and applicants for cosmetic surgery intended to determine whether the applicants were eligible for medical insurance.

I undertook this research in the Netherlands, which has a system of socialized medicine. Until recently, national health insurance covered from 50 percent to 100 percent of the costs of cosmetic surgery, provided the recipient fell into one of three categories: functional disturbance (for example, eyelids that droop to such an extent that vision is impaired), serious psychological difficulties (as certified by a psychiatrist), or "a physical feature which falls outside the range of what is considered normal" (as defined by a medical expert).

Whereas the U.S. fee-for-service medical system limits cosmetic surgery to those who can pay for it, in the Netherlands it is available to everyone regardless of her economic situation, provided she meets the criteria of eligibility. This means I was able to talk to women from a wider range of economic and social backgrounds than would have been possible in the United States.

5. I translated the following examples from transcripts originally in Dutch and have attempted to preserve the idiomatic quality of the speech. The names are fictitious.

6. The fact that Betty's general practitioner is so forthcoming about the risks of breast augmentations should undoubtedly be viewed against the backdrop of the current crisis of the Dutch welfare state where it is becoming increasingly difficult for the state to meet even the most basic health care needs. In the U.S. fee-for-service system, we might expect a rather different kind of interaction.

7. Obviously this is not true for operations that are complete failures; these can be very traumatic for the recipient. However, it is surprising how pleased women can be with the surgery even when it does not live up to their expectations. Betty, for example, ended up having one breast implant calcify, requiring another operation. Her initial reaction was optimistic: at least *one* of her breasts was perfect—just what she had always wanted!

8. The term *discursive penetration* is from Giddens (1984) and refers to actors' understanding of the conditions under which they live. Whereas much of this consciousness is practical—a tacit ability to know "how to go on" without being able to say why—part is also discursively available in actors' accounts. Actors often display understanding of authority relations or experiences of oppression through humor, sarcasm, or irony, indicating that the ideological wool has not been pulled over their eyes.

9. During this fieldwork, I was seated next to the door, giving me a good view of the applicants as they were ushered in by the physician. I had no prior knowledge of the applicants' medical history and therefore caught myself trying to guess as they entered the room what kind of surgery they wanted. With one exception—a man with a "cauliflower nose"—I was unable in a single case to detect the recipient's reason for the visit.

10. See Fraser 1989 for a useful approach to the problem of needs. She advocates treating them as essentially contested, multivalent, and contextual. Need claims should be evaluated in terms of the kinds of questions they raise rather than looking for definitive answers to them.

45

11. Vanessa is a glamorous and buxom sex symbol, movie star, and singer—the Dutch equivalent to Dolly Parton.

12. Whereas women in the United States seeking cosmetic surgery might amend their sense of entitlement with a "provided I can pay for it," in a system of socialized medicine, recipients tend to see health care as something they are entitled to by virtue of their citizenship. See, for example, de Swaan 1988 for a discussion of this particular feature of the European welfare state. Since cosmetic surgery is funded by medical insurance, it is not surprising that my respondents framed their defense of cosmetic surgery in the rhetoric of citizenship.

13. In the Netherlands, for example, where there is an ongoing public debate about whether cosmetic surgery should be included in the standard health care package, critics express reservations about undertaking expensive operations for what is often seen as a "luxury problem." Proponents, on the other hand, call for a reformulation, arguing that face-lifts and breast corrections are a kind of "welfare surgery."

14. The fact that otherwise quite disparate and even antagonistic feminisms also share similarities in some of their philosophical underpinnings is well documented by Jaggar 1983.

15. Obviously cosmetic surgery is not the only field where this kind of moral argument is applied. Recent discussions about euthanasia (in the Netherlands) or about the limits of medical intervention for those who are terminally ill are cases in point. Another long-standing philosophical debate concerns punishment and what constitutes a just measure of pain. See, for example, de Haan 1990.

REFERENCES

Baker, N. C. 1984. *The Beauty Trap: Exploring Woman's Greatest Obsession.* New York: Franklin Watts.

Banner, L. W. 1983. American Beauty. New York: Alfred A. Knopf.

Billig, M. 1987. *Arguing and Thinking: A Rhetorical Approach to Social Psychology.* Cambridge: Cambridge University Press.

Billig, M., S. Condor, D. Edwards, M. Gane, D. Middleton, and A. Radley. 1988. *Ideological Dilemmas.* London: Sage.

Bordo, Susan. 1989. "The Body and the Reproduction of Femininity: A Feminist Appropriation of Foucault." In Jaggar and Bordo (1989), 13–33.

Brownmiller, S. 1985. *Femininity.* New York: Fawcett Columbine.

Chapkis, W. 1986. *Beauty Secrets.* London: Women's Press.

Davis, K. 1991a. "Critical Sociology and Gender Relations." In *The Gender of Power,* ed. K. Davis, M. Leijenaar, and J. Oldersma, 65–86. London: Sage.

Davis, K. 1991b. "Remaking the She-Devil: A Critical Look at Feminist Approaches to Beauty." *Hypatia* 6(2): 21–43.

de Haan, W. 1990. *The Politics of Redress: Crime, Punishment and Penal Abolition.* London: Unwin Hyman.

de Swaan, A. 1988. *In Care of the State.* Cambridge: Polity Press.

Diamond, I., and L. Quinby, eds. 1988. *Feminism and Foucault.* Boston: Northeastern University Press.

Dull, D., and C. West. 1991. "Accounting for Cosmetic Surgery: The Accomplishment of Gender." *Social Problems* 38(1): 54–70.

Finkelstein, J. 1991. *The Fashioned Self.* Cambridge: Polity Press.

Foucault, M. 1980. *Power/Knowledge: Selected Interviews and Other Writings, 1972–1977,* ed. C. Gordon. New York: Pantheon.

Fraser, N. 1989. *Unruly Practices.* Cambridge: Polity Press.

Freedman, R. 1986. *Beauty Bound: Why Women Strive for Physical Perfection.* London: Columbus Books.

Garfinkel, H. 1967. *Studies in Ethnomethodology.* Englewood Cliffs, N.J.: Prentice-Hall.

Giddens, A. 1984. *The Constitution of Society.* Cambridge: Polity Press.

Haug, F., et al. 1987. *Female Sexualization.* London: Verso.

Henley, N. M. 1977. *Body Politics.* Englewood Cliffs, N.J.: Prentice-Hall.

Jacobus, M., E. F. Keller, and S. Shuttleworth, eds. 1990. *Body/Politics: Women and the Discourses of Science.* New York: Routledge.

Jaggar, A. M. 1983. *Feminist Politics and Human Nature.* Totowa, N.J.: Rowman and Allanheld.

Jaggar, A. M., and S. R. Bordo, eds. 1989. *Gender/Body/Knowledge: Feminist Reconstructions of Being and Knowing.* New Brunswick, N.J.: Rutgers University Press.

Lakoff, R. T., and R. L. Scherr. 1984. *Face Value: The Politics of Beauty.* Boston: Routledge and Kegan Paul.

MacCannell, D., and J. F. MacCannell. 1987. "The Beauty System." In *The Ideology of Conduct,* ed. N. Armstrong and L. Tennenhouse, 206–238. New York: Methuen.

Millman, M. 1980. *Such a Pretty Face.* New York: Berkeley Books.

Perrot, P. 1984. *Le travail des apparences: Ou les transformations du corps féminin XVIIIe–XIXe siècle.* Paris: Éditions du Seuil.

Perutz, K. 1970. *Beyond the Looking Glass: Life in the Beauty Culture.* Middlesex, England: Penguin.

Probyn, E. 1987. "The Anorexic Body." In *Body Invaders: Panicsex in America,* ed. A. Krober and M. Krober, 201–211. New York: St. Martin's Press.

Spitzack, C. 1990. *Confessing Excess: Women and the Politics of Body Reduction.* Albany: SUNY Press.

Starmans, P. M. W. 1988. "Wat gebeurt er met de esthetische chirurgie?" *Inzet: Opinieblad van de ziekenfondsen* 1:18–25.

Suleiman, S. R., ed. 1985. *The Female Body in Western Culture.* Cambridge: Harvard University Press.

Weldon, F. 1983. *The Life and Loves of a She-Devil.* Kent, England: Coronet Books.

Wolf. N. 1991. *The Beauty Myth: How Images of Beauty Are Used against Women.* New York: William Morrow.

DEVIANCY, DRESS, AND DESIRE

Elizabeth Wilson

She hung out at Gianni's, where the serious bulldykes went, the ones who were into cross-dressing. At least that's what they used to call it, before the style seeped into the upper classes and got renamed the 'androgynous look.'
—Jane DeLynn, *Don Juan in the Village*

LESBIANS AND GAYS IN THE EIGHTIES

On Easter Sunday 1991, the *Observer* newspaper in London reported that the first undergraduate courses in lesbian and gay studies had been set up at Sussex University. Predictably, negative responses came from figures ranging from a notoriously right-wing member of Parliament to a lecturer in literature at Cambridge, but as the organizer of the course, Dr. Jonathan Dollimore, commented, if lesbian and gay issues were really such a minority interest, why was everyone so steamed up about them.

The 1980s were full of contradictions for lesbians and gays. The resurgence of Christian fundamentalism and right-wing governments, and the appearance of the HIV virus clashed with a more general, growing tolerance in sexual attitudes in Western society. Britain is perhaps particularly anomalous in this respect. It has one of the highest divorce rates in Europe, and, as in Scandinavia, cohabitation is becoming more popular as rates of marriage decline. The number of single-parent families is also high—one in five children in inner cities will be part of such a family at some point during childhood—and worries about single parenthood are frequently expressed. A broad spectrum of "official" political opinion tar-

48

gets fathers who desert their families and refuse to take financial responsibility for them, but there is widespread recognition that it is impossible to roll the clock back and make divorce more difficult. Rape within marriage looks set to become a crime. The stigma of illegitimacy has all but disappeared. Homosexuality, however, has not achieved a similar degree of tolerance, and significantly, homosexuals in Britain, particularly men, have fewer rights in relation to the age of consent and decriminalization than homosexuals in almost all other European countries. It almost seems as if, now that adultery, fornication, cohabitation, divorce, and remarriage have become commonplace, homosexuality has had to bear the brunt of all the displaced moral indignation of the traditionally minded segments of society and, indeed, of the more liberal segments as well. One could almost say that lesbians and gay men have "carried the can" for the rest of British society in the sense that the moral sexual panics of the late eighties and early nineties focused particularly on them.[1] Britain affords an interesting contrast with the United States, where fundamentalist Christianity plays a more central role. Britain has long been known as one of the least religious countries in the world, and although the influence of Moslem, Jewish, and Christian fundamentalists is probably growing, it would be a mistake to perceive the situation in Britain as parallel to that in the United States. Yet because the vicious prejudice expressed against lesbians and gay men, especially by the tabloid press, is often clearly not motivated by religious feeling, it can be even more frightening.

In radical equal opportunity discourse, lesbians and gay men are often bracketed in with women and blacks, although in a sense gays and lesbians are more vulnerable, or at least their situation is different. In the first place, women and blacks (world wide) do not constitute a minority, as homosexuals do. Another feature peculiar to gays (and Jews to some extent) is that, again unlike women and most blacks, they are not immediately distinguishable from the rest of the population. For this reason, dress and appearance have played a special role in formation of the gay identity, and as more gays come out publicly, dress becomes an even more important signal to the world of one's identity. (Dress and appearance have, of course, also played a crucial role in the formation of black and Jewish identities.)

FASHION GENDER AND IDENTITY

Costume history in Britain was for many years characterized by painstaking empirical work. Within this tradition, the ways in which fashion was theorized were, on the whole, less sophisticated and less successful than its empirical grounding. Surprisingly, for example, use was often made of the work of Thorstein Veblen (1957), who hated and condemned fashion as pernicious "conspicuous consumption." This was surprising because we usually presume that those who devote their life to the study of a subject—fashion, in this case—take pleasure in it: yet Veblen condemned the fashions of his time outright. On the other hand, Veblen did take female subordination seriously, and was aware of the ambivalence for women of transforming themselves into objects to be looked at—one of the main functions of fashionable dress as he saw it.

Meanwhile other theoretical traditions belittled or trivialized the subject they purported to explain. Writers such as J. C. Flugel (1930) used psychoanalytic theory to explain fashion away; he viewed it as a neurotic symptom and looked forward to a utopian future in which we would be sufficiently psychologically mature to give up clothes altogether. More recently Alison Lurie (1981) concentrated on the unconscious meanings of dress, suggesting, for example, that although punk rockers might believe their style signified rebellion, in actual fact they dressed themselves like angry, unloved babies. This is the classic psychoanalytic put-down of all rebels.

Writers such as Quentin Bell (1947) and Cecil Beaton (1954) wrote about fashion in an informed, yet intuitive, anecdotal manner, treating the subject with refreshing wit and panache. Yet this somehow suggested that fashion was a "light" rather than a "serious" subject.

With the ascendancy of cultural studies, things changed. In Britain, cultural studies grew out of an interdisciplinary convergence of English literature, history, and sociology. Central to its concerns is the study of popular culture, which takes seriously the most apparently insignificant and vulgar aspects of everyday life. This area includes an exploration of the nature of pleasure and the way in which popular cultural objects and texts hook into individual and collective fantasies and fears.

The study of everyday life and popular culture soon came to include every sort of design, including fashion. Feminism played a key role in the formation of cultural studies, as did fashion, especially subcultural dress (Hebdige 1979). It was therefore not surprising that before long some feminists began to question the tradition that positioned them as hostile to fashion. Although some continue to believe that fashion is inescapably part of an oppressive consumerism which imposes coercive norms of beauty and conformity on women (see, for example, Brownmiller 1984 and Lovibond 1989), many feminists now argue that exploration of dress is important and valid and that dress and fashion are often used by

50

women to interrogate traditional and conventional norms. An interest in fashion may also be a feminist reaction against perceived prescriptions and proscriptions which seek to impose a "correct line" about what women should wear and how they should look. In general, the crude view of women as imprisoned and enslaved by fashion has given place to a more sophisticated recognition that fashion works in a complicated way in Western society to "produce" identities, including, very importantly, gender identities.

In the 1980s the development of identity politics—a political insistence on the importance of sexual, ethnic, and national identities in the construction of a sense of self, individually and collectively—flourished alongside these other cultural preoccupations. Yet paradoxically, the 1980s was also the decade of postmodernism. Postmodern theories such as poststructuralism and Lacanian psychoanalysis actually questioned the unitary nature of identity and emphasized its fluid, provisional, and fragmented aspects. The paradox arises because on the one hand some writers speak as if identities are fragmenting on all sides, yet others assume the coherence of black and other minority identities without question (see Huyssen 1988).

Thus cultural studies brought together a whole range of preoccupations, including fashion, and focused on the way individuals and groups do not merely passively ingest popular culture but actively use and transform it. Far from being brainwashed and oppressed by the entertainment industries and consumer goods, we adapt and reinterpret their meanings.

Cultural studies has come to include the sociology of the body—and clothing, socially speaking, normally "stands in" for the body. Body and clothes combine to create "appearance." The word *appearance* itself resonates with multiple meanings: we "take a pride in our appearance"; but ghosts also "appear," and another word for ghost is apparition, or appearance. So there is a notion of something either imaginary, hallucinatory, or insubstantial in the word, which gestures toward the spectacular and theatrical aspects of self-preservation. Yet at the same time we have no other means of representing ourselves. As Kaja Silverman (1986: 145) has pointed out:

> Clothing and other kinds of ornamentation make the human body culturally visible . . . clothing draws the body so that it can be culturally seen, and articulates it in a meaningful form. . . . Even if my sympathies were not fully on the side of extravagant sartorial display, I would feel impelled to stress as strongly as possible that clothing is a necessary condition of subjectivity—

51

that in articulating the body it simultaneously articulates the psyche. . . . Laplanche makes [this] point when he insists upon the need for an "envelope" or "sack" to contain both body and ego, and to make possible even the most rudimentary distinctions between self and other, inside and outside. . . . In effect, clothing is that envelope.

MAKING A QUEER APPEARANCE

Clothing and body together construct a gendered "appearance," and gender, so significant for all women and men, is especially significant for lesbians and gay men. Of course, as Gayle Rubin (1984) has argued, it should be possible to distinguish sexual preference from gender assignation, but in Western culture the two are usually collapsed together. So dress for gays—or as many of a new generation of radical lesbians and gay men now prefer to call themselves, queers—may be used to conceal sexual preference or to flaunt it, may reinforce or go against the grain of the wearer's anatomical sex to signify a "butch" or "femme" gender; but however it is used, it is always of moment. Partly for this reason, throughout the 1980s the attitudes of lesbians and gay men toward dress tended to be different from those of feminists. Many feminists simply wanted not to think about their clothes and chose styles whose main purpose was to avoid sexual objectification.

The links between dress, gender, and sexual preference were finally formed only in the nineteenth century. Although Western dress has always signaled gender, this tendency appears to have intensified about the time of the industrial revolution. Masculinity was redefined and more intensely coded in dress by the dandies of the Regency, and dark colors, beards, and a general functional sobriety soon became the norm for men. At the same time, the development of male homosexuality as a way of life or gender identity gradually replaced the earlier, more simple notion of unlawful sexual acts such as buggery. Many historians and sociologists of homosexuality argue that the "homosexual role" for gay men developed very slowly and became fully established only toward the end of the nineteenth century (Bray 1983; McIntosh 1981; Plummer 1981; and Weeks 1977). It is usually assumed that the lesbian identity emerged even later.

Yet while the self-presentation of lesbians and gay men cuts across "normal" biologically based sexual identities, it is also defined by them. If we look historically at the ways in which lesbians and gay men have presented themselves satorially, we find that they have often seemed imprisoned or at least restricted by existing masculine/feminine conventions of dress. Proust wrote of the surreptitious use of bracelets and cosmetics by late nineteenth-century homosexual men, although he also referred to the opposite solution of exaggerated masculinity (Proust 1981)—a theme that returned with the "clone" dressing of the 1970s. By the early twentieth century, when Proust was writing, a distinct lesbian identity was also emerging. Colette, whose lesbian relationship with the marquise de Belboeuf ("Missy") lasted for eight years, writes insightfully—and rather mockingly—of the satorial norms that governed the social group of upper-class lesbians with whom she associated at this period:

> How timid I was, at that period when I was trying to look like a boy, and how feminine I was beneath my disguise of cropped hair. "Who would take us for women? Why, women." They alone were not fooled. With such distinguishing marks as pleated shirt front, hard collar, sometimes a waistcoat, and always a silk pocket handkerchief, I frequented a society perishing on the margin of all societies. . . . The clique I am referring to . . . tried, trembling with fear, to live without hypocrisy, the breathable air of society. This . . . sect claimed the right of "personal freedom" and equality with [male] homosexuality, that imperturable establishment. And they scoffed, if in whispers, at "Papa" Lépine, the Prefect of Police, who never could take lightly the question of women in men's clothes. (Colette 1971:61)

The most famous literary expression of lesbian masculine attire is found in Radclyffe Hall's *The Well of Loneliness*, published in 1928. Indeed Hall herself was famous, or notorious, in the 1920s for her masculine style of dress. She devotes one passage of her novel to what almost amounts to an initiation rite, when Mary, who has come to live with Stephen, the lesbian hero/ine, inspects her new lover's wardrobe as though it held the key to the mystery of Stephen's sexual nature: "Mary opened the wardrobe, revealing a long, neat line of suits hanging from heavy mahogany shoulders—she examined each suit in turn with great interest. . . . On the shelves there were orderly piles of shirts, crêpe de Chine pyjamas . . . and the heavy silk masculine underwear that for several years now had been worn by Stephen" (Hall 1982:324). Stephen's apparel almost *is* her sexuality, and her sexual attraction is mediated through her masculine garb and accessories. These also denote a strong class loyalty, since Stephen's whole appearance is designed to make her look as much as possible like an upper-class English gentleman—but with a difference. For at the heart of this masculinity is the vulnerability of her gendered fault, her ambiguity:

> Stephen was . . . grooming her hair with a couple of brushes that had been dipped in water. The water had darkened her hair in patches, but had deepened the wide wave above her forehead. Seeing Mary in the glass she did not turn round, but just smiled for a moment at their two reflections. Mary sat down in an arm-chair and watched her, noticing the strong, thin line of her thighs, noticing too the curve of her breasts—slight and com-pact, of a certain beauty. She had taken off her jacket and looked very tall in her soft silk shirt and her skirt of dark serge. (Hall 1982:323)

The glance in the mirror, the double reflections, mark both sameness and difference, the whole passage creating simultaneously an Other and a narcissistic love ideal (see Rolley 1992).

Radclyffe Hall seems to have accepted the view put forward by the sexologist Havelock Ellis and others that "inverts," as homosexual men and women were termed, constituted a "third sex," marked out from birth. It followed that the masculine woman invert would inevitably fall in love with a "normal" woman—although one, Ellis speculated, who was not quite attractive enough to find a male lover! This theory focuses interest on the invert rather than her (in this case) partner. In Stephen, Hall created an idealized self, a noble anomaly of nature, but Mary's sexual identity remains unquestioned; she is a passive blank. Hence the impression of narcissism. Paradoxically, an emphasis on dress, so often understood as demonstrating the narcissism of the feminine woman, comes, in *The Well of Loneliness*, to signify the nonfemininity of the "third sex."

Androgyny and narcissism are also evident in another lesbian classic of the 1930s, *We Too Are Drifting* by Gale Wilhelm, in which the boyish heroine is tormented by her attraction to and for women. One of the women with whom she is involved is vacuous, the other predatory, but both are feminine. Jan, however, the artist heroine, is used as a model for a statue of Hermaphroditus (see Weir and Wilson 1992). It is not Jan's identity that is specifically indicated through her clothing; in this novel it is the femininity of her lovers that is emphasized through their use of lipstick and soft dresses.

The complex interactions of masculine/feminine within the lesbian community were reworked in the United States during the 1940s and 1950s. Following the experience of the Second World War, when many homosexual men and women were able, for the first time, to find both anonymity and a gay community in the big cities and in the armed forces, the emphasis moved from aristocracy, isolation, and pessimism to a new affirmation of gay identity, notwithstanding McCarthyism and the repression of the early cold war period.[2] This affirmation was more radical, more working class, less elitist, less self-oppressed. For the writer Quentin Crisp (1979), to be a homosexual man in the 1930s and 1940s was still to be, if not a woman trapped in a man's body, at least a "true" homosexual, whose truth was always to love a "real man" who could never return his love. Outrageous makeup and effeminacy translated this potentially tragic situation into a form of social rebellion and challenge. But in the 1950s, butch and femme roles in the lesbian community seem to have acted as strong statements of a specifically lesbian desire. Butch lesbians did not just ape men, and they were depicted in the novels of the period as ardent, vulnerable, and attractive to other women. By this time the desire of the femme lesbian was no longer absent, nor was the femme a pale and passive copy of the heterosexual woman (see Nestle 1989; Weir and Wilson 1992). These differences were, nonetheless, still articulated through dress. Butch and femme were ways of being that involved very distinct dress codes, some obvious, others extremely subtle.

Many of the heroines of the dime store novels of the fifties, whether butch or femme, were making for the bohemias of the big cities, where it was possible to inhabit a gay subculture. Edmund White remembers this—in fact it was a young bohemian lesbian who first introduced his (autobiographical) hero to a gay social scene in this novel of the fifties:

> I see her even now striding along in black pants and a man's white shirt spotted with paint, her hair slicked back behind her ears. . . . She's wearing white sneakers, also spattered with paint, a sailor's pea coat and no makeup, although her eyebrows have been slightly plucked. She looks very scrubbed and German but also faintly glamorous; the glamour clings to her like the smell of gitanes in wool. Is it the hard defiance in her eyes or just the slicked-back hair with its suggestion of the high-school bad girl that lends her this dangerous aura? (White 1988:1)

White here describes a style of dress which emerged in the 1950s and operated as an alternative to the rigidly binary oppositions of butch and femme. This was bohemian dress. Originating in postwar Paris with the existentialists, it soon migrated to London's Soho and New York's Greenwich Village.

In the 1970s, feminists created a myth about the 1950s as a decade of seamless repression for women, and Lillian Faderman (1991) has recently extended that view to include the history of lesbians and gay men. Popular culture in the 1980s, meanwhile, portrayed in advertisements and films an alternative 1950s as an American utopia in which kitsch cultural objects were embalmed in the rosiest nostalgia.

There was, however, a third fifties, a radical counterculture, influenced by existentialism and other subversive movements—surrealism, for example—and this in turn influenced the mainstream. The key Hollywood heroes of the period were bisexual men—Marlon Brando, Montgomery Clift, and James Dean—who became aesthetic icons of the Hero as Outlaw (McCann 1991). Their outlaw status was signaled primarily by one key garment: the black leather jacket. Audrey Hepburn was the female star who offered a less threatening gamine alternative to standard feminine Hollywood sexiness in films such as *Sabrina* (U.K.: *Sabrina Fair*) and *Funny Face*. In the latter she portrayed a Left Bank/Greenwich Village existentialist who gets taken up and transformed by characters based on the fashion photographer Richard Avedon and fashion editor Diana Vreeland of both *Harper's Bazaar* and *Vogue*. Although at one level fashion triumphs, the film satirizes the whole fashion circus, and Audrey Hepburn emerged as the fifties icon of bohemian style. Indeed, she proved an inspiration to the architects of 1960s unisex youth styles, according to Barbara Hulanicki (1984:54, 61), one of the key British designers of "Swinging London" and the creator of the famous shop Biba. She recalls that "*Sabrina Fair* had made a huge impact on us all at college: everyone walked around in black sloppy sweaters, suede low-cut flatties and gold hoop earrings . . . Audrey Hepburn and Givenchy were made for each other. His little black dress with shoestring straps in *Sabrina Fair* must have been imprinted on many teenagers' minds forever."

In the 1960s and 1970s this androgyny influenced lesbian and gay male circles, where there was a reaction against what was seen as an aping of conventional gender roles. Under the impact too of the women's movement and gay liberation, politically conscious lesbians and gay men undertook a revaluation of gender and gender roles. One dominant gay fashion was the "clone look," in which gay men dressed alike in a masculine style—jeans, lumber jacket, moustache, boots—in part to protest the "slur" of effeminacy. Lesbian feminists reacted against butch and femme role playing and opted for a more androgynous style. But perhaps the fashion for androgyny was less radical than it seemed, since this was a period when androgynous fashions ruled in the mainstream as well.

UNSETTLING GENDER IDENTITIES

To rework gender definitions was not easy. What has always been unsettling and disturbing to those outside lesbian and gay culture has been the way in which the cross-dressing aspects of lesbian and gay sartorial codes have revealed the way in which gender includes elements of masquerade, even for heterosexuals. The "out" gay identity—the resistant, transgressive gay identity—has nevertheless been identity as critique rather than as alternative, aimed at messing up prevailing gender identities rather than creating new ones. At the end of the day, lesbians and gay men are still bounded by the parameters of existing binary alternatives: masculine/feminine.

Nevertheless, the meaning of these terms is altered, extended, and questioned by lesbian/gay dress codes. It is no longer quite so easy to map heterosexuality directly onto conventional stereotypes of gender which in turn get mapped onto biology. To mix elements of masculinity and femininity in dress and appearance calls into question the existing norms, challenges the audience, and demands a different response. In radical lesbian circles, experimentation with butch/femme and even sadomasochistic styles has constituted avant-garde—and sometimes controversial—ways of extending the boundaries of masculine/feminine as well as of sexual pleasure. S/M styles make use of fetish wear and punk, especially the way punk style juxtaposes incompatible elements and creates such inverted notions of beauty as red eyeshadow and black lipstick. Inge Blackman and Kathryn Perry (1990:69) have recently described some of the conventions of S/M styles: "The style differs depending on whether the wearer wants to indicate that she is the top/butch or the bottom/femme. Top dress will reveal the body from the waist upwards: light vest, waistcoat (no shirt) or no clothing at all. By exposing her breasts, the top defies the pervasive western fetish of the female breast and flirts with the demand that breasts be kept hidden. She declares her sexuality but at the same time she makes herself vulnerable." Here the breast, a symbol of femininity and feminine sexuality, one of the most fetishized of heterosexual markers, becomes the signifier of a, so to speak, masculine role in lesbian sexuality, although the word *masculine* would not normally be used in that context. Leather and rubber are important in S/M styles, as are boots—Dr. Martens, biker boots, or cowboy boots.

The bottom or femme may wear similar clothes, but together with a very short skirt or dress, lingerie, and high heels. In this way, conventional symbols of masculinity and femininity, perversion, aggression, and submission are reworked to correspond with sexual identities that are also not clearly restricted to rigid roles—that is, there can be an exchange of roles or, if roles remain relatively stable, their meaning is nevertheless challenged. Thus it has been argued that the femininity of the femme lesbian carries a set of meanings that are distinct from the meanings of heterosexual femininity, which, in the world at large, is much more closely aligned to material relations of oppression and dominance. By contrast, in the alternative world of the lesbian and gay subculture, the ultimate equality of sameness can offer a field on which fantasies of and experiments with difference can be developed.

In any case, lesbian dress in the late 1980s was as much about the rehabilitation of femininity in a different context as about sadism and aggression. What caused the most uproar within the lesbian feminist community were not even the most contentious symbols of sadism; for many critics, even worse than the chains and swastikas were the signs of femininity. How could lesbians who were feminists wear lipstick, high heels, and cocktail dresses? Initially the wearers offered a celebratory defense of such practices, bringing notions of postmodern playfulness to the fore so that, at their most trivial, butch/femme dress codes became *just* style. This situation was different from that of the 1950s, from which these styles were copied or reworked. In the fifties, butch/femme was in deadly earnest.

A further reevaluation has now begun. Perhaps the adoption of roles signaled by distinct styles is very shallow; alternatively, perhaps it is a smokescreen for unresolved questions. "If difference is necessary for desire to exist," two femme lesbians ask, "*what* difference? Are butch and femme ways of organising certain differences between women and eroticising them? Or is butch/femme a simple matter of masculine and feminine identifications?" (Ardill and O'Sullivan 1990:81).

At one level this "messing up" of gender identification is playful and parodic, although it is interesting how consistently even playful countercultural dress codes can anger outsiders and arouse opposition. In the late sixties, long hair (on men) and unisex clothes caused apoplectic rage in onlookers, as did the punk spiked hair and torn clothes of the midseventies. Yet mainstream fashion then takes up these deviant forms of dress, reworking them into something unthreatening, then acceptable, and eventually boring and passé. Indeed, by a strange paradox, aspects of punk aggression styles became signatures of Thatcherite success in Britain—the hard haircuts, the black, the strong makeup.

Thus is fashion always on a knife-edge, and transgressive dressing too: it shocks, challenges, and subverts, yet is itself subverted, recuperated, and drained of its radical content. This paradox occurs partly because the meanings of dress are highly contextual and flexible (see Davis 1985, 1987, 1992). It also reflects the voracious nature of fashion design, which cannibalizes even the most unlikely sartorial forms: zoot suits can cause riots in 1940s Los Angeles, yet come to be a standard and fairly toothless part of pop music culture in a later period. As George Melly (1970) pointed out long ago, rebellion is defused and becomes merely style.

POSTMODERN IDENTITIES

Play and parody are seen as characteristics of postmodernism, and in theory, in a postmodern culture, gender identities should be flexible, free-floating, and unserious, in tune with the alleged fragmentation and bricolage of postmodern times. Writers such as Andreas Huyssen (1988) and Craig Owens (1985) have played up the positive and radical aspects of a fragmenting culture through whose cracks and fissures new, radical identities can appear—the "Others" of Western culture can find affirmation and a stronger sense of identity in this situation:

> It was especially the art, writing, film making and criticism of women and minority artists with their recuperation of buried and mutilated traditions, their emphasis on exploring forms of gender- and raced-based subjectivity in aesthetic productions and experiences, and their refusal to be limited to standard canonisations, which added a whole new dimension to the critique of high modernism and to the emergence of alternative forms of culture. . . .
>
> Women's art, literature and criticism are an important part of the postmodern culture of the 1970s and 1980s and indeed a measure of the vitality of that culture, the stability and sanctity of canon and tradition. (Huyssen 1988:198)

Yet Huyssen is also aware of the reaction against radicalism, experimentation, and questioning: "Actually, the suspicion is in order that the conservative turn of these past years has indeed something to do with the sociologically significant emergence of various forms of 'otherness' in the cultural sphere, all of which are perceived as a threat to the stability and sanctity of canon and tradition" (Huyssen 1988:199). And Fredric Jameson (1984) has described postmodern culture in hyperbolic terms as a kind of return of the repressed, the revenge of the whole detritus of capitalism, condemning us all to live in B-movie cities or eternal shopping malls.

In Britain the lesbian and gay community certainly has been at the cutting edge of the "conservative turn." In addition to coping with the AIDs crisis, it has fought the notorious Clause 28 of the Local Government Act, a law passed in 1988 to prevent local government from "promoting" homosexuality. Paradoxically, Clause 28, intended to intimidate, aroused a massive reaction from the lesbian and gay community. One further result was that Ian McLellen, the most famous and distinguished contemporary British classical actor, "came out" in protest and was subsequently invited to meet the prime minister, John Major, specifically to discuss the problems of lesbians and gay men, the first ever such meeting.[3]

On the other hand, in 1990 a group of gay men were given harsh prison sentences for consental S/M activity in private, sentences recently confirmed on appeal, and now before the House of Lords, the highest court of appeal. There have been further efforts to restrict the legality of homosexual activity through legislation and to restrict the right of lesbians to artificial insemination, although calls from the Right for the repeal of the 1967 Sexual Offences Act (which partially decriminalized male homosexual behavior) and for a ban to prevent lesbians having children have been unsuccessful.

The Right, in fact, is divided. Attacks on the gay community come largely from its fundamentalist Christian lobby. This lobby is unrepresentative of the Right as a whole, since the Tory party has a more liberal (in the American sense) wing, and there are also right-wing libertarians who object to any restrictions on the freedom of the individual. Yet, although unrepresentative, the fundamentalist lobby does have an influential following among right-wing members of Parliament.

Clause 28 has no doubt had an intimidatory effect on some public bodies, yet gay culture in Britain remains highly visible, and some even believe it was reinvigorated by the recent attacks. At present we see an ongoing and intensified contest between the alternative, visible lesbian and gay community and homophobia's traditional supporters. Dress remains central to this struggle and is used as an infinitely flexible symbolic instrument of outrage and sexuality. My local (London) newspaper, the *Hampstead and Highgate Express,* covering as it does Hampstead Heath, which contains both a gay cruising ground and an all-male bathing pond, carries weekly reports of skirmishes in this war of attrition. The following is from an 8 September 1991 article, "Gay Bathers Claim Pond Harassment": "A man was assaulted by an ex-member of the heath management team for wearing a T-shirt with a picture of a nude man. Property developer Sean Ross-Powell . . . was arrested near the pond two weeks ago for wearing the same T-shirt and charged with displaying an indecent design. But the charges were dropped at a hearing in Highbury Court on Monday." (It should be pointed out that the man in question was wearing his t-shirt in a nude bathing area!) Once again, dress is at the center of the dispute and symbolizes a new militancy on the part of gays. In an extraordinarily homophobic article in the supposedly liberal national daily newspaper the *Guardian,* however, the writer (himself apparently gay) condemns the way dress acts as the carrier of a potent message of defiance:

> For twenty years we have been mimicking the traditional force of oppression, the macho male. By sidling up close, by taking it home and fucking it we, in pantomime, had been destroying its power over us. Steve is a skinhead in clownsized DMs [Doctor Martens boots] who's a regular at the LA [the London Apprentice, a popular male gay bar]. "People look at me on the Tube [subway] like I'm trouble, like I might be about to kick their face in. I wonder what they'd say if they knew I was a poof."
>
> So successful had we become in this game, so unafraid, we took it out of the clubs and bars and paraded it on the streets where we watched our parody become the fashions of the men from whom it was originally stolen. No longer in pantomime but in reality, we had neutralised our oppressors. (Haselden 1991)

This article focuses on the destructive and nihilistic side of defiance; in fact, both the bleak and the optimistic views of lesbian and gay life in the 1990s are accurate. Huyssen and Craig Owens were too upbeat in their celebration of the postmodern scene as a stage for the emergence of a plurality of identities, and Jameson is correct to remind us of the violence, exploitation, and destructiveness of the capitalist world of which postmodernism is also expressive. Fragmentation in the postmodern world does not mean simply a diaspora, a liberation from monolithic forms of power into a world in which power no longer signifies. On the contrary,

61

power struggles intensify. Foucault's vision of micropower struggles in every arena of the social seems more accurate, although it too is, in its own way, insufficient.

Lesbian and gay alternative culture offers an especially clear example of the way the multiple, fragmented identities of the contemporary scene represent a constant process of contestation. The lesbian or gay identity may be a clear case of an identity that is fluid. Yet it is achieved in the context of rigid opposition and is both dangerous and vulnerable. Lesbian and gay alternative culture provides a space in which sartorial and other aesthetic experiments and explorations can redefine identities, but this redefinition is never achieved painlessly or easily. Lesbians and gays seem to be on the front lines of the tremendous, unfinished battle between those who believe in Nature—the essential, biological core of maleness and femaleness—and those who insist on the constructed and "unnatural" nature of gender. This conflict may well turn out to be *the* great cultural and ideological battle of the twentieth century.

The dress codes of lesbian and gay subculture offer a useful case study of the creation of an appearance which corresponds not to an assumed "nature" or even entirely to the social creation of a community or group through clothing, although that does figure. Above all, these styles appear as an attempt to assimilate dress to fantasy in a more conscious way than is usually the case. They constitute a text which aims to articulate lesbian and gay sexual desire. In spite of or even because of their marginality, it is possible to use them as a lens through which to view more general problems of gender. Probably all clothing in the Western world is chosen on an individual basis for some unconscious as well as conscious reasons, no matter how residual the unconscious element may be when the subject is, for example, a middle-class white man in a conventional suit. What is interesting about some lesbian and gay subcultural modes is the way there is almost an attempt to make the unconscious conscious and to explore in a manner that goes deeper than style just how fluid—or not— gender can be. At the same time, these styles go beyond the gender issue to speak a political position and to symbolize the demand for a right to an open existence, an aspiration still to be achieved.

NOTES

1. This article is based on a paper given at the International Sociological Association World Congress of Sociology in July 1990. It reworks aspects of several of my recent articles (Wilson 1991a, 1991b) and Weir and Wilson (1982).

2. This period is well documented in gay history. See D'Emilio 1983; Licata 1985; Licata and Petersen 1985; and Duberman, Vicinus, and Chauncey 1990.

3. In the context of Clause 28, it is of interest that according to a recent survey by the London-based Labour Research Department, "Trades unions are increasingly taking up the cudgels on behalf of their lesbian and gay members." Sixty percent of British trade unions surveyed in 1991 "had produced and distributed publicity among members about lesbian and gay issues and the same number had included such issues in their training courses. Eighty percent had taken action over the anti-gay Section 28 of the 1988 Local Government Act and thirty-two percent were actively opposing the discriminatory Clause 25 of the new Criminal Justice Bill" (*Morning Star*, 3 June 1991).

REFERENCES

Ardill, Susan, and Sue O'Sullivan. 1990. "Butch Femme Obsessions." *Feminist Review*, no. 34 (Spring) (lesbian issue).

Ash, Juliet, and Elizabeth Wilson, eds. 1992. *Chic Thrills: A Fashion Reader*. London: Pandora Press.

Beaton, Cecil. 1954. *The Glass of Fashion*. London: Weidenfeld and Nicolson.

Bell, Quentin. 1947. *Of Human Finery*. London: Hogarth Press.

Benstock, Shari. 1987. *Women of the Left Bank: Paris, 1900–1940*. London: Virago.

Blackman, Inge, and Kathryn Perry. 1990. "Skirting the Issue: Lesbian Fashion for the 1990s." *Feminist Review*, no. 34 (Spring) (lesbian issue).

Blankley, Elyse. 1984. "Return to Mytilène: Renée Viven and the City of Women." In *Women Writers and the City: Essays in Feminist Literary Criticism*, ed. Susan Merrill Squier. Knoxville: University of Tennessee Press.

Boffin, Tessa, and Jean Fraser, eds. 1991. *Stolen Glances: Lesbians Take Photographs*. London: Pandora Press.

Boyne, Roy, and Ali Rattansi, eds. 1990. *Postmodernism and Society*. London: Macmillan.

Bray, Alan. 1983. *Homosexuality in Renaissance England*. London: Gay Men's Press.

Brownmiller, Susan. 1984. *Femininity*. New York: Fawcett Columbine.

Colette, S.-G. 1971. *The Pure and the Impure*. Harmondsworth, England: Penguin. Originally published in French in 1932 as *Ces plaisirs*.

Couch Carl, and David Maines, eds. 1987. *Information Technology and Social Structure*. Springfield, Ill.: Charles C. Thomas.

Crisp, Quentin. 1979. *The Naked Civil Servant*. London: Heinemann.

Davis, Fred. 1985. "Clothing and Fashion as Communication." In *The Psychology of Fashion*, ed. Michael Solomon. Lexington, Mass.: D. C. Heath.

———. 1987. "Gender, Fashion and the Dialectic of Identity." In *Information Technology and Social Structure*, ed. Carl Couch and David Maines. Springfield, Ill.: Charles C. Thomas.

———. 1992. *Fashion, Culture and Identity*. Chicago: University of Chicago Press.

D'Emilio, John. 1983. *Sexual Politics, Sexual Communities: The Making of a Homosexual Minority in the United States, 1940–1970*. Chicago: University of Chicago Press.

Duberman, Martin B., Martha Vicinus, and George Chauncey, Jr., eds. 1990. *Hidden from History: Reclaiming the Gay and Lesbian Past*. Harmondsworth, England: Penguin.

Faderman, Lillian. 1991. *Odd Girls and Twilight Lovers: A History of Lesbian Life in Twentieth-Century America*. New York: Columbia University Press.

Flugel, J. C. 1930. *The Psychology of Clothes*. London: Hogarth Press.

Foster, Hal, ed. 1985. *The Anti-Aesthetic: Essays on Postmodern Culture*. Port Townsend, Wash.: Bay Press.

Hall, Radclyffe. 1982. *The Well of Loneliness*. London: Virago. Originally published in 1928.

Haselden, Rupert. 1991. "Gay Abandon." *Weekend Guardian*, 7–8 September.

Hebdige, Dick. 1979. *Subculture: The Meaning of Style*. London: Methuen.

Hulanicki, Barbara. 1984. *From A to Biba*. London: Hamish Hamilton.

Huyssen, Andreas. 1988. *After the Great Divide: Modernism, Mass Culture, Postmodernism*. London: Macmillan.

Jameson, Fredric. 1984. "Postmodernism; or the Cultural Logic of Late Capitalism." *New Left Review*, no. 146 (July/August).

Licata, Salvatore. 1985. "The Homosexual Rights Movement in the United States: A Traditionally Overlooked Area of American History." In *The Gay Past*, ed. Salvatore Licata and Robert Petersen. New York: Harrington Park Press.

Licata, Salvatore, and Robert Petersen, eds. 1985. *The Gay Past: A Collection of Historical Essays*. New York: Harrington Park Press.

Lovibond, Sabina. 1989. "Feminism and Postmodernism." *New Left Review* 178 (Nov.-Dec.): 5–29.

Lurie, Alison. 1981. *The Language of Clothes*. London: Heinemann.

McCann, Graham. 1991. *Rebel Males: Clift, Brando, and Dean*. London: Hamish Hamilton, New Brunswick, N.J.: Rutgers University Press.

McIntosh, Mary. 1981. "The Homosexual Role." In *The Making of the Modern Homosexual*, ed. Kenneth Plummer. London: Hutchinson.

Melly, George. 1970. *Revolt into Style: The Pop Arts in Britain*. Harmondsworth, England: Penguin.

Modleski, Tania, ed. 1986. *Studies in Entertainment: Critical Approaches to Mass Culture*. Bloomington: Indiana University Press.

Munt, Sally, ed. 1992. *Being There: New Lesbian Criticism*. Hemel Hempstead, England: Harvester Wheatsheaf.

Nestle, Joan. 1989. *A Restricted Country*. London: Sheba.

Owens, Craig. 1985. "The Discourse of Others: Feminism and Postmodernism." In *The Anti-Aesthetic: Essays on Postmodern Culture*, ed. Hal Foster. Port Townsend, Wash.: Bay Press.

Plummer, Kenneth, ed. 1981. *The Making of the Modern Homosexual*. London: Hutchinson.

Proust, Marcel. 1981. *Remembrance of Things Past*. London: Chatto and Windus. Originally published in 1922.

Rolley, Katrina. 1992. "Love, Desire, and the Pursuit of the Whole: Dress and the Lesbian Couple." In *Chic Thrills: A Fashion Reader,* ed. Juliet Ash and Elizabeth Wilson. London: Pandora Press.

Rubin, Gayle. 1984. "Thinking Sex: Notes for a Radical Theory of the Politics of Sexuality." In *Pleasure and Danger: Exploring Female Sexuality,* ed. Carol Vance. Boston: Routledge and Kegan Paul.

Silverman, Kaja. 1986. "Fragments of a Fashionable Discourse." In *Studies in Entertainment: Critical Approaches to Mass Culture,* ed. Tania Modleski. Bloomington: Indiana University Press.

Squier, Susan Merrill, ed. 1984. *Women Writers and the City: Essays in Feminist Literary Criticism*. Knoxville: University of Tennessee Press.

Vance, Carol, ed. 1984. *Pleasure and Danger: Exploring Female Sexuality*. Boston: Routledge and Kegan Paul.

Veblen, Thorstein. 1957. *The Theory of the Leisure Class*. London: Allen and Unwin. Originally published in 1899.

Weeks, Jeffrey. 1977. *Coming Out*. London: Quartet.

Weir, Angela, and Elizabeth Wilson. 1992. "Lesbian Fiction and 1950s Suburbia: The Greyhound Bus Station in the Evolution of Lesbian Popular Culture." In *Being There: New Lesbian Criticism,* ed. Sally Munt. Hempstead, England: Harvester Wheatsheaf.

White, Edmund. 1988. *The Beautiful Room Is Empty*. London: Picador.

Wilson, Elizabeth. 1985. *Adorned in Dreams: Fashion and Modernity*. Berkeley: University of California Press.

———. 1988. *Hallucinations*. New York: W. W. Norton.

———. 1991a. "Making an Appearance." In *Stolen Glances: Lesbians Take Photographs,* ed. Tessa Boffin and Jean Fraser. London: Pandora Press.

———. 1991b. *The Sphinx in the City*. Berkeley: University of California Press.

CLOTHING, CONTROL, AND WOMEN'S AGENCY: THE MITIGATION OF PATRIARCHAL POWER

Linda Boynton Arthur

It is "part and parcel of daily experience to feel both free and enchained, capable of shaping our own future and yet confronted by towering, seemingly impersonal, constraints."
—M. Archer, *Culture and Agency*

In this chapter, by examining how clothing can simultaneously symbolize agency and constraint, I examine the ways women move between both. I do so in a particularly rigid social context which seems to offer little opportunity for resistance—a conservative Holdeman Mennonite community.[1] Holdeman Mennonite women live within but also negotiate the boundaries of their lives, and they do so in a tightly controlled and highly patriarchal world.[2] Metaphorically referred to as "a mirror to the soul," women's clothing is considered by the Holdeman Mennonite community to be the external manifestation of inner attitudes. For Holdeman Mennonites, then, dress provides a visual display of religiosity.[3]

Sociologically speaking, it does more than this. Dress and, by extension, the body are the sites where different symbolic meanings are constructed and contested. This case substantiates Mary Douglas's thesis that the human body is a symbol for the social body, that is, that persons' bodies represent the values of the culture to which they belong. She explains that such symbols arise from pressures within a culture to create consonance between physiological and social experiences. The more value people give to social constraints, the more value they set on symbols of bodily control (Douglas 1970:67). Further, she argues that when social groups are threatened, they use the body in a symbolic manner to define and defend their boundaries (Douglas 1982a:9).

Thus the control of women's clothing by Mennonite ministers as well as the ways women resist this contest represent a negotiation of symbolic meaning for their society at large. From this perspective, neither social control nor collective resistance is a clear-cut phenomenon. These issues are negotiated in everyday interaction in even the most tightly controlled communities.

While compliance with group norms or personal control is required for all Holdeman Mennonites, for women of the community, constraints involve both formal and informal controls that regulate almost every facet of life. The church community regulates social roles and social activities. If there is no specific rule, then usually a custom dictates the correct procedure for any activity. Diversity in any manner is frowned on. Following tradition is the rule which leads to homogeneity. Nevertheless, the women experience a measure of ambivalence. They find comfort in sameness but yearn for variety, especially in clothing.

Although Mennonites as a group feel threatened by the outside world, Holdeman Mennonite women in addition feel threatened by the men of the community. Because the women's need for variety and self-expression is expressed through subtle variations in their dress, clothing is a source of conflict between men and women. In this conflict men exercise control, with ministers having the most power. Women, however, walk a fine line between obedience to the norms and self-assertion when they react to the control exercised by men.

Plagued by anxiety, women nevertheless maneuver in a subtle manner. Through individual and group deviance from the norms, they attempt to change the details of their traditional dress. In doing so they confront the established image and carefully fashion an alternative to the image defined by men, resisting what appear to be overwhelming constraints. Subtle changes in dress, then, function symbolically to establish solidarity among women and to circumvent patriarchal control.

Since resistance to change is characteristic of Holdeman Mennonite culture, the changes that do occur are, as we would expect, minute. Nevertheless the tension between agency and constraint, or power and resistance, becomes apparent in these subtle struggles over the symbolic meaning of women's dress.

POWER AND RESISTANCE

Power and resistance are often examined in terms of their public impact. Control of women, however, is also an intensely personal matter tied to conceptions of self. Merten and Schwartz (1982) note that by transgressing the conventional boundaries between public and private, symbolic process in nonritual contexts acquires power to represent the self. They argue that by implicating the self in the constitution of new metaphors, symbolic process in everyday life gives meaning to normative conflict. Symbolic processes involved in normative conflict are frequently not investigated in depth in the social control literature.

Most research on social control tends to be macroscopic in nature and focuses on the use of formal/legal means of control. Goffman (1963, 1971) was among the first to remind us that there is an alternative: we could focus more microscopically in order to investigate symbolic processes. From this perspective, social control would be conceptualized as a social process which, while normatively governed, occurs in everyday interactions. The norms governing social behavior in any situation are implicit. They go unnoticed until they are violated. Then sanctions can be applied to bring behavior back into normative compliance. Here infractions are discouraged by others.

Goffman goes on to specify three forms that normative controls can take. First, there is *personal social control*. The individual refrains from improper behavior by self-regulation. If she or he has acted improperly, the offense is admitted and reparations are undertaken in order to reestablish the social norms. Second, there is *informal social control*. When the individual begins to offend, peers may warn that disapproval is imminent and that sanctions may be applied. Increasing pressure may be exerted until the offender is brought into line, which reaffirms social norms (Goffman 1971:346–347). This feedback is one of the main mechanisms of socialization. Third, the threat that an offender introduces to the social order is managed through *formal social control*. These social sanctions are administered by specialized agents such as the police. Criminals break social rules and ideally are punished. In sum, personal, informal, and formal controls are the means by which conformity to social norms is effected. Deviation is inhibited or corrected, and compliance is assured (Goffman 1971:347–348). Similarly, Douglas (1982a:5) has argued that "people who've banded together . . . will tend to coerce one another to develop the full implications of their style of life."

Further, Douglas (1982b) claims that all conflict within families, churches, and social groups is really about the boundaries of each institution. The dissent centers on how to deal with normative behavior that becomes encoded as rules. The rules may be as simple as dress codes or as complex as laws. Nonetheless, social control measures are used effectively by society to protect the institution's boundaries. The social body, then, constrains the physical body. As a result, the body (including its care and grooming) is a highly restricted medium of expression.

One of the most significant boundaries in society is the line drawn between male and female. The gender system is defined by Schur (1984) as a pervasive network of interrelated norms and sanctions through which female (and male) behavior is evaluated and controlled. Gender-related norms maintain their dominance in society and influence the "micropolitics" of routine interactions (Emerson and Messinger 1977).

In this chapter I take Goffman's recommendation to examine social control microscopically as my analytic starting place. From this position, and using an analysis of dress, I explore both the cultural constraints on Holdeman Mennonite women and their resistance to those constraints. I argue that even in the rigid structure of Holdeman Mennonite life, where men in general and ministers in particular have the power to exercise formal social controls, women resist. Since self-control is a basic requisite of life in Mennonite societies, individual women exercise personal control. In addition, women working together in groups exercise informal collective control. These controls both reinforce dress code norms and contest them.

Holdeman Mennonite women resist not through massive insurrection, but through the most minute everyday practices. By examining how social control is both exercised and resisted within their community, we not only get a picture of the women's never-ending creativity, but we add to the theoretical discourses on social control. Drawing on the insights of Douglas (1970) and Mauss (1936), we can understand women's bodies as an image of society, as giving visual expression to sociocultural values. In other words, women's bodies must be analyzed in conjunction with this social dimension.

Thus control of the Holdeman Mennonite women's clothing by their ministers and the women's resistance to it represent a negotiation of symbolic meanings about both women's bodies and the social body. Negotiations about women's dress are also negotiations about gender and power. As ministers and women struggle over dress codes, ministers symbolically reinscribe themselves as powerful and women as other. Women's bodies, clothed as they are, are symbolically marked and located on the margins. The social body is male. As women resist the dress code, they also restrict their otherness, their location on the margins of power. These struggles take place in the context of an ever-present historical past, which continues to have a great deal of influence on the Holdeman Mennonites' everyday life. History and tradition are used to maintain the status quo and prevent change.

SOME HISTORY

Branded in Europe as heretics, Mennonites migrated throughout the Continent from the sixteenth century on, hoping to escape religious persecution. Eventually some came to North America, where they established isolated communities required to "live and dress simply in avoidance of the world" (Boynton 1986; Hiebert 1973:25). This separation was facilitated by strict social control measures.

The theme that links social control and clothing norms is the historical pattern of "avoidance" or separation from the world. Mennonites believe that there are two kingdoms—the kingdom of God and the kingdom of the world. Separation from "the world" was a simple matter while the Mennonites were physically isolated in remote communities. However, as non-Mennonites moved in among these sectarians, Mennonites began to feel their influence, and many became acculturated. For conservative Mennonites who saw acculturation as a threat, separation from the world became a divisive issue that led to several schisms, including the Holdeman schism of 1859.

Alluding to acculturation and citing the loss of Mennonite distinctiveness, John Holdeman and his followers left the Old Mennonite church. For them, separation from the world was accomplished symbolically by retention of many of the old traditions, including plain dress,[4] formalized in both proscribed and prescribed dress codes. According to Hiebert (pers. comm. 1980), in the early days of the sect Holdeman had prescribed a dress code for women which was characterized by a cape dress with a high neck, loose bodice, and fitted waist.

The historical pattern of modest and plain clothing has continued. Like other "plain people," the Holdemans believe that a lack of emphasis on external beauty leads to the expression of spirituality (Scott 1986:15). Clothing, as all of life, has to be brought under the scrutiny of New Testament standards. The most salient symbol of a woman's Christianity is her black head-covering, worn to symbolize her submission to God, to men in general, and to her husband in particular.

Within Mennonite culture, women have always been subservient to the men. According to the Holdeman Mennonites, male power and female submission are divinely ordered and are rooted in the Bible, the authoritative word of God. This belief results in gender-based segregation within the sect. Men hold all positions of formal power. A group of ten to twelve ministers and deacons are expected to define and eliminate deviance in behavior and appearance. For these patriarchs, control of deviance seems a straightforward matter. Guidelines are based on tradition and the communal goal of living a good Christian life. Through consensus among themselves they determine where the boundaries of deviance are drawn—boundaries that make most change deviant.

If men have the formal power in the family and community, women have informal power rooted in their age-sets. Deliberately emphasizing the corporate nature of social groups, age-sets are a particular type of social organization, a permanent grouping of individuals by age and sex. The Holdemans are patrilocal, so as women marry into a congregation, they are accepted into an age-set.[5] Usually persons enter the set as children and pass through the age-grades as a group; as a consequence, "I" becomes "we" and suppresses individuality (Gulliver 1968:157–161).

In church and other social situations, such as picnics and dinners at the social hall, the sexes remain separate.[6] A Holdeman Mennonite woman, then, interacts primarily in a world of women organized by age-sets. These groups comprise not just a social network, but a working social organization whose complex function is devoted to affirming social norms. It monitors its own behavior in order to insure compliance to religious norms, while at the same time supporting some infractions of the norms. As a consequence, the age-set provides an informal female channel that subverts the formal channels of male control.

THE STUDY COMMUNITY

I studied a specific Holdeman Mennonite community called Bend in northern California, a farming community of 310 persons on the Sacramento River.[7] The community is comprised of sixty-five families. Because land is inherited patrilineally, it is common for several generations of a family to live on farms near each other. Most of the men in the community are farmers, and all of the married women are housewives. Large families are the norm (five children average), and raising children as good Christians is the central focus for all.

The community interacts extensively with the other West Coast Holdeman Mennonite congregations beyond Bend. These communities are linked through a national church conference, missionary work, and marriage. Since the Holdeman Mennonites are religiously endogamous, approximately half the young women leave to marry men from other congregations. The combination of endogamy, patrilocal residence, and few converts creates a community in which most people are related (at least distantly) to each other.

I collected data in two phases. During the first phase of fieldwork,

71

which was intermittent and occurred over a forty-month period, I observed and conducted casual interviews with church members (1979–1984).[8] During the second phase, which occurred between 1985 and 1987, with follow-up interviews in 1991, I interviewed, in groups and individually, most of the local people who had left the church. Almost all of them had been formally expelled.[9] These interviews were tape-recorded and transcribed. Because these people had not returned to the church even under the intense pressure of shunning, they were acutely aware of the power of tradition, history, and social control in Mennonite society.

Tradition and control within the community overlap in the women's clothing. Dresses have changed little since the early days of the sect. Following the styles of their forebearers, women and girls wear shirtwaist dresses characterized by a wide, long skirt and a fitted bodice with buttons down the center to the waist. There is generally a small collar and belt. The uniform attire of Holdeman Mennonite women attests to separation from external society as well as separation of the sexes. Dress reflects the assumed natural gender differences that underlie patriarchal family and social systems.

A MIRROR TO THE SOUL: CONTROLLING THE IMAGE

Since nearly all members of the Holdeman Mennonite community attend every church activity, objective evaluation of a person's commitment to the faith is impossible, so symbolic measures such as dress codes are employed instead. The sexes have different standards as to proper Mennonite dress. While the women dress in a uniquely Mennonite style, the men dress in Levis and plaid shirts, much like outsiders. John and his wife were expelled for differing with the ministers over interpretation of doctrine. He explained: "It's always been that way. Women have always had to dress more carefully. It's a way of the men controlling the women. Holdeman men *need* to control women [because] they feel so controlled themselves." According to his wife, "The men feel like they're accomplishing something if they can get someone to do what they require of them. That is control—women's clothing shows they are being controlled—they have to dress plainer than the men."

A person's religious commitment is exhibited through personal control, so formal measures of social control are not often needed. However, cases such as those described below serve a preventative function in that they demonstrate to women the price they must pay for deviating from norms enforced by both informal and formal social control.

Formal Control

Ministers and deacons (all men) mete out in public formal measures of social control, including general displays of power, formal reprovals, denial of communion, a practice known as "church repentance," and expulsion. Most of their formal social control of women is related to Mennonite men's particular image of a "proper" Mennonite woman. She should be sober in demeanor and appearance. She is expected to be thin and modestly dressed, visually testifying to her self-control over what are termed "lusts of the flesh." Sensory enjoyment is considered sinful; consequently, such pleasures as eating and sexual and emotional expressions are repressed. Any activity done solely for fun, or to excess, is prohibited. Self-denial is the rule in Mennonite life and is expected to be visible in appearance.

A woman's head covering is a potent symbol of her self-denial, submission, and acceptance of group norms. The following incident over such a head covering, related by an expelled woman, reflects conflict between women and ministers:

> We went through a period of time where we were having some trouble about the head covering. It is a three-cornered black flat scarf, which only becomes round when you shape and fold it around the bun. If you have a lot of hair, this is hard to do—you pin it on at the top, bring it down, fold in each side, tie it under, tuck the bottom tail around, and then it looks like a cap. What we began to do was to sew caps so we could just slap them on and pin them down. That wasn't allowed because the ministers said it wasn't traditional—but they only look at history if they can use it to their advantage.

Women often get into "church trouble," which usually starts with public reprovals. These typically began at a staff meeting (a weekly meeting of all the ministers and deacons), where the men discuss behavior considered deviant. And because rigid conformity is the norm for this sect, it does not take much to be labeled deviant. Women who are so labeled are continually watched by the staff for symbols that are perceived as deviations from established rules. An individual's behavior is interpreted in light of the deviance label, and this results in unequal

73

enforcement of the rules. For example, Leah was in "church trouble" from the time she reached puberty until her midthirties, when she was expelled from the church. She recounted a reproval by the ministers:

> I was eight-and-a-half months pregnant and overweight, and I had borrowed a maternity dress from my older sister Jane [an orthodox member], and I was sitting there and they were giving me the third degree—asking why I do this, or that—and I was crying and they asked why couldn't I please my husband. And one of the ministers said, "Just take for instance that dress you're wearing." It was a decent dress, but he said, "That dress is loud—a woman like you wearing such a dress is offensive." Jane wore it many times after I did, and never was reproved for it. I was the only one who was; it was because they saw me as a threat, because I have always been attractive and not ashamed of it. Ministers always kept their eyes on me.

This incident occurred at the church and involved only the ministers, Leah, and her husband. Formal reproval most often occurs in this manner. It is also common, however, for the errant member to be brought before the entire congregation for a public reproval. "Men do not get reproved very often: women are reproved by men in order to control them," Sharon reports during a group interview. As a member becomes more recalcitrant, the increasingly public and formal nature of the social control becomes evident.

Denial of communion and "church repentance" are formal declarations of deviant status. Leah stated: "The last few years they weren't allowing me to go to communion. They didn't really have anything on me except for my clothes, which was what they harped on. And my clothes were pretty much like everyone else's." "Church repentance" is a period of formal censure. According to an expelled woman, "repentance is like purgatory, like hell, like being shunned, but not quite. You're untouchable. People look at you and weep, because they know you're going to hell." In general these measures are effective in controlling deviance. Some women, however, are unable to accept the power of the ministers and are expelled.

The most drastic form of formal social control, expulsion, is followed by shunning (social ostracism). After appropriate deliberations, ministers expel people at a members' meeting. In Bend, 22 percent of members are expelled, which supports the national figure of 20 percent cited by Hiebert (1973:402). When expelled, a person is not allowed to eat at the same table with the family or have social or economic interactions with church members. The intense pressure generally is successful in returning the member to the fold.

Becky, who has been expelled five times, is one such member. She stated she could foretell her own impending church trouble when she began to experience an increasingly negative attitude toward Mennonite clothing:

> It felt suffocating, as though when I put on the clothes, I put on the church's rules. I was a different person in worldly [fashionable] clothing—I was uncontrolled. The church's rules didn't apply to me. As I got back into the frame of mind that is expected, I grew to appreciate that God wants me in the church; as that happened, I no longer wanted worldly clothes. Eventually, putting on the Mennonite clothes and head covering felt right.

Thus Becky's crisis was apparent visually in her appearance. This illustration points to the ability of clothing to symbolize not just group affiliation, but the construction and affirmation of both personal and cultural identity.

Informal Control

Maintaining group norms is the expressed purpose of informal social control measures. Using methods ranging from gossip to reproval (formal criticism), women insure conformity to norms and function as social control agents within their age-sets. They spend a great deal of time in the company of their friends, and the other members of the community are the main topic of conversation. Since intense scrutiny is considered a sign of Christian love, nothing goes unnoticed. When she breaks a norm, a woman knows the transgression will be noticed and become a current topic of conversation. If that threat is ineffective in redirecting her behavior, a woman's best friends will talk to her directly and express their concern for her spirituality. Members are continually aware of clothing and use it to gauge a person's submission of self to the group. Anna stated that "when Leah was expelled, it was so sudden. There were no signs that she was in trouble. . . . Even her clothing was the same—I'd have expected to see some changes, like her dresses getting fancy or something, 'cause clothing was so important to her."

In the last months prior to her expulsion, Leah's conformity to clothing norms continued in spite of her ongoing difficulty with the ministers and deacons. This example illuminates a larger issue; women derive satisfaction from their social ties, and to retain them, the self is always subjugated to the will of the group. Deviation from the group standard is equated (negatively) with pride. Signs of individuality are seen as a rejection of group norms and values. Naturally, the expression of individuality in clothing is too obvious to be ignored. Charity, a minister's daughter who left the church in 1970 but still lives in Bend, concluded:

> If your clothes are straight down the lines as to the rules of the group, then everyone can see that you are submitting your will to the church. The Mennonite dress is like a uniform—it indicates that you're keeping everything under control. When you're having trouble with the rules, your clothing can show it. This is why everyone watches what everyone else is wearing and how they are wearing it, because clothing shows acceptance of all the rules of the church.

Some women resent the amount of control men exert over women, especially in regard to dress. Leah stated: "We have to conform to whatever the men want, whether it's the way we dress or our behavior. They think it's scriptural. I think it's just another way to *tame women down* [her emphasis]. The men say 'women, submit yourselves to your husbands.'" And submit they do to both formal public reprovals and informal private reprovals which generally occur between two women. One woman recalled: "On the first Sunday that my daughter wore little anklets with lace around them, Rachael reproved me. She was really on her toes to catch that the first time they were worn!" Rachael's daughter explained: "In her heart, my mother despises confrontations. She comes from a long line of ministers, and will do anything to avoid getting into conflict with them." In order to prevent such conflict with the ministers, Rachael reproved other women out of sisterly concern.

It is in the best interest of all the women to keep each other committed to the social norms, in order to insulate themselves from formal control by the ministers. An expelled woman described reprovals she experienced while still a member:

> I was reproved for wearing a low-neck dress—it was a dress which was unbuttoned to just below the collarbone. The woman who reproved me was wearing a neckline lower than mine—but reproved me anyway. . . . I was occasionally reproved for my daughter's dresses—I made her beautiful dresses which were a

little bit on the fancy side. She loved them! Now that I've been expelled, the Mennonite women make ugly, plain dresses for her that she prefers to wear. She won't wear anything that I made anymore.[10]

Women are reproved for any number of infractions, but clothing is one of the more frequent topics. Katie said that "for instance, if my sister or a friend started wearing shorter skirts, I would worry that she was losing her spirituality. I would express my concern about this, and she would probably lower her hems." Holdeman women do not see this gesture as interference; instead they accept the informal reprovals as indicative of sisterly concern. The consensus is that women maintain vigilance over each other to keep themselves from straying too far from the norms and risking formal reprovals.

Through vigilance within their age-sets, women informally control their own dress, whereas men exert formal control over women and their appearance. These forms of control function quite differently. By enforcing a particular image of "proper" Mennonite dress for women and not allowing deviations from the clothing norms, the ministers exert a great deal of power and try to inhibit resistance. As they control women's dress, men both reflect and reinforce a particular image of women's bodies and the social body—an image that sustains their patriarchal power. By contrast, when women control women's dress, they provide some resistance to that power. They offer an alternative, no matter how minute—an alternative that mitigates against patriarchal power. They assert collective independence by using hypertraditional dress in order to bring about changes in the less salient aspects of Holdeman Mennonite dress. Dressing more traditionally than men keeps women above male reproach. By informally enforcing dress codes among themselves, they actively deny men the opportunity to exert formal control. They actively deny men the opportunity to reinforce their patriarchal authority. Not only do women resist by depriving men of the opportunity to reinforce their definition, but they participate in shaping an alternative image of both women's bodies and the social body.

A MIRROR TO THE SOUL: SHAPING AN ALTERNATIVE IMAGE

By working together, Mennonite women are able to balance the restrictions imposed by ministers with some measure of individual expression.

This process is empowering and results in some deviations from the usually explicit dress code. While not all the women approve of these variations, they stand together and do not interfere with the changes. The most obvious deviations occur among young women.

The community generally understands that adolescence is a period fraught with tension. Men defer to their wives in raising daughters, and the girls are given some leeway with the dress code. Girls exhibit rebellion by secretly wearing "worldly" clothing. Mary recalled that when she went to public high school (late 1960s), many of the Mennonite girls kept worldly clothing in their school lockers. Charity agreed: "I'd sneak them out of the house; I kept some worldly things at school. I also wore two-inch-wide belts, so that when I rolled up the waistband to shorten the skirt, the roll wouldn't show. This way, dresses could be long around adults and short at school like the other [non-Mennonite] girls." Leah was in public school at about the same time as Charity and Mary and recalled that "It was in high school that I really wanted to dress different than the Mennonites. . . . My friends and I all dressed in worldly clothes when we got the chance. But they didn't have to sneak the clothes out as much as I did, 'cause my parents were so conservative. They could get by with fancier clothes . . . than I could."

Girls are not allowed to wear makeup, other than a medicinal foundation if they have acne. However, it is typical for Mennonite girls to use foundation and minimal makeup. According to Charity, "makeup has always been forbidden, but we used to sneak out mascara. . . . I would dye my eyelashes with this stuff called Dark Eyes. Mom wondered why my lashes got so dark! The girls in the church now are wearing makeup, but they're sneaking it. They only wear enough that it barely shows." The ministers are apparently unable to discern subtle makeup from the absence of makeup. Leah stated that "the ministers would ask, 'do you wear eyebrow paint?' I'd say no. I wore mascara but I figured that if they didn't know the name for it, I wasn't gonna help them out. They didn't even know the difference."

In addition to using makeup, young women have more latitude with their wardrobes. The most overt instance of rule bending concerned Charity's sister-in-law who converted just before she married. Although "she's a total Mennonite today, she did rebel a little, for a while [just after she married] she left her hair down and wore jeans." Although this is generally unacceptable, the women in the congregation knew about it and looked the other way.

Similarly, the more conservative women overlook the tendency for young women to invest a great deal of time, energy, and money in their wardrobes. While Mennonite women agree that it is required that clothing be modest, single women wear dresses that fit snugly. Charity remarked: "If you're single, clothes are for sexual attraction, but you can't be too obvious. Once you've caught a man, there's no need to put so much time in extensive wardrobes. . . . When you have to wear one basic style, the only way to get variety is to have a lot of dresses. Many girls have extensive wardrobes." Becky concurred: "girls spend a lot of time designing dresses to be different from everyone else's. We find details to add that won't be objectionable. That's one reason why our dresses look different from the married ladies'—they don't have the time, or need to attract male attention!" The differences alluded to include such structural details as tucks, pleats, and yokes. Applied details are never acceptable, although details that could be considered functional are overlooked. There is an understanding that the rules of modesty can be bent during this short time in a woman's life, since marrying is of utmost importance.

A woman is not considered an adult until she has borne a child, so until then she is able to bend the rules somewhat. With motherhood, however, comes full adulthood and the expectation that a woman will become more settled and submissive. This expectation is apparent in the clothing of married women; they exhibit greater acceptance of the dress code, which reflects the corporate nature of the age-set. When deviations do occur, they are typically collective in nature.

Shoes (other than tennis shoes) must be black or brown, following tradition. They may not have heels smaller than a dime, and no open heels or toes are permitted. This effectively limits shoe selection to flat, unfashionable styles. Most Mennonite women, however, are short and want to appear taller, so when three-inch-high wedge-heeled shoes came into style in the 1970s, they were quickly bought by Mennonite women. Anna remembered that "the ministers complained that these were too worldly, but what could they do? We'd found the perfect solution to get around the rules!" Additionally, when black and brown shoes were no longer fashionable and became unavailable, Mennonite women dyed white shoes in an apparent attempt to get the acceptable colors. However, the accuracy of shoe dyes left much to be desired and some color variation came into the wardrobes of grateful Mennonite women. Katie remarked that "I used brown dye but got mauve—and I like it! [The minister] couldn't say anything, 'cause it'd be a waste to throw them out!"

Adherence to tradition, a major goal of the ministers, runs into conflict when it comes up against technological change. For example, women may not replace buttons with zippers. Nevertheless, the women found a way to circumvent the ministers' decision: "Changes happen that the

79

ministers say don't follow tradition—we wanted to use zippers in the 1960s to save work. It takes a lot of time to make a dress that buttons," recalled Charity. (Several hours could be saved by constructing a garment that closes with a zipper rather than buttons.) However, the ministers sensed a redesign of the costume and could not be persuaded to accept the change, so the women agreed to keep the buttons and buttonholes down the front of the dress but to insert a zipper in the side seam to make getting dressed easier.

Traditionally, Mennonite women made their dresses out of printed cotton fabrics, but in the 1970s polyester knit fabrics were rapidly adopted when they became available. Not only is it quicker and easier to make dresses of polyester knit, but the fabric needs no ironing. Mennonite women consciously choose fabrics that resemble the old cotton calico prints they traditionally used in order to make a significant change without drawing the attention of the ministers.

Resistance to the image of the "proper" Mennonite woman as proscribed by the ministers is subtle. The most obvious examples of resistance are found in deviations from the clothing norms. In recent years, weight has also been a subject of quiet revoltion. According to the local physician, in the early 1980s the obesity rate for adult Mennonite women was 15 percent, compared to thirty-five percent for women in the surrounding community (J. Bradshaw, pers. comm., 1988). Mennonite women kept their weight down through weight-loss programs and exercise. Recently, however, the obesity rate of Mennonite women is increasingly noticed by their non-Mennonite neighbors, one of whom said, "It used to be that Mennonite women were always thin, and we were fat. Now, they're as chubby as we are!" (J. Perez, pers. comm., 1991). One Mennonite woman explained, "We spend most of the day cooking, and it's hard not to eat. But our husbands want us thin—that's so hard to do when we're always in the kitchen. It's getting hard to keep them [husbands] happy." The increased obesity rate of Mennonite women could be interpreted as a covert attempt to defy their husbands' control over their bodies.

The preceding examples demonstrate Holdeman Mennonite women's subtle resistance to both private (family) and public (societal) patriarchy. There is no mindless subjugation of self. While the women may appear submissive, their motivations are complex. They reinforce the dress norms while also resisting the image proscribed for them by the ministers. While there is overt submission, on a more covert level there is collective resistance which supports women's dissension. Women work together, within the age-set, to protect themselves from men's control by monitoring their own behavior. Through their own informal control, women protect themselves from male censure and fashion an alternative image to counteract the image proscribed by men.

While individual men spend much of their time alone, women are constantly involved with other women. Friendship between the sexes is exceedingly rare, and interaction between husband and wife is kept to a minimum. As a consequence, men are excluded from women's lives and are intentionally kept in the dark about things of interest to women. Women take advantage of male ignorance and through their age-sets are able subtly to circumvent the rules. Both resistance and reinforcement of the norms are possible because women's age-sets build solidarity. An individual alone is unable to bend the rules, but women as a group are able to make small changes in the dress codes. The result of this corporate resistance is creation of alternatives to male characterizations of both women's bodies and the social body. These alternatives resist rather than reinforce patriarchal authority.

CONCLUSIONS

The constraints on Mennonite women seem overwhelming. However, these women were raised to suppress individual needs and to yield to group control. The formal structure of the Holdeman Mennonite community as a whole is expressed by men, while the informal structure of the women's age-set supports both community norms and some deviance. The age-set is a first line of defense against the structure imposed by men. Clothing is a major source of conflict between men and women. It is the site of struggle—a struggle between the patriarchal social system and the collective agency of the women's age set-groups. It is also a source for building solidarity among women.

In these struggles, it is not only clothing per se that is negotiated. Dress is the site of conflict in which symbolic meanings are negotiated and contested. Dress is a metaphor; it is interpreted as a visual symbol of the suppression of the self to the demands of the community. In this conflict, the physical body becomes a symbol for the social body. In the case of the Holdeman Mennonites, women's bodies become the focus of a symbolic struggle over both personal and group identities—a struggle that draws attention to the ways freedom and constraint go hand in hand.

Freedom and constraint are apparent in conflict over the Mennonite dress code. While men exercise both private and public power over the female body, women help keep each other in line and overlook some deviations from normative behavior. Thus they both reinforce and resist normative constraints. There is a double nature to the agency of Mennonite women. Both actions resist the characterization of a social body ruled entirely by men. Both empower women and build solidarity within the age-sets and for women as a whole.

Religious dogma is used to rationalize admonishing women for infractions of a rigid dress code, since clothing is seen as evidence of either religious conformity or deviance. The greater the deviance from the dress code, the more likely the woman will be reproved by the ministers. The women's age-sets are able to enforce and mitigate that discipline, however.

Resistance of this kind points to the need to go beyond narrowly defined descriptions of agency. A singular focus on either structural constraints or personal agency seems inadequate to analyze the Holdeman Mennonite case. It is through a constant process of negotiation that boundaries are delineated, negotiated, and redefined.

NOTES

1. There are about 300,000 Mennonites in the United States today. The Mennonites are prone to schisms, and at least twenty major divisions represent liberal, mainstream, and conservative philosophies. One of the most conservative sects is the Holdeman Mennonites, who number over 10,000 in the United States (Scott 1986:35). Formally known as the Church of God in Christ, Mennonite, members of this branch are called Holdemans, Holdeman Mennonites, or (by the local outsiders) Mennonites. In this chapter, I generally refer to the group as Holdeman Mennonites. When the term *Mennonite* is used, it refers to the larger body of Mennonites.

2. *Patriarchy* is used here to indicate both a family system in which men control women and children in the private sphere, and a social system, characterized by the formal and public control of society by men. This usage follows Carol Brown's (1981) discussion of private and public patriarchy.

Brown distinguishes between public patriarchy (i.e., a patriarchal social system) and private patriarchy. She states that private patriarchy includes the individual relations found in the traditional family, in which men have control over women, their labor (productive and reproductive), and their children. However, Brown notes that patriarchy is not just a family system. In the social system, we find public aspects of patriarchy that function to uphold rights and privileges of the collective male sex. A husband's control of his wife's daily life is reinforced by the larger-scale monopolization of the social and economic world by men. In current U.S. family law, private patriarchy intersects with public patriarchy (Brown 1981:240). In most of the United States today, it is public not private patriarchy that is problematic for women. For the Mennonites, however, public and private patriarchy constantly intersect, which functions to keep power firmly in male hands.

3. For a discussion of clothing as a metaphor of religiosity, see Boynton 1989 and Poll 1962.

4. "Plain dress" is required by most conservative Amish, Mennonite, and Hutterite churches. It illustrates the values of modesty, piety, economy, and simplicity and provides visual testimony to the commitment and fellowship of the group. For further reading on this topic, see Scott 1986.

5. In Holdeman Mennonite society, the major age-sets for women are girls (sixteen and older, unmarried), mothers (married to age thirty-five), and older women (over thirty-five). Mennonite women refer to unmarried young women as girls. Spinsterhood is rare. It is acknowledged that, without a husband, a woman has few options and a nebulous status. The good things in life, family and children, only come to married women.

6. One woman in the community explained this separation in the following way: "well, you want to be with your friends, the ones you grew up with. After all, you can talk to your husband at home." It is only in the homes that the sexes mingle.

7. I've changed the names of persons and places to insure anonymity.

8. Sixty-three of the seventy-eight adult women, both married and unmarried, were interviewed.

9. A person who will not be controlled by the church is expelled and shunned, which means the expelled person is cut off socially and economically from everyone in the group. As a result of this pressure, the person usually begs for forgiveness and returns (85 percent return to the church). During the second phase of my fieldwork I interviewed 95 percent of the ex-Mennonites who lived within a hundred-mile radius of Bend.

10. This situation was highly unusual. The woman was expelled while she and her husband were having marital problems that ultimately ended in divorce. Initially she was unjustly accused of adultery, after which she became bitter and did have an affair. Eventually she left her husband and was denied access to her children, so the women in the community took over their care. In this instance, public and private patriarchy clearly intersected. Only one other divorce occurred in the history of this community.

REFERENCES

Archer, M. 1988. *Culture and Agency: The Place of Culture in Social Theory.* Cambridge: Cambridge University Press.

Boynton, L. 1986. *The Plain People: An Ethnography of the Holdeman Mennonites.* Salem, Wisc.: Sheffield Press.

———. 1989. "Religious Orthodoxy, Social Control and Clothing: Dress and Adornment as Symbolic Indicators of Social Control among Holdeman Mennonite Women." Paper presented at the American Sociological Association annual meetings, San Francisco.

Brown, C. 1981. "Mothers, Fathers and Children: From Private to Public Patriarchy." In *Women and Revolution: A Discussion of the Unhappy Marriage of Marxism and Feminism,* ed. L. Sargent. Boston: South End Press.

Douglas, M. 1970. *Body Symbols.* Oxford: Blackstone.

———. 1982a. *Essays in the Sociology of Perception.* London: Routledge and Kegan Paul.

———. 1982b. *Natural Symbols.* New York: Pantheon Books.

Emerson, R. M., and S. Messinger. 1977. "The Micro-Politics of Trouble." *Social Problems* 25 (December): 121–134.

Goffman, E. 1963. *Stigma: Notes on the Management of Spoiled Identity.* Englewood Cliffs, N.J.: Prentice-Hall.

———. 1971. *Relations in Public.* New York: Harper and Row.

Gulliver, P. H. 1968. "Age Differentiation." In *International Encyclopedia of the Social Sciences.* New York: Macmillan.

Hiebert, C. 1973. *The Holdeman People.* Pasadena, Calif.: William Carey Library.

Mauss, M. 1936. "Les techniques du corps." *Journal de la Psychologie* 32 (March/April): 372–383.

Merten, D., and G. Schwartz. 1982. "Metaphor and Self: Symbolic Processes in Everyday Life." *American Anthropologist* 84:796–810.

Poll, S. 1962. *The Hasidic Community in Williamsburg.* New York: Free Press.

Schur, E. 1984. *Labeling Women Deviant: Gender, Stigma and Social Control.* New York: Random House.

Scott, S. 1986. *Why Do They Dress That Way?* Intercourse, Pa.: Good Books.

NEGOTIATING DISCOURSES AT LOCAL SITES

GENDER, POWER, RESISTANCE: IS CARE THE REMEDY?

Sue Fisher

Caring, at least since the emergence of the "cult of domesticity" (Cott 1977), has been gendered. In rapidly changing times it has played an important role in shoring up the ideology of gender difference. As the informal, unpaid labor which women do to protect and promote the well-being of others, as a routine feature of the domestic economy, as a part of women's everyday life in the family and in the community, caring has contributed to the glorification of the home and women's roles in it. There has been, in addition, a strong association between caring and taking care of, including taking care of the health of others. Women have long been responsible for providing the domestic conditions necessary for both maintaining health and recovering from illness (Graham 1985).

During the social transformation from preindustrial to modern industrial work patterns, women began to turn their usual domestic occupations into paid work (Cott 1977). Health care was no exception. In her history of American nursing, Reverby (1987) argues that caring for others' needs out of love became transformed, for some, into caring for others as paid labor. In the early years, paid nursing was a trade "professed" in the marketplace, learned at home and practiced by older women with no formal training or schooling. When nursing moved out of the home and into the hospital, and especially after the Nightingale-based reforms, female character built on the obligation to care contributed to the sacrifice of nurses' autonomy on what Reverby refers to as the "alter of altruism." Caring has remained central to nursing. The later separation of nursing education from nursing service diminished neither the obligation to care nor nursing's position as a woman's occupation. Neither a university education nor the move toward professional autonomy eliminated the cultural identification of nursing with caring.

During the 1960s, when federal policies in the United States were directed toward countering societal inequities, including inequities in health care, a new health professional came into being—the nurse practitioner. While nurses had long been subordinate to physicians by custom and law (Melosh 1982), nurse practitioners sought to establish themselves as fellow professionals. The medical profession has, as Freidson (1970) points out, "an official approved monopoly to the right to define health and illness and to treat illness"—a right based on its control of medical knowledge and technical skill and on its freedom from outside control, that is, professional autonomy. On what grounds, then, could nurse practitioners establish themselves as medical professionals? If nurse practitioners share a body of medical knowledge and technical skills with physicians and if they are positioned in relationship to them as physician extenders, on what could their professional autonomy rest?

Nurse practitioners turned caring from an obligation to a virtue. Operationalized as psychosocial skills, patient education, and prevention, caring provided the knowledge and skill they could control and upon which their declaration of professional autonomy could rest. Nurse practitioners claim to offer a system of care which adds caring to curing, and this does not seem to be an empty assertion. Ample literature demonstrates that nurse practitioners provide medical care that is comparable to the care provided by primary-care physicians—care that is high quality, efficient, effective, and economical (Shamansky 1985; Diers and Molde 1979; Sackett 1974). In addition, nurse practitioners are generally acclaimed for their psychosocial skills (Lohr and Brooks 1984). It is this combination of medical and psychosocial skills which is said to differentiate nursing from medical practice and which is used to ground nurse practitioners' claim for professional autonomy.

Caring, then, couched in terms of qualities understood as natural— qualities that could jump from the private to the public spheres without threatening the identity of its bearer—has been vital to important transitions for women. While remaining pivotal to women's identity, caring has taken women from the home to nursing in the paid labor force. Now, when women's participation in the public sphere as nurses working in a secondary labor market is more accepted, caring has emerged as central to another battle—the battle nurse practitioners are fighting for professional status. Caring has been at the heart of the campaign to move from doctor's handmaiden (Melosh 1982) to autonomous medical practitioner.

It grounds the identities of nurse practitioners as women and is foundational to their struggle for professional autonomy. In the nurse practitioner's fight, caring provides the basis for both a new political reality—the nurse practitioner as autonomous medical provider—and a different kind of provider-patient relationship, one that integrates medical and psychosocial skills. These claims, however, are problematic.

To pose a system of care as the justification for a different kind of provider-patient relationship, the grounds for professional autonomy, and the basis for professional identity is to participate in the reinscription of two convergent sets of social relations. These claims also reinforce a sexual division of labor and women's participation in a secondary labor market as nurses and fortify what some refer to as the public patriarchy (Brown 1981). In addition, they raise questions about whether caring, which has embedded in it some of the deepest dimensions of traditional gender differentiation in our society (Tronto 1989), could modify the asymmetry so characteristically associated with the medical relationship and, in so doing, empower patients by maximizing their voice. These questions are, at one and the same time, empirical and theoretical.

EMPIRICAL QUESTIONS: CARING AS PRACTICE

Researchers, myself among them, have concentrated overwhelmingly on the doctor-patient relationship. We have gathered an impressive array of empirical materials—materials which suggest that the medical relationship is characterized by an asymmetry between provider and patient and by an almost exclusive concern with medical topics to the near total exclusion of the social, biographical context of patients' lives (Todd 1989; Mishler 1984). This medical relationship rests on a medical model which presents illness as the organic pathology of individual patients. From this perspective neither nonorganic complaints nor the social context of patients' lives fits comfortably. The medical problem to be solved is located in the individual's body—organs malfunction in mechanistic style. Diagnosis identifies the specific etiology—the specific pathological disturbance—and treatment optimally returns the system to its normal state of balance.

The system of care which nursing claims to offer challenges this model. Nurse practitioners argue that the problems patients bring to examining rooms cannot be separated from the complex social and psychological lives people lead. A nursing practice that integrates the social-psychological and medical aspects of care is said to eliminate the spurious distinction between the medical and the social, the physiological and the psychological.

Since delivery of health care is essentially a communication event, this challenge to the medical model implies skills that are linguistically based. To gain access to biographical information, nurse practitioners must encourage patients to speak about their lives. Could a nursing practice that adds caring to curing, then, minimize the asymmetry in the provider-patient relationship? And in so doing would it maximize the patient's voice, providing a discourse that adds the social, contextual to the medical found to characterize doctor-patient discourse? If so, would it provide a discourse upon which to redefine the medical model and the clinical practice that flows from it?

There empirical questions are without ready answers. They ask what a nursing practice which adds caring to curing would look like and whether it could provide the bases for a different kind of provider-patient relationship. But while studies have evaluated the quality and effectiveness of nursing practice, there is very little systematic information about what nurse practitioners actually do in examining rooms. Without such data, we do not know how caring or, for that matter, quality and effectiveness translate into nursing practice. Nor can we understand what consequences, if any, such translations might have. It is one thing to posit that nurse practitioners offer a system of care, it is quite another to display what this system of care looks like in practice.

THEORETICAL QUESTIONS:
A DISCOURSE OF THE SOCIAL

At another level the ways we understand the relationship between provider and patient, the medical and the social, and medicine and society pose theoretical issues—issues central to three recent sociological studies by Mishler (1984), Silverman (1987), and Waitzkin (1983). While each of these studies focuses on the doctor-patient relationship, the issues they raise are directly applicable to questions about power and resistance in the nurse practitioner–patient relationship.

Mishler (1984) describes the practice of medicine as divided into two separate discourses—the voice of medicine and the voice of the lifeworld. Doctors oriented almost exclusively to the technical bioscientific aspects of medicine have the dominant voice—they speak in the voice of medicine. Patients, who are subordinate, have difficulty being heard, have difficulty inserting their voices—the voices of the lifeworld. Reformers, like Mishler, challenge the dominance of the medical model and call for a more humanistic, patient-centered medical practice which includes both social-psychological and medical aspects of patients' lives.

If patients are treated as whole persons rather than sick body parts, if the medical and social, the pathological and the psychological, are valued equally, if the emphasis on diagnosis and treatment is extended to include education and prevention, if patients are recognized as the experts on their own lives, if doctors ask open-ended questions, if they share medical information, if they listen to what patients have to tell them, and if they encourage patients to participate, then an asymmetrical relationship could become more equalitarian. Providers could maximize the patient's voice by broadening the medical model, by exhibiting a more humanistic attitude, and by minimizing their power and sharing their knowledge. Patients would then be able to participate in the diagnostic-treatment process and, therefore, enhance their potential for agency. This recommendation sounds much like the system of care nurse practitioners claim to provide.

Silverman (1987) is critical of Mishler's remedy to the problems in the medical encounter. He argues that the call to humanize medical practice by encouraging patients to speak about their lives relies on faulty assumptions. It poses the social in opposition to the medical, assuming that doctors speak in the medical and patients speak in the social voice. Encouraging a "discourse of the social" as an authentic (it speaks the truth) voice is presented as inevitably liberating. Calling for, inciting, a discourse of the social, then, could correct the imbalances in the medical relationship.

Rather than relying on these polarities, Silverman suggests that we see in the medical consultation a plurality of voices, each interrupting and interpenetrating the other. Doctors and patients can and do speak in both medical and social voices. Speaking in a common language, they produce a field of power which governs them both.

Waitzkin (1983) is also critical of Mishler, but has a different conception of how power works than Silverman does. Doctors and patients do not speak in a common voice. They do not form a field of power which governs them both. Nor does the voluntary inclusion of a more humanistic discourse of the social resolve the troubles in the medical relationship. Both positions present the medical relationship as if it is independent from the larger social context; both accept the context of patients' lives uncritically.

91

Since the medical relationship does not occur in a vacuum, larger social contradictions penetrate its purported intimacy. During medical consultations doctors routinely do ideological work that reflects and reinforces dominant structural arrangements, especially economic arrangements, encouraging patients' consent to them. Both social and medical discourses, then, are deeply political.

For Waitzkin, the remedy is for socially conscious doctors to engage in ideological work that reveals and resists oppressive structural arrangements. The starting place for social change is a new form of medical practice which redirects patients toward political action. Doctors *help* patients break the ideological chains that bind them.

Positioned against the background of Mishler's call for a discourse of the social and Silverman's and Waitzkin's very different theoretical stance, I perform a detailed empirical analysis of two cases—one with a family practice doctor and one with a nurse practitioner. I interrogate this data to illuminate the ideological work of this communication. By juxtaposing the ways nurse practitioner and patient versus doctor and patient communicate during medical encounters, I shed light on both empirical questions about what nurse practitioners actually do in examining rooms—about caring as medical practice—and theoretical questions about the viability of caring as a discourse of the social which remedies the problems in the provider-patient encounter by empowering patients.

BACKGROUND INFORMATION

I chose the two cases I am about to discuss for their comparability.[1] Both the doctor, Dr. Aster, and the nurse practitioner, Katherine Heinz, are primary-care providers—family medicine and community medicine respectively. Family practice shares with nursing a commitment to patient-centered holistic medicine which integrates the medical and social-psychological. In these cases, then, the stated intent of both the medical and nursing practices is similar.

The patients, Wendy Foster and Prudence Batson, are young women—twenty-five and twenty-seven years old respectively. Both are married, are mothers, and live in an intact nuclear family. While Wendy is a new mother of a first child, Prudence has three small children. Each lives out a double day, working and having primary responsibility for childcare and housework. Wendy works part time for her husband, and Prudence works full time alongside her husband in a factory. Both are Caucasian and working-to-middle class, a fact evidenced in their ability to pay for health care.

Both the doctor and the nurse practitioner are meeting their respective patients for the first time. In each case, on this initial visit the patients are seeking medical attention for vague and nonspecific complaints. Wendy's presenting complaint is that she felt faint, nauseated, and nearly passed out. Prudence's primary complaint is fatigue. Complaints of this kind, where no organic pathology is found, are often attributed to psychological rather than physiological distress. They are seen as social rather than medical in nature. Such attributions provide a fertile site for exploring the ways the social is dealt with in medical and nursing encounters—the ways the social provides a site at which power and resistance are negotiated.

THE MEDICAL CONSULTATION

After the doctor introduces himself and asks what he can do for the patient, the patient presents her complaints. She says:

> Well, this morning I nearly passed out and my whole body felt like it was going numb (D: Uh huh) in here it goes through this sort of tingle (D: Uh huh) I just felt like that all over. Then my arms started hurting and I couldn't open my hands, mostly my left hand but my right hand was doing a little bit but ... (D: Ok, ok) I felt a little bit nauseated but that's passed but I got real feverish.

Here the doctor interrupts to ask medical questions: whether the symptoms began all of a sudden and what the patient was doing when they began. Once he finds out that the onset was sudden and that the patient had been feeding breakfast to her six-month-old baby when they began, he abandons medical questions for social ones and the patient offers no resistance.[2] The doctor does not ask for additional information about nausea and fever. Instead he asks if there are any other children and if the baby is healthy. Rather than asking open-ended, probing questions to find out what is going on in the patient's life, the doctor locates the problem narrowly in the patient's domestic arrangements. This location then shapes the questions he asks, limiting the exchange of information and leaving the way open for his assumptions to structure subsequent exchanges. These assumptions can be seen from the beginning. The doctor questions whether the baby is healthy, how many children the patient has, and whether anything else is going on, "like having to get your husband off to work or anything." He does not ask how it feels to be a new mother, but he does ask whether the baby "was eating all right."

Both the questions and the silences—the questions not asked—perform ideological work. They recirculate dominant cultural assumptions about the identities of doctors and patients and the nature of the medical relationship. An asymmetrical medical relationship with a dominant doctor and a subordinate patient is reinscribed. In addition, they justify the traditional nuclear family which has at its center a mother, whose very sense of herself as healthy or sick is tied to her domestic responsibilities. By implication, when babies don't feed well, or when a woman is confronted with both a small child and the responsibility of getting a husband off to work, the stress may be too much for her and so she somatizes—she makes herself unwell. The medical interaction, then, is functioning as an ideological forum in which culturally contradictory versions of woman, mother, and family are worked out. As the interaction continues, the ways the medical interview functions as an occasion for recirculating hegemonic discourses emerge much more clearly.

During the medical history the doctor learns that Wendy is breast-feeding her baby (information she tacks onto a question about whether she takes any medication regularly). He also discovers that she works part time for her husband and that they are both sales representatives. He proceeds to ask a few more questions about what the baby eats and how well he eats it. The patient seems to hear these questions as the doctor's search for a social-psychological "cause" for her presenting symptoms and as a challenge to the way she has accepted her new motherhood role—a challenge which she questions. She asks: "You think I might have some (laughs) (D: What?). You think I might have some mental problems with (slight pause) the baby?"

The patient names what has been implied—that her problems are social-psychological in nature and tied to motherhood. A struggle ensues. However, it is a struggle in which the patient does not prevail. Rather than answering the question the patient has asked, the doctor responds by making his diagnosis:

> Well I'll just tell you what I'm thinking right now, uh, what you're describing sounds like a classic hyperventilation syndrome, which is, usually happens *when you're upset about something* and you cannot be aware of it but you're breathing too fast, and when you do that you blow off too much carbon dioxide and that makes you feel weak, makes your hands tingle,

feel numb, and can make you feel dizzy (P: Uh huh). Uh, but like I say it can happen really without being aware of it or really without being upset, but I just wanted to find out if that was anything you were upset about, you know, if something was (P: Not) going on.

The patient reads this as a request for information and responds:

Not really this morning, it's just that, well, like the last couple of weeks my husband's been out of town opening a new store so I had to fill in more hours (D: More hours) and I think, that's what I thought my headaches were from (P: laughs; D: laughs) because I had so much to do. But this morning I felt nauseated, but I just, it was just like dry heaves you know (D: Uh huh, uh huh). I never really did get sick so my husband told me to put your head between your legs and breath slower and I felt better.

Here we have a medical solution to a problem identified as emotional, and we have a diagnosis which locates the cause of Wendy's symptoms in her emotions. When *you're* upset about something, *you* breathe too fast, blow off too much carbon dioxide, and cause the symptoms *you* describe. What we do not have is much information about why the patient was upset. We know, because she found a way to squeeze it into the discourse, that she has been feeling tense, that she attributes this tension to the fact that her husband has been away opening a new store, and that she has had so much to do that she has worked more hours. She laughs as if to indicate her discomfort with the explanation she is providing and concludes that the stress of her husband being away and the extra burden of work *may* have produced her tension headaches.

While doctor and patient seem to agree that the cause for her symptoms resides in the social context of her life, their agreement ends here. For Dr. Aster, Wendy's domestic arrangements produce an emotional conflict which cause her to hyperventilate. This description supports a culturally hegemonic view of women as ruled by their emotions and blames the patient for her problem. If she could control her emotions she would not hyperventilate. Wendy resists this definition of the situation. For her there have been life problems which generated situationally relevant stress and may have produced tension headaches. Her explanation is much less global than the doctor's. It blames the situation, not her inability to control her emotions, providing an alternative to the dominant cultural view of women as ruled by their emotions—an alternative which resists both Dr. Aster's definition of the situation and the asymmetry of the medical relationship.

Moreover, a diagnosis of tension and hyperventilation does not, for Wendy, tell the whole story. She continues by saying: "*But* this morning I felt nauseated." We do not know what the nausea means to her. We do know that she has mentioned it twice, once in her presenting complaint and again now and that she has expanded it here by saying she had the dry heaves. The doctor does not pick up on this medical topic; rather he comments on her husband's recommendation to put her head between her knees and breathe slower. He says: "That's a good thing to do." The patient tries to interrupt, saying "but," and the doctor continues, "that's a real good thing to do."

Both what is attended and what is not perform interactional and ideological work. The medical interaction is functioning as a site to reproduce dominant cultural assumptions. Just as the doctor is refigured as the dominant participant in an asymmetrical medical relationship, the husband is presented as the dominant participant in the family. Both the doctor and the husband/father know what is best for Wendy. While these presentations reinforce dominant cultural assumptions about the identities of doctor and patient, the nature of the medical relationship, and the domestic arrangements of the traditional nuclear family, they do not attend to Wendy's medical complaint—her nausea.

Later in the consultation the doctor again reinforces a traditional discourse about domestic arrangements when he says: "Well, you know, if *this* continues to be a problem, you know, if you have any more episodes, then you know you might need to look into ways that *you could limit the amounts of any work that you have to do,* uh and I think that that would be a good place to start."

Wendy has tentatively linked the stress of her husband's unusual absence and the *extra* burden of work that it produces for her to provide a context which explains her increased tension. These tentative links are transformed by the doctor. Wendy's work becomes the problem. The doctor recommends that if "this" continues, and the "this" implied is the tension that makes Wendy sick, she "could limit the amount of any work" that she does. Here a social problem—tension—is transformed into a medical one, and a social-contextual issue—the conflict between domestic responsibilities and participation in the labor force—is transformed into both an individual problem and a specific medical etiology. While this is done without determining the meaning of work in this patient's life, it functions to reinforce the doctor's authority to define social reality—a reality which foregrounds one version of domestic life—and in so doing recirculates and reinscribes the doctor's institutional authority and culturally dominant domestic arrangements. The doctor continues by asking:

Are you and your husband getting along fairly well?

Wendy responds, tacking on what may be the reason for her visit. She says:

Yeah, fine. Well, see, there is the problem that I'm still getting up with the baby (D: Huh) at night, you know, and that wears me out, so I didn't realize (D: Yeah), *I thought I was pregnant again* (P: Laughs) (D: Laughs). Oh no.

Now the patient's concern with nausea makes more sense. She was afraid she was pregnant. In fact this fear, rather than the fact that she works, could account for her tension, her headaches, and her hyperventilation. The doctor responds medically to this new information by saying: "Well (pause) well, I'll tell you that it is a possibility and I think it's remote (unintelligible) breast-feeding, but since you are here we might as well go ahead and check it, if its ok with you (P: Yeah), you know, just to be safe."

He continues by giving her some information about breast-feeding as a form of contraception and advising her that *after* she has stopped breast-feeding she can come back and talk about birth control with him. This information is dubious at best, especially since the patient is weaning the baby and is down to one breast-feeding a day. Whether the information the doctor provides is accurate or not, he speaks in the voice of medical authority. This voice reinforces his identity as medical expert and implies that the patient is inappropriately concerned, fortifying the view that she is an overly emotional woman.

Toward the end of the consultation the doctor asks: "Do you have any questions?" It is in the doctor's responses, here, that the interactional and ideological messages are the strongest. The patient asks: "No, I just didn't realize that that could do to you, a little bit of stress (D: Yeah). It just seemed like a little bit to me (D: Uh huh) but . . . "

The doctor interrupts her to correct her mistaken impression that she is under just a little bit of stress. He says: "Well actually it may seem like a little bit to you, but to most people I think I'd be a great deal really, being a mother, you know, and a six-month-old and working too and, you know, breast-feeding. All those are really, that's, those are lots of demands on your body, really. So I'd really try to think about ways that you could try to reduce that." And the patient responds: "Well, it was, you know, it might just be because I had to work so much these past two weeks."

What you see here is the continuation of their struggle. Doctor and patient have been struggling over the contested meaning of wife, mother, and the nuclear family and in so doing struggling over the asymmetrical nature of the medical relationship. But while the patient has resisted, the doctor has prevailed, and in the process both his reading of the dominant culture and their identities as doctor and patient interacting in an asymmetrical medical context have been reinforced. For the doctor, Wendy's stress is to be found in the conflicting demands of work and domestic roles—demands that can be eliminated if she does not work. He calls upon common understandings to support his position, saying that *most people* would find being the mother of a six-month-old, breast-feeding, and working stressful.

Wendy agrees that the situation produces "a little bit of stress," but the problem for her is neither work per se nor the conflict between being a mother, even the mother of a nursing infant, and working. The conflict is to be found in the situationally produced increase in her isolation and responsibility and the iatrogenically produced fear that she is pregnant. Her husband has been away more than usual and responsibilities at work have increased proportionally at a time when she is unable to get an uninterrupted night's sleep and is more tired than she would usually be. In addition, she has been told that she needs birth control only *after* she stops nursing—an impression reinforced in this medical consultation. She is weaning the baby, has felt nauseated, and fears that she is pregnant again. In this context it is not hard to understand why the fear that she is pregnant and the thought of another baby could produce the tension headaches and hyperventilation she has described.

Early in this encounter the doctor identifies Wendy's problem as social-psychological rather than medical and narrowly locates the problems in her domestic arrangements. In so doing he largely abandons the discussion of medical topics. He does not pursue Wendy's nausea, even though she mentions it more than once, and he only suggests a pregnancy test after Wendy tells him that she thinks she may be pregnant. While Wendy leaves this consultation reassured that she is not pregnant, she leaves without a prescription for birth control and without accurate contraceptive information. The recommended treatment is that she stop working to reduce her stress. While Wendy struggles against Dr. Aster's definition of the situation, these interactions leave dominant cultural assumptions about the identities of doctor and patient, and about the nature of the medical relationship and of women, work, and the nuclear family, firmly in place.

THE NURSING CONSULTATION

The nursing encounter begins with Katherine Heinz, the nurse practitioner, introducing herself to Prudence Batson, the patient. Provider and patient then communicate to establish the meaning of the presenting complaint. Katherine opens this sequence by asking:

K: I see on the little slip that Martha [the receptionist] made out that, uh, you're feeling tired a lot.
P: Yeah, just tired.
K: When did it start?
P: Um, a few weeks ago. Cause I'm falling asleep early at night. Usually I can stay awake till eleven, eleven-thirty, and it doesn't bother me. And I've been falling asleep, like almost literally passing out. Eight, eight-thirty, nine o'clock. And I'm sitting [unintelligible] and it's like I just run out (laughs).
K: Um hm. Has this been true every night?
P: Mnn, well, it's almost every night. Just about. I get tired, I don't know, I don't know if it's the job or what?

The consultation opens very much like the last. The nurse practitioner, like the doctor, encourages the patient to expand on her presenting complaint. Both patients describe symptoms usually coded as psychosomatic. And the provider in each case probes to get a little more information. Here the similarity ends. The doctor provides very little space for the patient to explain what her symptoms mean in the context of her life and lets both contextual and medical cues pass unexplored. The nurse practitioner maximizes the space for the patient to explain what her symptoms mean as she pursues cues.[3] In the next exchange Katherine picks up the patient's cue, "I don't know if it's the job or what?" and uses an open-ended question which she follows with a series of probes. She asks: "Tell me, go back about your job and tell me, fill me in a little bit about what your life is like now."

In response Prudence describes what she calls a "normal" day, and

Katherine learns that the patient's day starts at 5:30 A.M., that she has total responsibility for domestic arrangements from taking the children to the baby sitter to taking care of house and family, and that she also has a job outside the home that involves physically hard labor. When the children go to bed around eight o'clock, her responsibilities end, and that's when she feels tired. While being tired seems easy to understand, she describes her day as: "You know, just the normal things that I've always been doing. I don't know, I'm just tired. I don't know if I need vitamins or what?" Katherine responds: "And then you fall face forward on the floor."

Katherine does not pick up the medical cue—whether the patient needs vitamins. To do so would be to medicalize and individualize a social problem.[4] Instead she legitimizes the patient's experience, implying that anyone, after putting in a day like the patient describes, would be tired. She then probes, looking for what has changed. She asks what the patient does when she gets home from work at three-thirty, whether she cooks dinner and whether she cooks it alone, whether Prudence's husband helps with "the kids, or dinner or any of that," how long she has been working, and whether anything has changed recently. She finds that Prudence's schedule and her domestic responsibilities are essentially unchanged. She also discovers that Prudence works next to her husband during the day and that she has been confronting him at night about taking a more active role at home. She is angry and describes her anger in the following way:

> I'm just getting so mad at him, though, he's, he's not very helpful sometimes, a lot, he well, he is, but sometimes you know, when it comes to cooking, and just being able to walk out of the house and go work on the lawn mower, or the motorcycle or something. It's a lot, it's freedom to him, you know, it's, that's what I look at it as. Because he's got the freedom to just walk out the door and, you know, go talk to his friends or something. I don't have that. I've gotta stop and say (K: Sure) somebody's gotta watch these kids you know (K: Sure). I just can't leave them all free there or you know I'll come home to a mess (laughs).

Once again Katherine picks up on the social cues and probes for more information. She asks what's different with Prudence's husband now. As the patient answers she begins to diagnose herself. She describes herself as "just wanting to stay away" from her husband in the last few weeks and concludes:

100

Maybe that's why I'm falling asleep so early (laughs) so I don't even have to listen to him or anything. But he gets mad at me, like at night, sometimes I want to sit there and read a book or something and he gets mad.

Again Katherine probes:

What's his anger?

Prudence explains:

He thinks his sex life is crazy. He thinks "Why do you want to read books, when you know it . . . "

Her voice trails off and Katherine finishes her sentence:

When you could be having sex.

In the discussion that follows Katherine learns that Prudence wants what she describes as her freedom "to go out and do something, not with other men or anything, you know, with my friends," that she feels as if she is suffocating by spending twenty-four hours a day with her husband, that she is trying to change jobs so she won't have to work next to him, and that her husband is critical of her work both in the factory and at home. Both husband and wife are angry—an anger that is being argued out over sex and is perhaps being acted out in Prudence's fatigue.

What emerges here is a picture of a husband and wife struggling over the changing meaning of being a wife/mother and husband/father in an economic climate that makes it increasingly necessary for both husband and wife to be wage earners. While the economic context has changed, the social changes that make domestic duties a shared responsibility are much slower to develop. Prudence has moved into her husband's work place. She is angry because he resists moving into the domestic arena traditionally seen as her work place. She is angry because her husband has the "freedom" to be with friends and do things that he enjoys—like working on his motorcycle. Yet when she wants to be with friends or do things she enjoys, like reading or playing with the children, her husband gets angry. Katherine sympathizes, saying:

101

I can certainly understand that (P: Yeah). I can tell you that I, and most women I know, would not survive well on that kind of atmosphere.

Unlike Dr. Aster, Katherine neither moves rapidly toward diagnostic closure nor does she narrowly locate the patient's presenting complaint in her domestic arrangements. Instead she repeatedly gives Prudence the opportunity to talk about her life and in so doing to explain her presenting complaint. As the story unfolds, Katherine both elicits social/contextual information and responds to it. In addition, while Dr. Aster consistently reinforces dominant cultural assumptions about women, Katherine does not. She does not tell Prudence that her symptoms are caused by a conflict between her domestic responsibilities and her participation in the paid labor force. She does not intimate that Prudence's problems are the result of her out-of-control emotions, and she does not even imply that Prudence's stress would be reduced if she stopped working and stayed at home. Quite the contrary, Katherine legitimates both the reasons for Prudence's fatigue and her anger.

Katherine, like Dr. Aster, is clearly the dominant interactional partner. She initiates topics for discussion and controls the conversational floor. But where Dr. Aster consistently relates to Wendy in ways that recirculate his authority, Katherine does not. Katherine reinforces her authority; however, at the same time and even in the same interactions, she distances herself from it, minimizing her professional status. While Katherine and Prudence relate to each other as provider and patient, by saying that she and most of the women she knows would not survive well in Prudence's life, Katherine locates herself in a community of women and in so doing positions herself as a woman like Prudence. The nurse practitioner both personifies the institutional authority associated with her professional status and works to establish and maintain a gender solidarity based in women's common experiences. Since this is a professional consultation, not a meeting between friends, a certain tension between these discourses seems unavoidable (see Davis 1988), and where there is tension a struggle often follows.

While it is the patient, not the provider, who makes a diagnosis, pinpointing the problem in the ongoing conflict between husband and wife—a conflict she escapes by going to bed early—it is Katherine who, whether talking as a provider or talking as a woman, asks a series of probing questions about the way this anger is expressed and about possible treatment options. It is Katherine's professional status which positions her to ask these questions. She begins with:

Did you ever think of leaving him?

Prudence responds:

> Yeah, I thought of it a couple of times. But I don't know, it just
> gets so—I don't know, I want to stay, but, . . . you know, I mean
> we got married when I was fifteen, you know and it's like I never
> had other boyfriends. I never—I don't know. I've always been a
> mother, a wife and a housecleaner. I want to do something else
> (laughs). You know?

Katherine legitimatizes her feelings:

> You know that's absolutely understandable. That's, that doesn't
> (P: "Good," laughs) make you a bad person.

Prudence continues:

> Good (laughs), that's one reason I went out and got a job in
> September, 'cause I couldn't handle it being home all the time,
> you know, I was, just no adult conversation.

Again Katherine legitimatizes her actions:

> You know that's a real growth step for you, to realize those needs
> and then to go take some action, to do something about them.
> Do you see that as a growth step?

As this line of discussion continues, Katherine learns that some time ago
Prudence's father had left her mother and that after the first year her
mother's life improved greatly. Prudence admits that at some level she
thinks the same could happen to her, except:

> I want to know what I'm going to do with three kids, a car pay-
> ment, the rent. You know, I . . . no way I can cut it on my own
> with, you know, just one salary. Forget it. There's no way.

A little later Katherine concludes:

> So it's economic?

And Prudence agrees:

Yeah.

This is a particularly interesting sequence. Katherine solicits information about the social biographical context of Prudence's life. What emerges is a complex picture of a woman who both reinscribes and resists the dominant discourses about being a wife, mother, and worker. On the one hand, Prudence describes her identity and financial security in traditional terms. She explains that while she has thought about divorce, she wants to stay. She was married at fifteen, had never had any other boy friends, and has "always been a mother, a wife, and a housecleaner." In addition she presents herself as unable to afford ending her marriage. She explains that one salary is not enough to cover car payments, rent, and the needs of three children.

While the reality Prudence depicts is all too familiar to many of us, her characterization reinscribes the dominant discourse which reinforces the traditional nuclear family and women's roles in it. At the same time, when Prudence delineates her reasons for getting a job in the paid labor force, her portrayal is oppositional. She claims that she wants to work because she feels suffocated, because she wants adult conversation. In the dominant cultural discourse which foregrounds women's domestic responsibilities, work may be an economic necessity, but it should not provide an opportunity for pursuing "selfish," individual interests.

Prudence describes marriage and motherhood as the source of both her definition of self and her economic stability. While Katherine does not explicitly challenge the traditional reasons Prudence gives for not leaving her marriage, when the opportunity presents itself she supports Prudence in views that are far from traditional. She affirms that it is a sign of real growth for Prudence to realize and take the necessary steps to meet her needs. Here Katherine's support again circulates an alternative discourse as she legitimates the pursuit of Prudence's self-interest.

The picture of Prudence's life that emerges here is a distressing one. Prudence is angry and frustrated. These emotions are expressed in a physical symptom, fatigue. Katherine has explored the possible treatment options of a divorce and of therapy and neither seems feasible. Prudence does not want and cannot afford to end her marriage; nor is therapy an option. She explains that her husband refuses to go, does not want her to go, and "knows every move she makes." These potential treatment options now seem closed. Katherine raises the topic of divorce once again, however, and a struggle ensues. First she asks, "Are you pretty clear that if the economics of the situation were different you would leave?" Prudence responds by explaining that she is *not* at all sure. Later the following interchange occurs:

K: How long can you keep this up?
P: I don't know because I am getting sick and tired of going to sleep early. It's been a long time.
K: I suspect that's not the only way you're showing your anger. I suspect that other parts of your body are closing down as well. It's just not as easy for you to see. I'm really concerned that this kind of strain over time will have a really negative effect on you. I absolutely understand that the economics of the situation . . . so that's why I was asking if the economics of the situation were taken care of, if that was out of the question, would you leave?
P: I don't know, I, I thought about it, but if it came right down to it, I don't know if I could.
K: Not right now anyway.
P: Yeah, probably not, not right now. I've been thinking about it. And it's getting more and more serious in my own mind, you know. At first, it's like, you know just playing around with the idea. But it's getting more and more concrete as the time goes on.

This series of exchanges is telling. Although Katherine has recirculated the institutional authority associated with her professional status, she has assiduously refrained from imposing either her medical expertise or her definition of the situation. In addition she has consistently avoided closure and resisted the temptation to make a medical diagnosis. Instead, whether speaking as a medical provider or as a woman, she has supported Prudence. Yet after divorce and therapy are rejected as possible treatments, Katherine's approach seems to change.

In this exchange the nurse practitioner switches from a social to a medical register. In so doing she brings all of the authority associated with her professional role to bear as she presses her definition of the situation—albeit an alternative one. First she asks Prudence how long she can continue to live in an untenable situation. Next she tells her that being tired and falling asleep early are not the only ways she is showing her anger: "other parts of your body are closing down as well." The image here is both unpleasant and frightening. Katherine continues by expressing her concern that the stress Prudence lives with "will over time have a really negative effect."

These messages from a medical provider take the form of a diagnosis and a treatment recommendation and as such carry a heavy load of cultural baggage. Even as they resist dominant cultural assumptions about women, work, and the nuclear family, they rely on and recirculate dominant assumptions about the identities of providers and patients and about the asymmetrical nature of the medical encounter. Prudence resists both the oppositional message about her life and the traditional message about the nature of the provider-patient relationship, and at least for the moment she prevails.

It is hard to know if Katherine's next questions pick up Prudence's frustration or her own, but in either case she does not avoid the emotions associated with the patient's presenting complaint, as Dr. Aster does. Instead she probes, and in doing so she provides a site for Prudence to speak about her life. Hearing that Prudence feels trapped and suffocated, Katherine asks her to consider what she does with that anger. Is she taking it out on her children in the form of child abuse? Is she taking it out on herself in the form of depression? Is she considering suicide? Hearing that husband and wife are struggling over the contested meaning of wife/mother and husband/father and that both are very angry, she asks whether Prudence's husband is acting out his anger by battering her. These questions are unusual for a medical encounter. It is much more common for providers to avoid these deeply troubling issues.[5]

With these questions asked and answered, Katherine seems able to accept Prudence's definition of the situation. After exploring both the possibility of divorce and of therapy and finding these options blocked, Katherine relies on her status as a medical expert to suggest that Prudence find a friend or two she can talk to so she can "unload some of the feelings." She impresses on Prudence that long-term stress and repressed anger can over time produce physical symptoms. She advises that Prudence continue to try changing her job so she no longer works next to her husband and that she take up running again. Both a job change and exercise would reduce her stress. Running would also provide a positive outlet for her anger and help with her depression.

Talking with friends, exercising, and changing jobs are the treatment recommendations agree on *after* nurse practitioner and patient have struggled over divorce and therapy. All three recommendations have caused prior trouble in Prudence's marriage. Her husband pouts and punishes her because he sees them as an expression of her independence. Katherine points out that since she is damned if she does and damned if she doesn't, she might as well do what is good for her, and talking with friends, exercising, and changing jobs would be good for her. Here the provider is offering an alternative discourse, one that in its alterity holds the potential to challenge more dominant discourses. While her earlier oppositional recommendation—divorce—was not successful, Prudence agrees to this compromise.

CARING AS PRACTICE REVISITED

Throughout the consultation Katherine has encouraged/incited Prudence to speak about her life, to add the social-contextual to the medical so characteristic of the provider-patient relationship. While this discourse of the social is just the kind that Mishler (1984) recommends and many of us would prefer in our own health care, neither the medical model nor the asymmetry usually associated with the provider-patient relationship has disappeared. In the medical and the nursing consultations, Katherine and Dr. Aster both rely on and recirculate the medical model. To reach a diagnosis and recommend treatment they search for the *cause* of the patient's presenting complaint in the form of a specific etiology, but they do so quite differently.

In the medical encounter the doctor consistently recirculates dominant cultural assumptions about the identities of doctor and patient and the nature of the medical relationship. From this position of institutional authority, Dr. Aster does not ask open-ended, probing questions to determine what Wendy's presenting complaint means in the context of her life. Instead he diagnoses Wendy's problem as social-psychological *rather* than medical in nature and narrowly locates the social in the patient's domestic arrangements. Without inquiring about the meaning of work in her life, he determines that work is the problem. *Working* and the out-of-control emotions it produces cause Wendy to hyperventilate, and hyperventilation explains her presenting complaint of dizziness. Both the diagnosis and the recommendation for treatment recirculate hegemonic assumptions about women, work, and the nuclear family.

It seems the doctor is drawing on a binary logic here. Either the presenting complaint has a medical basis or it does not. Either Wendy's problem is located in her body or in her psyche. Either Wendy is a wife and mother or she is a worker in the paid labor force. This logic, when combined with the persistent revivification of his institutional authority, has both medical and social consequences. Once Wendy's presenting complaint is identified as social-psychological, Dr. Aster abandons the medical in favor of the social. He performs only a cursory physical examination, and he misses Wendy's medical cues about nausea. In the end a social problem—tension—resulting from a situational specific conflict between Wendy's domestic responsibilities and her participation in the paid labor force, is transformed into a specific medical etiology. This etiology then becomes the basis of the treatment recommendation that she stop working and stay at home with her child.

At first glance the nursing encounter looks quite different. The nurse practitioner does not move rapidly toward diagnostic closure. She neither abandons medical topics for social-psychological ones nor narrowly locates the presenting complaint in Prudence's domestic arrangements. Instead she persistently asks open-ended, probing questions that maximize the space for Prudence to explain what her presenting complaint means in the context of her life. What emerges is a richly textured narrative in which the patient, not the provider, locates her presenting complaint in her domestic arrangements and diagnoses herself. Provider and patient agree that Prudence is living in an untenable situation, one that makes her angry. This anger is now making her tired and has the potential to make her sick eventually. However, while they agree on the diagnosis, they disagree about Katherine's treatment recommendation of divorce.

The binary logic that characterizes the medical encounter seems entirely lacking in the nursing encounter, which is clearly more multi-layered, complex, and fluid. For Katherine the medical and the social interrupt and interpenetrate each other. In addition, Katherine does not simply reflect or unambiguously negate the institutional authority usually associated with medical providers. Instead she relates to Prudence in ways that both foreground the institutional authority associated with her professional status *and* highlight her distance from it. Moreover, she and Katherine do not associate *only* as provider and patient; they also relate to each other as women. It is from this position that Katherine legitimates Prudence's anger. Finally, although Katherine consistently promotes an alternative discourse about women, she supports Prudence whether she is circulating traditional or alternative discourses.

While in each case the patient resists the provider's definition of the situation and a struggle ensues, the outcomes are quite dissimilar. Where Wendy struggles with Dr. Aster's definition, the doctor systematically prevails. By contrast, Prudence struggles with both herself and Katherine. While the struggle with herself may be inconclusive, the struggle with Katherine is not.

Katherine uses both her status as a medical provider and her location as a woman like Prudence to push for her definition of the situation.

At first she is not successful. Prudence retains control and remains am- bivalent about a divorce. Where Dr. Aster sticks to his definition of the situation, notwithstanding Wendy's resistance, Katherine does not. After asking whether the anger is acted out in domestic violence, she accepts Prudence's definition of the situation and changes her treatment recom- mendation. She suggests talking with friends, changing jobs, and getting more exercise as ways to treat Prudence's presenting complaint. Prudence accepts this reformulated recommendation and in so doing accepts the oppositional message that, since her husband pouts in any case, she may as well do what is good for her.

These differences between the medical and nursing encounters are not insignificant. The disparity between a discourse that reinscribes hege- monic assumptions about women and one that offers oppositional alter- natives is meaningful. The potential to establish a solidarity based on gender, to legitimate the patient's feelings, and to support her opposi- tional understanding is useful. The distinction between a medical con- sultation that consistently reinscribes the asymmetrical nature of the provider-patient relationship and a nursing encounter that both recircu- lates and resists this asymmetry is notable. And the dissimilarity between the binary logic that characterizes the doctor-patient encounter and the more multilayered, complex nature of the nurse practitioner–patient consultation is also important.

These differences are most evident when patients contest the provi- der's definition of the situation and a struggle ensues. While in both the medical and the nursing encounter, providers and patients struggle, the outcomes are quite different. Where Wendy and Dr. Aster never reach agreement on what caused her presenting complaint or how to treat it, Katherine and Prudence reach a compromise agreement.

Despite these differences, there are striking similarities in the way Katherine communicates with Prudence and Dr. Aster talks with Wendy. In both cases it is the provider who is interactionally dominant, control- ling the topic under discussion and access to the conversational floor. It is the provider's location in the institution of medicine which positions him or her, providing a site of access to institutional resources. Patients have no similar access. And it is the provider who calls his or her own status into play and speaks as a medical expert or, in the case of the nurse practitioner, distances herself from this status. While providers and pa- tients struggle over contested concepts—concepts that need translation— in the end it is the provider's definition which prevails. Wendy never successfully challenges Dr. Aster's recommendation that she stop work- ing, and Prudence finally accepts Katherine's compromise recommendation that she stand up to her husband. Their perspectives are quite different. Nevertheless, doctor and nurse practitioner each defines the correct way to deal with problems in the patient's life, and in so doing neither one is a neutral objective provider of medical care. In each case the ways doctor and nurse practitioner communicate with patients are thoroughly social. They are also deeply ideological and political.

Notwithstanding the differences in the medical and the nursing encounters, empirical support for the claim that nurse practitioners offer a system of care which, while maximizing the patient's voice, minimizes the asymmetry in the provider-patient relationship is far from clear. While Katherine certainly makes space for Prudence's voice, while she actively solicits information about the social context of her life, this shift in focus in no way diminishes her control.

CARING AS A DISCOURSE
OF THE SOCIAL REVISITED

The system of care that nurse practitioners claim to provide resembles the discourse of the social that Mishler (1984) and other reformers advocate. For these reformers, problems emerge in the provider-patient encounter because providers do not probe beneath the surface of the medical relationship. They do not gain access to biographical information, laying bare the socio-emotional context of the patient's symptoms. But even though Katherine does all these things, her interactions with Prudence are not automatically liberatory.

As we have seen, whether coded as a system of care which adds caring to curing or as a discourse of the social, neither the medical model nor the asymmetry associated with the provider-patient relationship has disappeared. By itself, social talk does not make power disappear, nor does it redefine the practice of medicine, humanizing it in the process. This finding leaves little support for the claims that what differentiates nursing from medical practice is a system of care or that a discourse of the social can remedy the problems so characteristic of medical practice.

Furthermore, by dichotomizing the voice of medicine and the voice of the lifeworld and declaring that the social is found in the lifeworld, reformers direct our attention away from the very issues that arise in these transcripts, away from how the social is already incorporated into the discussion of medical topics, and leave intact the assumption that medical talk is objective. Thus they obscure how political medical discussions are and how in and through them gender and professional status are negotiated.

It seems clear that neither nursing's claim nor Mishler's recommendation is sufficient to resolve empirical questions about caring as medical practice or theoretical issues about the relationship between the provider and the patient, the medical and the social, and medicine and society. Silverman (1987) and Waitzkin (1983) point us in the right direction; however, they too leave important issues unaddressed.

As Silverman (1987) explains, the distinction Mishler makes between the lifeworld and medicine is itself problematic. For Silverman, the social and the medical are not oppositional voices. These voices "interrupt and interpenetrate each other" (Silverman and Torode 1980:104). While this insight is important, once Silverman makes it he shifts his focus away from the social and toward the medical. He claims that the distinction Mishler makes ignores "the place of medical discourse in modern societies and, indeed, the ways it has entered our own account of ourselves" (Silverman 1987:198).

By arguing that providers do not speak solely in the medical voice and that patients cannot speak the truth about their lives in authentic social voices and thus liberate themselves, Silverman points us in the right direction. However his claim that medical discourse has become part of our cultural understanding makes only part of the argument. There is little doubt that the language of medicine has entered our own accounts of ourselves; however, in both the doctor-patient and the nurse practitioner–patient consultations, a social/cultural discourse about women, work, and the nuclear family is brought into the medical setting, where it interrupts and interpenetrates what is presumably a medical discourse.[6] Although Silverman's theoretical perspective does not preclude an analysis of the social, he, like Mishler, fails to specify how the social is already incorporated into medical practice, how the provider draws the social into what is presumably medical discourse, and how the social becomes a site for struggle—a struggle in which gender disparities as well as cultural notions about femininity are both constructed and resisted. These failures obscure how thoroughly ideological and political social topics are and how they are negotiated during what is presumably an objective discussion of medical issues.

In addition, Mishler's distinction between the lifeworld and medicine ignores the relationship between voices. Silverman, by contrast, claims that both doctor and patient can speak in either voice, that the medical

111

and the social interrupt and interpenetrate each other, and that in each case the discourse is shaped in this process. This description of the relationship between voices relies on a particular, and not uncontested, understanding of power. Drawing from Foucault (1981, 1979), Silverman argues that power is neither something that can be possessed nor something that operates from above through constraint and repression. It is "capillary," circulating everywhere and in everyone. It operates in everyday social practices at the lowest rather than the topmost extremities of the social body and works as much through encouraging as repressing speech.

If, as Silverman claims, doctors and patients are "compelled to speak to one another in a common language around which a field of power forms to govern them both" (quoting Arney and Bergen 1984), in Silverman 1987:198), then medical domination no longer provides an appropriate model for understanding either the medical relationship or challenges to it. It follows that neither medical providers nor social scientists can engineer new forms of practice or new forms of discourse. Change can come only through practical struggles. Quoting Foucault, Silverman concludes, "the problem is one for the subject who acts" (Foucault 1981:12–13, quoted in Silverman 1987:203).

Once again Silverman seems to have pointed us in the right direction. Certainly it seems that power can work as much through encouraging as repressing speech. Undoubtedly the medical relationship is a site for struggle. While Silverman does not take full advantage of it, it is this notion—the medical relationship as a site for struggle—which provides the theoretical justification to examine the ideological and political struggles between providers and patients. Clearly these struggles about gender and professional status do not disappear if the patient is encouraged to talk about her life. But an important question remains unanswered: Does agreement here imply total reliance on a notion of power as productive? If the social provides a site to reinscribe and resist hegemonic discourses—a site for struggle—theoretically do we have to reject any concept of medical domination and instead accept a shared capacity for action?

From Silverman's perspective the answer to these questions is a resounding yes. However, it is hard to reconcile his arguments about medical domination, his conception of the subject, and his notion of power with the consultations just discussed. If one looks at the nurse practitioner–patient consultation and discounts the nurse practitioner's interactional dominance, then power, at least the power to disseminate hegemonic and alternative discourses about women, may circulate every-where and in everyone. But this look may be deceptive. While Prudence is caught between hegemonic and alternative discourses about women, Katherine is not. She consistently supports Prudence's resistance and per-sistently pushes oppositional understandings about women, work, and the nuclear family. Prudence resists and on occasion prevails, but in the end the nurse practitioner's oppositional position wins out. Is the nurse practitioner, then, the subject who acts? And if so, what ramifications would this have for Silverman's claims?

If one looks at the doctor-patient consultation in terms of shared capacities for action, the notion of power as productive is even harder to support. Throughout the medical encounter Dr. Aster tenaciously rein-scribes one version of reality. He foregrounds the traditional nuclear family with a woman who is defined by her domestic responsibilities and with men, whether doctor or husband, who know what's best for her. Wendy does not passively accept this definition of the situation, she reso-lutely resists, but she does not prevail. Even though she struggles, the doctor's representation of the dominant order prevails. If this is not medi-cal domination, is it produced by a subject/patient through her failure to struggle sufficiently?

How are we to understand the finding that despite the patients' resis-tance, in the end both providers prevail. The asymmetry so characteristic of the provider-patient relationship is recirculated to sustain their defini-tion of the situation. It seems clear that while doctor and patient and nurse practitioner and patient may share a common medical language, a field of power does not form to govern them both. From a Foucauldian perspec-tive, questions about institutional authority, about domination and subor-dination, cannot be posed let alone adequately answered. Fraser (1989a), for example, argues that a conception of power as productive, unavoid-able, and therefore normatively neutral is problematic. From this per-spective, it is neither possible nor desirable to specify "who is dominating whom and who is resisting or submitting to whom" (Fraser 1989a:29).

We are left with two additional questions. First, if doctor and nurse practitioner persistently put forth their definition of the situation and if in the end that definition prevails, how do we account for the fact that these definitions are quite different or justify a preference for a com-mitment to one side as opposed to another? Fraser (1989b:283–286) argues that while such justification is desirable, from a Foucauldian per-spective it is not possible. For Foucault, normative neutrality allows ar-guments about neither power nor morality. Fraser finds this disturbing, particularly since she sees the Foucauldian notion of resistance as already implying a normative standard.

Second, if providers and patients are engaged in a practical struggle, where does their power come from? Since Silverman is relying on Foucauldian conceptions, neither power nor resistance are expressions of some preexisting structural or symbolic order. Without any notion of power as other than productive, as domination or constraint, Silverman's analysis lacks a conception of society. There is no way to understand how or why the institutions of medicine and nursing provide very different sites for the delivery of care. There is therefore no way to specify how or why doctors and nurse practitioners wield power differently and how or why one patient resists successfully but the other does not. As Hall (1986) argues, without a conception of society, one cannot assess how strong the power is, how strong the resistance is, or how the balance changes between them.

Here is where structural criticism confronts Foucauldian analysis. The relationship between society and the practice of medicine is central to a structural criticism. From this perspective it is not difficult to locate which groups have power or why they wield it as they do. Nor is it difficult to justify a preference for one side over another.

Waitzkin (1983), for example, argues that medical discourse does not exist in a vacuum—that it reflects and reinforces broader social relations. During medical consultations, when patients talk about troubles in their lives, doctors have an opportunity to do ideological work. Using the symbolic trappings of scientific medicine, they can encourage patients to consent to behaviors that are consistent with traditional or alternative expectations; in so doing, they reproduce or undermine the patients' material conditions, especially economic conditions. If doctors analyze the social roots of suffering, if they avoid medicalizing nonmedical problems, and if they stimulate patients to become actively engaged in organized resistance, then they can become socially conscious agents of change.

Waitzkin, like Silverman, seems to point us in the right direction—albeit a different one. He provides a notion of power as other than productive and links it to both a conception of society and the institution of medicine. He argues that ideological work—work that reflects and reinforces structural arrangements—occurs in medical encounters. In the consultations just discussed, it seems apparent that ideological work is being done; doctor and nurse practitioner do this work very differently, however. It is hard to reconcile this difference with Waitzkin's theoretical formulations.

At the heart of Waitzkin's argument is the Marxian assumption that institutions reflect and reinforce material conditions. At one and the same time, Waitzkin relies on this assumption and turns it on its head to argue that power can authorize resistance. Medical providers, whose power reflects and reinforces their location in broader social relations, can capitalize on patients' social talk by encouraging them to undermine these structural conditions. This formulation is internally contradictory and does not help us understand the consultations just discussed.

It is fairly easy to see how Dr. Aster functions as an agent of social control. He consistently guides Wendy toward behavior that reflects and reinforces dominant structural arrangements. It is more difficult to see how he can simultaneously become an agent for social change, encouraging her to engage in organized political activity, especially considering his position on women, work, and the nuclear family. On these gendered topics, there is nothing in the slightest bit revolutionary in his approach. By contrast, it is hard to see Katherine as an agent of social control and easier to see her as an agent of social change. She consistently speaks an oppositional discourse, encouraging Prudence to resist the oppressive conditions in her life.

The problems do not end here. Waitzkin, like Mishler and Silverman, fails to specify how social talk is already incorporated into the discussion of medical topics. Presumably doctors are advised to capitalize on patients' social talk because a medical discussion is fact based and value neutral. Here the social/medical distinction is maintained as is the notion that providers are objective medical experts.

Furthermore, and perhaps most importantly, Waitzkin's position implies that power flows primarily in one direction—from provider to patient. In the name of revolutionary social change, the institutional authority so characteristically associated with providers is retained. While this perspective certainly does not preclude the possibility of resistance, the dual focus on the provider as the agent of social change and the agent of social control directs our attention toward the ways providers authorize the patient's resistance and away from the ways the patient resists in the face of asymmetrical relations.

Moreover, if power reproduces material conditions, especially economic conditions, the differences in the medical and nursing encounters must be understood largely in material, that is, economic, terms. It is Katherine's and Dr. Aster's economic location that determines their behavior. It is their material position that accounts for the disparate ways they talk about gender. This location enables Katherine to discover the truth about society and, as a political actor, to speak this truth in an authentic voice. It also provides for Katherine's greater willingness to

115

support Prudence's resistance. It is Katherine's material location that explains why Prudence's resistance is usually successful, while Wendy's is not. But if Katherine is the revolutionary actor because she is economically marginal, then why does Waitzkin present doctors, but not patients, as revolutionary actors? Doctors are certainly not economically marginal, and many patients, especially women patients, are.

While Silverman and Waitzkin may provide more questions than answers, taken together these theorists have the potential to loosen the concept of ideology from its fixed association with a material base. From this perspective the provider-patient relationship is multilayered and complex, while the discourses about gender, power, and resistance which circulate through it are contested.

GENDER, POWER, RESISTANCE: A SOMEWHAT DIFFERENT PERSPECTIVE

Hall (1986) argues that ideology is not reducible to its economic determinants. It is a social process in thought which enables us to represent to ourselves and others the way the system works, why it functions as it does. From this perspective the differences just discussed are cast in another light. Doctor, nurse practitioner, and woman are not just preexisting identities and the roles assigned them preexisting realities. They are contested categories which require translation. The institutions of medicine and nursing—institutions which were constituted historically as gendered professions—provide different sites for the production of knowledge about gender, for the fixing of identity, for the differentiation of men from women, doctors from nurses.

Historically it is widely recognized that doctors gained their professional dominance in the nineteenth century by competing in a loosely organized field of medical providers—a field not dominated by any one group (Stevens 1966; Starr 1982). "Regular" doctors tied by class, race, and gender to powerful men in foundations and government gained control through a state-supported monopoly to practice medicine. Their ascendancy was more of a social and political victory than a medical one—a victory in which medicine was constituted as a gendered profession.

Nursing has no similar history. It evolved in the context of a medical monopoly, and as a woman's occupation it had few ties to the powerful in society. In addition, while united by gender, nursing from its inception has been stratified by race, class, and professional status. This history leaves nursing without the political clout and internal cohesion of the medical profession. It also places nurses in a different position economically. The medical profession gains from its location in a capitalist economy because doctors provide medical care in a fee-for-service system. Nurses rarely practice autonomously and rarely gain economically. Rather they are usually salaried employees—a position doctors encourage and hospitals and insurance companies reinforce. While this arrangement may place less time pressure on their practice, as time for them does not mean money—an apparent benefit—it is tied to a distributive injustice: nurses are underpaid, especially in relation to doctors.

Perhaps most importantly, caring, whether as an obligation or a virtue, played a pivotal role in this history. It has contributed to the glorification of the home, to the movement of women into the paid labor force, to the emergence of nursing as a woman's occupation, and to the battle by nurse practitioners for professional autonomy. Represented as a natural quality of women, it has functioned to shore up the ideology of gender difference, to bifurcate reality into separate, but unequal, spheres. The notion that women care but men reason reinscribes a gender hierarchy and a sexual division of labor. In other words, a discourse of caring has played a central role in the constitution of nursing as a gendered profession.

This history suggests that doctor and nurse practitioner are professionals whose identities are produced by their location in a gendered profession. It is their position as social actors and members of a gendered professional group that provides a different relationship to the system of knowledge called medicine and to their patients—that provides the basis for an institutionalized pattern of interpretation.[7] Providers and patients represent to themselves and to their patients how the system works. They speak social structure (Molotch and Boden 1985), and they do so differently in the medical and nursing encounters just discussed.

The doctor persistently re-creates both his status as medical expert and his dominance as a man and medical provider. He also just as persistently re-creates the patient as other, as layperson, as woman, and as subordinate. In so doing he consistently reinscribes hegemonic discourses about the subordination of women, and he does so under the guise of a medical discussion. While from time to time the patient resists these representations, she does not prevail. To prevail would be to challenge traditional discourses about the ways women are to be patients and the ways they are to live their lives as women. This challenge would undermine both the doctor's professional status and his dominance as a man.

The nurse practitioner has much less at stake. As a woman and as a medical provider she is located at the margins of dominant discourses. From this position she is able to move more easily between hegemonic and alternative discourses. In so doing, she reinforces the status associated with her professional role and resists it by relating to the patient woman to woman. But whether speaking as a medical provider or a woman, she invariably speaks and supports an oppositional discourse. From time to time the patient resists these representations and prevails. In the end, however, the nurse practitioner's oppositional discourse succeeds, and this success is not insignificant. While engaging in a presumably value-free medical discussion, she undermines hegemonic discourses as she encourages the patient to resist them. In contesting traditional discourses about the ways women are supposed to be, she provides an oppositional translation for the concepts woman, work, and the nuclear family—a translation which supports the patient's resistance in the examining room and encourages it in her everyday life.

These institutional patterns of interpretation are the sites at which gender, power, and resistance are constructed, undermined, and invested with meaning. It is here that the doctor, the nurse practitioner, and the patients are constituted as objects of knowledge and subjects who act and that professional and gendered meanings—doctor/nurse, masculinity/femininity—are clarified. This interpretive process is very different in the institutions of medicine and nursing.

NOTES

Another version of this chapter was published as Fisher 1991. In both papers all names have been changed to preserve confidentiality. Both papers primarily discuss the same data, but caring is a more central category of this analysis. In addition, my understanding of the data has evolved and my reading of it expanded. Earlier I was content to see the differences in the ways doctor-patient and nurse practitioner–patient recirculated or resisted the dominant discourses about women, work, and the nuclear family. While this interest remains central to my task here, I now see the provider-patient relationship as more multilayered, complex, and contested than I did before. In this chapter I suggest that women, work, and the nuclear family are concepts which require translation, that translation is a contested process, that this translation involves power and resistance, and that the medical and nursing encounters provide different sites for it. Both discussions work out ideas central to my book *Caring Gone Public: The Case of Nurse Practitioners,* published by Rutgers University Press. In both I have appreciated the comments of Kathy Davis and Joe Rouse.

1. With the permission of provider and patient, I audio- and video-taped consultations and transcribed the tapes for later analysis.

2. It is interesting and telling that from this time on in the interaction, the doctor defines the patient's symptoms as social-psychological, and abandons the medical altogether.

3. While the nurse practitioner does not pursue every medical symptom as it is presented, she performs a thorough physical examination. By contrast, the doctor neither pursues medical cues nor performs a thorough physical exam. His physical examination, like his medical history, is cursory at best.

4. In the prior encounter I criticized the doctor for not pursuing the patient's medical symptom, nausea. Here I seem to be praising the nurse practitioner for a similar lack of attention to a medical cue. But nausea and a need for vitamins are not equivalent. Nausea is a symptom, a clue in the search for a differential diagnosis. Vitamins are a treatment recommendation. Dr. Aster might have gotten medically relevant information by pursuing Wendy's nausea. There is no similar gain in exploring whether Prudence needs vitamins. At this point in the consultation, Katherine does not have enough information to discuss their potential benefits.

5. And Katherine does not stop here. While doing the exam, she asks about birth control. If Prudence feels backed against the wall, another pregnancy might tip a precarious balance.

6. Whether provider and patient can both speak in the medical voice is an open empirical question which will be dealt with in subsequent work. Prior work, however, suggests that at least for doctors and patients there is not a shared capacity for medical talk. A patient's ability to enter the domain marked as medical varies by gender and is probably influenced by other factors as well, such as race, class, and professional status (see Fisher and Groce 1990).

7. I am indebted to Fraser 1989a for this insight, although she is talking about social work and I am talking about medicine.

REFERENCES

Arney, W., and B. Bergen. 1983. "The Chronic Patient." *Sociology of Health and Illness* 5(1): 1–24.

Brown, C. 1981. "Mothers, Fathers and Children: From Private to Public Patriarchy." In *Women and Revolution*, ed. L. Sargent, 239–268. Boston: South End Press.

Cott, N. F. 1977. *The Bonds of Womanhood.* New Haven: Yale University Press.

Davis, K. 1988. *Power under the Microscope.* Rotterdam: Foris Publications.

Diers, D., and S. Molde. 1979. "Some Conceptual and Methodological Issues in Nurse Practitioner Research." *Nursing and Health* 2 (March): 73–84.

Fisher, S. 1991. "A Discourse of the Social: Medical Talk/Power Talk/Oppositional Talk." *Discourse and Society* 2(2): 157–182.

———. Forthcoming. *Caring Gone Public: The Case of Nurse Practitioners.* New Brunswick, N.J.: Rutgers University Press.

Fisher, S., and S. Groce. 1990. "Accounting Practices in Medical Interviews." *Language in Society* 19 (June): 225–250.

Foucault, M. 1979. *The History of Sexuality.* Vol. 1. London: Allen Lane.

———. 1981. "Questions of Method." *Ideology and Consciousness* 8: 3–14.

Fraser, N. 1989a. "Foucault on Modern Power: Emperical Insights and Normative Confusions." In *Unruly Practices: Power Discourse, and Gender in Contemporary Social Theory,* ed. N. Fraser, 17–34. Minneapolis: University of Minnesota Press.

———. 1989b. "Women, Welfare and the Politics of Need Interpretation." In *Unruly Practices: Power, Discourse, and Gender in Contemporary Social Theory,* ed. N. Fraser, 144–160. Minneapolis: University of Minnesota Press.

Freidson, E. 1970. *Profession of Medicine.* New York: Dodd Mead.

Graham, H., 1985. "Providers, Negotiators and Mediators: Women as the Hidden Carers." In *Women, Health and Healing,* ed. E. Lewin and V. Olesen, 25–52. New York: Tavistock Publications.

Hall, S. 1986. "The Problem of Ideology: Marxism without Guarantees." *Journal of Communications Inquiry* 10(2): 29–43.

Lohr, K. N., and R. H. Brooks. 1984. "Quality Assurance in Medicine." *American Behavioral Scientist* 27:583.

Melosh, B. 1982. *The Physician's Hand.* Philadelphia: Temple University Press.

Mishler, E. G. 1984. *The Discourse of Medicine: Dialectics of Medical Interviews.* Norwood, N.J.: Ablex Publishing.

Molotch, H., and D. Boden. 1985. "Talking Social Structure: Discourse, Domination and the Watergate Hearings." *American Sociological Review* 50(30): 273–288.

Reverby, S. M. 1987. *Ordered to Care: The Dilemma of American Nursing.* Cambridge: Cambridge University Press.

Sackett, D. L. 1974. "The Burlington Randomized Trial of the Nurse Practitioner: Health Outcomes of Patients." *Annal of Internal Medicine* 80(2): 137–142.

Shamansky, S. L. 1985. "Nurse Practitioner and Primary Care Research: Promises and Pitfalls." In *Annual Review of Nursing Research,* Vol. 3, ed. H. Werley and J. Fitzpatric. New York: Springer Publishing.

Silverman, D. 1987. *Communication and Medical Practice: Social Relations in the Clinic.* London: Sage Publications.

Silverman, D., and B. Torode. 1980. *The Material World: Theories of Language and Its Limits.* London: Routledge and Kegan Paul.

Starr, P. 1982. *The Social Transformation of American Medicine.* New York: Basic Books.

Stevens, R. 1966. *Medical Practice in Modern England: The Impact of Specialization and State Medicine.* New Haven: Yale University Press.

Todd, A. D. 1989. *Intimate Adversaries: Cultural Conflicts between Doctors and Women Patients.* Philadelphia: University of Pennsylvania Press.

Tronto, J. C. 1989. "Women and Caring: What Can Feminists Learn about Morality from Caring." In *Gender/Body/Knowledge: Feminist Reconstructions of Being and Knowing,* ed. A. M. Jaggar and S. R. Bordo, 172–187. New Brunswick, N.J.: Rutgers University Press.

Waitzkin, H. B. 1983. *The Second Sickness: Contradictions in Capitalist Health Care.* New York: Free Press.

WOMEN'S AGENCY, SOCIAL CONTROL, AND THE CONSTRUCTION OF "RIGHTS" BY BATTERED WOMEN

Linda Gordon

Despite the fact that violence against women remains widespread, a great majority of Americans today condemn wife beating absolutely and under all circumstances—a consciousness which represents considerable progress from several centuries ago, when wife beating was widely accepted. This delegitimation of a once common patriarchal privilege was not a gradual, epiphenomenal result of "modernization" or individualism, but mainly the result of political activity by organized feminists of both "waves." Less often noticed was the contribution to this change by victims of wife beating, including some of the poorest and generally most wretched of women. In this chapter I hope to give these women their due, to recognize the bravery, ingenuity, and perseverance of women often seen mainly as victimized and defeated. Their activism has implications for several important issues in feminist scholarship, particularly the meanings of patriarchy and social control, and the construction of what historians sometimes call "agency."

When I wrote *Heroes of Their Own Lives* (Gordon 1988b), a history of family violence, I was conscious of contending with social control analyses. More specifically, I was challenging 1960s and 1970s left-wing and feminist appropriations of earlier social control views. The original social control theorists of the early twentieth century thought of social control as inevitable and entirely positive (Ross 1901). Enforcing some degree of conformity, it was argued, was a sine qua non of any societal coherence. This insight seems undeniable, but it is of course difficult to distinguish between enforcing coherence and enforcing regimes of domination and exploitation. This critique of social control only became common seven decades later when New Left–influenced scholars focused on the ideological and cultural forms of domination. These scholars wrote their critical social-control analyses from what they saw as the standpoint of the controlled and the subordinated, charging that professions such as social work, psychology, and education in fact served the interests of ruling and superordinate groups as against those of their subjects. The general features of these analyses, as elaborated incisively by Stanley Cohen (1989:349–350) include the conception of social control as "an active, autonomous force that has to be explained, not with reference to the character of the 'deviance' but by its . . . relationship with the wider social order"; a "refusal to take ideology, claims, pretentions, intentions and programmes wholly in their own terms, . . . a characteristic 'hermeneutics of suspicion'" which views the true purposes of social control as hidden; and a tendency "to see the object of social control . . . as a *tabula rasa.*" In the case of family violence a social control approach sees the boundaries of child abuse and appropriate responses as constructed by the controllers, not by the objects of their efforts. The focus is shifted from the relations among participants in family violence to those between controller and deviant.

This kind of analysis seemed to me an entirely inadequate expression of what I read in family violence records, and I told quite a different story. Because I adopted a feminist standpoint, I was aware of and interested in fissures and tensions within families, while most social control analyses treated families as homogeneous units. Thus in my narrative the nature of, say, child abuse or wife beating was defined as much by its participants, victims, and assailants as by the social controllers; also the participants often articulated strategies and tactics for solving these problems which were quite distinct from those offered by the social controllers. Most importantly, my story was not alternative to but supplementary to a social control analysis. The charity and social work agents had great power over their "clients" and, as I argued in my book, usually succeeded in influencing the definition and outcome of the problems. In such an account, however, the play of forces is not necessarily diadic and, in individual cases, indeterminate in outcome. Moreover, the social control operatives had to fit their approaches to meet the initiatives and resistances of the objects of their control.

Since finishing the book I have begun to see deconstructionist approaches to social problems as offering new variants of social control analyses—extremely insightful but incomplete. In the classic social-control story, we are invited to seek out ideologies and structures representing interests "behind" social control efforts. Social control analyses are usually functionalist, and visible instruments of control—courts,

123

social workers, legal definitions—are often seen as veils hiding "real" master interests. By contrast, a deconstructionist approach denies the existence of master structures or interests, but also denies literal, commonsense definitions of problems such as child abuse. Poststructuralist and structuralist analyses agree that there are no evident, obvious definitions, that the meaning of acts of family violence is not immanent in the behaviors. A poststructuralist approach would go on to view family violence as entirely discursive, constructed through hegemonic discourses. Such an approach, if followed consistently, would deny that the historian could identify determinate social disagreements, such as might be called a class difference or a race difference in standards of what counts as abusive. As Stanley Cohen (1989:350) writes, "deconstructionism leads not to the identification of any one of these hidden master forces, but to the conclusion that the deconstructed fragments defy any reassembly at all." For example, a review of my book charged that I had exaggerated the agency of family violence participants and failed to recognize it as a "discursive effect . . . of social workers' constructions of families, gender, and family violence" and that I suggest that individuals "are the autonomous origins of their own actions" (Scott 1990:850–851). These criticisms restate a social control position that people on the receiving end of domination cannot act or form ideas autonomously of their controllers.

Of course this autonomy I identify is relative and extremely malleable; it is not isolation or independence. Individuals are social creations. The premise of my work on my family violence has been that what counts as abuse has been constructed differently to be sure, but that these constructions are identifiably *social* and produce patterns of agreement and disagreement among and between different social groups and different historical moments, as in the construction of anyone's sense of self. The forms of coercion used in families and the responses to them have been various. Thus agency is endlessly variable. But I would doubt that one person's "agency" is over entirely constructed by another—for example, by a social worker. I cannot conceive that I would call a human a creature without agency.

I have no ontological theory of agency, nor am I trying to construct one. Indeed, as a historian I confess that I rather like the mystery involved in the ultimate unpredictability of resistance, accommodation, and social movements. For me the obstacles agency creates for social explanation are an enjoyable challenge and a source of hope. This subjectivity is historical, and it is by no means inexplicable; indeed it is important to try to explain it. But it is not entirely reducible to structural position or degree of oppression or privilege or discursive construction. It is of course

124

not a unified subjectivity or guaranteed to be positive; the historical record includes much self-destructive agency, and among social movements there are more mass leaps into authoritarian and aggressive consciousness than toward freedom. Still this free and never quite unpredictable human will is what we are stuck with.

In the case of family violence, moreover, one source of will may be the body. Perhaps part of the theoretical significance of family violence as a topic is that because it often involves physical pain, reactions against it are not exclusively cultural. Women do not need a conceptual breakthrough from patriarchal culture, as was necessary for them to want to vote, in order to dislike being hit. The problem of wife beating is an example of the importance of the body and a reminder not to be so threatened by charges of essentialism that we forget physicality. In looking at violence we see subjectivity without postulating a soul or a mind that can be separated from the body.

Thus I begin from an assumption that there was agency among the battered women I studied. The exercise of this agency, the forms of the women's response to their predicaments, showed the influence of the social workers, whose social power was greater than theirs, as well as the force of values and strategies autonomous of those social workers and formed by autonomous histories. In this chapter I look at changes in battered women's responses to wife beating and make a historical argument about the changes.

The particular argument I advance here also reflects a scholarly debate about the use of rights claims, which has arisen since I finished my book in 1987. In this chapter I argue that rights talk was not used by these battered women during the first fifty years of my study, although they might well have heard it in the discourse of social workers and social reformers, who were widely influenced by feminist consciousness; that without an articulation of rights claims they nevertheless actively resisted their abuse; and that these battered women evolved a notion of a right not to be beaten which fit their changed historical circumstances of the last thirty years of this study. Recently critical legal scholars have argued that rights are usually constructed as possessions of individuals, thus fostering a conception of society as composed of individuals and organized through property relations; that rights talk is usually ahistorical and makes social change more difficult to understand and imagine; that it may interfere with the ability to conceive of more solidaristic, communitarian goods. Looking at this critique socially, they have suggested that rights discourse is a classically liberal, even bourgeois phenomenon, unfit and possibly counterproductive for use by subordinated groups. A gender analysis further reveals that rights talk usually defends individuals vis-à-vis the state, while the greatest threats to women often come not from the state but from other individuals. Still, a look at women's social movements produces an opposite interpretation. Surely it is significant that those now critical of rights concepts are themselves in privileged positions and that they are arguing to reject rights just as less privileged groups begin to grab them. Moreover, some subordinate groups have used rights talk effectively in their political struggles, and used it to build, not to erode, solidarity and community. In particular the work of Elizabeth Schneider (1990) can be read as a sequel to my book in demonstrating the role of rights discourse in the movement against wife beating in the last two decades. My own work shows no such collective use of rights talk because my subjects were by their nature atomized, through their construction as social work "cases." Even so, their stories show how deeply notions of rights were at times able to intensify and solidify their grievances and sense of purpose in taking action against them.

Thus in this chapter I take material from a study whose topic is wife beating and use it differently. I rotate the evidence about these battered women to an oblique angle and subject it to a different set of questions: how social control works when examined from a perspective that acknowledges that no party to it is a tabula rasa; how forms of resistance emerge from a variety of historical influences; what conditions are necessary for an extremely subordinated group to find it advantageous to talk of rights. These battered women present a good example for examination because they are in a uniquely difficult position. Disproportionately poor and oppressed, they were also unusually isolated in their victimization because wife beating mainly occurs in private and because they had to contend with a dominant culture that has rendered this problem unspeakable.

The characteristics that make battered women a "good" subject for an examination of resistance also made it difficult to find out about them. The battering victims in my study were overwhelmingly poor, because the victimization of well-to-do women was better hidden by the collusion of relatives, friends, and professionals concerned with respectability. I could see battered women only when they left tracks through the doors of charity and social-work "child-saving" agencies. My evidence comes from a study of the case records of child welfare agencies in Boston from 1880 to 1960. Societies for the Prevention of Cruelty to Children (SPCCs) originated in the United States in the 1870s with the discovery of child abuse and quickly sprang up throughout Europe as well. Other groups, such as placing-out (foster care) and child guidance agencies, also began to devote themselves to these problems. At first they tried to limit their jurisdiction to child mistreatment. But their clients, mostly mothers, virtually dragged the child protectors into wife-beating problems, with the result that one-third of their cases involved marital-violence incidents.

In order to get a close look at how family violence was constructed and reconstructed as a social problem, I randomly sampled the case records of three child-saving agencies in Boston: the Massachusetts SPCC, the Boston Children's Service Association, and the Judge Baker Guidance Center. These records changed substantially over the time period of this study. Those of the late nineteenth century consisted of handwritten comments in bound ledger books. Remarks about a particular case might be scattered among many volumes, and these notes were extremely brief and haphazard. There was little system governing what kinds of information were recorded, individuals were hard to trace because foreign names were repeatedly misspelled, for example, and even children's given names and ages were taken down incorrectly. Diagnoses were often given in shorthand without evidence, for example, "father drinks, mother low type." Beginning in the second decade of the twentieth century, professional social work and the typewriter began to transform these case records: they became folders, with new material interpolated through the years and with related cases cross-referenced. Standardized intake forms began each folder, and results of psychological testing, court records, and correspondence were included. These twentieth-century case records could be over a hundred pages, but the average was ten to twenty typewritten single-spaced pages.

Yet the new social-work professionalism did not end the moralism and bias of these records. The agency workers, whether volunteers or professionals, were until the 1930s virtually all Protestant, well educated, prosperous native-born Americans and their clients mainly Catholic, poor immigrants. Even allowing for some shifts over time, one can accurately say that the child savers believed domestic violence to be primarily a problem of the urban degraded poor, and whether they saw the problem as hereditary depravity or environmental deprivation, they looked down on their clients.

Thus the historian's task in reading these texts is complex and the results imperfect. Most of the case records are notes by social workers who understood the clients' words, behavior, and environment through their own class and cultural lens. Furthermore, the social workers' notes were intended to be read by supervisors, so we cannot take these notes as an accurate rendition of what the social workers did. Many workers could not understand the broken or accented English of their clients. Only rarely do we find direct statements by the clients, such as correspondence, in the case records, and even these are suspect since virtually all clients had something to hide from the social workers—or at least they had a particular spin they wanted to impart to their narratives. And yet these records in their bias, incompleteness, and many-layered texts are not so different from the records historians use to describe wars, diplomatic negotiation, or labor struggles. What I have done here—an act of interpretation, what may now be called a "reading"—is part of the classic tradition of historians.

THE NINETEENTH-CENTURY FEMINIST DISCOURSE ON WIFE BEATING

The very "discovery" or invention of family violence in the 1870s was conditioned by the women's rights movement. The identification of child abuse as a problem was a part of a discourse that condemned corporal punishment and opened the family and "home" to scrutiny. This women's movement contained a substantial campaign against wife beating, a campaign that has been underestimated because it produced no separate organizations and operated largely from within a discourse about temperance, voluntary motherhood, and social purity (Pleck 1983). The image of the beaten wife, the indirect victim of drink, was prominent in temperance rhetoric from the 1830s. In the later half of the century, particularly in the work of the Women's Christian Temperance Union, drinking was a veritable code word for male violence (Nadelhaft n.d.; Bordin 1981:162; Epstein 1981:114). The child protectors were usually temperance advocates who considered family violence the inevitable result of drink. Putting a temperance frame around criticisms of male behavior allowed feminists to score points obliquely, without attacking marriage or men in general. Male brutality, not male tyranny, was the target. The problem came from exceptional, "depraved" men, not from the male sex in general. Nevertheless, temperance agitation made drunkenness a gendered voice—male—and its victims quintessentially female. Considered as a veil thrown over challenges to male supremacy, temperance was a thin cloth indeed.

Another frame in which shocking narratives about wife beating were told was the feminist campaign for divorce. Feminist divorce advocates actually harped more on marital rape (although they did not use this term but rather discussed brutality and "excessive demands") than they did on wife beating, probably because they believed the latter had remedies in criminal law, while the former had none. Women's rights leaders publicized particular cases, usually those whose victims were of high social standing or popular appeal. Feminists sheltered runaway wives, agitated in divorce and child-custody cases, and held a few public meetings about egregious cases (DuBois 1981:95; Pleck 1983).

Women's rights advocates also agitated against wife beating in the context of child-raising discourse. Elizabeth Cady Stanton (DuBois 1981: 95) summed up a common view when she said that "the condition of the child always follows that of the mother." Mothers of any properly operating families were not conceived to have interests separate from, let alone antithetical to, those of their children. Damage to one was damage to both.

The very feminists who talked of women's right to vote, the right of married women to own property, and women's right to an education spoke less often and less militantly of women's rights vis-à-vis their husbands. The voluntary motherhood slogan called for women to be able to refuse their husbands sexually because involuntary sex was immoral, unnatural, and produced inferior babies, yet there was little talk resembling what we would today call reproductive rights. When feminists condemned wife beating, they did so in a chivalric mode, positioning women as vulnerable and men who would abuse their wives as monstrous and depraved, lacking in true manhood. Some spoke of a woman's "ownership" of her body but not of her right to freedom from violence (Gordon 1990).

By the end of the nineteenth century the public discourse surrounding wife abuse showed significant feminist effect, although that influence cannot be accurately measured by suffrage or other legal reforms. Contrary to some common misconceptions, wife beating became radically delegitimated in the middle classes during the century; it was not generally accepted as a husband's prerogative but regarded as a disreputable, seamy practice (Pleck 1979). And despite the fact that reformers avoided the language of women's rights, by the 1870s courts commonly denied men the right to physically chastise wives (Gordon 1988b:255, 364n.).

VICTIM'S DISCOURSE

If wife beating was not widely considered legitimate, neither was public discussion of it. Most feminists as well as more conservative moralists preferred that it remain a hidden, euphemistic, or at least whispered sub-

129

ject, and this preference characterized the child protectors as well. At times they may not have "heard" women's complaints of abuse, which in turn forced clients who sought help from them to find a language they would hear. At other times, however, case records show female clients reluctant to see themselves as abused when the social workers offered that construction of their family life. This reluctance is common still today, as women who are stuck with abusive men may understand that their lives only become harder if they name themselves victims, so many may prefer to deny the abuse. Perhaps more important, or at least more evident in the case records, many of these clients rejected a view of themselves as victims and preferred to present themselves as strong.

The class and cultural differences between poor immigrant clients and social workers may have affected their differing views of marital abuse. Most preindustrial communities had tolerated a male privilege to hit ("punish") wives. This does not mean that prior to modern feminism women never objected to or resisted beating. Perhaps the best way for us to understand this traditional "tolerance" of wife beating is as a tense compromise between male supremacy and female resistance in a system which rested to a great extent on mutual interest in cooperation between men and women. Communities had standards as to what constituted excessive violence. Recently, such notions as the "rule of thumb"—that a man might not use a stick thicker than his thumb to beat his wife—have been cited as evidence of women's total humiliation and powerlessness. On the contrary, such regulation was evidence of a degree of women's power, albeit enforceable mainly through the willingness of others to defend it. But women often had allies within a patriarchal community. If that much abused word *patriarchy* is to have any usefulness, it must be employed to describe a system larger than any individual family, a system that requires regulation even of its privileged members. While patriarchal fathers could control their households, they in turn were subject to sanctions—social control—by the community, whose power brokers included not only fellow patriarchs but women, particularly senior women. The agency clients were accustomed to appealing to fathers as well as mothers, brothers as well as sisters and friends, for support against abusive husbands.

Nevertheless, in the nineteenth and early twentieth centuries, many women clients did not seem to believe they were entitled to freedom from physical violence. When social workers expressed disgust at the way they were treated, the clients sometimes considered that reaction naïve. They spoke of the inevitability of male violence. Their refusal to condemn marital violence in moral terms must be interpreted carefully; it did not mean that they were fatalistic about beatings. They often resisted assault by fighting back, running away, attempting to embarrass the men in front of others, and calling the police or other authorities. And they expressed moral outrage if the men crossed some border of tolerability. There is no contradiction here. Traditional societies tended to have few absolute individual entitlements but many overlapping, even competing social rights. The exact measure of any individual's or group's exercise of traditional prerogatives was determined by conflict and bargaining. Because the client women did not conduct a head-on challenge to their husbands' right to hit them does not mean they liked being hit or believed that their virtue required accepting it. Failure to make this distinction is the result of flat and ahistorical conceptions of what patriarchy and female subordination have been like. There was no society in which women so "internalized" their inferiority, to use a modern explanation, that they did not try to improve their situation. All systems of domination—gender, class, race, wage labor, slave—are systems of conflict.

In the last thirty years of the study, after about 1930, a new tactic was discernable in women's struggles against abusive men and women's complaints to social workers. This new discourse claimed an entitlement to *absolute* freedom from physical molestation and was grounded in terms of a "right." In the context of this particular study—dealings with social work agencies—this new discourse means that clients felt entitled to ask for help in leaving their abusive marriages. This was a claim women began making only when they had some reasonable expectation that they could win; until then, strategies other than head-on confrontation with a husband's prerogatives were more effective. Furthermore, this rights claim expressed the erosion of certain other forms of protections that had been characteristic of more patriarchal societies.

Women's invention of a right not to be beaten came from a dialectic between changing social possibilities and aspirations. When women's best hope was their husbands' kindness, because they were economically dependent on marriage, they did not protest violations of their individual rights but rested their case on their importance as mothers. One might categorize this earlier discourse about marital abuse as a kind of social "needs" talk (Fraser 1990). Women appealed to social necessity, for example, women's importance in raising healthy, disciplined children, as the reason wife beating was bad. As women's possibilities expanded to include wage earning, remarriage after divorce, some control of childbearing, and aid to single mothers, women's best hopes escalated to focus on their own, individual aspirations, including escape from marital violence altogether.

For example, in the earlier decades of this study, several women clients complained bitterly about their husbands' obscene language and its effect on children. A 1916 wife who had left her husband agreed that she would "keep his house if he would treat her respectfully and use decent language before the chn" (case 3,646). A 1920 mother thought her husband's "dirty mouth" was "the hardest thing we have to bear in this house, harder even than [his] not working" (case 3,240).

By fare the most striking and consistent women's complaint, however, until the 1930s, focused on husbands' nonsupport rather than abuse. Nonsupport cases involved married women whose husbands did not adequately provide for them, for reasons that might include unemployment, illness, drunkenness, hostility, or negligence. In 1910 a mother who was permanently crippled by her husband's beatings, who had appeared to the police and her priest so badly bruised that they advised her to have him arrested, complained to the MSPCC only about his failure to provide (case 2,027). In 1901 a young mother complained only about nonsupport; yet the abuse discovered was so severe that an MSPCC agent began making secret plans to sneak the mother and two children out of the house after the father had gone off to work (case 3,363).

The emphasis so many women placed on nonsupport does not necessarily mean that they considered it more unbearable than beating. Rather, they had strategic reasons for their claims. First, in approaching child-saving agencies, they knew they had to present evidence of mistreatment of children, not just of themselves. Some women apparently calculated that foul language and nonsupport were violations of norms of child raising that social control agents could be expected to defend. Second, they may have believed, and with a great deal of evidence, that nonsupport was more criminal and actionable to social workers and courts than wife beating. They themselves likely felt more entitled to support than to bodily integrity. They believed that they had a claim on the community, as represented by the social work agencies, for their support by husbands, but not to protection from physical violence in marriage. (Although court precedents against wife beating had been established, these precedents did not necessarily prevail in the lower courts; also, likelihood of conviction was high only in egregious cases or ones that included nonsupport or intemperance.)

Without directly challenging male authority, women tried to get social control agencies to support their bids for autonomy. An 1893 wife complained she had left her husband "with his permission," but that later he broke his word (case 1,040). In 1917 a wife and children were beaten for not fulfilling the father's work demands, but the woman complained only about his demands, not about the beatings. She asked the case workers to persuade him to take in fewer boarders, as the work was too much for her. Her logic differed from that of the agency, which was willing to investigate the violence but told her that the "agency was not in [the] business" of regulating his labor demands (case 2,523).

Surprisingly, women's direct complaints to agencies about wife beating grew in number just as feminism was at its nadir. In this study the 1930s form a divide after which the majority of women clients complained directly rather than indirectly about wife beating, and after which the records increasingly show formulations about rights and willingness to press criminal charges. In 1934, for example, a young mother of three, married through a matchmaker at age sixteen to an Italian-born man, repeatedly made assault and battery complaints against him. He too was also a nonsupporter, but her logic differed from that of earlier clients, and it was the beatings that appeared to her actionable. This American-born woman was much younger than her immigrant husband, and she may have had less patriarchal expectations than average among the largely immigrant family-violence clients. Her husband's probation officer described her as a "high-type Italian," and the case worker thought she expected "people to do things for her" (case 4,007A). Women continued to allege child abuse in order to get agency help, but in the ensuing investigations they protected about their own abuse more strongly than previously. One MSPCC agent complained in 1940 that the mother was not really very interested in her son's problems but only wanted to talk about herself (case 4,584).

In other cases that year women rationalized their battering in new ways—not as an inevitable part of the female condition or the male nature, but as something they individually deserved. One woman said, "This is my punishment for marrying against my mo.'s wishes" (case 4,284). Thus even in their self-blaming they expressed a new sensibility that wife beating should not be the inevitable lot of women.

Wife-beating accusations stand out still more because of the virtual disappearance of nonsupport complaints, even in the midst of the Great Depression. This striking inverse correlation between nonsupport and wife-beating complaints stimulates an economistic hypothesis: economic dependence prevented women's formulation of a sense of entitlement to protection against marital violence, but it also gave them a sense of entitlement to support; by contrast, the growth of a wage labor economy, bringing unemployment, transience, and dispersal of kinfolk, deprived women of a certainty that they could get support from their husbands, but allowed them to insist on their physical integrity. It is a reasonable hypothesis that the Depression, by the leveling impact of its widespread unemployment, actually encouraged women regarding the possibility of independence and therefore of individual rights claims. (That a distinct increase in wife-beating complaints to social workers appeared in the 1930s does not, of course, constitute evidence against the influence of organized feminism. Organized feminism was and remains a complex influence, continuing to work even as feminist organizational forms diminish, and always combining, as I have argued, with a sense of the possible largely determined by economic and social opportunities for independence.)

Progress is rarely homogeneous, and a change is noticeable here: the increase in battered women's claims to a right not to be beaten coincided with a decline in complaints about marital sexual abuse. I noted earlier that nineteenth-century feminists spoke a great deal about marital rape, condemning men's "unnatural" and "excessive" demands. There were many complaints in the case records, too, about husbands' sexual abuse. These complaints were less visible in more recent decades. Social workers brought to family cases a new sense of "normal" marital sex which was vigilant against female frigidity and tolerant of a wide range of male-initiated heterosexual activity. But clients too had lost a basis from which to condemn any particular amount or range of sexual demands from husbands: few things were immoral, and there was no longer a feminist discourse about the appropriateness of wives' refusal. From a contemporary feminist perspective, this appears as a contradiction, since we are inclined to consider sexual pressure a form of violence, and because we know that many women are beaten over sexual disagreements. The formulation of a "right" was delimited within particular boundary lines.

THE CONSTRUCTION OF RESISTANCE

There is no evidence that these battered women were taught this application of rights language by organized feminists. We have seen that nineteenth-century feminists did not discuss family violence in terms of rights, and the rights talk appeared among the battered women at a low ebb in feminist discourse. But the appearance of rights talk among battered women in the 1930s did not escalate their overall resistance. On the contrary, we see continuous and relatively steady levels of resistance from the beginning to the end of this study. Moreover, a second continuity across the eighty years is that the wife-beating complaints to social work agencies produced little help for most women. Most were unable either to change the man's behavior or to leave the relationship.

The difficulties these women experienced were essentially those faced by single mothers. The biggest obstacle for most women living with abusive men was that they did not wish to lose their children; indeed, their motherhood was for most of them (including many who were categorized as abusive or neglectful parents) their greatest source of pleasure, self-esteem, and social status. In escaping they had to find a way simultaneously to earn money and raise children in an economy of limited jobs for women, little child care, and almost no reliable aid to single mothers. They had to do this with the often low confidence characteristic of women trying to take unconventional action. Moreover, these women had the added burden of defying a social norm condemning marital separation and encouraging submission as a womanly virtue.

Consider one woman's dilemma. Mrs. O'Brien (not her real name), whose story began in Charlestown in 1910, changed her mind repeatedly about how she wanted to deal with her husband's abuse. One might imagine her inconsistent behavior was interpreted by social workers as a sign that she was masochistic or at least passive, not really wanting to escape her victimization. Scrutinized more closely, her seeming ambivalence reflects the lack of options she and so many others had. Both she and Mr. O'Brien were born in Ireland; he worked as a freight handler for the B&M Railroad. They had three surviving children in 1910, and four more were born as the case continued, with three of them surviving. The beatings she suffered were so apparent that several outside authorities— the police, her priest, the MSPCC—all took her side. The police advised her to have him arrested; but she responded, speaking for thousands, "She does not want to lose her chn. however and the little money which she does receive from fa. enables her to keep her home together." Instead, she tried to get the MSPCC agent to "scare" him into treating her and her children "right," even though previous jail terms had not "reformed" him. She agreed to another prosecution at one peak of rage—"would rather starve than endure the treatment"—then changed her mind and agreed to let him return to live with her if he would give her all his wages. The MSPCC got her to agree that it would collect $10 per week from him and give it to her. When he agreed to this, she raised her demand to $11, evidently dreading taking him back. But he agreed to this too. Three months later he was sentenced to six months for assaulting her;

she was pregnant and soon began campaigning to get him out of jail. This pattern coninuted for years. In 1914 and again in 1920 she was threatening to murder him, describing herself as in a "desperate state of mind" (case 2,027).

Mrs. O'Brien's ambivalence was a rational response to her situation. Her children, numbering six by 1920, literally forced her to submit to her husband. Her problems illustrate the limited usefulness of prosecution as a remedy in the absence of economic provisions for single mothers. (It also suggests why prosecution might have different meanings today, when greater employment opportunities, ADC, and shelters offer women somewhat more chance of survival alone with their children.) But Mrs. O'Brien, like many victims, believed in the potential benefit of prosecution as a deterrent; this was not an option forced on her by social control agents.

And her contradictory behavior was typical. Many women who successfully prosecuted their husbands for abuse then quickly petitioned for their pardon, and the numbers who withdrew their complaints before trial or whose husbands were not convicted must have been even greater but were untraceable. To cite but one of scores of examples: Arnold W., a second offender whose wife had testified that she was afraid for her life, was sentenced to five months in 1870 by a judge who considered him "incorrigible." But Mrs. W. returned within two months to say she had testified against him "while angry" but now needed his release on grounds of poverty; the district attorney, supporting her petition, wrote that "certainly she is right, if the starved appearance of her children is any indication" (Executive Council Records 1969–1970).

Batterers often realized that women could not prosecute for fear of losing economic support. One husband threatened that "if she ever sues for divorce or separation or if she ever has him brought into court . . . he will throw up his job and then she will be without support" (case 6,040). Others derided their wives' chance for independence: "if you want to come back, all right, if not all right, we will see who wins out in this deal. . . . I work for W. C. Hill, when you want me arrested," one wife beater wrote in 1911 to his wife who had left (case 2,024).

Short of and more common than prosecution, women sought to use the police to threaten prosecution, hoping to frighten the men. Police were called in 49 percent of these wife-beating cases (with very little change over time in the rate of police involvement). Women had no other agency to call for emergency help, but what they got was almost always unsatisfactory. Their stories sound familiar: The police implicitly (and sometimes explicitly) identified with the husband, and while urging him to moderate his violence and to sober up, sympathized with his frustra-

136

tion and trivialized his assaults. They often removed the angry man from his home for a while and calmed him down, and this service was of some limited value to women. Sometimes the police threatened men with arrest and jail. Often, too, the police knew that little they could do would be useful to the women, who could not survive without these men. At times the police were worse than useless: in one 1910 case a woman who went to the station to complain about her husband was arrested herself for drunkenness (case 3,040). Often the police simply refused to respond to domestic disturbance calls. In 1930 one officer told a social worker, "she is always calling on the Police for the slightest things and the Police will no longer go to the home when [she] requests them to" (case 3,560A). Or as another woman reported in 1960, the police pacified her husband in another room and did not talk with her at all (case 6,041).

Mrs. O'Brien's ultimate desire was for a "separation and maintenance" agreement, as such provisions were then known: she wanted the state to guarantee her the right to a separate household and require her husband to pay support. Such plans were the most common desire of the beaten wives in this study. As another woman explained, "She did not wish him to be put away as he is a steady worker but wd. like the case arranged so that he wd. live apart and support her and the chn." (case 3,040). Mrs. O'Brien managed to get aid from the new Massachusetts mother's pension program in 1920, but only after she had been struggling against her husband's abuse for at least ten years, he having built up a record of convictions and jail terms for assault and nonsupport.

Failing to get separation-and-maintenance agreements and unable to collect support even when it was promised, the remaining option—called desertion—was taken only by the most depressed, disheartened, and desperate women. A moralistic nomenclature no longer common, desertion meant a woman leaving a husband *and* children. Female desertion was extremely uncommon in these cases, especially in contrast to the prevalence of male desertion. The low female desertion rate revealed the strength of women's attachments to their children. Moreover, the guilt and stigma attached to such action usually meant that women "deserters" simultaneously cut themselves off from friends or kin. All in all, it was unlikely that ridding themselves of the burdens of children would lead to better futures for wife-beating victims.

Another response to beatings was fighting. The incidence of mutual combat and female aggression in marital violence has been obscured by the legacy of victim blaming in the interpretation of the problem. For differing reasons, both feminists and sexists have been reluctant to recognize or acknowledge women's physical aggression. Moreover, poor women of the past may have been more comfortable with fighting than "respectable" women and contemporary women. Of the marital violence cases I studied, 16 percent contained some female violence—8 percent mutual violence and 8 percent husband beating.

Most of women's violence was responsive or reactive, as distinguished from men's violence, which grew out of mutual conflict, to be sure, but was more often a regular tactic in an ongoing power struggle. In these records I found three patterns in women's violence toward their husbands. The most common pattern comprises women's active, ongoing participation in mutual violence. Consider the 1934 case of an Irish Catholic woman married to a Danish fisherman. He was at sea all but thirty days a year, and there was violence whenever he returned. One particular target of his rage was Catholicism: he beat his sons, she claimed, to prevent them from going to church with her and loudly cursed the Irish and the Catholics—he was an atheist. The neighbors took her side and would hide her three sons when their father was in a rage. The downstairs tenant took his side. They reported that she swore, yelled, hit him, and chased him with a butcher knife, that she threw herself down some stairs to make it look like he had beaten her. Amid these conflicting charges it was certain, however, that she wanted to leave her husband, but he refused to let her have custody of the children; after a year of attempted mediation, the MSPCC ultimately lent its support for a separation (case 4,060; see also, e.g., cases 2,008, 2,561, 3,541, 3,546, 5,085). In this case the woman responded with violence to a situation she was eager to leave, while he used violence to hold her in the marriage. Her violence, as well as her maintenance of neighborhood support, worked relatively effectively to give her some leverage and ultimately to get her out of the situation. An analogous pattern with the sexes reversed could not be found—indeed probably could not occur. Women's violence in these situations was a matter of holding their own or hurting a hated partner whom they were not free to leave. The case records contain many plaintive letters from wife beaters begging for their wives' return: "the suspense is awfull at times especially at night, when I arrive Home, I call it Home yet, when I do not hear those gentle voices and innocent souls whisper and speak my name" (case 2,024).

The second pattern consists of extremely frightened, usually fatalistic wives who occasionally defended themselves with a weapon. In 1960, for example, the MSPCC took on a case of such a woman; she was underweight, malnourished, and very frightened of her husband, who had a record for drunkenness as well as a diagnosis of mental illness. Profane and abusive, he was hospitalized as a result of a powerful blow she had given him on the head (case 6,042; see also cases 3,363, 5,543). This is the pattern that most commonly led, and leads, to murder.

In a third pattern, the least common, women are the primary aggressors. In one 1932 case a mother, an obese, unhealthy woman described as slovenly, kicked and slammed her six children around, locked them out of the house, knocked them down the stairs, and scratched them as well as beating her husband and forcing him and an oldest daughter to do all the housework. His employer described him as "weak and spineless, but very good-hearted." Ultimately this woman was committed to a state mental hospital, at her own request, as a psychotic (case 3,024; see also cases 4,261, 4,501, 6,086). I cannot resist the only partly humorous observation that if there is a pattern of "masochism" in violent marriages, it describes male better than female behavior since it is mainly the men who appear to want to continue the violent relationships.

Of the three patterns of female violence, the latter two usually involved extremely distressed, depressed, even disoriented women. The fighting women in mutual violence cases were not depressed and may have been better off then the more peaceful ones. They were often struggling, albeit sometimes ambivalently, for separation, defending rights their husbands were challenging (for example, an outside job), or battling over resources and labor.

Over the period of this study there appears to have been a decline in mutual violence and women's aggression (Straus 1980; Pleck et al. 1978). Particularly noticeable is the disappearance of cases of women attacking other women. In the first decades of this study there were several cases like that in 1910 of an Irish-American woman who had "drinking parties" with other women which not infrequently ended in name-calling and fights; she and her daughter fought physically in front of an MSPCC agent; and her daughter was arrested for a fight with another girl (case 2,047). This decline was offset by an increase in women leaving marriages. A likely hypothesis is that a trade-off occurred between women's physical violence and their ability to get separations or divorces.

Although women usually lost in physical fights with men, the decline in women's violence was not a clear gain for women and their families. Condemnation of female violence went along with romanticization of female passivity, which contributed to women's participation in their own victimization. Historian Nancy Tomes found that a decline in women's violence in England between 1850 and 1890 correspond to an increase in women's sense of shame about wife beating and their reluctance to report or discuss it (Tomes 1978). In this area, feminism's impact on women in violent families was mixed. The delegitimization of wife beating increased battered women's guilt about their inability to escape; they increasingly thought themselves exceptional, adding to their shame. First-wave feminism, expressing its relatively elite class base, helped construct a femininity that was oppressive to battered women: by emphasizing the superiority of women's peacefulness, feminist influence made women loathe and attempt to suppress their own aggressiveness and anger.

Few battered women attempted to resolve their problems privately with their husbands, whether violently or otherwise. That neighbors, kinfolk, and friends were of limited help was not because the victims failed to ask. Beaten women often asked for places to stay, the minimum condition for escape. One 1910 incest and wife-beating case developed in part *because* of a woman's lack of a place to live. She had previously left her abusive husband to stay with her mother but was left homeless when her mother died; she returned to her husband in 1911; in 1914 he was convicted of assault and battery on her and in 1916 of incest with their oldest daughter (case 2,054A).

Or women might ask for money to help maintain their own households. Close neighbors, landladies, and relatives might be asked for child care, for credit, or for food. One very young wife, at age twenty-one already a four-year veteran of extreme abuse, had at first displayed the typical ambivalent pattern, leaving several times to stay with her relatives and always returning. Taking a firm decision when she discovered that he had infected her and her young daughter with venereal disease, she left for good, able to return to a household that still contained a mother, sister, and brother who supplied child care as well as a home. This support was her ticket to success: four years later, in 1914, she was managing on her own, her daughter cared for by her sister while she worked as a stenographer (case 2,058A). But kinship support was no guarantee of safety. In Charlestown in 1917 a beaten wife stayed with her parents and took a job, but whenever her payday came, the estranged husband would arrive to demand her money. When her father refused to let him in, the wife would meet him secretly and give him money (case 2,520). In a 1940 case, a battered wife had already left her husband and gone to live with her mother, but he threatened and attacked his mother-in-law too until she became frightened to have her daughter with her; he also terrorized the welfare workers who were, in his view, supporting his wife's defiance (case 4,502).

Occasionally I found cases in which there was more direct intervention by relatives; these were more frequent in the first forty years of this study. In 1910 one extremely patriarchal Italian father tried to stop his son from assaulting his wife (case 2,042). In 1893 a woman's brother traveled to another part of Boston each night to protect her from her husband, "who would lie in wait for her with a club" (case 1,040). But relatives also set clear limits on their involvement. In 1917 an Italian-born husband who had battered his wife for years ended their relationship by committing her to a mental hospital (despite the attempts of a thirteen-year-old daughter to convince an MSPCC agent that abuse was her mother's main mental problem). The wife's parents lived close by, and the wife had fled to them on several occasions. They vociferously condemned her husband in speaking to a social worker, and when the wife's mother died they blamed it on her anguish at her daughter's abuse. But when the husband demanded the wife's return, her parents were unwilling to interfere with his authority so far as to shelter her. Moreover, after committing his wife, the husband retained his right to be accepted by her relatives as a member of the family (case 2,800A).

More important than the material help offered by neighbors, friends, and relatives was their influence on how victims defined the standards of treatment they would tolerate. The reactions of confidants, or even of neighbors who heard the fights, affected the responses of victims and assailants. Some counseled resignation and passivity, while others, by their outrage of partisanship, suggested that battering need not be accepted. Parents like those above who expressed their commitment by their willingness to take their daughter in, but nevertheless deferred to her abusive husband's ultimate authority, were telling their daughter that beatings should be tolerated. By contrast, in another Italian-American family, the mother and sister of a battered woman not only took her in with her six children but brought her to complain to the MSPCC (case 6,300).

Battered women sometimes turned to child welfare agencies because their informal networks could not protect them, but often they added these agencies in to a reservoir of resistance strategies, just as they had added rights claims to others. Sometimes they benefited from the agencies, mainly when they were able to obtain legitimation and financial support for leaving their marriages. Such benefits were owing sometimes to the skill and insight of social workers, but more to the ingenuity of the victims. Indeed, sometimes the victims taught the social workers the best helping techniques, chipping away at their hostility to separation, divorce, and female-headed households, just as the victims learned from social workers what aspirations might be within their reach (Gordon 1988a).

I do not mean to suggest that clients were equals in their contacts with the child protectors; on the contrary, cumulatively the agencies were more successful in imposing their standards, just as men could not usually be brought to change their behavior. We must be clear that concepts like agency and resistance do not mean victory; nor should they work to soften the ugly and painful history of victimization. Indeed, many forms of resistance were probably poor choices, although one might argue that the impulse to do *something,* however ineffective, was usually preferable to resignation. The problem so evident in women's history—and in much other scholarship from the standpoint of subordinated groups—of romanticizing either victimization or resistance is closely associated with moralism. Historical accounts need to avoid moral categories whenever possible. Oppression may be evil, but victims are not therefore "good" or "nice" or "wise."

What can we learn from this enumeration of forms of resistance to wife beating? First, we see that resistance is itself an interpretation, a construction, one participated in by the historian and reader, certainly, as by the wife-beating victim herself. To resist is to experience autonomy, to experience oneself as planning against one's assailant, and to interpret the assault as something avoidable or controllable. One expert on contemporary wife beating has explained how a victim may appear to be provoking an assault—as, for example, by belittling a violent and insecure husband—when her (experienced) intention is to control when, where, and how severe it will be (Walker 1979). The same actions might have quite a different meaning in a different context—if, for example, she does not expect to be beaten, or if she wants to be beaten (a hypothetical for which I found no evidence). At the very least, the range and stubbornness of some of these modes of resistance are too great to be constructions exclusively of social workers.

Second, we see that rights claims seemed to emerge under certain specifiable conditions. Feminists and battered women alike seemed to avoid rights talk about wife beating while social and economic conditions made it difficult and disrespectable for married women to become independent of their husbands. Moreover, rights talk seems to fit best with absolute claims—no physical coercion at all should be tolerated. This position simply did not fit the life conditions of many women, for whom putting up with a husband's fists might not be worse than the poverty and loss of one's children attendant to separation. This reading of the evidence suggests that battered women's claim to rights, a claim upon the state to protect them from violence, arose precisely because of the weakening of patriarchy, while other forms of resistance had been an essential part of patriarchal systems.

REFERENCES

Bordin, R. 1981. *Women and Temperance: The Quest for Power and Liberty, 1873–1900.* Philadelphia: Temple University Press.

Cohen, S. 1989. "The Critical Discourse on 'Social Control': Notes on the Concept as a Hammer." *International Journal of the Sociology of Law* 17:347–357.

"Debates on Marriage and Divorce, 10th National Women's Rights Convention, 1960." In *The Concise History of Women Suffrage*, ed. Mari Jo Buhle and Paul Buhle, 170–189. Urbana: University of Illinois Press.

DuBois, E. C., ed. 1981. *Elizabeth Cady Stanton, Susan B. Anthony: Correspondence, Writings, Speeches.* New York: Schocken.

Epstein, B. L. 1981. *The Politics of Domesticity: Women, Evangelism, and Temperance in Nineteenth-Century America.* Middletown, Conn.: Wesleyan University Press.

Executive Council Records, Commonwealth of Massachusetts. 1969–1970. Pardon, Communication, and Parole files, unnumbered box, Massachusetts State Archives, Boston.

Fraser, N. 1990. "Struggle over Needs: Outline of a Socialist-Feminist Critical Theory of Late-Capitalist Political Culture." In *Women, the State, and Welfare*, ed. Linda Gordon, 199–225. Madison: University of Wisconsin Press.

Gordon, L. 1988a. "The Frustrations of Family Violence Social Work: An Historical Critique." *Journal of Sociology and Social Welfare* 15:139–160.

———. 1988b. *Heroes of Their Own Lives: The Politics and History of Family Violence, Boston, 1880–1960.* New York: Viking.

———. 1990. *Woman's Body, Woman's Right: A Social History of Birth Control in America.* 2d ed. New York: Penguin.

Nadelhaft, J. N.d. "Domestic Violence in the Literature of the Temperance Movement." Manuscript quoted in Elizabeth Pleck, *Domestic Tyranny: The Making of American Social Policy against Family Violence from Colonial Times to the Present*, 98–101. New York: Oxford University Press, 1987.

Pleck, E. 1979. "Wife Beating in Nineteenth-Century America." *Victimology* 4:60–74.

———. 1983. "Feminist Responses to Crimes against Women, 1868–1896." *Signs* 8:451–470.

Pleck, E., J. H. Pleck, M. Grossman, and P. B. Bart. 1978. "The Battered Data Syndrome: A Comment on Steinmetz' Article." *Victimology* 2:680–683.

Ross, E. A. 1901. *Social Control: A Survey of the Foundations of Order.* New York.

Schneider, E. M. 1990. "The Dialectic of Rights and Politics: Perspectives from the Women's Movement." In *Women, the State, and Welfare,* ed. Linda Gordon, 226–249. Madison: University of Wisconsin Press.

Scott, J. W. 1990. Review of *Heroes of Their Own Lives. Signs* 15:848–852.

Stanton, E. C. 1981. "Address to the Legislature of New York on Women's Rights." In *Elizabeth Cady Stanton, Susan B. Anthony: Correspondence, Writings, Speeches,* ed. Ellen DuBois, 49. New York: Schocken. Originally published in 1854.

Straus, M. 1980. "Victims and Aggressors in Marital Violence." *American Behavioral Scientist* 23(May–June): 681–704.

Tomes, N. 1978. "A 'Torrent of Abuse': Crimes of Violence between Working Class Men and Women in London, 1840–1875." *Journal of Social History* 11:328–345.

Walker, L. 1979. *The Battered Woman.* New York: Harper and Row.

TELLING CRIMINAL STORIES: THE *FEMME CRIMINELLE* IN LATE NINETEENTH-CENTURY PARIS

Ann-Louise Shapiro

In fin-de-siècle Paris, crime had become an imaginative obsession. Criminal stories proliferated across a broad cultural field that included journalistic, literary, legal, medical, and social scientific writings. Criminals were the subjects of popular ballads; they wrote memoirs from prison and figured prominently in illustrated supplements to mass circulation newspapers. Forensic psychiatrists probed the medical dimensions of criminality in published case histories; former chiefs of police wrote multivolumed memoirs that celebrated, in ironic juxtaposition, both crime and its containment; a specialized daily newspaper, the *Gazette des Tribunaux,* reported on the most intriguing or scandalous court cases, quoting the texts of criminal indictments and providing a reconstructed version of the interchanges of the courtroom; the *fait divers* of the popular press—those condensed stories about terrifying accidents, natural disasters, sensational crimes, mysterious disappearances, miraculous escapes, and otherworldly occurrences—came more and more to focus on violent and criminal events; popular theater featured criminal melodramas in its staple fare; novels and serialized *romans feuilletons* elaborated on real and fictional crimes; and professionals in law and criminology issued a steady stream of expert testimony in the courtroom and in journals, monographs, and reports from international conferences.

This wide-ranging discussion of criminal activity not only made good press, providing the occasion for vicarious psychic and social adventures in transgression, but was more importantly part of broader processes of cultural definition. As Dennis Porter (1981:121) has explained, a crime always has the status of a symptom, one that functions as an insistent question, inviting a discussion of causes and motivation. Criminologists, responding to this invitation from several different disciplines, saw crime as offering a mirror of society, the most vivid, accurate representation of customs and inclinations, "a pathologically enlarged version of the tendencies of the day" (Sighele 1899: 195–96), and presented criminal stories as "social physiologies [in which] the vices of our society are laid bare with a documentary exactitude."[1] In their minds, studies of crime and criminality would produce a prophylactic knowledge with which to address a broad range of perceived social threats or social pathologies (alcoholism, venereal disease, prostitution, degeneration, suicide), while producing a scientific taxonomy of human sentiments (hate, greed, vengeance, love, despair), and a normative description of healthy and viable social arrangements, including the appropriate relations between men and women and among social classes. In the service of this project of social hygiene, they would produce a vast literature of criminal stories.

My particular interest here are the varied accounts of female criminality. Although crime rates for women remained fairly stable (or declined slightly) in the final three decades of the nineteenth century, the discussion of the female criminal expanded—inviting us to ask, in Porter's terms, exactly what question women's criminality posed for contemporaries. Of what was it a symptom? What were the cultural meanings of the alleged "problem" of women's crime? Or, why did so many people, with diverse interests and intentions, discuss at such length "the criminal woman"? Following the work of Joan Scott, Mary Poovey, and others, I suggest that "those issues that are constituted as 'problems' at any given moment are particularly important because they mark the limits of ideological certainty" (Poovey 1988: 12). While contemporary commentators explained the pervasive fascination with crime, *le prestige du mal,* in terms of voyeuristic pleasures and scientific curiosity and even as a sign of the growth of a subversive popular culture, I argue that this preoccupation suggests, above all, a moment of struggle, even crisis, in the self-definition of the emerging bourgeois culture of the Third Republic. And I place "women" at the center of this struggle.

In effect, stories of and about criminal women resonated so broadly because deviant women had come to symbolize a condition of national danger during this period. I begin by looking at the ways in which contemporaries understood criminal women as mirrors of a more generalized social pathology and set themselves the task of solving this problem. Next I explore the processes by which the criminal stories were constructed, emphasizing the contest for interpretive authority between culturally sanctioned narratives and more oppositional stories. Finally, in

146

order to understand how oppositional stories became effective—that is, gained cultural weight—I examine the conditions that made the fact of female criminality and the stories of criminal women central, rather than marginal, in a time of political and cultural transition. In sum, I argue that, in forging a link between debates about the position of women in the new Third Republic and the nature and viability of republicanism, criminal women gained an audience for their stories that they might not otherwise have had.

FEMALE DEVIANCE AND THE FATE OF THE NATION

The political culture of the early Third Republic contained ideological conflicts that we can read in the literatures on crime. In the aftermath of the Commune,[2] all political parties presented themselves as parties of order pledged to simultaneously uphold traditional values and restore French power in the international arena. But Radicals, Republicans, and other parties of the left and center were vulnerable to conservatives' charges that republicanism—with its assertion of the rights of the individual and its anticlerical spirit—weakened both the family and the nation. In this context, the precise meaning of order became less clear. Did republican citizenship imply the same rights for all? Including women? And if women were given the same rights as men, what would happen to traditional patterns based on the patriarchal family? If republicanism meant freedom, then what were the limits of this freedom?

New agitation about the position of women revealed in concrete terms the difficulties of reconciling the ideals of personal freedom with the desire for social discipline. Within the framework of such unresolved questions, the viability of the Republic was linked, in effect, to the ability of republicans to solve "the woman question." A reinvigorated women's movement was beginning to demand women's right to divorce and to bring paternity suits, to decry unequal standards of justice in adultery cases and unequal power in the marketplace, while a tiny minority of feminists sought equal civil status and full citizenship, including the right to vote.

In a twist that seemed quite logical to contemporary observers, the female offender was linked rhetorically and thematically to the problem of unruly women who were demanding greater rights.[3] The female criminal had increasingly come to symbolize a condition of national disorder that was evident not only in the presence of women as defendants in the

147

criminal courts, but in the slippery social/political/civil status of women in the final three decades of the century. In this discourse, the feminist and the criminal seemed to merge, representing but slightly different versions of the same social malady.[4] Like feminists, criminal women—women who defied the familial and the legal order—raised the issue of female disabilities. In so doing, they challenged republican aspirations to unity and stability and exposed contradictory commitments to freedom and supervision, to equality and hierarchy, that coexisted in an unstable equilibrium within republican ideology.

In a somewhat different register, criminal women similarly became symbolic vehicles for exploring wide-ranging anxieties about a perceived condition of national decadence. While the precise political meanings of republicanism were being negotiated, the government promoted the myth of a harmonious national community. At the same time, however, others wrote with equal conviction of national decay. Doctors and social scientists posited a national disease, *dégénérescence*—a condition characterized not only by physical deterioration but by parallel moral and intellectual decline—that provided a counterdiscourse to the rhetoric of progress. In their terms, degeneration was both the disease of particular individuals and the condition of modernity itself, manifest in persistent social divisions, the irrational behavior of crowds, urban crime, and insanity. According to Daniel Pick (1989:230), theories of *dégénérescence* "flirted and flitted between the dreams of purity and danger . . . in socially specific ways," suggesting sometimes that "degeneration involved a scenario of racial decline (potentially implicating everyone in the society) and [alternatively] an explanation of 'otherness,' securing the identity of, variously, the scientist, (white) man, bourgeoisie against superstition, fiction, darkness, femininity, the masses, effete aristocracy." Degeneration was a pervasive concern precisely because it could not be reduced to one message or to one context; rather, it emerged to conceptualize "a felt crisis of history" (Pick 1989:54) that could be seen equally in the national defeat by Prussia in 1870 or in the nation's intractable social problems. With such a diffuse etiology, degeneration theorists could link political fears about repeated revolution, unruly crowds, anarchism, and violence to anxieties about depopulation, alcoholism, crime, prostitution, insanity, and feminism. Republican optimism notwithstanding, the modern world seemed doomed by a self-reproducing pathological process.

In the presence of these worries, social and cultural authorities pursued strategies that were essentially cathartic, that is, they mobilized anxieties around a set of problems that could be solved.[5] Increasingly, a cultural consensus began to emerge that identified Woman as the mirror through which the nation could recognize itself, "the woman question" as the center of the problem of national weakness. Henri Thulié (1885:i) provides us with a fairly complete description of a perceived syndrome that had gained considerable credibility:

> Scientists have finally aroused public attention. Cries of alarm are heard everywhere: the size of the population is diminishing; infant mortality is increasing; infanticide and abortion have become, as in America, routine phenomena of daily life; prostitution is growing; people seek shameful and sterile pleasures; the vitality of France has been undermined. . . . From another perspective, women defend themselves against men with vitriol and with the revolver. They no longer seek legal justice which does not have the power to protect them; hence they take vengeance. This weakening of the nation, these vices and violences, are symptoms of a profound sickness from which France is suffering.

National anxieties could be collected around the condition of particular deviant women who needed to be recuperated in order to cure the French *mal de siècle*.

In study after study, criminologists slid from general observations about contemporary criminality directly into discussions of a disorder that was particularly female.[6] The malaise of modernity and the malady of the modern female converged: "woman becomes more delinquent with the advance of civilization which gives her more initiative, more freedom to exercise it and more needs to satisfy" (Toulouse 1904:292). This focus on femaleness was grounded in well-entrenched patterns of thought that conceived of women as uniquely capable of reflecting back the contours of social life. Experts spoke of women as "more readily penetrated by the influences of their environment than were men," more suggestible, more easily swept away by the fantasies produced by urban glitz and less resistant to the lure of urban vice, more corruptible by literature, theater, and leisure than were men (Puibaraud 1899; Chevalier 1893). In this analysis, female criminals were the signs and instruments of a particularly modern demoralization that seemed quite directly responsible for national decline. Contemporary anxieties which were focused on the phenomenon of female criminality opened, then, a problematic in which professionals and popularizers worried over the essence of "femaleness," delineating in some detail the character of the "normal" and the "un-

149

natural" woman and cataloging in a new, and charged, political context the hallmarks of sexual difference.

CRIMINAL STORIES AND THE PENAL PROCESS

If we examine the various representations of the female criminal, we can begin to fill in the details of a process through which sexual stereotypes were confirmed, constructed, and deployed, invoking and building upon what Michèle Ouerd (1978) has called "the persistent fantasies and formulaic nightmares" that inform discourses about the deviant woman. At the same time, however, it is crucial that we move beyond an analysis of the production of stereotypes—even as they were reinterpreted in new historical contexts. Rather, we must attempt to evaluate the effective cultural weight of these stories so as to understand how they worked in cultural and political terms. Criminal stories were told within a cultural frame informed by social values and expectations; they were inflected by the literary representations of high and low culture and by the writing of bourgeois professionals (criminologists, magistrates, lawyers, forensic psychiatrists); official stories were ultimately orchestrated by the structures of the penal process itself (the pretrial investigations, the formal documents of the judicial dossier, the hearing). These stories were presented to juries and, through the press, to diverse popular audiences who understood them within particular social and cultural conditions that rendered the stories intelligible. We have, then, not only different interpretive communities, but different kinds of tellings that were produced in different contexts.

Various experts told stories to reveal the essential qualities of body and mind that characterized the criminal woman. Although sometimes perceptive, occasionally subtle, these writings made sense largely because they represented reality through stereotyped literary and cultural conventions that had wide currency.[7] They reinvigorated myths about "women" that set the narrative frame for the official tellings of criminal stories. It is not coincidental that bills of indictment and popular retellings of crimes were so formulaic, uniform in their presentation of motivation and plot development. But stories, even those broadly credible within the culture, always exist in tension with other stories (Steedman 1987:12). Even within the dominant classes, the discourse about criminal women was not homogeneous; most important, female defendants themselves responded to the official, public stories that allegedly made sense of their lives in quite different ways. Some women told defiantly oppositional

150

stories—accounts that directly called into question the conclusions of their accusers. But others read their scripts perfectly, repeating the rhetorical and social conventions that typically organized perceptions of women's criminal acts. As Natalie Davis (1987:81) has shown in her recent discussion of sixteenth-century pardon tales, women characteristically have had a problematic relation to their own violence and incorporate this ambiguous positioning into their self-presentation as perpetrators of crime. In many cases, then, women made use of received story lines—explained their motivation and behavior in terms of well-understood plots that fulfilled, to a great extent, the expectations of their accusers. And because these expectations were also, inevitably, internalized, the repetition of recognizable plots must have been both intentional and unconscious. The stories of and about criminal women are, then, inevitably stories-in-contest.

With a new attention to the effects of narrative, legal scholars have recently begun to explore "the perceptual fault lines" that inform criminal stories and to expose, in the deeply patterned activity of legal storytelling, the ways that the ideology of social and cultural authorities passes for neutrality.[8] For some, the cure is to invoke counterhegemonic stories that reveal the ideological assumptions embedded in and produced through the legal process itself. But the effects of such storytelling are not at all self-evident. It may, in fact, be too simple to decontextualize the negotiation between accused and accusers, too simple to frame the negotiation as between two opposing interpretive communities. For example, we need to know what conditions are necessary for counterhegemonic stories to be heard. By what criteria can we measure the effects of such alternate tellings? And how do individual stories translate into effective cultural resistance?

It seems to me that the relationship between power and language requires a more subtle examination—one that sets this relationship in a historical context complicated by the play of parallel and perhaps unrelated processes that are all negotiating around the articulation of cultural meanings. In looking here at the stories of female crime, we are able to see both the way that the criminal process produced these narratives and the cultural field that gave them authority. At the same time, we can look at the relationship of female defendants to the stories told about them, revealing their connections both to the authorities who framed the stories of their behavior and to alternate stories that derived largely from the values and expectations of their own working-class communities. In sustaining these multiple perspectives, we have, I think, a clearer picture in a specific historical moment of the effects of discourse on social relations,

151

of the operation and force of structural constraints and social relations that precede discourse, and, finally, of the possibilities for effective resistance in interactions between unequal parties.

In her perceptive study of eighteenth-century crime, Arlette Farge has warned of the seduction of the judicial archive,[9] of its ability to generate illusion. Through its recovery of the forgotten or neglected details of ordinary life, of "the exceptional normal" made visible in criminal behaviors, we are led, she argues, to give both too much and too little weight to these "pieces of the real." In the end, Farge concludes, we must see the voices of the archives as speaking within a system of power relations that governs the production of discourse, revealing, above all, not any specific truth about their subjects, but rather the imbrication of private and official worlds in a way that produces these descriptions (Farge 1986:7–8). I am arguing, in an extension of Farge's insight, that the criminal story emerged, in effect, through a kind of enforced collaboration between accused and accusers. The defendant passed through police interrogations, which were followed over a period of months by extensive questioning by the *juge d'instruction*, the investigating magistrate charged with compiling the state's case; the defendant then arrived at the court hearing where she was interrogated by the presiding judge, the Président de la Cour. In each of these settings, the different modes of examining elicited different kinds of responses and different types of information. At each level, different (and sometimes random) principles governed the inclusion or withholding of pieces of the story. And at each level, contradictions might be resolved, ignored, or suppressed. There was not, then, a single or even a linear story of any individual case. The dossiers are themselves anarchic, presenting not only the interactions between defendant and interrogators, but also the depositions of numerous collateral parties which were equally contradictory and inconclusive. What we have, then, is a view of the process that produced an official version of the crime and the disparate voices that contributed to this version.

Nineteenth-century criminologists were preoccupied with classification, with creating taxonomies, and even physiognomies, that provided a reliable set of personality traits by which to identify specific criminal types. By the end of the century, contemporaries shared a fairly consistent description of the deviant or unnatural woman, someone predisposed to commit a violent crime. According to criminological testimony, she was likely to be sharp-tongued, insufficiently deferential, and publicly critical of her husband; she might invert appropriate female behavior by refusing domestic responsibilities or by engaging in questionable sexual behaviors; she was prone to slip into excess, unable to contain or control the emotions generated by her reproductive system; or, she might be moved by a much discussed, particularly vicious, particularly female vengeance.[10] The criminal stories produced in the penal process both participated in this work of cultural mythmaking and responded to well-established and enduring assumptions. The official story of the crime, reported in the summary documents by the investigating magistrate, not only set the terms by which to understand the myriad details and counterstories contained in the individual dossier, but also promoted particular narrative models that conveyed the desired social judgments most effectively. According to one critic who noted the already interpreted information of the indictment, "It is a summary that the law wanted; it is a novel that was substituted" (Cruppi 1895:72).

In effect, the stylized format of the questioning of the judicial investigation worked toward confirmation of familiar images of the devious and dangerous woman. The three formal interrogations of the accused proceeded with questions from the juge d'instruction that articulated the terms of the state's case in the form of declarative statements to which the defendant responded. The questions were not open-ended, did not seek to explain so much as to confirm what the earlier police investigation had unearthed. Rarely did defendants respond with more than a single sentence. We can see something of this format and its effects in the case of Marie Fournet. In June 1886, Marie Fournet murdered her former lover and business partner.[11] During her preliminary interrogations, Marie explained that "I was outraged to see that all my savings were lost and that I had been duped by Biver, and it was because of this that I killed him." Her interrogator responded: "Weren't you, on the contrary, particularly overexcited because Biver had refused to continue the intimate relations that you had established?" Again, Fournet countered this suggestion: "No, I had had relations with Biver when we were together in the employ of M. Courtois; but these relations ceased when his wife arrived in Paris." The interrogator, undeterred, continued: "When Biver rebuffed your advances and announced the intention of living with his wife, it was from this moment that your jealousy awoke and you began to threaten him and his wife about money." Fournet repeated her story: "This is a two-faced man—telling his wife one thing and me another. I wanted to settle accounts and break with him." In the hearing in the Cour d'assises, the presiding judge persisted in the official line of inquiry: "You have killed this man for jealousy?" The defendant's response: "No monsieur, because he had compromised my situation and dissipated my savings" (*Gazette des Tribunaux*, 6–7 October 1886). At no point could Marie Fournet dislodge the conclusions of an already emplotted narrative.

As cases such as Marie Fournet's were prepared for court, the particular phrases and causal assumptions that linked the defendant's character, motives, and behavior in the official documents became, in essence, formulas that situated the stories within a credible system of meaning. The *acte d'accusation* (indictment) typically began with a capsule assessment of the character of the defendant, based especially on a summary review of past behavior. Women were either *honnête* (respectable, honorable, with no sexual history to report) or characterized by *une légèreté de moeurs* (disreputable). Setting the context for an analysis of her character, the indictment for attempted murder against Marie Arnoult began, for example, with reference to a damaging moral lapse: "Following an intrigue in her hometown, her mother sent her to Paris." This information was followed immediately by the statement that, several months later, Marie Arnoult became the mistress of a man whom she met in Tuilleries gardens. There can be little doubt that Arnoult's morals were meant to be an issue in the trial, especially because her lover was a married bourgeois (AVP, D2 U8:211, 12 November 1886). With comparable effect, the indictment against Marie Charrier opened with a description of the defendant that represented, above all, the investigator's assessment of the evidence: "The sordid avarice of the accused, her slovenly demeanor, and her unjustified jealousy alienated her husband." Nowhere did the official documents record Marie Charrier's countercharges of neglect, infidelity, and cruelty.

Typically, the indictment reported many of the pertinent conclusions that appeared in the final summary documents of the *instruction* (judicial investigation), the *sommaire* (summary), and the *réquisitoire définitif* (final charges against the defendant). But the indictment was the result of an elaborate process of selection that not only might omit evidence (as in the case of Marie Charrier's alternate version of events), but might come to conclusions that directly contradicted information that had been preserved through every stage of the investigation up until the writing of the summary documents. In the case of Rose Méhu, for example, a laundress accused of burning her former lover, Paul Lelong, with vitriol (aggravated assault), the indictment concluded by stating that "the accused claimed that she wanted to avenge herself for the desertion of her lover. But he claims that he did not dream of ending their common life and never told his mistress of such an intention" (AVP, D2 U8:288, 30 January 1892). In fact, the sommaire states that Méhu learned Lelong had renewed relations with a former mistress; that when Méhu asked him not to abandon her (because she was pregnant with his child), he taunted her in response; that without informing Méhu, Lelong went to take another apartment after their landlord had given them notice.[12] These omissions are especially noteworthy in light of the sympathy characteristically afforded young pregnant women, seduced and abandoned.

And finally, in the case of Rose Chervey (AVP, D2 U8 : 144, 29 March 1883), a former barmaid who had a long-standing liaison with a middle-class entrepreneur, Paul Parquet, the indictment carefully defined the context in which the disruptions surrounding the termination of this relationship should be seen: "This liaison had, for the two lovers, only an ephemeral character, and it was never a question of their becoming a couple." From the beginning, it is to be understood, Chervey could not have expected anything other than the separation that did, in fact, occur. The juge d'instruction, for example, told Chervey that her situation did not compare to that of other women: "Here it is not a question of betrayed promises, nor of seduction, nor of a shameful abandonment, nor of disavowed paternity." Chervey's case could not be assimilated to categories that would legitimate her action. He continued: "You knew perfectly well that this liaison would end. . . . When a woman wants to be protected against an abandonment, she finds a means in marriage; but if you had wanted to marry, you would have been obliged to marry a man of your station and to work for your living. Instead you preferred to take the risk of a free union with a rich man." Although Chervey agreed that she did not expect marriage, she had indicated in her depositions that Parquet had told her "one hundred times" that they must have a baby to win his mother's consent to marriage. In the end, however, it is Parquet's right to leave her that discounts any other testimony. The investigating magistrate reminded Chervey that, even if Parquet did not conduct himself well, "you are guilty because he has only exercised his right in seeking to extricate himself from an irregular situation that was distressing to his family." In so reinforcing Chervey's marginal social status, the indictment invoked, above all, their class differences, providing an interpretive grid that would necessarily marginalize Chervey's grief and finally undermine her explanation of the attack.

The indictment, then, was more than a formal statement of charges. By selection, omission, and emphasis it announced the state's conclusions. By invoking conventional narrative and social codes, it interpreted criminal acts and situated behavior in contexts that were familiar. In theory, bringing a case to court meant there was sufficient cause to believe the defendant might have committed a crime. But in practice, and in contrast to the Anglo-Saxon system, the presumption of guilt was greater. Recommendation of an indictment by the *instruction* carried with it the assumption that the defendant was guilty until proven otherwise.[13] Thus the summary documents of the *instruction* (and especially the acte d'accusation) that were read in the courtroom were extremely influential in shaping responses to the case. And most important, the interpretive authority of the judicial investigation was reinforced by the practices of the hearing itself. Nowhere was the editorial power of the official story more visible than in the courtroom interrogation of the defendant by the Président de la Cour.

Although the Président's role was supposed to be impartial and supervisory, in practice he exercised enormous authority that could determine the outcome of the case. Before 1881, following the presentations by the prosecution and the defense, the Président made a lengthy summation to the jury, a practice that drew considerable criticism because, in effect, the impartial arbiter had become too influential, interpreting the case for the jury without the possibility of rebuttal by the defense. In 1881 this summation was abandoned, only to be replaced by an informal practice that, ironically, enhanced rather than reduced the Président's impact on the case. Instead of a summation, the Président engaged in an extensive interrogation of the defendant immediately after the reading of the indictment and before the first witness was called. Because this practice was essentially extralegal, it followed no prescribed rules; the Président might refer at will to material from the dossier not included in the official case, leaving the defendant no way to deal with damaging allusions.[14]

The hearing in the Cour d'assises typically confirmed the details selected by the pretrial investigation as the Président reiterated the claims of the indictment. In the case of Melanie Lerondeau, for example, accused of poisoning her husband, the *juge d'instruction* had concluded his interrogation of the defendant by stating that "your vanity, your avarice, and above all, your wantonness led you to hate your husband; your hatred, becoming more inflamed each day, finally led you to crime." We can hear echoes of this perspective in the Président's questioning, which reproduced the representation of Melanie Lerondeau as an unnatural woman:

Q: Your household became a hell for him.
A: I loved him very much, even too much.
Q: You insulted him; you hit him.
A: Never.

Q: You threw stones to chase him away.
A: Oh! . . .
Q: You sent him at midnight to the barn.
A: That is a falsehood.
Q: He was very poorly clothed.
A: That I agree with. I did not maintain his clothes well enough.
Q: He was forced to eat here and there.
A: Because he worked here and there in the countryside . . .
Q: You said: "Ce c . . . .-là, it is more than three months since he has touched me."
A: No. That is an invention of neighbors . . .
Q: Your hatred seemed to grow. . . . Your husband feared you, feared that he would be poisoned.
A: I cannot believe that . . .
Q: You were violent and out of control [on the morning of the death].
A: That's true, I agree. I am a little quick-tempered, I shout . . .
Q: Everyone in your district accused you of killing him.
A: From jealousy . . . In small villages, those who succeed a bit are envied. (*Gazette des Tribunaux,* 30 June 1878)

In looking at this kind of courtroom interrogation we can see most clearly both the conceptual limits of a believable story—what could be heard and understood—and the way the criminal narrative became a form of social transaction, shaped by the social relations between teller and audience in the particular context of the telling. The Président organized the story that the court would hear and lectured broadly on the social codes and customs—not the laws—that were relevant to the case, providing both the language for interpreting criminal behavior and the assumptions that gave this language meaning. In the case of Marie Sivadon, who had shot her husband's mistress, the Président lectured both the errant husband and his mistress on their complicity in the violent episode:

[To Mme Millet, the mistress:] You claim . . . that when Sivadon took you as his mistress, you were several months pregnant. . . . We have already seen that [behavior] in the history of the Roman emperors. It is disgusting!

[And to the husband:] You had an honorable and excellent wife and, if she is here today, you are the cause. You left her to go with this other woman . . . it is always the same . . . you have destroyed your honor yourself. . . . You knew that she [Mme Millet] was pregnant and that did not prevent you from taking her as a mistress? Well! (*Gazette des Tribunaux*, 23 February 1887)

The Président's interactions with Marie Sivadon were equally pointed. A visible display of repentance was often a required aspect of the courtroom drama (female defendants frequently carried small statues of the Virgin, for example); but when such contrition was not immediately forthcoming, symbolically or verbally, it was more directly elicited by the Président. When the Président asked Marie Sivadon if she regretted what she had done, the defendant responded, according to the *Gazette des Tribunaux,* in a whisper, "Oui Monsieur." He next asked if she had intended to kill Mme Millet (and her husband, whom she had pursued without success). Without hesitation, Marie Sivadon admitted, apparently in a more normal voice, that that had been her desire. We can only speculate on the meaning of the reporter's editorializing; nevertheless, it does seem that the Président accomplished multiple objectives with his interrogation. He had at least elicited the obligatory expression of regret, however compromised by the softness of voice, and created a context for identifying the conduct of husband and mistress as finally more offensive than the shooting. The *Gazette des Tribunaux* announced the case in a headline that urged an interpretation: "A woman deceived by her husband. Attempted murder." The jury brought in an acquittal.

THE POSSIBILITIES FOR ALTERNATIVE STORIES

The dossier of Victorine Lelong is particularly useful for exploring the implications of various modes of "telling," highlighting not only discrepant versions of the story of the crime, but the conditions that elicited and constrained both the narrative and the behavior of teller and audience (AVP, D2 U8:38, 9 July 1875). Lelong was charged with the murder of Constant Langlois, at whom she had hurled a bowl of vitriol (a charge later reduced to aggravated assault causing death), and was sentenced to five years imprisonment. Lelong and Langlois had lived together for seven years; at the time of the attack, they had been separated for four years, although he continued to visit her and to send her some money to support their child, a detail that appeared prominently at the very beginning of the indictment. The most important aspect of the prosecution's case against Lelong, however, was the large amount of vitriol that she had purchased (two liters) and her apparent vehemence during the attack. She emerges in these documents as exceedingly vicious, a monster. When the Président interrogated her in the courtroom, he noted that "Langlois died after horrible suffering. It was a great misfortune for him to have met a woman like you" (*Gazette des Tribunaux*, 10 July 1875).

Lelong did not succeed in disrupting this image either in her interrogations or in her performance at the hearing; nevertheless, the pattern of question and response in this case allows us to see something of the social transactions that worked to confirm the official story. Lelong stands out because, unlike most defendants, she refused to sign many of the depositions that were placed before her during the *instruction*. When her interrogator insisted that she must have intended to kill Langlois, for example ("If you had only wanted to wound him, you would not have bought two liters of vitriol"), Lelong explained that she did not bring all of the vitriol to Langlois's house. She claimed that, after making the first purchase, she became frightened and spilled most of it into the toilet, noting that the police commissioner had in fact found a mostly empty bottle at her house. The next day, she bought another bottle, and, according to her testimony, the police found her second bottle still almost full after the attack. To this response, her interrogator asked, as if she had not spoken, why she had armed herself with two bottles of vitriol. Lelong did not reply to this question. Her interrogator continued with a discussion of the kind of bowl that she had used, concluding that she chose it in order to have a more accurate aim. Lelong remained silent. Finally, the interrogator asked: "Do you persist in your claim that you did not intend to kill Langlois?" To which Lelong replied, "Yes." Her interrogator continued: "We have a different opinion." In the end, Lelong withheld her signature from the transcript, no doubt unsure about whether her story had been recorded in any way that made sense to her. In an ironic coda to this set of interactions, the Président lectured Lelong in front of the court on the inappropriateness of her silences: "Instead of closing yourself up in your silence and in your pride, you would perhaps do better to ask the pardon of the jury" (*Gazette des Tribunaux*, 10 July 1875).

Nine days after Lelong's unsatisfactory interview by the juge d'instruction, she sent him a lengthy letter from prison, stating that she had not yet been able to speak as she wished, and laid out her account of the crime. In a style that often characterized women's testimonies in the looser structure provided by preliminary police investigations, Lelong took her story back in time, beginning with the period which marked the unhappiness that was, for her, the source (and explanation) of her crime.

The story Lelong tells is one of suffering and deprivation; she identifies in quite specific terms her claim on the sympathy of her listener, assuming the moral high ground to Langlois's shoddiness, and, while never justifying her act, explores her experience of profound grievance at Langlois's hands. Her story begins with the serious illness of her daughter, during which Langlois "never spoke a kind word or offered to spend the night with me, even though it was his child as well as mine." Following the funeral of the child, Langlois left to visit his mother for eight days. Lelong seems to have felt especially deserted in her grief. She then moves on to what seems to be the center of her story. During the summer of 1870, in the midst of war, Langlois was unemployed. Lelong reports: "We had only my wages; I worked day and night, and he never lacked for anything even though he was not working." In the difficult winter of that year, according to Lelong, although she was two months pregnant, she gave Langlois her portion of meat as well as a small bit of wine provided by a generous benefactor "because he was so delicate and in such poor health." With the outbreak of violence during the Commune, she helped him to flee Paris so as to escape harm.

Lelong continues by describing a time when both she and her second child were ill, a time in which she appealed to Langlois for assistance, which he gave, but in a fairly restricted and grudging way; following her ability to resume work, she once again paid for her own meals so as not to be a burden. At this time, Langlois no longer lived with Lelong, but she continued to do his laundry which he regularly brought to her. Her account describes her increasing need for Langlois's help and his growing distance from her, culminating in his advice to give up the child to public assistance. When the child died, Langlois refused to pay for the burial. Lelong found herself alone, having lost her two children, and abandoned by her lover who had taken another mistress. In her despair, Lelong reports, she began to think that if Langlois were disfigured, he would return to her, knowing of her abiding devotion. Shaken by the sight of Langlois and his mistress, "seeing her enjoying the happiness that I deserved," she hurled the pot of vitriol at Langlois as he mounted the stairs to his home.

The details that Lelong provides in this letter place her crime in a context that attempts to establish a set of principles by which to evaluate her deadly act. Her emphasis on the ways that she cared for Langlois and her belief that he owed her loyalty and support in return are unmistakable markers of a way of understanding the world that Lelong expects will be cogent, if not compelling, for her listener. The story itself is self-serving; nevertheless, it conveys a code based on mutual responsibilities that seems crucial to Lelong, but without obvious meaning to her accusers who understood the case through a set of conventional assumptions that were about female jealousy and vengeance. This dossier suggests, then, the possible disparities between the kinds of explanations offered in official narratives of crime and the codes that organized behavior among ordinary people who necessarily experienced their lives both within and, more importantly, beyond the cultural myths that were invoked to explain them.

Like Lelong, Rose Chervey wrote to the juge d'instruction in order to tell her story outside the format of the interrogatory. And again like Lelong, she began with an extended history of domestic patterns and expectations that she believed had to be set in place in order to understand her failed attack on her former lover, Paul Parquet (AVP, D2 U8 : 144). She wrote: "I kept his house, cooked for him, even shined his shoes, and took care of him when he was sick." She explained her "petits économies" (cooking ragouts instead of chicken) and how she had pawned her possessions to support their ménage because Parquet gambled away his money. Above all, she noted that she had been as devoted to him as any legitimate wife, especially caring for him when he had a "shameful disease" (one which she eventually contracted), consenting "to wash his linen in order to spare him certain humiliations." Instead of the reciprocal loyalty that she believed she deserved, she found herself abandoned in a particularly humiliating manner, that is, via an emissary who showed her little respect.

The accounts of Lelong and Chervey reveal precise social codes that organized each woman's perception of her situation. Their narratives allowed them to establish motivation and give meaning to their acts in ways that attest to the strength of very different assumptions held by women who were separated from their accusers (and in the case of Chervey, from their victims) by both gender and class. These women may have shared some of the perceptions of the court personnel who represented them in terms of their self-evident social and sexual subordination. And they were most likely familiar with the canonical stories of jealousy and vengeance proliferating in the popular press. But it seems clear that this perspective did not encompass fully their own sense of identity nor did it exactly coincide with their own ways of giving meaning to the events of their social experience. They not only contradicted the assumptions of the indictment,[15] but began to put in place alternative explanations that referred implicitly to personal hopes and desires and explicitly to the expectations and values of the communities in which the defendants lived. Even when the most intimate experiences and feelings ultimately elude our analysis, we can, nevertheless, glimpse interpretive

161

tensions between accused and accusers that emerge especially out of differences of position and perspective.

Carolyn Kay Steedman (1987:5) has written compellingly about the problem of accounting for lives "lived out on the borderlands, lives for which the central interpretive devices of the culture don't quite work." She has sought to confront the difficulties of people who need to tell themselves stories about how they got to the place they currently inhabit, while recognizing, on some level, that these stories are in deep conflict with the official interpretive devices of the culture. Such cultural dissonance was clearly a part of the experience of the penal investigation for the women we have been looking at. Most women who committed violent acts during this period immediately turned themselves in to the local *commissaire de police*. At this initial interrogation, it is striking that women tended *not* to discuss the crime itself, but rather to rehearse a litany of long-standing grievances captured in a selected sequence of events that were meant, above all, to account for the crime in some much broader sense than the immediate provocation. By means of narratives such as those told by Lelong and Chervey, women identified the particular moments that gave coherence and legitimacy to their own lives, even when the logic of the story was quite different from the more public versions that were constructed through the penal process itself.

But these alternative stories could not simply displace more familiar accounts. In examining the stories told by female defendants, what we see most prominently are the many ways that cultural expectations and the social relations of the arenas of the telling impinged. Criminal narratives remained for the most part strikingly formulaic, peopled by stock characters caught in familiar situations who responded in predictable ways. The stories told by female criminals, even those entirely suppressed in the official documents, did not necessarily stand starkly apart from the kinds of interpretations either imposed by the structure of the penal investigation or inflected by the cultural reference points that informed the narratives throughout. Some women modeled their defense, for example, in the precise terms offered by their accusers, merging their voices with those of their interrogators in ways that produced contradictions and ambiguities that elude final resolution. This would usually require that their own narrative include an admission of being *surexcitée*, out of control or mad—even as they described other motives—followed, quite regularly, by profound expressions of regret. Such stories incorporated, at the least, personal needs, community values, the expectations of the court, models of criminal stories readily available in popular cultural forms, and, no doubt, some measure of calculation. Female defendants

162

who could not speak through the interference of already emplotted narratives may not have been able to find accessible cultural information that would have enabled an oppositional story.

But some defendants, as we have seen, did tell stories quite different from the ones that appeared in the courtroom. These women denied the validity of official accounts and persisted in refusing throughout the language and style that was expected of them—insisting finally in the courtroom that they only regretted that their attacks had not fully succeeded. The implications of Marie Sivadon's whispered regret were drawn more explicitly by others who neither disavowed their intentions nor begged forgiveness. They persisted in their claims that the wrongs to which they had been subjected outweighed their crimes or that the story needed to be told in a context and time frame that rendered their acts reasonable. Yet it is not at all clear that such defiance produced any immediate effects. Often these stories were entirely omitted from all official accounts or so reinterpreted by court personnel and by the press as to be unrecognizable. And many, perhaps most, of these defendants were acquitted, an outcome that enabled the court to dismiss their alternative accounts and to assume their repentance even when it could not be publicly elicited.

In another kind of resistance, defendants occasionally attempted to forestall the direct interventions of both the juges d'instruction and their courtroom interrogators. With unusual fortitude, Célestine Béal interrupted the Président to remark that "it is not worth the trouble of questioning me if you are already sure [of my guilt] and if you do not want to believe me" (Guillais 1986:314–315). This breach in deference was rare in an environment that was both formal and austere, filled with symbolic reminders of the authority and power of the state and its representatives. More usual were the awkward non sequitors, the discordant patterns of question and response that appear again and again in so many transcripts. This nondialogue signals, above all, an ongoing contest over meaning that attested to cultural divides, exacerbated by class and gender differences between accused and accusers, but did not necessarily affect the outcome of the case or disturb the larger balance of power of which these narrative disjunctions were emblematic.

MELODRAMATIC NARRATIVES
AND POLITICAL CHANGE

What are we to conclude, then, of the political and cultural meaning of these various forms of resistance? In order to assess the effect of women's alternative stories, we need to look at the relationship between the courtroom and the immediate environment that produced the stories on the one hand and the political context in which these criminal dramas were being enacted on the other. The stories must be seen as part of a broader negotiation about power and authority. The courtroom itself provided what was, in effect, popular theater, one specializing in domestic melodrama, in which desired gender and class hierarchies could be reaffirmed and, in part, restored. Like melodramas, courtroom proceedings recited a dramatic story, fueled by emotional hyperbole, that served in the end to make visible the moral universe (Brooks 1976:11–12, 45). The courtroom narrative provided, ideally, a moment of ethical clarification in which behavior was simplified, stripped of ambiguity and complexity in order to underline cultural and ethical imperatives. The presiding magistrate typically spoke, ex officio, to reiterate the rules of social relationships: to define the obligations between unmarried persons from the same social stratum, the differences in these obligations in cross-class alliances, the rules for what constituted a promise, the differences between a legitimate and an illegitimate abandonment, and so on.

Even more, the effect of the courtroom drama was to personalize the stories. Drained of social meaning, accounts of crime became, in effect, love stories, underlining in the end the powerlessness and dependency of female defendants, a powerlessness that had been momentarily interrupted by their acts of violence. Léon Métayer has argued, for example, that the female heroine in nineteenth-century melodrama was necessarily also a victim who required the intervention of a male protector. Within the formula of the melodramatic narrative, the appropriate power relations were fixed by the right of a male character to pardon as well as to punish—"the fate of the woman is only assured by the good will of a man" (Métayer 1987:44). According to Métayer, the symbolic importance of the pardon derives from the assumption that a woman is naturally tender and forgiving, while the pardon of a male, less readily available, more discriminating, stands in for the will of society. The analogy to the courtroom seems evident. The accused, in this scenario, is not only a criminal but, more important, had been the victim of an overpowering male will and was, once again, at the mercy of a (male) court. In evidence here is what Judith Walkowitz (1987) has called the erotic triangle of nineteenth-century melodrama—the villain, the daughter, and the outraged father who, in the end, acts to restore the patriarchal order. By assuming the right to pardon, by speaking as the voice of society, the court was able to restore the order that had been disrupted by the woman's crime. In actual practice, prominent defense lawyers such as Charles

164

Lachaud spoke quite directly to this point, explicitly reminding jurors of their role in the courtroom drama. In a style that came to define the genre, Lachaud first established the image of the victim: "Have courage, *my child,* life is difficult because this man has taken everything from you, your honor, your future, your spiritual peace. You have suffered greatly." His conclusion then, with inexorable logic, directed attention to the (paternal) power of the court: "I deliver this unfortunate [woman] to your hands, gentlemen of the jury, and I await your verdict with confidence" (Lachaud 1885:458; emphasis is mine). Whatever the outcome, the rules of the social order had been reasserted and the *femme criminelle* had been, in effect, redomesticated.

Courtroom (and discursive) practices thus sought to stabilize gender relations, reaffirm behavioral codes, and validate the institutions that would mediate conflict. Such practices could not, however, live up to their goals. By the close of the century, critics of the penal process were increasingly alarmed about growing acquittal rates for women, about the possibility of growing female lawlessness, women out of control, taking the law into their own hands, defining justice themselves (Moreau de Tours 1889; Aubry 1894). Legal scholars and criminologists began to make finer and finer distinctions between the kinds of cases that warranted judicial leniency and those that did not. And in a growing chorus of voices that suspected women made use of theories of female criminality for their own purposes (that is, feigned uncontrollable passion, irresistible impulses), magistrates demanded to know whether defendants had, from their reading of press reports, assumed that they would automatically be pardoned in the Cour d'assises. Worried critics noted that some women flaunted their criminal acts, making themselves heroes of their own lives, refusing the role of victim, refusing even the required remorse. It seems that women who had acted on their anger found in the penal process an invitation to tell their stories. Medical experts and lawyers complained that many female criminals looked forward expectantly to their day in court and, in a perverse refusal to express the obligatory devastation and regret, only lamented that they had not succeeded in killing their victims. Commentators like Luis Puibaraud (1899:407) worried that "in taking vengeance, they believe that they are taking vengeance for all betrayed women. They imagine that they are accomplishing an act of integrity. You will nearly never meet a woman repenting for having assassinated or attempted to assassinate the one who has been unfaithful or treacherous. The words 'my conscience reproaches me for nothing' are frequently on their lips."

In a newspaper column, Gaston Jollivet fantasized a grand conspiracy of women. Arguing against the trend to acquit women, he imagined the postcourtroom scene: "She will leave the Cour d'assises, her face uplifted, . . . to hold forth in the evening at some meeting of the League for the Rights of Women where she will retell, superbly, her emotions as a person who has rendered justice, who has redressed wrongs."[16] And humorists noted with sharp-edged irony that seduced and abandoned women no longer thought of asphyxiation or throwing themselves into the Seine, "games" that had become *démodé*, but chose instead to vitriolize their former lovers.[17] The woman who suffered in silence seemed to have disappeared. A satirical novelist alerted his readers to a changing context. Before, he notes,

> when you wanted to break with a woman [you would] simply take the train without making a song and dance of it and allow 24 hours for her to get over wanting to shoot you. During these 48 hours she shrieks, she storms, she buys laudanum, she poisons herself, she makes a mess of it. As in all things, she doubles the dose, but when you return, you have been replaced. But today, *les revolveriennes* are no longer so nice; the 24 hours of the revolver has elongated considerably; they no longer buy laudanum but the latest model pistol and wait patiently; if you take the train, they are capable of following you. (Rabinowicz 1931: 138–39)

All these examples foreground the possibility that women might reject the victim's role required by the melodramatic scenario—might, in fact, substitute a more heroic scenario while escaping legal accountability.

Critics had begun to perceive that courtroom practices and official narratives could not restore traditional gender hierarchies. If women—justified generically as victims or persons *surexcitées*, not fully responsible for their acts—could commit crimes with impunity, how were social relations and social roles to be made finally secure? If women were routinely acquitted, how could distinctions between good and bad women be preserved? And if women could set their own terms of justice, what happened to male authority? These contradictory implications of penal practices derived especially from the court's implicit recognition that women's crimes emerged from the conditions of their lives. Acquittals acknowledged the asymmetries in social and economic power that provoked women's crime, even when the stories told by female defendants—stories that typically described vulnerability and abuse—were discounted, erased, or transformed in the penal process itself. As these tensions increasingly called penal practices into question, the official narratives—personalized stories that emphasized character and emotions—inadvertently led back to politics. While the details of the alternative stories offered by criminal women may have been effaced, the women's presence in court continued to refer to a larger contemporary debate about the position of women in marriage and their rights as citizens in the new Republic.

Thus while some commentators worried that verdicts in Paris reflected, above all, an "esthétique théâtrale" (Escoffier 1891:12), romantic and melodramatic, juries claimed, in acquitting so many femmes criminelles, to be bringing the law into harmony with public opinion—a public opinion that believed justice could be served only by recognizing the special circumstances that defined the parameters of women's rights and means of redress. These special circumstances included the persistence of a double standard of sexual morality, built into the law on adultery in the penal code,[18] the prohibition until 1884 of divorce, the outlawing of paternity suits, wide-ranging exclusions in the civil code that gave women the status of minors in the eyes of the law, and various exclusions and restrictions in the workplace that promoted female economic dependence. Increasingly, many of the professionals who had participated in the construction of the criminal woman—surexcitée, driven by vengefulness and disappointed love—had themselves come to recognize the broader struggles embedded in these criminal stories and in their trajectory through the penal process. Efforts to personalize and domesticate the issues raised by female crime and the formulaic narratives that sustained this effort could not, then, fully succeed, as verdicts responded to the social and political as much as to the personal.

Although intended to restore gender hierarchies, these trials and the stories that explained female crime did not, finally, reconfirm traditional values; rather, they facilitated the assimilation of change. By implicitly raising questions about female dependency, the courtroom provided an arena in which the jury, and even courtroom spectators, both created and responded to shifting popular opinions about such issues as the responsibilities of paternity, standards for judging adultery, and the rights of women in both marriage and irregular liaisons. Court verdicts reflected more accurately a contestation around issues of gender and domesticity, economic inequalities and social rights, than they did a confirmation of existing rules. So it seems the melodramatic text with its closed moral universe and pretensions to ethical clarity could lead to unintended political outcomes—to a recognition of the connections between women's "passionate" violence and questions of economics and politics.

167

It was, then, the intensity of political discussion around the question of women's legal status in the Third Republic that gave the stories told by criminal women their potential to disrupt the formulaic cultural conventions that shaped official criminal narratives. In their behavior and in their position as defendants, female criminals challenged social and legal codes and challenged the tropes, literary and cultural, invoked to tell their stories. In their explanations of their antisocial acts, they revealed the artificiality of the separation of the personal from the world of economics and politics. In their interrogations and court appearances, they undermined the interpretations of their acts offered by court personnel, forcing experts to compete among themselves and with public opinion for interpretive authority. And in their violence, they brought to the fore women's painful experience of the disparity in power between men and women in both public and private spheres. In pointing to the special circumstances that gave criminal women extraordinary access to judicial leniency, the stories of female defendants joined the larger discussion of women's place in French society.

Republican ideology insisted on the freedom of the individual and equality of rights and opportunities. But the persistent legal disabilities of women continued to threaten to explode the contradictions of republican rhetoric and the discrepancies within republican practice. The female criminal focused public attention on these inequities and demonstrated—sometimes purposefully, sometimes inadvertently—the inability of the official narratives to contain the tensions they were constructed to manage. The criminal acts of women and the varied representations of these acts reveal, then, a society in which the stories told by criminologists, journalists, and court personnel suggest as much cultural dissonance as do those of female defendants. Without the broader debate about the meaning of republicanism and women's place in French society, the competing stories about criminal women might have remained marginal, without cultural weight. In the context of the ferment of fin-de-siècle society, women's stories in all their diversity became part of a process of cultural transformation.

NOTES

1. Archives de la Préfecture de Police, Series BA, 1165: Macé. Hereinafter cited as APP. All translations of both archival and bibliographic material are by the author unless otherwise noted.

2. In 1870, Napoleon III's Second Empire ended when France was defeated

by Prussia in the Franco-Prussian War. This humiliation was followed by a short-lived but bloody civil war. The radical government of the Commune, created in this war, was succeeded by the Third French Republic.

3. The Commune provided the most important model making this connection: women had usurped political power, taken up arms, occupied public space. Conflated in this multivalent image are the themes of women's emerging demands (civil, economic, political and, perhaps, sexual) on the one hand and criminal violence on the other. In succeeding decades, the issues of divorce, adultery and paternity, female education, and political and economic rights for women would be discussed within a conceptual frame haunted by the condensed image of the criminal (Communard) woman.

4. In an appendix of supporting documents for a general study of "crime and debauchery" in Paris, the author included a list of women who had received university degrees between 1870 and 1878. The author connects the higher education of women to crime, with no explanation for this linkage (Demaze 1881).

5. Roberts 1991 provides an interesting discussion of the cultural effects of the cathartic strategy.

6. See Demaze 1881; Corre 1891. Corre's chapter on female crime is organized into the following headings: "Criminality"; "Differences between Men and Women"; "Prostitution"; "Plight of the Poor Working Girl and Eventual Corruption"; "Women's Rights."

7. See Stephen Heath's discussion of plausible texts: A readable text is one "which repeats the generalized text of the social real institutionalized as Natural," a discourse "that copies the discourse assumed as representative of Reality by the society" (Heath quoted in Porter 1981:115).

8. See, for example, the collection of articles in "Legal Storytelling" 1989.

9. Judicial dossiers for the Cour d'assises (the primary criminal court) typically included reconstructed accounts of the initial police interrogations of all witnesses; accounts of three interrogations of the defendant by the *juge d'instruction,* the investigating magistrate preparing the state's case; the depositions of witnesses; medical and forensic reports; all documents that referred to the investigation, including letters; and official documents of the state's case, including the *requisitoire définitif* (final charges) and the *acte d'accusation* (indictment), as well as a summary of the investigation.

10. For a more extended discussion of the female criminal type, see Shapiro 1991, 1989; Harris 1989; Guillais 1986.

11. Archives de la Ville de Paris et du Département de la Seine, D2 U8: 207, 6 October 1886 (hereinafter cited as AVP).

12. This same information is included in the réquisitoire définitif but was dropped from the acte d'accusation.

13. See Lailler and Vonoven 1897; Lacaze 1910; Saillard 1905; Martin 1990. The presumption against the defendant was further exacerbated by the fact that until 1897, the *instruction* was secret (that is, the defendant was not privy to the information gathered against her), the defendant was not accompanied by a lawyer during the interrogations, and the defense lawyer might not see the file until

169

just before the court appearance. Critics of these policies argued that the protracted isolation of the defendant awaiting trial led to full confessions if not suicide attempts.

14. Cruppi 1895:76, 139; "Juges et criminels," *Le Petit Parisien*, 2 September 1880; Lailler and Vonoven 1897:146. Critics of this interrogation referred especially to the close connections between the men chosen as Présidents de la Cour and the prosecutors.

15. The acte d'accusation in Chervey's case presents, for example, a picture of a kept woman whose lover took care of all her needs, "who lacked for nothing." There was no reference to either his gambling debts or her contribution to their domestic economy.

16. Bibliothèque Marguerite Durrand, dossier, "Criminalité."

17. In the words of satirists Henry Buguet and Edmond Benjamin (1886:163), "Customs have changed, things have progressed. Henceforward, when the church organ emits its joyous sounds as the Don Juan puts an end to his career in marrying the daughter of a rich chocolatier, Ariane waits at the exit with her small bowl of vitriol, ready to hurl it at his head. . . . The drama ends in the Cour d'assises where the judges, always gallant, acquit the young woman who sustained this vengeful fury."

18. Whereas the criminal code established that a husband's adultery could only be punished (by a fine) when the act had taken place within the marital home, an adulterous wife could be fined and imprisoned for her behavior (no matter where it took place) and her murder could be excused, especially if she were found in flagrante delicto.

REFERENCES

Aubry, Paul. 1894. *La contagion du meurtre: Etude d'anthropologie criminelle.* Paris: F. Alcan.

Brooks, Peter. 1976. *The Melodramatic Imagination.* New Haven: Yale University Press.

Buguet, H., and Edmond Benjamin. 1886. *Paris enragé.* Paris: Jules Lévy.

Chevalier, J. 1893. *L'inversion sexuelle: Une maladie de la personalité.* Lyon: A. Storck.

Corre, A. 1891. *Crime et suicide.* Paris: Octave Doin.

Cruppi, Jean. 1895. *La cour d'assises.* Paris: Calmann Lévy.

Davis, Natalie Zemon. 1987. *Fiction in the Archives: Pardon Tales and Their Tellers in Sixteenth-Century France.* Stanford: Stanford University Press.

Demaze, Charles. 1881. *Le crime et la débauche à Paris.* Paris: G. Charpentier.

Escoffier, Paul. 1891. *Les crimes passionnels devant le jury.* Orleans: Georges Jacob.

Farge, Arlette. 1986. *La vie fragile: Violence, pouvoirs et solidarités au XVIIIe siècle.* Paris: Hachette.

Guillais, Joëlle. 1986. *La chair de l'autre.* Paris: Olivier Orban.

Harris, Ruth. 1989. *Murders and Madness: Medicine, Law, and Society in the Fin-de-Siècle.* Oxford: Oxford University Press.

Lacaze, Charles. 1910. "Des enquêtes officieuses et des officiers de police judiciaire qui y procèdent." Ph.D. diss., University of Toulouse.

Lachaud, Charles. 1885. *Plaidoyers de M. Lachaud.* Ed. Félix Sangnier. Paris: G. Charpentier.

Lailler, Maurice, and Henri Vonoven. 1897. *Les erreurs judiciaires et leurs causes.* Paris: A. Pedone.

"Legal Storytelling." 1989. *Michigan Law Review* 87 (August).

Martin, Benjamin. 1990. *Crime and Criminal Justice.* Louisiana: Louisiana State University Press.

Métayer, Léon. 1987. "La leçon de l'héroïne (1830–1870)." *Europe: Le Mélodrame,* nos. 703–704 (November–December): 39–48.

Moreau de Tours, Dr. Paul. 1889. *De la contagion du crime et sa prophylaxie: Mémoire présenté au Congrès des Sociétés savantes.* 12 June.

Ouerd, Michèle. 1978. "Dans la forge à cauchemars mythologiques, sorcières, praticiennes et hystériques." *Les Cahiers de Fontenay,* September, pp. 139–213.

Pick, Daniel. 1989. *Faces of Degeneration: A European Disorder, c. 1848–1918.* Cambridge: Cambridge University Press.

Poovey, Mary. 1988. *Uneven Developments: The Ideological Work of Gender in Mid-Victorian England.* Chicago: University of Chicago Press.

Porter, Dennis. 1981. *The Pursuit of Crime.* New Haven: Yale University Press.

Puibaraud, Louis. 1899. *La femme criminelle.* Reprint from *La Grande Revue,* 1 May.

Rabinowicz, Léon. 1931. *Le crime passionnel.* Paris: Marcel Rivière.

Roberts, Mary Louise. 1991. "The Great War: Cultural Crisis and the Debate on Women in France, 1919–1924." Ph.D. diss., Brown University.

Saillard, Paul. 1905. *Le rôle de l'avocat en matière criminelle.* Paris: Larose et Forcel.

Shapiro, Ann-Louise. 1989. "Disordered Bodies/Disorderly Acts: Medical Discourse and the Female Criminal in Nineteenth-Century Paris." *Genders* 4 (Spring): 68–86.

———. 1991. "Love Stories: Female Crimes of Passion in Fin-de-Siècle Paris." *differences* 33:45–68.

Sighele, Scipio. 1899. *Littérature et criminalité.* Paris.

Steedman, Carolyn Kay. 1987. *Landscape for a Good Woman: A Story of Two Lives.* New Brunswick, N.J.: Rutgers University Press.

Thulié, Henri. 1885. *La femme: Essai de sociologie physiologique.* Paris: A. Delhaye et E. Lecrosnier.

Toulouse, Dr. E. 1904. *Les conflits intersexuels et sociaux.* Paris: E. Fasquelle.

Walkowitz, Judith. 1987. "Melodrama and Victorian Political Culture: 'The Maiden Tribute of Modern Babylon.'" Paper presented at the Pembroke Center Conference on Melodrama, Popular Culture and Gender, 15 January.

"TRYING TO PUT FIRST THINGS FIRST": NEGOTIATING SUBJECTIVITIES IN A WORKPLACE ORGANIZING CAMPAIGN

Nina Gregg

Recent American popular culture offers viewers a variety of images of women's workplace resistance, from films such as *Silkwood, Norma Rae,* and *9 to 5* to television's sarcastic waitresses at Mel's diner on "Alice," Roxanne Mellman's leadership of a walkout of clerical workers on "L.A. Law," and Rosanne Connor's frequent confrontations with patrons at her various pink-collar and food service jobs. These dramatizations of women's workplace resistance stand out because they are relatively rare, drawing our attention to women acting autonomously, in their own interests, in what is still often regarded as the male domain of work. In the everyday realities of women's work lives, resistance is less rare than on television or in Hollywood movies, but occasions of employed women acting autonomously, in their own interests, still stand out. This chapter takes one such occasion, the organizing of a clerical and technical (C&T)[1] workers union at Yale University, and explores women's responses to the organizing of Local 34 of the Federation of University Employees.[2] Drawing from interviews with women at Yale who supported and opposed the union, the discussion illustrates relationships between subjectivity, agency, and resistance. These women's stories show how they made sense of the situation in their workplaces by negotiating among the possibilities and constraints of the personal relations and social structures of their everyday lives. Thinking and acting within and across multiple subjectivities, the women at Yale took up positions regarding the union to affirm possibilities and resist constraints in their lives.

The women's stories illustrate how the possibility of resistance and the forms resistance takes in the workplace are products of subjective *and* material positions, discursive *and* socioeconomic realities. When union organizers told Yale C&Ts that Yale did not respect them and that the only way to secure respect was to organize together, organizers were suggesting to these women that their assumed places in a given reality were not only inaccurate but could be improved. Women working at Yale began to think about their subjective experiences in new ways, evaluating competing representations of reality: Did anyone at Yale respect them? Were they receiving fair and equitable treatment and how could they know? Could working conditions be different? Could workers obtain respect and more concrete changes individually, or was collective action necessary? With these questions came also the necessity of reconciling contradictions between Yale University's image as an embodiment of "Lux et Veritas" (Light and Truth) and the administration's efforts to undermine the union, between better paid unionized blue-collar campus workers and white-collar workers' perceived higher status, between the union's claim to represent the entire bargaining unit and the desires of individuals to represent themselves, between the ideology of the American dream and the actuality of individual achievements. In the women's discussions of these issues, their experiences of the multiple subjectivities of gender, race, and class are linked to themes of autonomy, solidarity, and status. These themes and connections have implications for practice as well as theory, for understanding the different contexts within which people resist and the varied means by which they do so is fundamental to building any movement for social change.

ORGANIZING AT YALE

For over thirty years clerical and technical workers at Yale University were the focus of several labor organizing campaigns.[3] More recently, in the early 1980s, the United Automobile Workers (UAW) and Hotel Employees and Restaurant Employees (HERE) ran overlapping organizing drives, competing to secure the right to represent more than two thousand Yale employees. Wages and salary compression were central issues, as in the case of one clerical worker who was still in the same salary grade as when she was first hired, after sixteen years at Yale and the completion of an associate's degree in business administration. After UAW organizers withdrew from the Yale campus, pro-union C&Ts, staff organizers from the Hotel and Restaurant Employees (HERE) union, and blue-collar Yale

173

workers who were members of HERE Local 35[4] went on to organize around issues such as wages and pay equity, job classifications and promotions, pensions, health and safety, and job security. Their efforts culminated in a union certification election on 18 May 1983. The final election tally gave Local 34 of the Federation of University Employees (FUE) a thirty-nine-vote margin of victory. FUE, affiliated with HERE, became the bargaining agent for more than two thousand Yale clerical and technical workers.

Twenty months passed between the May 1983 election and contract ratification in January 1985. The first contract negotiating session took place on 11 October 1983, five months after the certification election. Six months later, frustrated by the lack of progress, Local 34 members set a strike deadline of 28 March 1984. This deadline was postponed for twenty-four hours and followed by a vote to strike on 4 April 1984. On 3 April the strike was averted by the ratification of a revolutionary "partial contract," settling many noneconomic issues but leaving wages, benefits, pensions, and job security still to be negotiated and the right to strike intact (Gilpin et al. n.d.: 48–50; Ladd-Taylor 1985: 474). On 13 September, after a summer without progress and at the start of a new semester, Local 34 members voted overwhelmingly in favor of a 26 September strike deadline. Talks broke down at 10:30 P.M. at the seventy-third negotiating session on 25 September, and the following morning eighteen hundred members of Local 34 went on strike over Yale University's failure to negotiate a contract. For the next ten weeks, more than half of Local 34's members did not go to work; many of them walked the picket lines daily (Cupo et al. 1984; Gilpin et al. n.d.; Ladd-Taylor 1985).

Nearly four months later, in January 1985, the membership of Local 34 and Yale University agreed to a three-year contract providing (among other things) wage increases and job classification changes designed to remedy extreme job compression that most severely affected minority employees in job classifications dominated by women (McClure 1985).[5] When contracts with Locals 34 and 35 were renegotiated and renewed in early 1988, both locals made important gains in affirmative action and secured further adjustments to the job classification system (Tynan 1988: 16; see also McClure 1989). When the second contract expired early in 1992, members of both locals worked without contracts and considered strike action while negotiations continued (Tuhus 1992). On 12 February 1992, the same day Locals 34 and 35 won a third strong contract, union members joined the Graduate Employees and Student Organization in a three-day walkout over the university's refusal to recognize or bargain with graduate teaching assistants, many of whom had publicly supported Local 34 and honored the picket lines in 1984 (Colatosti 1992:14; see also Tuhus 1992).

For nearly five years—during the Local 34 organizing campaign, negotiations for the first contract, and the strike—Yale C&Ts confronted the possibility of changes in their workplaces and opportunities to participate in the initiation and evolution of those changes. Yale employees and New Haven residents were targets of two opposing strategies: the university's efforts to wear down union members and foster opposition to the union, and union supporters' extensive communication networks that informed bargaining unit members and the New Haven community of every administration move and turned routine communication into an organizing tool. Pointing to delays in negotiations precipitated by university actions, the union argued that only an organization of workers could hope to wrest fair treatment and improved working conditions from the university. University representatives made the familiar anti-union claim that no third party was necessary in the relationship between Yale administrators and other Yale employees, and the university provost, acknowledging that economic equities existed, announced that this was not Yale's problem to solve (Federation 1984).

How did the women at Yale make sense of the competing claims made by the university and the union? Positioned by occupational status, income, gender—and for women of color, race—on the social and political margins of the Yale University community, each woman negotiated among the exigencies and possibilities of her everyday realities on the job and elsewhere in evaluating the options created by the existence of the union. The assessment of individual power to effect change was part of that negotiation; as one clerical worker said, "I kept thinking I was going to convince my boss in my own way, to do something about my job, to recognize my value. Then [Local] 34 came along, reached in behind closed doors, and I was ripe." Faced with the oppositional choice to join the union or not, what was at stake in allying with one side or the other? Short of leaving their jobs, there was no third option, and both of the remaining choices involved taking a visible position within the dynamics of power and resistance. As technical worker Jane Bevins explained, being active in the union "jeopardized how your employer looks at you. She looks at you differently, you're working at something pro and con, against or for." While the choices these women made differed, each made sense of the presence of the union and the university in her life by evaluating which institution offered a position from which to act on her own behalf and fulfill her own needs and objectives.

In their responses to the Local 34 organizing campaign, the strike,

175

and its aftermath, the women at Yale suggest ways to think about women's agency, power, and resistance. However, while casting women's responses to the organizing of Local 34 as examples of agency and resistance invokes the history of labor organizing in general and women's labor history in particular, the discussion here does not center on working women's resistance to the authority exercised by an employer (which certainly merits and has received analysis elsewhere).[6] Rather, my focus is the more individualized interpersonal (and intrapersonal) and structural contexts in which these women made sense of the union's and the university's places in their lives and how these contexts influenced the actions they took. The stories told by opponents and supporters of the union provide examples of the relationships between experience and meaning, of connections between women's realities, the choices they perceive and the actions they take. Their meanings and their actions offer evidence of the varied ways in which those ordinarily considered at the margins of power can and do resist institutional and social practices that structure their everyday lives.

RESISTANCE, AGENCY, AND SUBJECTIVITY

Resistance "can mean rather diverse things, translating into different practices and strategies that must be assessed and developed each in its concrete sociohistorical situation," notes Teresa De Lauretis (1986:3). For example, resistance is expressed in women's agency as makers of meaning, through the reconciliation of competing representations ofreality with women's own experiences. This is a site of struggle, but it is not the only one. Resistance is also expressed as agency in individual women's attempts to work out a coherent, consistent identity in the context of several possible and often contradictory options. Subjectivity is implicated in both kinds of resistance, in the process by which a negotiation of experience, meaning, and possibility is effected. The organizing of Local 34 at Yale offers a concrete sociohistorical situation in which to explore women's agency as both kinds of resistance, generating meaning and creating identity.

The development of theory that locates women as subjects of, not just in, their own lives has yielded a new awareness of the relationship between women's experience and their activities in making meaning.[7] From different and overlapping subject positions as workers, mothers, activists, and citizens, the women's accounts—what I call their "stories

176

about reality"—make visible the contested meanings of self and identity. It is by negotiating among multiple and contradictory subject positions that women create room for the contestation of meanings, opposition, and change.

Central to this analysis is a reworking of theories of the subject to account for gender and related reworkings of the concept of subjectivity.[8] By subjectivity I mean the continuous process by which we experience the world and make sense of it—not an entirely individual or autonomous activity, but rather the interaction of material, structural, and interpersonal encounters and relations *understood* as personal. For some feminist theorists, the subjectivity of women's experiences is the location of both the ongoing construction of Woman (as a cultural and social object) *and* the site of alternative, resistant constructions of self, woman, and knowledge (Gross 1987:126).[9]

When defined as "that process by which one places oneself or is placed in social reality" (De Lauretis 1984:159), the concept of subjectivity assumes that an individual does not possess an essential, coherent self, but rather that individual subjectivity is situationally and temporally specific, constructed and reconstituted continuously through a variety of signifying practices. Subjective experience is understood, then, as both the sites where individuals "inhabit" numerous discursive positions simultaneously (O'Sullivan et al. 1983:74), and places in which established (everyday) discourses—those of class, race, gender, age, and sexuality, for example—give meaning to subjective experience by suggesting appropriate subject positions from which to make sense of one's life. Acting from a constellation of subject positions, individuals engage in practices that reproduce, reconstitute, and contest those meanings.[10]

Wendy Hollway (1984:236) proposes that "discourses make available positions for subjects to take up," thereby placing a certain degree of agency in the subject. For example, women may "choose" particular subject positions (in the present case, for or against the union) because of the power a particular position promises relative to her "investment" in other "subject positions" determined by material needs, the maintenance or attainment of status, and personal history.[11] The combination of placing oneself and being placed in social reality contributes to identity, through the negotiation of subjectivities in order to develop a coherent and powerful story about one's life.

These formulations of subjectivity open up space for the articulation and acknowledgment of the complexity of gendered experience and possibilities for agency. The everyday management of multiple—and at times

177

contradictory—subjectivities (or subject positions) becomes visible as an example of women's agency. In Daphne Patai's terms, each woman is "struggling to make sense of events that are beyond her control and to establish a place for herself in terms of the things that are within her control" (1988:163).[12]

Once one assumes women are acting subjects, the question of women's resistance becomes one of examining the subject positions from and within which women act, and the significance of gender, race, class, age, and other social factors for those subject positions. These social factors contribute to the material conditions of these women's lives in a variety of ways—as wage earners, as single parents, or as college-educated[13] white-collar workers—as well as to their experiences as individuals seeking confirmation of their value as workers and as knowers.

In the discussion that follows, we see each of these women negotiating within and across multiple subjectivities, attempting to sustain a coherent identity in the face of competing and contradictory "ways of being an individual" (Weedon 1987:3). Components of identity such as gender, race, and class work within, across, and against social and cultural contexts, offering grounds for autonomy as well as solidarity.

Laura Morrison, a white single parent in her forties, opposed the union. Among her reasons was the threat a strike presented to her family's financial security. Nonetheless, she observed the initial three days of the strike as a gesture of support for her co-workers. Jane Bevins, who opposed the union and did not strike, was also a white single parent; she rejected the union's characterization of C&Ts as individually powerless. Susanna Folsom, another white single parent about the same age as Morrison and Bevins, supported the union, seeing in it an opportunity to act on a feminist analysis of the waged work system and effect changes within that system. May George, a young black Yale alumna who supported the union, expressed her belief that "the struggle did not begin, did not end with Local 34 organizing and winning a contract." She drew on her knowledge of the civil rights movement in the South to contextualize the union campaign at Yale within a larger struggle for global justice. Linda Wilson, a black woman in her midthirties, initially opposed Local 34 because of the racist history of labor unions in the United States. Wilson later came to support the union as a protective hedge against the "fickleness" she perceived on the part of her supervisor. Rita Kushner, a white mother of four who grew up in a working-class family and worked her way through college, opposed the union. Seeking to preserve a sense of autonomy in her workplace, Kushner was determined to differentiate herself from union supporters whose behavior she found inappropriate. Sara Brach, a single white woman in her forties who attained a life-long professional goal when she was hired at Yale, requested a demotion ten years later in order to be active in the union.[14] The stance each of these women took regarding Local 34 reflects a synthesis of her concrete lived experience and perceptions of possibility. When acted upon, this synthesis of positions is an assertion of identity.

GENDER AND OTHER IDENTITIES

Although the women's descriptions of their experiences belie the presumed homogeneity of female experience, each woman also "continue[s] to become Woman, continue[s] to be caught in gender" (De Lauretis 1987:10). While a number of women (particularly those opposed to the union) resisted identifying themselves by gender—asserting a preference to think of people as people—the material conditions of the lives of all the women I interviewed, pro- and anti-union, bore markers of gender dynamics: single parenting, periods of unemployment while raising children, few opportunities for advancement in either blue- or white-collar employment, difficulty obtaining jobs appropriate for their skills and training, and compensation below that of comparable jobs held by men. Consciousness of social and cultural gender dynamics is present in many of the women's stories, including the stories of women who opposed the union. In addition, many women mentioned unequivocal support for equal opportunity and equal pay guidelines. For example, Margaret Connolly, a white clerical worker nearing retirement who was actively opposed to the union, offered an indignant analysis of the double standard with respect to wages and the very different social expectations of men's and women's professional wardrobes. "There is something to this business of single women being treated like second-class citizens. You know, that's not all talk," Connolly explained:

> Because when you think about it, if you go to rent an apartment, you get a price mentioned, right? Fine. But if you're female or if you're male, the price stays the same. Whereas if you go for a job, the price doesn't always stay the same. You know, that's so basic it's not even funny. It's amazing how few people actually think that food costs the same whether you're male or female, rent costs exactly the same. In fact, a female is almost expected

179

to have more changes of costume than a man ever has. So in effect what you've got is lower income and more expectation of using money than a man has.

At the same time, negotiation among subject positions takes place in the everyday social and cultural contexts in which there is "slippage between Woman as representation . . . and women as historical beings . . . governed by real social relations" (De Lauretis 1987:10). Women's gender subjectivity is experienced within the context of the additional ideological and material dimensions of any particular woman's life. The union's documentation of the compression of women employees into lower labor grades and the unpredictability of promotions and raises confirmed (for those opposed to the union as well as for union supporters) gender-based wage discrimination at Yale.[15] Indeed, several women's stories suggest that their responses to the union's representations of their lives were grounded in both their precarious financial status as single parents and a broader cultural definition of what was possible for them individually—definitions that are influenced by class, race, culture, and age. As clerical worker Susanna Folsom recounted, "I was amazed at the different ways you're treated if you're married to a professional male or you're an artist, single, female, living alone. Night and day."

Seeing these women's responses to the union as something worked out among available subject positions suggests that resistance is a negotiation among positions already taken up ("invested" in, as Hollway puts it) and possibilities for the future. But while the cultural and social category (or position) Woman has consequences for all women, and the union's efforts to organize around those consequences elicited support, those same efforts also engendered resistance. For some women neither gender subjectivity nor worker solidarity offered a subject position in which they could or would invest. Making sense of the possibilities represented by the university and the union took place within and against individual experiences of historical, social, and material realities. For example, Jane Bevins was one of several union opponents who credited the union with drawing attention to gendered wage inequities, but she pointed to her location on the margins of economic stability as one reason she could not support the union and risk a strike. As Bevins explained, "Being divorced with two children to support, I had to work. . . . I needed the paycheck, no question about that. Whether or not I agreed with what the union was doing, I felt I had no choice in the matter."

ASSERTION OF IDENTITY AS A FORM OF RESISTANCE

Given the multiple subject positions women occupy, the active assertion of a coherent identity can be a form of resistance to the "otherness" of alternative subject positions. Both Rita Kushner and Laura Morrison explained their opposition to the union by describing how their lives, experiences, and self-images differed from those who supported the union. "I feel I'd lose my sense of self if I approached my problems [the way union members do]," explained Rita Kushner. "The flip way they picketed, it didn't say 'serious' to me at all," said Laura Morrison.

Union supporters similarly explained their stances by describing how their support of Local 34 was consistent with how they saw themselves. Sara Brach described her decision to leave a supervisory job that was not in the bargaining unit for a clerical position within the bargaining unit as a conscious self-placement in a power relationship. "What I'm doing now," she explained, "[is] not to be, to avoid being in any position of power over people." For Brach, joining the bargaining unit and the union was an act of "trying to put first things first . . . [and] translate that into action day to day." The subject positions offered by the union fulfilled a long-awaited opportunity for Susanna Folsom, who said the union provided "a chance to express something I'd been wanting to express all my life." Linda Wilson's consciousness as a black woman first led her to oppose the union, but the insecurity of her employment as a Yale clerical worker later led her to join Local 34.

For all of these women, formulating a response to the union required assessing which position assured a place for herself. The sense made by each woman was a product of negotiation between current truths, available discourses, material necessity, and other, simultaneously occupied subject positions.[16] The resultant meaning secured a location where each woman could continue to be herself in (her) social reality.

NEGOTIATING MULTIPLE IDENTITIES

In taking positions for or against the union, women at Yale were negotiating multiple subjectivities to produce coherent stories about their experiences. Their attempts to secure locations in and from which their identities could be sustained may also be read as acting in the interest of solidarity or autonomy. In the next sections, the women's responses to the organizing of Local 34 show how the meanings made of gender, race, and class identities are situationally specific and have material consequences. The women's responses are linked to but not bound by these social categories, which offer simultaneous but not always compatible grounds for action. Their stories suggest that looking to gender subjectivity as *the* way to understand women's agency and resistance is looking too narrowly and too exclusively, missing the broader implications of a theory of subjectivity. Women do not experience gender or any other single subjectivity (or subject position) in isolation, and so the assertion of an identity—whether autonomous or collective—is never simply achieved.

Gender Identities and Autonomy

Laura Morrison, a recently divorced single parent, evaluated the union from the perspective of her everyday reality. In this evaluation individuality was central: "While I believe in many things the union is promoting, especially for women in clerical and support staff positions at the university, I have to balance all that . . . with my role as a mother and how I do best as an employee. It's a very individual thing," she explained. Like many other women, Morrison experienced difficulty when she returned to the workforce after raising two children. "I term myself as a professional volunteer, because I was extremely active in the community and the school," she said. She continued: "Of course none of that counted when I went to look for a job. They didn't care about the eight years I had worked before my children were born. . . . it's to me a real crime. Because some of the skills I obtained doing volunteer work have enabled me to do some of the things on my last job. . . . For that to go unrecognized as not being worthy of any kind of recognition in a hiring for paid work situation is a crime."

Morrison described the circumstances under which finding paid work became a necessity and her identity as an individual took shape: "I was unemployed, living with a husband who had opened his own business . . . with three other partners in the space of three months' time, without any real discussion with me and no income coming into the family. We lost everything but the house. . . . So, that's what I meant by having to work. And the savings were going down and down and down. And that's when I became very individual, apart from my marriage, because our survival depended on me."

Morrison especially resisted what she perceived to be the union's characterization of all bargaining unit members as alike. She underscored the importance of individual needs and choice to her perspective on the union when she described what striking would mean to her: "If I had gone out on strike I would have lost the one thing I had left for my kids' future, which was a house," she explained. "And I wasn't willing to take that risk on their future." In an account of how several union supporters refused to acknowledge a co-worker's desire not to attend union meetings, Morrison remarked, "It's a nonawareness of people who can't, who say, 'This is how I am,' within your ranks. I don't want to be a clone of a clone of a clone. And the inability [of some union supporters] to recognize that spoke very loudly to me."

Morrison's experiences returning to the workforce and becoming the primary wage earner in her family framed her response to the union. While the circumstances of her life were conditioned by social and economic dynamics of gender which the union acknowledged, for Morrison both the necessity of maintaining her autonomy (in order to bring home a paycheck) and her belief that she could accomplish her goals on her own overrode the possibility that the union could address those conditions in a material, or any other, way. The self-sufficiency Morrison developed during the end of her marriage was reinforced by her work experiences. She rediscovered her capabilities and along the way received five raises and two promotions in three years at Yale:

> I think I respect myself more than I did, because I know what I can do and I've had a chance to apply it, not just think about it. And I've had the opportunity to do that and it's been very meaningful to have an opportunity to do things I'm capable of doing—because that's the ultimate reassurance that indeed you are. So I just think of it as adding to a tool kit, and the tool kit's always strapped around my waist and I'll just take that tool kit with me wherever I go. Those things belong to me.

Consistent with Morrison's response to the union's inadequate acknowledgment of the specificities of the individual lives of C&Ts, the tool kit metaphor asserts Morrison's self-containment, self-sufficiency, and autonomy. By adopting this metaphor, Morrison is "investing" in a subject position of autonomous and capable woman, a position the union's rhetoric of solidarity did not easily accommodate, and resisting the alternative subject position the union offered her. The separation from dependencies within her marriage that Morrison described extended to a separation from other perceived dependencies. Morrison's response to her new circumstances asserted her identification as an individual who was independent and could act on her own behalf: "If a job isn't going well does not necessarily mean it's because of the presence of the union or the lack of presence of a union. It may have to do with that job, and you are in control as to whether you stay in that job or not. And you have the right to make a choice to stay there or leave. That to me is a much more powerful thing, to remain in control of your own life."

When Morrison honored the picket line for the first three days of the strike, she negotiated among available positions and found a way to maintain her own economic stability while simultaneously demonstrating her support for some of her co-workers "who felt they needed it [the union]." But for Morrison, joining the union would have meant surrendering control over her own life. In addition to choosing to stay on the job or leave, defining her work situation was a way to exercise control. For example, when a supervisor did not fulfill a promise to provide Morrison with computer training, she "went into the director's office and rolled her computer out and sat down with a Wordstar training manual and did a few simple things that I wanted to do to help me perform my job." Drawing on her own positive experiences as a Yale clerical worker, Morrison rejected the union's characterization of C&Ts as individually powerless. As an acting subject and from a position of economic marginality, Morrison resisted a workplace structure that constrained her. Negotiating among subject positions that were ideological as well as material, Laura Morrison found in the union's representation of reality neither confirmation of her successful autonomous experiences nor assurance of the combination of flexibility and stability necessary to her everyday life.

Jane Bevins, whose living circumstances were similar to Morrison's, also sought to maintain autonomy and rejected the union's call for worker solidarity. Bevins felt she could not risk the visibility of union activism. Financial necessity and experience with a union in another workplace informed Bevins's response to Local 34: "I found [in a previous workplace] I didn't have that big a say [in the union] unless I got *very* active—and that jeopardized how your employer looks at you. She looks at you differently, you're working at something pro and con, against and for. . . . And sometimes I do feel that I'd need to get active for it to be of any benefit." Moreover, since her divorce Bevins had experienced "a complete change in my way of thinking about myself and my family," a change that placed her in a position different from the one the union appeared to suggest she occupied: "I am intelligent—I had to tell myself, you aren't a stupid crumb under the rug somewhere. . . . I didn't realize what I had done to myself in the relationship. I put behind me a lot of my own thoughts and feelings for the relationship, not realizing I was denying myself my existence. You are smart, you can make decisions, you don't have to rely on togetherness, you can be an independent individual." From Bevins's point of view, there was no place in her life for the union and the kinds of oppositional relationships the union proposed. At Yale, Bevins said, "I was able to negotiate what I would get for salary, what I would do. I thought I would make out better as an individual than with a group."

While the union's case for better wages and working conditions included the assertion that clerical and technical workers were able and competent (and therefore deserved better treatment), the more salient message for Laura Morrison and Jane Bevins was that individual workers could not obtain decent treatment on their own. Both Laura Morrison and Jane Bevins rejected this message, even though each woman acknowledged gender-based wage discrimination and the union's success in drawing attention to pay inequities. "In retrospect," admitted Bevins, "[the union] was valuable in bringing up points, for instance equal pay for equal work . . . and the inequity in job descriptions—they pointed out the concentration of women in certain jobs." Nonetheless, each asserted her own position as an example of what sufficiently motivated women could accomplish independently. Morrison and Bevins found no acknowledgment of their self-images, successful autonomous experiences, and realities as single parents and heads of households in the union's insistence on group solidarity. The union's representation of reality cast Morrison and Bevins as powerless and—even more important—wrong in their knowledge of their own lives. By resisting the union's characterization of their individual abilities and experiences, Morrison and Bevins claimed the validity of their own points of view and their lived experience as a legitimate basis for knowledge and action.

Laura Morrison's and Jane Bevins's desire to maintain independence and flexibility is a complex response to their subjective experiences as women in a culture where female independence—economic, social, political, emotional—is simultaneously discouraged and necessary. When I asked each of them about the meaning of being a woman, both Morrison and Bevins resisted identifying themselves by gender. "I don't think I've ever thought of being a woman. I think of people as human beings," said Morrison. Similarly, Bevins preferred not to make gender distinctions: "I like not to think of male and female differences, but more of individuals and what they can contribute," she explained. For Laura Morrison and Jane Bevins, negotiation of their personal experiences of gendered subject positions reasonably resulted in refusing both the union's claim of individual powerlessness and the parallel limitations that collective gendered identity implies. This is not an example of "false consciousness," but rather, as Paul Smith (1988:40) suggests, a form of resistance "produced by and within the ideological. Where discourses actually take hold of or produce the so-called 'subject' they also *enable* agency and resistance." Situated materially and discursively as women, workers, mothers, and citizens, Morrison and Bevins acted within the discourses of U.S. political ideology and liberal feminism, both of which assert individual possibility and autonomy, and against the discourses of collective worker and gender identity.

Gender Identities and Solidarity

In contrast with Morrison's and Bevins's responses to the union, Local 34's organizing campaign confirmed Susanna Folsom's gender subjectivity. Folsom was also a single parent and had been divorced for a number of years before Local 34 was established at Yale. She described those years from the perspective of gender: "I came into the world just being very naïve . . . I was shocked by early experiences and attitudes of men, landlords, and the way a single woman is viewed. . . . I've been shocked at the different treatment, the lot of women who are not protected in some way. . . . You're automatically one down if you don't have something protecting you: career, money, marriage, family." Folsom believed the union would make possible the realization of a lifelong desire: "I was thrilled [to hear about the union organizing]. Usually people's politics are quite separate from anything terribly real in their own life, and I had been sort of an armchair political person. . . . even if I was fighting for civil rights or a particular candidate or something, that didn't affect my life in a real way, in as real a way as this. It gave me a chance to express something I'd been wanting to express all my life."

Where Laura Morrison equated pressure from union organizers to make a commitment to group identity and solidarity with a loss of individual control (becoming a "clone"), for Folsom the economic pressures of daily life threatened her survival and her ability to provide a decent home for her child. And where Morrison did not make a direct association between her gender, the material circumstances of her life, and her opposition to the union, Folsom's gender identity informed her assessment of the union and how its organized power could be used to aid

186

individual women. Paralleling Morrison's account, Folsom described her return to the workforce:

> I naïvely thought that the job world would welcome women who had been raising kids. . . . Now [in my forties] I'm in my first secretarial job I've ever had, when it should be a time of my life when I'm getting somewhere. In the last couple of years it's been very painful to have had a good professional start [before having children]. Instead, I suddenly found myself being used as a secretary. Jobs I applied for demanded my professional background, my editing and writing skills, and yet I was slotted in the low clerical levels and paid accordingly.

Laura Morrison also felt she was inappropriately placed in a clerical position—"I'm better used not typing," she said—but Susanna Folsom associated her own employment status with institutional practices the union could transform. She did not share Bevins's confidence in making out "better as an individual"; rather, Folsom believed that Yale was "one of many institutions taking advantage of women," asserting that "we had to organize to take on something as big as Yale." Out of similar subject positions, these three single parents—all white and all in their forties—acted in different ways to assert their identities, confirm possibilities, and resist constraints. While their common (and gendered) locations on the margins of financial security drove each to seek economic stability, the positions Laura Morrison, Jane Bevins. and Susanna Folsom took up as acting and resisting subjects are not simply gendered responses to a material reality of structural and structured inequities; they are products of complex negotiations, illustrations of what Daphne Patai (1988:163) says "we all do . . . forging human relations within the situations that constrain [us]."

Taking the experiences of Laura Morrison, Jane Bevins, and Susanna Folsom as examples, gender appears to be only one of several subject positions within and from which women may act and resist. Even though these three women acknowledged the existence of their (and others') gendered (subject) positions and Local 34's role in drawing attention to wage discrimination, they were far from agreeing whether such positions offered a place with which to identify, from which to "act politically" (Alcoff 1988:422), or even from which to speak. As Susan Bordo (1990:150) notes, "gender never exhibits itself in pure form but in the context of lives that are shaped by a multiplicity of influences, which cannot be neatly sorted out." For example, the experience of subjectivities of race as well as gender is evident in the relationship between identity, agency, and resistance in the responses of May George and Linda Wilson to Local 34.

THE INTERSECTION OF GENDER AND RACE

May George went to work at the university (in a C&T position) after completing an undergraduate degree at Yale and promptly became involved in union activities. George did not seek a place for herself in the union's representation of reality, but rather saw the union as assuming a place within her own worldview. As a member of Local 34 she advocated attention to minority concerns, to which she felt the union had assigned a low priority:

> There have been very definite problems working with the union—our membership is predominantly white—on this issue [affirmative action], and also because the visible indicator in our bargaining unit is gender. Gender has sort of overridden race in this whole organizing effort and efforts to secure the goals that we set out for ourselves. I remember a while back wondering if in fact lip service was being given to the issue of race discrimination. . . . But it was something that a clear strategy hadn't been developed on, and something that a clear strategy still needs to be developed on.

Working with Local 34's Affirmative Action Committee, George and several other black women attempted to draw the union leadership's attention to "the everyday problems, the systemic problems" of racism. Offering her own employment experience at Yale as an example of the interpersonal dynamics involved in the hiring process, George described "an attitude they can select who they want to, the person they feel most comfortable with, usually that's someone who resembles them, resembles their background, [someone] the person feels they can somewhat more easily manipulate." She had been hired by a black professor:

> And I think the motivation for him was, here's a black woman who graduated from the university, and he wanted to fulfill his affirmative action commitment. It was really ironic, because he'd just gotten rid of a black female C&T who . . . did not work out . . . and he just didn't get along with her at all. Here I was, a

person with the Yale degree, and I guess he felt he could use my skills and talents but at the same time mold a personality and have someone conform to his way of acting—which didn't happen.

George also wanted Local 34 to take a place in the global struggle for workers' rights, beyond its role as an arbiter of relationships and power dynamics in the workplace. She acknowledged that the diversity in the union's membership might make consensus on such issues difficult to achieve:

> I think we get sort of stymied, we limit ourselves when we just deal with a labor issue in a small limited context and don't try to broaden that context to see how all of these things relate. I've had struggles trying to get the union to take more political stands on issues to support, for instance, workers' causes in El Salvador. . . . Before, it always was "we negotiate with our employers, we're not going to get involved with other issues." . . . [I think we should work toward] just having a consensus that we will work for the rights of working people wherever they are, whatever situations they are taking on. And that's something I see as fundamental. It's something, because we're all from different political, religious, and so forth, backgrounds, we've had to struggle [with] as a union.

For May George, the union was both a means of personal, individual protection and an organization that could contribute to the movement for social responsibility beyond the university. The intersection of race, gender, and class in the possibilities she perceived for her own life informed her understanding of the relationship between minority and women's issues and what the union might accomplish. "In my mind I always saw these two issues as integrated: women, minorities, are always . . . marginalized, people who are manipulated and used to set a certain standard, usually a low standard for pay, for entry," George explained. This understanding made her sensitive to how women's and minority issues were separated in Local 34's early organizing and bargaining strategies.[17] While George did not see the union as the solution to her concerns, she hoped that attitudes would change and concrete developments would follow: "We're not going to find any sort of panacea, but maybe something that will alleviate the problems that are out there. And something that moves beyond a mere PR strategy for the university

189

and the union, into something that is concrete, and [we] begin to show some real successful changes."

May George's support of Local 34 was an affirmation of the desirability of an alternative workplace reality, the achievement of which the union could assist. However, in considering the union as a tool of resistance, George also evaluated whether this organization could or would speak to the local interests of people of color in particular and the global interests of working people in general. May George's lived reality was one in which race as well as gender mattered; because of the lack of support for minority women in the sciences, as an undergraduate George had changed her major from engineering to literary studies. Acting from multiple subjectivities of race, gender, and class George found herself simultaneously engaged in resistance within and against both the university and the union. This meant that the union fit into her life as only one of several strategies of resistance. George's expectations of what the union could make possible reflected the continuing condition of female minority experience which Linda Wilson, another black clerical worker, described as "double jeopardy":

Being a woman is something you grow into. You know what I mean? You're born female, but you grow into being a woman. Being black, I've always been. So it's only now I can look at things and say, this is a women's issue, and it be not black or white. I can look at other things and say, this is a black women's issue. And it's scary—because things can happen because you're a woman, others—a woman and a black woman. And it's scary, it's like double jeopardy. 'Cause when you find out how horrible [being] a woman is, well, multiply that by two when you say a black woman.

Linda Wilson did not support the union in the early months of the organizing campaign. She collected and read fliers produced and circulated by the union and the opposition, but in keeping with her characterization of herself as "quite a loner" she maintained a distance, and no one from the union contacted her. Wilson explained her opposition to the union: "The reputations of unions, they're historically racist. My uncle and father were not union people, so it was initially coming from what they told me. . . . My father belonged, but he still was not a union person, not gung-ho. My youngest uncle . . . supports unions but he knows that there's a lot of work to be done within unions."

Eventually Wilson signed a union membership card, joining Local 34 as a means of self-protection. Even so, Wilson was uncertain whether Local 34 would accommodate the perspectives of those who were not close to the union's leadership:

> At a meeting not too long ago . . . I became aware that certain people come across as leaders. . . . If the majority hush and let one group have their way, that's a big fear of mine. If you have a group of people that are willing for you to hush and say "we'll run the show," and you're willing to be complacent and just sit back, there's a danger. . . . They feel they have to be in control all the time, of everything. . . . That's dangerous and I don't think any one group should have that kind of power.

While Wilson's skepticism about the inclusiveness of Local 34's leadership was grounded in her experiences as a black person, she also acknowledged a growing awareness of the significance of gender in her life. Gender subjectivity provided an additional explanation for some of her experiences. "I never thought of myself as a woman—nothing so unique about it," she said, "But lately, I think about it all the time Like 'I know this is happening because I'm a woman.' In a store, you ask to see the manager and people talk to you as though you're handicapped. They powderpuff you. A man commands respect. As a woman, I have to get hysterical or come across as cocky."

As had May George, Linda Wilson evaluated the union in terms of whether it could accommodate her identity as a black woman and found it wanting. While joining the union may have been an act of resistance against the university's unpredictability as an employer, like several opponents of the union Wilson also rejected the union's claim to represent all Yale C&Ts.

THE INTERSECTION OF GENDER, CLASS, AND STATUS

Along with the contributions subjectivities of gender and race make to identity, agency, and resistance, the relationship between class and status figured in several women's responses to the union. The university's and the union's competing representations of reality and possibility raised serious challenges to identity and status claims. Evaluating these competing subject positions compelled people to consider their locations in a world of real differences in social standing and power. C&Ts were being invited to situate themselves against or within a social structure embracing blue-collar workers, treating as equals in status, intelligence, and social possibility the mostly male maintenance and food service workers represented by Local 35 of the Hotel Employees and Restaurant Employees Union. Allying oneself with this group was a controversial and potentially threatening proposal, since such an alliance had serious implications for claims of privilege and status and belief in personal potential.

Some women resisted the union's representation of C&Ts as coequal with Yale's blue-collar workforce, while others distinguished themselves on the basis of behavior from their co-workers who supported the union. By describing picket line behavior as "inappropriate" or "unacceptable," union opponents invoked a gendered expectation regarding women's behavior and affirmed their own status as reasonable and worthy (female) members of a rational society.[18] Rita Kushner, a white clerical worker, was working to help pay for her children's college educations. Several of Kushner's relatives had been union members, but she felt strongly that an organization "isn't always the answer for a group of people." In this case, the group involved was one to which Kushner did not want to belong.

Rita Kushner described most of the union supporters in her workplace as "people with difficulties, people with a chip on their shoulder, almost a paranoia about authority of any kind." Comparing herself to picketers, Kushner secured her own identity as a reasonable person: "I wonder why they haven't found recognition without the banners and the buttons. I feel I'd lose my sense of self if I approached my problems [the way union members do]."

Laura Morrison also pointed to the behavior of union supporters to demonstrate how her approach to life differed from theirs: "They behaved very badly, as far as I'm concerned, during the strike. I talked to people over here who wanted to come to work who couldn't. People who were verbally abused, people who were physically abused. There's no place for that, absolutely no place. The flip way they picketed, it didn't say 'serious' to me at all."

In criticizing the "disorderly" behavior of strikers, Kushner and Morrison were expressing views similar to those of delivery men who crossed the picket line. Shouting that the women on strike should "go home to their husbands," the hecklers reinforced some strikers' sense that picketing was a statement regarding their subjective experiences as women who were not respected for the work they did.[19]

The assertion of autonomy in responses to gendered subjectivity described earlier reappears here in combination with the additional dimensions of class and status. Anti-union criticism of strikers' behavior underscored union supporters' belief that the privileges, possibilities, and acceptance connoted by middle-class status would not automatically be conferred upon them. Engaging in such an open act of resistance was unacceptable to women (and men) whose negotiated identities depended on believing in the material and social rewards of professing allegiance to, and behaving in conformity with, standards of acceptable female (and middle-class) conduct.

In contrast, Rita Kushner's description of her interactions with her employer represented acceptable conduct: "I have had my problems at Yale, but I have never had difficulty in dealing on my own with the powers that be. I don't find the administration difficult to deal with. I don't always get what I want, but that's not intolerable—it's a reality of life."

One reality of life that Rita Kushner found less tolerable was the visibility of distinctions between managerial Yale employees and C&Ts. Status differences suddenly became apparent when managers crossed Local 34 picket lines and C&Ts did not. For Kushner, this was one of the "most objectionable" things about the Local 34 campaign: "only at the strike did I learn the [job classification] levels of some people," she remarked. As long as those job classifications remained unknown, Kushner's negotiations of her own identity and her interactions with co-workers did not have to account for her status as a C&T.

Sarah Brach, a white single woman in her forties, made a reverse status claim when she sought a job demotion from a position classified by Yale as professional to one as a clerical worker. As a professional employee, Brach was prohibited from engaging in union activity. This restriction on her behavior was only part of Brach's reason for leaving her job; she objected as well to the framework within which she was expected to function at work: "The decision to stay out on strike was an end of a time in my life. I kind of knew I would do it, [it] represented a sort of fulfillment of a lot of things I was feeling and thinking. . . . I came to feel I had to get out of that job, I couldn't be professional . . . I had a desirable job, but I was suspicious, uncomfortable with the professional position and role of being a nice, helpful, gracious person." Brach attempted a form of on-the-job resistance to reconcile the conflict she was experiencing between her identity and the expectations of professional job performance:

> For a brief time in [the work site], I was "supervisor" of one C&T. This person and the situation deeply changed my life. . . . I was supposed to rationalize her, and I found I would not do it. I realized it didn't seem to matter, in a big sense, but also whether

people got [what they needed from her work site]. I don't know why. But there was no way I was going to act the authority with this person. I started to imitate her. I was supposed to do [an evaluation] on her. I did one on both of us. [My supervisor] said, "you can't," and he rewrote it.

In rejecting a prescribed role, Sara Brach was refusing to be someone she was not, resisting the subject position her job title bestowed. The workplace scenario and her actions there parallel Brach's discomfort as a young woman with expectations of gender-appropriate behavior:

Since adolescence, [being a woman] always meant I was ex-pected to dance some sort of dance I can't do. At the time—girls behaved certain ways vis-à-vis men. It made no sense to me. The first inkling that I would be probably a marginal person, one way or another, came to me at that time, around twelve or thirteen. I felt for so many years, I can't do this thing, I'll just miss out on this part of life. . . . The fact of refusal to behave like an adoles-cent girl was frightening. It meant no love in my life. It was so important not to be [something I wasn't]—if what I have to do in order not to submit is be alone, it's a lousy bargain, but I'll do it.

As a young woman and as an adult Sara Brach actively and con-sciously positioned herself, through her resistance, as "marginal" in a reality that had little room for who she was and who she wanted to be. With the arrival of the union at Yale, Brach welcomed the opportunity to locate herself among others who were similarly out of place with respect to traditional expectations of women's workplace behavior. Brach placed collective gender identity above professional status and repositioned her-self in a way that made her everyday life an act of resistance. On the picket line in particular she recalled "acceptance, unquestioned accep-tance on a certain level. . . . You were alright because you were there. That habit, of evaluating everybody else, was put into another context. There was an automatic 'here we are together.'"

Having found solidarity on the margins, Brach now had to consider how to provide for herself:

What I'm doing now, not to be, to avoid being in any position of power over people. . . . I'm trying to put first things first: [I care

194

about] rottenness in the world, translate that into action day to day. . . . I'm forty-five years old, I can't pay the rent. This may be a step in putting first things first, but it also could be a step in becoming a bag lady. . . . my work has to do with directions that have become important. And it's marginal.

Consciously choosing one sort of marginality provided a way for Brach to resist other, imposed forms of marginality. She achieved a congruence between her political identity and her material location, but that congruence came at a cost.

IDENTITIES ON THE MARGINS OF POWER

Feminist theorists ask how gender permeates the meanings women make of experience and the possibilities those meanings suggest for women's lives. The importance of subjectivity for feminist theory resides in the way this concept makes visible the situations in and processes through which women may and do act as agents, generating the meanings and the possibilities for action in their lives. To recognize a connection between experience and meaning in the accounts women gave of their responses to union organizing at Yale is to call attention to the ongoing construction of reality, and the placing of oneself within it, that takes place in everyday life. Investigating the relationship between experience and meaning as a negotiation of subjectivities contributes to theory building about women's agency; as I discuss in the concluding sections, such inquiry also has implications for strategies for social change.

By insisting on the legitimacy of their different realities and experiences as the basis for their positions vis-à-vis the union, women at Yale asserted ways of making meaning that both challenged and sustained traditional definitions of authoritative knowledge.[20] Each woman employed by Yale actively evaluated the representations the union and the university made of her experience and its meaning.[21] The expectation of employee (female) accommodation to the power of the employer (male) to determine truth and meaning regarding the value of work and the place of the worker was altered. The conditions and meanings of subjective experience were open to challenge and change. The articulation of subjectivities of gender, race, and class by clerical and technical workers, institutionalized within the union and the organized opposition to the union, became part of the ongoing negotiating and transformation of the power relations of gender, race, and class.

The Politics of Identity

The instability of subject positions outlined in the women's stories works against naming and organizing around issues from a perspective of shared identity, which is the appeal of identity politics. The continuous struggle to maintain a coherent and stable identity by negotiating between subject positions requires vesting some subjectivities with greater legitimacy than others. This implies that any identity politics similarly invokes a hierarchy of subjectivities, and as such invites resistance, as is illustrated by women's responses to the particular "identity politics" employed by union and university alike.

Whether the strategy is one of a politics of gender or some other characteristic of identity, identity politics calls for a unity that both experience and individual meaning-making challenge. Even though Local 34's proposition of the necessity of unity for action was ultimately successful, the resistance engendered by the campaign raises important questions for organizing in general and for organizing women in particular. In terms of the theoretical framework of subjectivity and subject positions outlined earlier, identity politics may turn subject positions into boundaries, reinforcing the very locations (geographic as well as discursive) that could be the subject of "a radical inquiry into the political construction and regulation of identity" (Butler 1990: xi). The women who most vigorously resisted identifying with the subject positions put forward by the union did so from locations that sustained their identities as autonomous and flexible. This meant that any social possibilities they perceived tended to be individual and personal. In such a context, the union, rather than representing desirable change, became an obstacle. One could explain these women's opposition to the union as resistance to the identity politics of the organizing drive, an identity politics which set up barriers and distinctions among the union's own constituency. As Judith Butler would predict, the identity politics of the organizing campaign invited resistance by insisting on a unified identity not all members of the bargaining unit shared. Multiple positionality is not easily accommodated by an identity politics, and in this instance the exclusionary effects of identity politics meant that support for the particular social vision the union represented came only from workers who could see a desirable place for themselves in that vision.

What the women at Yale had in common, however, was their attempt to maintain stability in an unstable world. Maintaining a coherent identity is a matter of negotiating the inconsistencies and contradictions between subject positions and everyday realities, making sense of one's life and the options available in both discourses and practices. The negotiation of subject positions, while in the service of constructing a coherent identity, takes place from and within particular locations.

Feminist philosopher Linda Alcoff (1988) argues for acknowledging positionality as a feature of women's identity and the generation of meaning. If we extend this suggestion, a politics of location[22] might be a promising approach for theorizing and exploring relationships between identity, resistance, and agency.

The Politics of Location

A politics of location was at work in women's responses to union organizing at Yale and their negotiation of experience, meaning, and identity. In a number of instances location worked against, rather than with, an identity politics grounded in group solidarity or gender. Each woman's account offers a window on the work done to (re)produce the social relations and subject positions that make diverse identities both possible and sustainable. From different and overlapping subject positions as workers, mothers, activists, and citizens, women at Yale told stories about their experiences that make visible the contested meanings of self and identity within the interplay of subjectivities and within particular material and ideological contexts. The perspective of a politics of location enables us to recognize how subject positions are discursive and structural sites, the construction and maintenance of which women (and others) invest in, resist, and negotiate.

Taking a cue from the women's accounts of their own experiences, a politics of location offers an alternative basis for action as well. Rather than reinforcing the distinctions between pro- and anti-union women, working-class and middle-class women, women of color and white women, a politics of location would look beyond these categories to accommodate the specificities as well as the commonalities of women's lives. A politics of location means seeing identity as positionality; moreover, as Judith Butler (1990:147) writes, "identity is an effect, that is produced or generated." As accounts of the relationship between experience and meaning, the women's stories make this latter point, and in so doing insist on the possibility and variety of agency and resistance. When we acknowledge identity as situational and contested, multiple and fragmentary, generated and produced, we admit more stories about reality into the arenas of theory and political strategizing. These stories enable us to recognize and affirm the many forms of women's agency and resistance, forms for which gender, race, and class are not defining categories. The boundaries of these positions are necessarily porous; as a result, rather than knowing for certain how to put first things first, we are met by and must contemplate concurrent possibilities and competing opportunities for the assertion of solidarity and autonomy.

NOTES

I thank Kathy Davis and Sue Fisher for their assistance in revising this article.

1. The designation "clerical and technical" or "C&T" refers to Yale employees in the bargaining unit represented by Local 34 of the Federation of University Employees. C&Ts at Yale perform a wide variety of jobs, including clerical, editorial, accounting, laboratory, and library work.

2. This chapter is drawn from my Ph.D. dissertation (Gregg 1991), which is a study of women's subjectivity and the generation of meaning. Included in the larger study are forty-six interviews with female and male employees of Yale University, several of which are excerpted here. The three interviews with men did not contribute significantly to my analysis. The majority of women I interviewed were white, as are the majority of members of the bargaining unit represented by Local 34. To protect confidentiality, all names of interviewees are pseudonyms. All quotations are verbatim from interview audiotapes, with editorial clarifications in brackets and any editorial emphases noted. In Gregg 1992, drawn from the same study, I discuss the contributions of gender, race, and class to women's generation of meaning.

3. The Distributive, Processing, and Office Workers' Union ran a campaign to organize Yale C&Ts in the 1950s. Other organizing efforts included Local 35 of the Hotel Employees and Restaurant Employees (HERE), which financed the Association of Clericals and Technicals (ACT) in 1967–1968; in 1969–1971, the Yale Non-Faculty Action Committee; from the mid-seventies through 1979, the Office and Professional Employees International Union (OPEIU); and between 1979 and 1982, the United Automobile Workers (UAW) (Gilpin et al. n.d.: 16–17; Wilhelm 1985).

4. HERE represented about a thousand maintenance and food service workers on the Yale campus. These workers had organized as part of the United Mine Workers (UMW) District 50 in the 1930s and affiliated with HERE in the late 1950s (Wilhelm 1985).

5. This series of events at Yale University was preceded and followed by organizing campaigns on a number of university campuses across the country. Regarding Columbia University, see Bernstein 1984 and Serrin 1984; regarding Harvard, see Glieberman 1983, Heller 1984, McCain 1984, McClure 1988, and

Serrin 1985. That industrial unions are turning to educational institutions as potential organizing sites is an indication of the rapidly shrinking manufacturing base in this country and a simultaneous growth in what is referred to as the "service" sector of the economy (even though clerical employment isn't necessarily increasing as a result: at Yale, the number of clerical and technical employees increased 9 percent over a recent ten-year period, while for the same period the number of managerial and professional employees—a job classification category at Yale—increased 48 percent; see Federation of University Employees 1984:16). Successful efforts to provide union representation to clerical and technical workers in universities and the insurance industry, nursing and support staff in hospitals, and workers at all levels of public employment also reflect the growing numbers of women in the labor force overall and the conditions of their employment that make union representation attractive.

6. For examples, see Cobble 1991, Costello 1987, Gannagé 1986, Hall 1986, Milkman 1985, Sacks 1988, and Westwood 1984.

7. These developments in feminist theory were encouraged by rejection of an earlier feminist version of a universal Woman by women whom it did not represent, including women of color, poor and working-class women, lesbians, women with disabilities, and non-Western women. On the latter, Martin and Mohanty (1986:193) write: "what is increasingly identified as 'white' or 'Western' feminism unwittingly leaves the terms of West/East, white/nonwhite polarities intact. . . . The potential consequence is the repeated failure to contest the feigned homogeneity of the West and what seems to be a discursive and political stability of the hierarchical West/East divide."

8. See Benhabib and Cornell 1987; De Lauretis 1984, 1986, and 1987; Henriques et al. 1984; Jardine 1985; Riley 1987; Smith 1988; and Weedon 1987.

9. The forms and significance of women's resistance in everyday life are the focus of a number of feminist studies. See, for example, Aptheker 1989, Bourque and Divine 1985, Gannagé 1986, Hall 1986, and Westwood 1984. Jaggar and Bordo's collection (1989) explores gender as a basis for being and knowing.

10. For example, Bettina Aptheker (1989:169, 174) discusses resistance in women's daily lives, "creating the conditions necessary for life" and "informed by the logic of survival."

11. Hollway defends her use of the term *investment* for its avoidance of problems with biologism and dualism, agency, and rational decision-making implicit in terms such as motivation, drive, instinct, and choice. However, *investment* implies the availability of some discretionary "capital" over which the individual (subject) has some control and, more important, can afford to risk. I am not at all certain that the taking up of subject positions by women and other less powerful groups involves the degree of autonomy suggested by the term *investment*. The classic example is that of a woman who bases her class identity on her husband's employment, not on her subject positions as wife, her own employment status, her race, or other material or cultural locations. She defines the meaning of her experience in terms of the experience of the male with whom she is associated, terms allowed by the dominant discourse, and terms which subsume her experience within his.

12. Due to space limitations I am unable to discuss here each woman's story as a narrative that relocates her, as Patai (1988:163) notes, "not only through her actions but also through her representation of those actions via language." Personal Narratives Group 1989 offers additional perspectives on the construction of self through narrative; Kauffman 1992 and Paget 1983 discuss the construction of self in the interview context.

13. More than three-quarters of the women I interviewed had attended or completed college. I have been unable to determine whether this is representative of the bargaining unit overall.

14. At the time Local 34 was organized, Yale University staff job classifications included clerical and technical (C&T) positions, most of which were in the Local 34 bargaining unit, and managerial and professional (M&P) positions, which were not. Employees in the latter classification were prohibited from engaging in union activity.

15. See Federation of University Employees 1984.

16. Kristin Luker (1984; see esp. 116–117) found a similar negotiation at work between identity and historical moment in her study of pro- and antiabortion activists. Sarah Eisenstein (1983:46–47) uses Frank Parkin's (1971:92) formulation of negotiation in the production of working-class consciousness to explain women's negotiation of experience, relationship, and tradition with dominant ideologies.

17. George's remarks are in reference to Local 34's initial organizing campaign and first contract. According to one press account, Local 34's second contract (January 1988–January 1992) contained an agreement "to reclassify jobs to redress economic discrimination against women and minorities." This agreement followed the release in fall 1987 of "an independent union-funded study . . . [that] documented that Yale pays Black women as much as $1,980 less per year than white men doing comparable work" (Tuhus 1988:10). As described, such a contract provision is a considerable achievement, but does not resolve two of George's concerns: racist behavior and affirmative action. The second contract also provided for a community training and hiring program aimed at Latinos and blacks. See also McClure 1989 and Tynan 1988.

18. See Hall 1986 for a discussion of women's labor militancy in the Appalachian South as a case of "disorderly women."

19. Bell Hooks (1989:5–9) writes that the act of speech is an assertion of self against the expectation of silence. Similarly, Paul Smith (1988:137) writes that "if women begin to speak and act from the same ground of . . . subjectivity and identity as men have traditionally enjoyed, a resistance is automatically effected in a sense." Both Hooks and Smith are acknowledging the agency of women's speech or, as Bell Hooks puts it, that in speaking out a woman is the author of her speech and her own voice. Whether women can speak at all, much less in their own voices, when language and its logic and the rationality of traditional discourses are the products of male-dominated culture and reasoning, is discussed by Jardine 1985, Spender 1980, Spivak 1988, and Weedon 1987.

20. *A Report to the Community* (Federation of University Employees 1984),

produced by Local 34, contains vivid examples of pro-union women articulating their gender subjectivity in both concrete and abstract terms. Anti-union and neutral or inactive women did not create parallel public documents or texts, but, like their pro-union counterparts, in interviews with me relied on their experiences, realities, and needs as rational bases for generating meaning and justifying their positions.

21. I am sensitive here to Denise Riley's admonition regarding the risks of consolidation. Riley (1987:44) cautions that "the collectivity which distinguishes you may also be wielded, if often unintentionally, against you. Not just against you as an individual, but also you as a social being." This discussion of subjectivity inevitably consolidates, creating opportunities for subjection as well as subjectification, possibly compounding opportunities occasioned when women are distinguished collectively from men by culture and social practices. And as I discuss in Gregg 1991, chapter 5, it is precisely the opportunity for subjectification created by the union campaign that has implications for strategies for organizing women.

22. Rich 1985 discusses the meaning of a politics of location.

REFERENCES

Alcoff, Linda. 1988. "Cultural Feminism versus Post-structuralism: The Identity Crisis in Feminist Theory." *Signs* 13:405–436.

Aptheker, Bettina. 1989. *Tapestries of Life: Women's Work, Women's Consciousness, and the Meaning of Daily Experience.* Amherst: University of Massachusetts Press.

Benhabib, Seyla, and Drucilla Cornell, eds. 1987. *Feminism as Critique.* Minneapolis: University of Minnesota Press.

Bernstein, Nell. 1984. "Columbia Battles Union." *Yale Daily News,* 21 September, p. 1.

Bordo, Susan. 1990. "Feminism, Postmodernism, and Gender-Scepticism." In *Feminism/Postmodernism,* ed. Linda J. Nicholson, 133–156. New York: Routledge.

Bourque, Susan C., and Donna Robinson Divine, eds. 1985. *Women Living Change.* Philadelphia: Temple University Press.

Butler, Judith. 1990. *Gender Trouble: Feminism and the Subversion of Identity.* New York: Routledge.

Cobble, Dorothy Sue. 1991. *Dishing It Out: Waitresses and Their Unions in the Twentieth Century.* Urbana: University of Illinois Press.

Colatosti, Camille. 1992. "Yale Workers Win Contract, Then Call Three-Day Strike." *Labor Notes* 157:1, 14.

Costello, Cynthia B. 1987. "Working Women's Consciousness: Traditional or Oppositional?" In *"To Toil the Livelong Day": America's Women at Work, 1780–1980,* ed. Carol Groneman and Mary Beth Norton, 284–302. Ithaca, N.Y.: Cornell University Press.

Cupo, Aldo, Molly Ladd-Taylor, Beverly Lett, and David Montgomery. 1984.

"Beep, Beep, Yale's Cheap: Looking at the Yale Strike." *Radical America* 18(5): 7–19.

De Lauretis, Teresa. 1984. *Alice Doesn't: Feminism, Semiotics, Cinema.* Bloomington: Indiana University Press.

———, ed. 1986. *Feminist Studies/Critical Studies.* Bloomington: Indiana University Press.

———. 1987. *Technologies of Gender.* Bloomington: Indiana University Press.

Eisenstein, Sarah. 1983. *Give Us Bread but Give Us Roses: Working Women's Consciousness in the United States, 1890 to the First World War.* London: Routledge and Kegan Paul.

Federation of University Employees, Local 34. 1984. *A Report to the Community from the Members of Local 34, Federation of University Employees, AFL-CIO.* September.

Gannagé, Charlene. 1986. *Double Day, Double Bind: Women Garment Workers.* Toronto: Women's Press.

Gilpin, Toni, Gary Isaac, Dan Letwin, and Jack McKivigan. N.d. "On Strike for Respect: The Clerical and Technical Workers' Strike at Yale University, 1984–85." Manuscript.

Glieberman, Erik. 1983. "Unions Organize at Colleges." *Yale Daily News,* 29 April, p. 5.

Gregg, Nina. 1991. "Women Telling Stories about Reality: Subjectivity, the Generation of Meaning, and the Organizing of a Union at Yale." Ph.D. diss., McGill University.

———. 1992. "Telling Stories about Reality: Women's Responses to a Workplace Organizing Campaign." In *Women Making Meaning: The New Feminist Scholar ship in Communication,* ed. Lana F. Rakow, 263–288. New York: Routledge.

Gross, Elizabeth. 1987. "Philosophy, Subjectivity and the Body: Kristeva and Irigiray." In *Feminist Challenges: Social and Political Theory,* ed. Carole Pateman and Elizabeth Gross, 125–143. Boston: Northeastern University Press.

Hall, Jacquelyn Dowd. 1986. "Disorderly Women: Gender and Labor Militancy in the Appalachian South." *Journal of American History* 73:354–382.

Heller, Scott. 1984. "Union Leaders Eye New Campus Gains by Clerical and Technical Employees." *Chronicle of Higher Education,* 9 May, pp. 23f.

Henriques, Julian, Wendy Hollway, Cathy Urwin, Couze Venn, and Valerie Walkerdine. 1984. *Changing the Subject: Psychology, Social Regulation and Subjectivity.* London: Methuen.

Hollway, Wendy. 1984. "Gender Difference and the Production of Subjectivity." In *Changing the Subject,* ed. Julian Henriques et al., 227–263. London: Methuen.

Hooks, Bell. 1989. *Talking Back: Thinking Feminist, Thinking Black.* Boston: South End Press.

Jaggar, Alison M., and Susan R. Bordo, eds. 1989. *Gender/Body/Knowledge: Feminist Reconstructions of Being and Knowing.* New Brunswick, N.J.: Rutgers University Press.

Jardine, Alice A. 1985. *Gynesis: Configurations of Women and Modernity.* Ithaca, N.Y.: Cornell University Press.

Kauffman, Bette J. 1992. "'Feminist Facts': Interview Strategies and Political Subjects in Ethnography." *Communication Theory* 2(3):187–206.

Ladd-Taylor, Molly. 1985. "Women Workers and the Yale Strike." *Feminist Studies* 11:465–489.

Luker, Kristin. 1984. *Abortion and the Politics of Motherhood.* Berkeley: University of California Press.

McCain, Nina. 1984. "Impact of Yale Clerical Strike on Other Schools Is Debated." *Boston Sunday Globe,* 21 October, p. 33.

McClure, Laura. 1985. "A Breakthrough Contract for Clerical Workers." *The Guardian,* 6 November, p. 7.

———. 1988. "Harvard Organizer Tells How." *Guardian,* 31 August, p. 12.

———. 1989. "Affirmative Action." *New Directions for Women,* November/December, p. 5.

Martin, Biddy. 1982. "Feminism, Criticism and Foucault." *New German Critique* 9:3–30.

Martin, Biddy, and Chandra Talpade Mohanty. 1986. "Feminist Politics: What's Home Got to Do with It?" In *Feminist Studies/Critical Studies,* ed. Teresa De Lauretis, 191–212. Bloomington: Indiana University Press.

Milkman, Ruth, ed. 1985. *Women, Work and Protest: A Century of U.S. Women's Labor History.* London: Routledge and Kegan Paul.

O'Sullivan, Tim, John Hartley, Danny Saunders, and John Fiske. 1983. *Key Concepts in Communication.* New York: Methuen.

Paget, Marianne A. 1983. "Experience and Knowledge." *Human Studies* 6: 67–90.

Parkin, Frank. 1971. *Class Inequality and Political Order.* New York: Praeger.

Patai, Daphne. 1988. "Constructing a Self: A Brazilian Life Story." *Feminist Studies* 14:143–166.

Personal Narratives Group. 1989. *Interpreting Women's Lives.* Bloomington: Indiana University Press.

Rich, Adrienne. 1985. "Notes toward a Politics of Location." In *Women, Feminist Identity, and Society in the 1980s,* ed. Myriam Diaz-Diocaretz and Iris M. Zavala, 7–22. Philadelphia: John Benjamins.

Riley, Denise. 1987. "Does a Sex Have a History? 'Women' and Feminism." *New Formations* 1:35–45.

Sacks, Karen Brodkin. 1988. *Caring by the Hour: Women, Work, and Organizing at Duke Medical Center.* Urbana: University of Illinois Press.

Serrin, William. 1984. "Columbia Faces Threat of Strike in Mid-January." *New York Times,* 31 December, p. 27.

———. 1985. "Labor Pact at Yale: Winning of Contract by Clerical Union Draws Attention of Other Universities." *New York Times,* 24 January, p. B4.

Smith, Paul. 1988. *Discerning the Subject.* Minneapolis: University of Minnesota Press.

Spender, Dale. 1980. *Man-Made Language.* London: Routledge and Kegan Paul.

Spivak, Gayatri Chakravorty. 1988. "Can the Subaltern Speak?" In *Marxism and the Interpretation of Culture,* ed. Cary Nelson and Larry Grossberg, 271–313. Urbana: University of Illinois Press.

Tuhus, Melinda. 1988. "Organizing Never Stops at Yale." *Guardian,* 23 March, pp. 10–11.

———. 1992. "Yale Unions Prepare for Another Strike." *Labor Notes* 155:16, 15.

Tynan, Roxana. 1988. "Yale University Unions Make Big Gains in Affirmative Action in New Contracts." *Labor Notes* 110:16.

Weedon, Chris. 1987. *Feminist Practice and Poststructuralist Theory.* London: Basil Blackwell.

Westwood, Sallie. 1984. *All Day, Every Day: Factory and Family in the Making of Women's Lives.* Urbana: University of Illinois Press.

Wilhelm, John. 1985. Interview by Jack McKivigan and Toni Gilpin, 12 March. Local 34 office, New Haven, Conn. Access courtesy Jack McKivigan.

SKIDDING/COPING/ESCAPING: CONSTRAINT, AGENCY, AND GENDER IN THE LIVES OF HOMELESS "SKIDDERS"

Rob Rosenthal

From the close of the Civil War until the early 1980s, most popular and academic inquiries into homelessness focused on the personal characteristics of those without homes. Accounts of tramps and hobos of the late nineteenth and early twentieth centuries spoke at best of their "wanderlust" (Anderson 1923; Reitman 1937), at worst of their social incompetence or moral depravity (see Bahr 1973:39–86). Researchers of the post–World War II era, although dealing with a very different population largely found on Skid Rows, maintained this focus on personal characteristics and similarly emphasized a more or less consciously chosen isolation from mainstream society. People—largely meaning men—were said to "drift" to Skid Row to avoid censure for their drinking habits, sexual preference, unwillingness to work, or other forms of "deviance" (Wallace 1965, 1968; Rooney 1961; Peterson and Maxwell 1958; Wiseman 1970; Bahr 1970, 1973), or owing to a lifelong social incompetence (Pittman and Gordon 1958; Vexliard 1956; Bahr 1970; Caplow 1970). Indeed, according to the leading theorists of the time, such "disaffiliation" was the characteristic common to all homeless people (Bahr 1969, 1970, 1973; Caplow, Bahr, and Sternberg 1968). While a few researchers such as Donald Bogue (1963) pointed out the high incidence of disabilities among those on Skid Row, lessening the sense of individual *blame*, structural explanations were rarely considered. For the most part, homeless people were seen as those either unwilling or unable to do the work of life, as "slackers or lackers" (Rosenthal 1993).

The enormous growth in the homeless population beginning in the late 1970s[1] called into question this emphasis on individual characteristics. It defied common sense to believe that hundreds of thousands—

perhaps millions—of people had suddenly caught irresponsibility or incompetence like the flu. Beyond the numbers, the 1980s saw what New York Governor Mario Cuomo (1984) has called a "democratization" of the homeless population: the post–World War II population, thought to be largely composed of older alcoholic white men, was augmented by increased numbers of women, young men, people of color, mentally ill persons (including deinstitutionalized mental patients), veterans, suburban dwellers, and families.[2]

In response, many researchers began stressing the *involuntary displacement* of individuals by large-scale macro processes beyond their control, including unemployment (often tied to deindustrialization), holes and cutbacks in the welfare system, the mental health policy of deinstitutionalization, changes in traditional family structures, and—beyond everything else—the demise of affordable housing.[3] Disaffiliation came to be regarded as a *result* of homelessness rather than its principal cause.[4] This structural emphasis changed the analysis of observations common to both perspectives. Where those looking at the individual found mental illness as a cause of homelessness, for example, those searching for societal factors were more inclined to look at the policy of deinstitutionalization; similarly, while both schools may see the "inability to get along with others" as an important precipitating factor, a displacement perspective emphasizes the social roots of competition for resources which mandate that those with perceived problems will be losers in the game (see Baumohl 1989).

In stressing structural roots and displacement instead of individual characteristics and disaffiliation, researchers have implicitly or explicitly rejected "blaming the victim." But in minimizing the role of personal blame, displacement theorists have correspondingly emphasized a picture of victimization, rendering an image of homeless people as almost universally hopeless and helpless against the macro forces which grind them down. That is, while older academic theories gave great weight to individual agency and little or no weight to societal constraints, displacement theorists appear to have created a polar image which gives great weight to constraint and little or no weight to individual agency.

TOWARD A THIRD PERSPECTIVE

For almost five years in the mid-1980s, I spent much of my time working and passing time with homeless people in Santa Barbara, California. I eventually collected forty-four in-depth oral histories from people I had come to know; in addition, I had access to more than five hundred intake sheets for those using a series of church-sponsored shelters, and over two hundred telephone log entries of a local self-help group of homeless and potentially homeless single parents (overwhelmingly women), the Single Parent Alliance. Neither a picture of slackers and lackers nor one of helpless victims resonated with what I was seeing in the field. While some—particularly those suffering mental illnesses—were certainly quite isolated, many more appeared to be constantly attempting to hold on to their past roots and networks and, when and where those were severed, to create new ones. Most appeared to have significant ties to other homeless people, to housed people, and to institutions of mainstream society, at least on an intermittent basis.[5] I began to believe that the methodological practices of researchers—primarily a heavy reliance on one-shot surveys, usually in "captive environments" (Liebow 1967) such as shelters—were producing a distorted picture of homeless life, one that stemmed from and reinforced the image of wide-spread isolation and impotence (see Rosenthal 1991).[6] My ongoing experiences in the field led me instead to see homelessness as a process framed by the dialectic between agency and constraint. Constraints do not simply "operate like forces in nature, as if to 'have no choice' were equivalent to being driven irresistibly and uncomprehendingly by mechanical pressures" (Giddens 1984:15).[7] They limit agency, they shape agency, but they certainly did not preclude agency among the homeless people I came to know.

For women, gender is one such constraint. But gender, of course, informs the agency of individuals as well. Increasing evidence suggests that homeless women and men display significantly disparate aggregate data concerning background, paths to homelessness, survival tactics, and escape strategies (see Crystal 1984; Owen, Mattessich, and Williams 1987; Burt and Cohen 1989). I explore this gendered dialectic of agency and constraint by looking at the struggles of homeless women, in particular at one subgroup[8] in Santa Barbara which I call Skidders: female single parents[9] who fell from an upper-working-class or middle-class existence into homelessness, usually through the breakup of their marriage or relationship and their subsequent inability to meet expenses on their income alone. Once evicted for nonpayment of rent (or in a few cases, mortgage), their "skid" is continued by the difficulty of getting into a new place because of discrimination against children, high rents, and the inability to save enough to afford "first, last and deposit."

Such persons rarely appear in public discourse about "the homeless," which is dominated by images of mentally ill people and those who use the street resources of missions, soup kitchens, and so forth—subgroups

I refer to here (following their street labels) as Wingnuts and Street People. Skidders, in contrast, generally remain invisible. They steer clear of soup kitchens, maintaining a "housed" outward appearance and finding shelter in a succession of friends' or relatives' homes, a week here, a week there, moving constantly until they are able to find and afford a place of their own (or, in relatively few cases, they wear out their social networks and actually enter street life).

This invisibility is not a new phenomenon for homeless women. While recent works suggest that women may have made up a substantial proportion of the "transient" population in this country until after the Civil War (Jones 1984; Clement 1984), homeless females are rarely mentioned in either the literature on the tramps and hobos of the late nineteenth century to early twentieth century[10] or the post–World War II literature on Skid Rows. Although most researchers agree that homeless women were in fact quite scarce compared to homeless men for most of this century (see Bogue 1963),[11] the women's desire to remain hidden and the methodological predilections of (largely male) sociologists (Bahr 1973) may well have contributed to an underestimation of their actual numbers.

More recent research indicates both a tremendous increase in the proportion of homeless people who are female (see U.S. Conference of Mayors 1984, 1987, 1989; Owen, Mattessich, and Williams 1987; National Coalition for the Homeless 1986b, 1987a, 1987c; Crystal and Goldstein 1984) and a continuation of their relative invisibility, often through their own deliberate strategies of concealment or camouflage (Shulman 1981; Hand 1976; Rousseau 1981).[12] We can begin to illuminate these usually hidden lives by tracing Skidders' vulnerability and paths to homelessness, their lives while homeless, and their struggles to escape homelessness.

WOMEN'S PATHS TO HOMELESSNESS

While post–World War II theorists argued that gender-associated norms and roles minimized homelessness among women (see Blumberg, Shipley, and Barsky 1978), research in the 1980s began suggesting ways in which femaleness as a social category helped to create the explosion of homelessness. In particular, numerous studies note that women far more frequently than men report the breakup of their primary relationship as the major factor leading to homelessness (see Goplerud 1987; King County Housing and Community Development Division 1986). The breakup it-

208

self may be related to issues of gender and gender conflicts, most obviously when it involves physical abuse—overwhelmingly of women by men, and clearly tied to gender roles of dominance and submission (see King County Housing and Community Development Division 1986; Alameda County Emergency Services Network 1987; Lantz 1986; Woods and Burdell 1987; U.S. Conference of Mayors 1987). But whatever the cause of the breakup, separation typically undermines the woman's financial stability rather than the man's. As Pearce and McAdoo (1981:17) note, "the same divorce that frees a man from the financial burdens of a family may result in poverty for his ex-wife and children." Weitzman's (1985:323) study in California indicates that in the first year after a divorce, the standard of living of the average ex-wife declines 73 percent, while her ex-husband's standard of living rises 42 percent.

There are a number of gender-related reasons why separated women experience financial instability—and thus have a greater chance of ensuing homelessness. If a coupled woman works outside the home, she almost certainly earns less than her male partner.[13] But the chances that she does not work outside the home, or does so on only a part-time basis, are much greater than for her male partner (see Crystal 1984; Joe and Rogers 1985:11–13), a phenomenon related to the ideological norms of gender in society and the resulting expectations of the proper roles of men and women in couples. Women in such couples who "aren't working" obviously *are* working a job, that of housekeeper. But in the household division of labor, the "breadwinner" whose job results in financial remuneration can survive a split far more easily than his or her partner can. Available data suggest that many mothers who become homeless have most recently worked as homemakers. For example, in Burt and Cohen's study of homeless users of soup kitchens and shelters in twenty cities, single men and women had been jobless on average only seven months longer than they had been homeless, while for women with children there was a thirty-one month difference, implying "reliance on welfare programs or *the incomes of other household members* for perhaps as many as half of these women prior to becoming homeless" (1989:514, emphasis added).

Finally, and quite significantly, women almost always assume major or total responsibility for children in the case of dissolution of the household. For example, 18 percent of the single women (including those divorced or separated) at the Santa Barbara church shelters had children with them (with another 6 percent pregnant) compared to only 1 percent of the single men guests, a pattern found in local studies across the nation (see Research Atlanta 1984; Goplerud 1987; King County Housing and

209

Community Development Division 1986; Bassuk, Lauriati, and Rubin 1987). Although children offer women a strong incentive to work, they also make working problematic, especially when funds for day care and spaces in existing centers are limited or lacking. While 19 percent of the single mothers in the church shelters were employed, compared to 10 percent of childless women guests, this percentage falls to 7 percent for single mothers with children under the age of six.

For those women who separate and keep their children, child support is supposed to be the device that will prevent their role as parent from weighing more heavily on them financially than it does on their ex-partner. A 1981 U.S. Census Bureau study, however, indicates that less than half of the mothers awarded child support by the courts receive their full payments, and a quarter receive nothing at all, figures consistent with data reported by homeless mothers in Santa Barbara. In theory, women who are unable to work and who receive little or no child support are still protected from homelessness through public assistance, particularly AFDC. As I discuss shortly, however, such aid is difficult to obtain and often provides insufficient protection.

Even if a mother were to achieve some financial stability through employment, public assistance, child support, or otherwise, discrimination against children in housing may yet render her family homeless, as Skidders in Santa Barbara constantly complained:

> Lynn: Let's just say that [children] are one step above or one step below having a pet. I don't have any pets, I don't need two strikes against me, but according to the Unruh Act [actually a court decision], it is now illegal to discriminate against people with children, but they still do. You ask them what the rent is and they go, "How many *people*?" And if you say two, they assume it's two adults, and if you say three, they assume it's one child and the rent goes into the unaffordable range.

The role children play in increasing the vulnerability of Skidders (and other women) to homelessness suggests that parental status (defined here as *current* responsibility for children) is the important variable for a number of these problems (see Research Atlanta 1984; Burt and Cohen 1989), but a variable confounded by gender. While the few male parents I met often voiced similar problems regarding antichild discrimination (as well as financial problems associated with high rents and deposits), the definition of female in popular discourse is so intwined with parental responsibilities and the reality of parental responsibility resting with

210

women is so pervasive (as the figures cited above indicate) that, both practically and ideologically, the two cannot be easily separated.

A final gender-related vulnerability for previously coupled women stems from the identification of women with the private household sphere. In relationships where gender roles have been extremely strong, women may have been so restricted from public life that initially following separation they have little idea how to go about securing the necessities of life from either the market or the state. Watson (1986), for example, finds in England a strong correlation between ignorance of the public housing system and previous marriage and/or lack of employment for homeless women.

While gender thus interacts with structural and cultural constraints to create an extra series of vulnerabilities to homelessness for women, there are also a number of ways in which being female (as socially constructed) may help some potential Skidders resist those constraints and avoid homelessness, that is, ways in which gender offers women the *opportunity* for greater agency. It appears that kin and friends of potentially homeless unattached women are more prone to take them in (presumably due to their perceived extra vulnerability on the streets), particularly if children are involved.[14] It may be that women's gender identity allows them to ask for and enables them to receive help more easily than men can. Their greater likelihood of contributing to the household through child care and domestic responsibilities, for instance, may make them less of a drain on those who offer shelter.

Obtaining public assistance is considerably more likely for women than men when children are involved. Receiving welfare, however, requires a good deal of initiative and resolve to navigate the long hejira through the entitlement bureaucracy (a journey that typically took between seven and twenty-four months in the early 1980s according to California state legislative testimony) (Shelby 1983:1). Most homeless people—in fact, a majority of eligible housed people (Harrington 1984; U.S. Conference of Mayors 1982)—do not receive the entitlements they are eligible for, for reasons ranging from lack of information to active discouragement by welfare workers (Rosenthal 1993). For instance, almost half of those coming to the Santa Barbara church shelters with serious mental or physical disabilities and over three-quarters of those with children received no public assistance of any kind, including food stamps.[15]

Even successfully applying for public assistance, however, does not necessarily mean avoiding homelessness. In some cases entitlement payments are simply too low to enable a woman with children to make ends meet, particularly in high-rent areas. Those women contacting the Single Parent Alliance who were receiving AFDC *and* had found shared housing reported still paying an average of 75 percent of their income on housing (Santa Barbara Single Parent Alliance 1983), a "shelter poverty" (Stone 1983) so profound that the slightest financial setback would almost invariably result in homelessness.

COPING WITH HOMELESSNESS

Once homeless, Skidders face, on the one hand, the same problems and constraints other homeless people face. Work is more difficult to obtain (since all homeless people are "suspects rather than prospects," as one told me). Welfare is more difficult to obtain because of the suspicion of public bureaucracies and the difficulty in proving local residency without a bona fide address. The simplest, most basic tasks of life become tactical questions: How does one "go to the bathroom" when one does not have a bathroom? And always, of course, the question looms: Where will I sleep tonight?

Skidders additionally face problems that are specifically related to their gender or parental status. Many are unable to present a potential employer with a recent work history (they were homemakers while their mates worked paying jobs). Further, their ability to find or keep work is even more problematic than for other homeless people due to the presence of children. Once homeless, there is even less likelihood of finding convenient and affordable child care, while the informal reciprocal arrangements one may have created with neighbors are no longer possible.

Finding a place to sleep is a concern for all homeless people, but it is of particular importance for Skidders since both women and children are especially vulnerable sleeping on the streets. Jahiel (1987:112) reports estimates that "the incidence of rape in the homeless population is 20 times higher than that in the general population." The manager of the Salvation Army's homeless shelter in Santa Barbara estimates that half the females who come there have been raped.[16] Aside from threats of physical harm and the elements, most Skidders also seek to avoid notice by the authorities for fear of losing their children, a trend apparently increasing nationally in recent years (U.S. Congress, Committee on Government Operations 1985; *Safety Network* 9[August 1990]:1). While such incidents are rare in Santa Barbara (and not official policy of the Child Protective Service), they are not unknown, and fear of such action is widespread among homeless parents.

Another important part of coping with homeless life for Skidders is making their children's lives as "normal" as possible. They have no need to be acquainted with the growing volume of literature on the deleterious effects of homelessness on children and family relationships (see U.S. Conference of Mayors 1987:9–10; Melnick and Williams 1987:32; Bassuk, Lauriati, and Rubin 1987:23; Wright and Weber 1987:110; Kozol 1988:30). They see it daily before their eyes:

> Juanita: I was snapping at the kids. The kids were talking back, it was affecting us. . . . They were hyper and unhappy. One of my kids one time sat down and cried: "Why do we have to go through life like this? Why doesn't God love us anymore?"

Many homeless parents consequently report grave feelings of guilt over their failure to provide a conventional home for their children:

> Liz: I am supposed to have a career and have a place to live for my kid. I'm supposed to have some kind of security for her, so she doesn't turn into a basket case. All these things I'm supposed to be doing for one reason or another, I'm not doing. The guilt is real heavy.

While Skidders are dramatically affected by an intertwined web of constraint—constraints that are inextricably linked to their homeless status, gender, and parental responsibilities—they are not merely passive reactors. They resist and in so doing claim some agency in the face of formidable constraints. In their desire to preserve a semblance of stability in their children's lives, for instance, many go to enormous lengths to preserve a schedule despite constant changes in their living situations, actively resisting the disorganization that could so easily accompany homelessness. Lynn and her children, for example, stay in a succession of friends' homes, sometimes house-sitting while her friends are away for several weeks, more often staying a few days in someone's living room and then moving on. But wherever she finds herself, Lynn maintains the same schedule, rising around seven, getting her children dressed, fed, and off to school, and then attending classes at the local community college from nine to noon. After noon she takes a bus to a suburb north of Santa Barbara where she works in a low-income medical clinic until five, takes a bus back to her children's school where she picks them up and brings them to wherever they're staying for dinner and bedtime.

But even with the best of intentions and organization, a "normal" life requires resources, beginning with an income. Given the difficulties outlined above, few Skidders work full time and a majority are not wage workers at all; in fact, homeless women and parents are considerably less likely to be *seeking* as well as finding work than men and nonparents.[17] However, of the six subgroups I looked at in Santa Barbara, Skidders were by far the most likely to be receiving welfare (in the form of AFDC), a testimonial both to their sense of entitlement and relative lack of fear of bureaucracy (perhaps from their previous class standing) and to their current "deserving poor" status as mainly low-income women with children. Further, Skidders typically have lived in Santa Barbara for an extended period of time (a common finding regarding homeless women) and thus find it easier to prove "present residency," a requirement for receiving most kinds of public assistance. Lineworkers are also generally more sympathetic to Skidders than to single people, particularly men, and more apt to approve their claims. As a result of all these factors, the proportion of Skidders who receive AFDC is significantly higher than, for instance, Street People who receive General Relief, or Wingnuts who receive Supplemental Security Insurance for the disabled, though in theory virtually all such people should be covered by one of the other program. Gender and parental status thus appear to contribute to both the willingness to seek aid and the likelihood of receiving it.

Since Skidders and other homeless families[18] are the most likely of the homeless population to have lived in Santa Barbara for extended periods,[19] they are the most likely to have networks of friends from their previous housed lives. These friends can be called on periodically for help with child care, clothing, an occasional shared meal (as well as shelter, as I discuss shortly), but doing so successfully requires initiative, tact, and good people management. As in securing welfare payments, opportunity becomes translated into actuality only through the skills of the individuals involved. Again, Skidders do not passively accept the conditions of their homeless status but creatively cope with (and sometimes actively resist) them.

Considerable creativity is also required for meeting the task of concealing one's homeless status, for managing information to prevent one's covert "discreditable" status from becoming an overt "discredited" status (Goffman 1986). Concealment may be necessary to protect or gain material resources, for example, when dealing with a potential employer. It may be necessary to protect the family unit, as when homelessness is hidden from authorities such as the Child Protective Service. It may be necessary to avoid labeling and embarrassment for one's children, as an organizer discovered when she first set up an appointment with the news media to interview some of the people who had contacted her through the Single Parent Alliance:

> They were especially interested in shooting footage of children living in cars and such. And most of the people who I know who are living in cars *don't* want their picture on TV. Especially the women. Two were women there with teenaged kids, and the teenaged kids don't want their friends to know that they've been living in their vehicle. Or that they're living with friends or whatever. That their mother is desperate.

Given their own vulnerability and that of their children, spurred by the prevalent desire to make their children's lives as normal as possible, and generally committed to concealment as a coping strategy, Skidders spend a great deal of time finding sleeping arrangements which provide both safety and "invisibility," including the homes of friends or family, hotels and motels, and, as a last resort, their vehicles. They are rarely found on the streets or in shelters (other than temporary transitional stays for some in the battered women's shelter). Over two-thirds of those calling the Single Parent Alliance reported currently staying with friends or family, with an additional 15 percent in motels, hotels, or their cars, while only 13 percent reported staying in shelters (primarily the shelter services for battered women) and 3 percent on the streets. Homeless parents coming to the church shelters in Santa Barbara were a fourth as likely as childless adults (12 percent to 48 percent) to report having spent the previous night sleeping on the streets. Studies across the nation show women, particularly women with children, likely to be found in hidden arrangements rather than in shelters or on the streets (see King County Housing and Community Development Division 1986; Research Atlanta 1984; Robinson 1985; Hope and Young 1986; Goplerud 1987; Owen, Mattessich, and Williams 1987).[20]

Staying with friends or family, however, is not easy. Women in such arrangements know full well they are dependent on the good will of their benefactors and must be careful not to take up too much room, physically or psychically. Since guests eventually wear out their welcome, no matter how unobtrusive they try to be, a pattern of episodic homelessness is common. Christine and her baby, for example, lived in her van at a house (paying rent), moved her van to another house (no longer paying rent), moved into a group living situation (paying rent), moved into her van in a friend's front yard (not paying rent), house-sat for a friend for a month, house-sat for another friend for a month, house-sat for a third friend for three weeks, moved in with a couple for several months (paying rent), and then began living clandestinely at another friend's place—all in a sixteen-month period. This is close to a typical pattern for the Skidders I met. Successfully arranging this continual process of residential ping-pong requires immense planning, including developing an extensive knowledge of the family situations of their closest friends, enabling Skidders to plan when they might use each home for a few nights. As consuming as this constant search may be, Skidders devote whatever time and energy it requires, fueled by their perceived necessity of avoiding the streets, as women and as parents.

Only when the situation is desperate do Skidders even consider the shelters. Their fear of the environment, the constraints of shelter regulations,[21] and their conception of themselves as middle class militate against using the shelters and limit their stays, when unavoidable, to the briefest amount of time possible. For the most part they are able to avoid the shelters through their creative planning, particularly through use of their networks of contacts, their vehicles if necessary, and the little money they have from time to time.

While the double-jeopardy status of female/parent involves additional constraints for Skidders, it also affords some advantages in coping with homelessness (as it did for prevention). The joint status of woman/parent confers an assumption of responsibility, good will, and innocence rarely granted to other homeless people. For instance, Skidders are virtually never ticketed for "illegal sleeping,"[22] and certainly never jailed for such offenses, even when they cannot find a conventional residence to use and end up in their vehicles for a night or two. In part this is because Skidders attract less attention, given their middle-class appearance. But even when detected, they are much more likely to be simply told by police to move on, whereas Street People are liable to face arrest or, minimally, a warrant check. More generally, once the widespread existence of homeless women and children was finally established and accepted by public policy formulators, this group typically received preference for whatever services were being made available to homeless people. Homeless families are more likely to be perceived as homeless due to situations beyond their control; combined with traditional notions of their greater vulnerability, this absence of fault establishes a special claim on the conscience of the community.

Skidders also possess an unusual ability to remain invisible, that is, to blend in with housed people rather than standing out as homeless. Women may use traditional female roles of "shopping, sorting, selecting,

[and] collecting to gain access to urban facilities" (Shulman 1981:11, based on Hand 1976). Sheltering one's children from inclement weather, for example, may rest on a Skidder's ability to appear to be an interested shopper in a downtown store, a subterfuge Street People, by contrast, are hard-pressed to accomplish. "In the world of the streets," Hombs and Snyder (1983:8) have observed, "invisibility equals access, and those who can pass unnoticed into public places suffer less abuse and harassment."

Concealing their homeless status is also generally easier for Skidders than for most homeless people because they can usually avoid the two most obvious signifiers of homelessness to the housed world: carrying one's "home" (including bedding, change of clothes, etc.), and an unclean appearance. Skidders are able to leave clothes and other possessions in the homes of friends, they rarely if ever sleep on the streets and so don't carry bedding, and their pattern of episodic stays at friends' homes allows for regular bathing and maintaining personal hygiene.

This ability to appear housed—even middle class—affects both material resource gathering and Skidders' reception by housed others, both of which greatly affect their own self-image. Homeless people generally are acutely aware of how housed people perceive their state and how this perception extends to a degrading of their personal worth. By escaping this judgment in most of their daily rounds, Skidders are able to minimize its effect on their self-conception. They often avoid a common downward cycle of homeless life in which lack of access to housed resources (such as showers or a home address) leads to an appearance of homelessness, leading to diminished social acceptability, hence diminished access to resources (such as an income through a job), furthering both one's self-concept and appearance as homeless.

Living in the homes of friends and kin generally helps Skidders remain connected to the mainstream world they had inhabited before becoming homeless. They continue to identify themselves with the friends whose homes they use; they evince little solidarity with (and often great hostility toward) more visible homeless people.[23] The psychological strains of being in this world, but not fully of it, are profound. But whatever the toll and costs, it cannot be said that they are isolated from mainstream society. Their children usually continue to go to the same schools; those working usually continue to work the same jobs; their peer group usually remains the same (unless and until they descend into street life). In contradiction to either of the dominant images, Skidders do not become homeless because they are disaffiliated, nor do they become permanently disaffiliated as a result of homelessness.[24]

217

ESCAPING HOMELESSNESS

The (relative) advantages of female/parent status are also of some help in escaping from homelessness, beginning with the belief of housed people that Skidders (and homeless families in general) are fundamentally different from other homeless people,[25] an echo of the traditional Benthamite distinction between the "deserving" and "undeserving poor." Public debates of the Santa Barbara City Council, for example, invariably included comments to the effect that while everyone was interested in helping women and children, no one should have sympathy for "Fig Tree types," meaning Street People.[26] As a result, Skidders are more likely to receive benefits (individually and collectively) that may aid escape, including welfare, outreach programs, and so forth.

The barriers to escape, however, are formidable. Most obviously and importantly, Skidders have a difficult time finding a permanent place to live due to the gap between market rents and their incomes. While Section 8 and rent voucher programs may help in some areas, they are typically of little to no use in areas of high rents (Boston Emergency Shelter Commission 1986). Additionally, reentering the housing market is much more expensive than continuing in an apartment. In an area like Santa Barbara, most landlords require a payment of two to three times the amount of the monthly rent to move in (to cover "first, last, and deposit"). In the mid-1980s, move-in costs for a one-bedroom apartment ran around $1,500, well beyond the means of most Skidders—and actually $500 more than those receiving AFDC were legally allowed to have in savings.

Thus escape from homelessness often requires finding sources of income larger than welfare programs provide, meaning essentially combining incomes with another adult (either as a romantic couple or as friends) or finding full-time employment that pays fairly well. But the latter, again, is unlikely due to lack of a recent work history and problems finding affordable child care (see Goplerud 1987:31; Alameda County Emergency Services Network 1988:13; King County Housing and Community Development Division 1986:50). Thus (ironically, given their sympathetic portrayal in the popular press compared to that of other groups) unemployed Skidders are the least likely of homeless adults to be seeking escape through work.

As when attempting to avoid initial homelessness, some Skidders find that even with an augmented income, the presence of children greatly complicates finding a suitable home, again in part due to persisting dis-

218

crimination against children. Although such discrimination is now illegal in many areas (including Santa Barbara during most of the period of my fieldwork), homeless people have few resources for combating it:

Pat: I came [to Santa Barbara] mostly for the change in environment, and I realized how expensive [it would be, but] I wasn't aware that landlords didn't want to rent to people with children. That's been a major factor.
Q: Do they say right out front that they don't rent to kids?
Pat: No, they say, "We only rent to one person," or "to two persons." It was basically that they didn't want children, that was the main reason. Because there were places I saw that would have been very suitable but they wouldn't even consider renting to me because of the children.
Q: Did you have any discussion with any of them about that being illegal?
Pat: They are so careful about it, mentioning just one person or two persons. They were just real careful about it.

Liz: I knew someone . . . [who] didn't want any first and last and all that kind of stuff, but my daughter had to be eighteen. . . .
Q: Were you aware at the time that it was illegal to discriminate against kids?
Liz: Yeah, I am aware of it. But at the same time, who has the time and the money to go after something like that?

Finding housing may be further complicated by parents' assessment that available and affordable housing is unsuitable for their children's needs in one way or another:

Liz: I don't like Goleta. I don't like Isla Vista [both suburbs of the city]. I may be picky about that, but it's too far out for my daughter. I don't want to disrupt her from school again, I've done that four times. I've moved her out of her school, out of her neighborhood. I don't want to do that again.

Escape for Skidders, as for virtually all homeless people, may also become more difficult due to the adaptations they have made to their homeless lives, but their pattern seems to be markedly different from

219

other subgroups. For instance, Skidders (and other parents) are much less likely to develop drinking problems as a result of homelessness (see Wright and Weber 1987:70–74; Goplerud 1987:15, 51; King County Housing and Community Development Division 1986:48) or to become engaged in illegal activities to raise money (see Goplerud 1987:15; Rosenthal 1993). On the other hand, the dangers of a reactive depression seem especially pronounced for Skidders in the first few months after displacement, when "the combination of factors that gives one sustenance and worth in one's own eyes and in the eyes of others, melts away with the advent of homelessness" (Hombs and Snyder 1983:4). Coming from a lifestyle so distant from homelessness (which is not the case for all other subgroups), the change is so overwhelming that paralysis sometimes results. The presence of children, however, appears one of the more effective antidotes to despair (see Rosenthal 1993; Kozol 1988).

Again, it is within these constellations of constraints, of potential liabilities and assets, that Skidders plan and carry out their individual escape strategies. Their basic coping strategy of finding shelter with friends and families is in itself extremely helpful for a number of escape tasks. Those meeting a potential employer or landlord are able to present a clean appearance and furnish a "home" telephone number; those seeking public assistance are able to provide a "home" address, satisfying residency requirements. Their links to a network of friends and kind additionally provide more options for resource gathering than persons in the shelters or on the streets possess, thus minimizing the likelihood of engaging in the more severe and dangerous resource-gathering adaptations (such as crime) or adaptations of despair (such as substance abuse).

Yet even those who do not fall into adaptations of desperation or despair understand that they are playing a game they are unlikely to win, particularly if they respect the rules. Escape strategies, therefore, often entail subterfuge of one kind or another. For instance, given that AFDC regulations call for loss of benefits if one's savings exceed $1,000 (in California in the mid-1980s), while securing an apartment requires minimally $1,500 for first, last and deposit, Skidders arrange imaginative ways of hiding their savings with friends and families. Similarly, most Skidders have discovered that honesty when dealing with potential landlords is an extravagance they cannot afford:

> Pat: By that point, I decided that I would just mention that I had one child. I would say that the other one was somewhere else and that he would be there at a later date, which I didn't like doing. But it was getting to be necessary.

Sonya: He asked what my income was. I said 800. I had to lie a little bit. My experience has been that if you don't make four times what the rent is, they don't want to rent it to you.

Q: Are people hesitant to rent to you when they find you are on [some form of public assistance]?

Sonya: Oh, that is the worst. A lot of times you will find a receptive landlord who might not mind having a child or being a single mother. I can't tell them that I am on welfare. To them that is just all in the same category. They all think that you are just a lowlife bum. I tell them I'm on child support. It sounds a little more respectable, I guess.

Finally, in keeping with their previous lifestyles and backgrounds, many Skidders pursue formal education as their primary path to escaping not merely their present homelessness, but lower-class life entirely:

Christine: I'm taking Montessori school, to become a Montessori teacher. . . . I'm not totally enthused about it, but it's something to get me out of this *rut*. At least it'll be one option.

Lynn: I don't like being on welfare, and if I went back to work I could afford to leave here, but my education right now is more important. I want to go into the registered nurses program and possibly be a certified nurse-midwife. I want to get my A.S. degree here and transfer to South Oregon State College for my master's. That's the five-year plan.

COLLECTIVE STRUGGLES

While homeless people's agency may lead to individual solutions, they may also attempt collective solutions. Unlike individual escape strategies, collective strategies seek to change the prevailing definitions and institutional arrangements which frame the boundaries of constraint and the possibilities for agency. Collective action by homeless people was considered virtually unthinkable by disaffiliation theorists (see Caplow 1970: 5–6; Bahr 1973:15, 30); the growth of such social movements in communities across the nation in itself calls into question characterizations of homeless people as largely isolated and disaffiliated (either as cause or effect of homelessness).

Yet clearly organizing collectively is fraught with difficulties and dangers for homeless people: resources are extremely limited, political contacts and leverage are usually slight, and activism requires surrendering precisely the type of invisibility that most homeless people (and particularly Skidders) work so hard to achieve. Still, the trials of homeless life spur some to sacrifice invisibility and whatever meager time and resources they have to engage in collective action:

> Sonya: I guess I've gotten to the point that I am so angry and tired and drained. From my own experiences. I know that a lot of other [homeless] women are desperate and are getting worse. I know that there are going to be more people joining them. It looks like the economy and everything and Reagan and unemployment and housing—I think people have to start doing something about it. At least trying.

Santa Barbara saw the creation of two organizations of homeless people, both built on generally accepted social categories: the Homeless People's Association (HPA), created by and representing mainly Street People (predominantly childless males); and the Single Parent Alliance (SPA), created by and representing mainly Skidders (overwhelmingly female parents). Their tactics further assumed and exploited these categories. While the HPA emphasized militancy and civil disobedience, the SPA emphasized self-help and networking, often operating less as a social movement organization than as a social service agency. Invoking the image of innocent women and children, the SPA was able to receive an influx of resources from outside its ranks, ranging from favorable media coverage to private and government funding to finance their office and activities.

For a short period of time, the HPA and SPA (along with interested individuals) were actively allied in an umbrella group, the Santa Barbara Homeless Coalition, working on their joint interests and attempting to overlook their important differences. In organizing their separate groups, activists had already made use of the social categories that often act as constraints on individuals' agency; in creating the alliance between groups they actually transcended those categories and constraints, particularly in rejecting the deserving versus the undeserving distinctions implied by their social categories. Such transcendence of social categories and public definitions, however, is quite difficult and thus usually transitory. In this case, the SPA-HPA alliance broke down within eighteen months. The clash of previous and present lifestyles (and accompanying self-images) between many Skidders and Street People made joint work increasingly difficult; more importantly, the desire of the SPA to capitalize on the relatively favorable public definitions of their gender and parental status conflicted with the HPA's tactics of militant challenges and demands.[27]

While collective action has not lead to escape from homelessness for homeless women as a group or homeless people as a class, it has clearly aided escape for many individuals. By challenging the prevailing definitions of the situation, collective action has reduced the power of labeling (particularly in the form of "blaming the victim") to subvert escape attempts by individuals. By making the hidden homeless population visible, it has led to far greater (though still insufficient) resources being made available to that population.

AGENCY WITHIN CONSTRAINT

Coping with and escaping homelessness require considerable creativity on the part of the homeless individual, yet the possibilities for that resistance are largely demarcated by the rules and roles of mainstream society. The resources necessary for survival and escape are primarily found within the institutions and networks of mainstream society, and thus the institutions, structures, and definitions of mainstream society lay down the boundaries of conduct for homeless people. They frame the possibilities for action: Which strategic possibilities are most likely to meet with success, but further, which are most likely to be even considered.

At each stage of the process of homelessness, the social categories "woman" and "parent" both impose constraints on Skidders' possibilities for action and, to a lesser extent, provide opportunities for active resistance. Within those constraints, and sensitive to where relative opportunity lies, Skidders attempt to secure their goals: short-term survival, retaining maximum normalcy amid what they believe to be an abnormal situation, and as speedy an escape as possible. To paraphrase Marx, women make their own history, but they do not make it precisely as they please.

NOTES

This chapter is based on material drawn from my work *Homeless in Paradise* (Temple University Press, 1993). My thanks for help and support of various kinds go to Kit Tremaine, Dick Flacks, Roger Friedland, Harvey Molotch, Sunny Banwer, Sue Fisher, Doug Welch, Patty St. Clair, Matt Salo, Alexandra Todd, Kathy

Davis, and the necessarily anonymous homeless people who gave me their time and information.

1. Given extremely formidable problems of definitions, concealment, flux, and so forth, all estimates of homeless populations should be cautiously approached. Yet whatever the actual numbers, evidence of an explosion in the late 1970s and early 1980s is persuasive. See Cuomo 1984; U.S. Conference of Mayors 1984, 1987, 1989; National Coalition for the Homeless 1987b, 1987c, 1989.

2. Among the literally hundreds of local and national studies documenting the increase in these subgroups, see Crystal 1984; U.S. Conference of Mayors 1984, 1987, 1989; National Coalition for the Homeless 1986a, 1987a; Baxter and Hopper 1982; Manhattan Borough President's Task Force on Housing for Homeless Families 1987; Ropers 1988; Lamb 1984; Bachrach 1984; Bassuk, Rubin, and Lauriati 1984; Robertson 1987; Kerr 1985.

3. Nearly all recent works on the subject examine most or all of these social roots. See Hope and Young 1986; Rosenthal 1993; Kozol 1988; Sloss 1984; Ropers 1988; Hombs and Snyder 1983; Hopper and Hamberg 1984; Rossi 1989; Wright 1989; National Coalition for the Homeless 1987a. Relatively few researchers still mention people who are "voluntarily" homeless (see Gaido, in U.S. Congress 1984; Winograd 1984; Chicago Task Force 1983).

4. Some theorists retain social isolation as a contributing cause as well as effect. See Rossi et al. 1987.

5. For similar analyses, see Snow and Anderson 1987, Lovell 1984, and Cohen and Sokolovsky 1989.

6. For other critiques of theoretical assumptions and methodological practices which have potentially exaggerated the appearance of isolation among homeless populations, see Cohen and Sokolovsky 1989, Wiseman 1970, and Hoch and Slayton 1989.

7. Rendered as part of his critique of structuralists.

8. Classifications of homeless people have generally been unsatisfactory. I have argued elsewhere that such typologies must minimally be created for each stage in the process of homelessness—path into homelessness, life while homeless, and escape strategies and attempts. Within the second of these stages I found in the Santa Barbara homeless population six subgroups, largely determined by what resources they used to survive: Skidders, Latino Families, Street People, Kids, Transitory Workers, and Wingnuts. Even within these groupings, of course, there is considerable variation. For a detailed discussion, see Rosenthal 1993.

9. In other works (see Rosenthal 1993) I have included a small number of males with similar characteristics other than gender in the Skidders group. I have omitted them here in order to focus on questions of gender.

10. For a rare exception, see Reitman 1937.

11. The lone exception to this general trend seems to have been the Depression years; see Hoch and Slayton 1989:75.

12. Ironically this invisibility may result in greater hardships for homeless women by engendering beliefs that women don't become homeless. Thus those

few who are visible must be "even more derelict than homeless men, and thus, the most socially undesirable of all marginal people" (Stoner 1984:4; see Shulman 1981).

13. Not only are women more likely to be employed in lower paid jobs or paid less for jobs of "comparable worth," but they are also half as likely to work lucrative overtime shifts and less likely to belong to unions and thus make union wages (Pearce and McAdoo 1981:5).

14. Rossi and Rossi found that in the general population, "among all kin, respondents acknowledged the strongest obligations to provide financial aid to unattached daughters and mothers" (Rossi 1989:120 reporting findings of Rossi and Rossi 1989). My data from the church shelters and the collected oral histories show homeless women three times as likely as men to receive shelter occasionally from friends or family, while parents were almost ten times as likely to do so as those without children. I have argued elsewhere (Rosenthal 1993) that those living in doubled-up arrangements in which they enjoy no legal rights to tenancy should be regarded as homeless. My purpose here is merely to show the greater availability of this resource to women and parents than to men and childless adults without engaging the question of whether such people are literally homeless.

15. In general, homelessness is made more likely by various welfare regulations, such as those that penalize working or staying together as a family unit. For instance, until 1990 many states barred payments to two-parent families; many still deny payments to homes where one parent is employed. The cutbacks in public assistance during the Reagan years, of course, greatly exacerbated this ongoing problem. The American Federation of State, County, and Municipal Employees (1984:1–3), for instance, estimates that from 1981 to 1985, 493,000 parents and children were dropped from the AFDC program.

16. All homeless people are extremely vulnerable on the streets. Nearly everyone I interviewed in Santa Barbara whose typical sleeping place was on the streets had been victimized, most a number of times. In their national study Wright and Weber (1987:128) report that homeless people were over twenty times as likely to die from homicide as were members of the general population. But females are at special risk.

17. For example, only 61 percent of church shelter mothers reported looking for work, compared to over 90 percent of all other guests, a fairly typical finding. See Piliavin, Sosin, and Westerfelt 1988:21; Owen, Mattessich, and Williams 1987:10–11; U.S. Conference of Mayors 1987:8, 34; Alameda County Emergency Services Network 1987:4.

18. The other major subgroup of homeless families in Santa Barbara includes those I call Latino Families; they are characterized by their use of resources available within the Latino community (raw foodstuffs from Catholic Social Services, the garages of kin for shelter, Latino friends for jobs) rather than by mere ethnicity. See Rosenthal 1993.

19. For example, half of those calling the Single Parent Alliance for help had lived in Santa Barbara for more than five years, and virtually all in a conventional residence.

225

20. Some researchers report increased shelter use by women and/or parents beginning in the late 1980s as their plight received greater attention (see Alameda County Emergency Services Network 1988:5; Burt and Cohen 1989:518–519). The use of shelters by women and women with children (in fact, by all subgroups) appears to vary widely from locality to locality, depending on such factors as perception of safety, reputation for welcoming certain subgroups, regulations, alternatives, and so forth.

21. For example, some shelters housing women and young children exclude males over the age of ten; see Research Atlanta 1984:11; Hope and Young 1986:102.

22. Laws in Santa Barbara, as in many towns and cities, forbid sleeping outside of a conventional residence between ten at night and five in the morning. Such laws were the object of ongoing political demonstrations by homeless people. See Rosenthal 1989, 1993.

23. For instance, no Skidder I interviewed said that many or all of her friends were also homeless, and about half said they had no homeless friends at all. In contrast, only one of the eleven people (nine single men and a couple) who made up the Street People subgroup reported that his friends were not mainly or all homeless. Similarly, 42 percent of the women interviewed by Watson (1986:106) in homeless hostels in England did not see themselves as homeless, a term they felt applied instead to "little old men with bags on their shoes."

24. Although this is more generally true of Skidders and Latino Families than any of the other subgroups I found in Santa Barbara, I have argued elsewhere that homeless people of all subgroups are considerably more linked to mainstream society than most recent accounts suggest. See Rosenthal 1991, 1993; Lovell 1984; Cohen and Sokolovsky 1989.

25. This belief is based on ideology, but also on observable aggregate differences (as much of this chapter illustrates). It nonetheless obfuscates reality in two important ways: by stereotyping individuals' behavior (which varies widely) by aggregate group characteristics; and, more importantly, by ignoring the crucial point of displacement theory that structural factors explain far more of the rise in homelessness than individual characteristics. While their personal stories may differ, the same macro processes—above all, the demise of affordable housing—underlie the homelessness of most Street People as most Skidders. Whatever their personal stories, fifteen years ago most members of either group would at least have been housed.

26. Fig Tree Park is a popular gathering place for Street People in Santa Barbara. See Katz 1989 for an excellent extended discussion of how poverty has been defined over the years.

27. Ironically, although the Single Parent Alliance was disturbed by being linked to the Homeless People's Association, and increasingly divorced itself from that image, it seems clear in retrospect that the limited support the SPA received from the city and other funding sources was due in large part to its position as a respectable alternative (representing women and children) to the HPA. Typically, the HPA would raise hell and be denounced by political officials, who would then look more favorably on requests from the Single Parent Alliance or other mod-

erate groups. They may well have received nothing at all if the HPA was not constantly raising the issue of homelessness in such a visible fashion. See Rosenthal 1989, 1993.

REFERENCES

[Alameda County] Emergency Services Network. 1987. *Homelessness in Alameda County: Needs Assessment Study, 1987.* Oakland: Emergency Services Network of Alameda County.

———. 1988. *Homelessness in Alameda County, 1988.* Oakland: Emergency Services Network of Alameda County.

American Federation of State, County, and Municipal Employees. 1984. *The States, the People, and the Reagan Years.* Washington, D.C.: American Federation of State, County, and Municipal Employees.

Anderson, Nels. 1923. *The Hobo: The Sociology of the Homeless Man.* Chicago: University of Chicago Press.

Bachrach, Leona L. 1984. "Interpreting Research on the Homeless Mentally Ill: Some Caveats." *Hospital and Community Psychiatry* 35(9): 924–916.

Bahr, Howard M. 1969. *Homelessness and Disaffiliation.* New York: Bureau of Applied Research, Columbia University.

———. 1970. "Homelessness, Disaffiliation, and Retreatism." In *Disaffiliated Man,* ed. Howard M. Bahr, 39–50. Toronto: University of Toronto Press.

———. 1973. *Skid Row: An Introduction to Disaffiliation.* New York: Oxford University Press.

Bassuk, Ellen L., Alison Lauriati, and Lenore Rubin. 1987. "Homeless Families." In The Boston Foundation, *Homelessness: Critical Issues for Policy and Practice,* 20–23. Boston: The Boston Foundation.

Bassuk, Ellen L., Lenore Rubin, and Alison Lauriati. 1984. "Is Homelessness a Mental Problem?" *American Journal of Psychiatry* 141(12): 1546–1550.

Baumohl, Jim. 1989. "Alcohol, Homelessness, and Public Policy." *Contemporary Drug Problems* 16(3): 281–300.

Baxter, Ellen, and Kim Hopper. 1982. "The new Mendicancy: Homeless in New York City." *American Journal of Orthopsychiatry* 52(3): 393–408.

Blumberg, Leonard U., Thomas E. Shipley, Jr., and Stephen F. Barsky. 1978. *Liquor and Poverty: Skid Row as a Human Condition.* New Brunswick, N.J.: Rutgers Center of Alcohol Studies.

Bogue, Donald. 1963. *Skid Row in American Cities.* Chicago: University of Chicago Press.

[Boston] Emergency Shelter Commission. 1986. *Boston's Homeless: Taking the Next Step.* Boston: City of Boston.

———. 1987–1988. *Making Room for Boston's Homeless.* Boston: City of Boston.

Burt, Martha R., and Barbara E. Cohen. 1989. "Differences among Homeless Single Women, Women with Children, and Single Men." *Social Problems* 36(5): 508–524.

227

Caplow, Theodore. 1970. "The Sociologist and the Homeless Man." In *Disaffiliated Man,* ed. Howard M. Bahr, 3–12. Toronto: University of Toronto Press.

Caplow, Theodore, Howard M. Bahr, and David Sternberg. 1968. "Homelessness." In *International Encyclopedia of the Social Sciences,* 6: 494–499. New York: Macmillan.

[Chicago] Task Force on Emergency Shelter. 1983. *Homeless in Chicago.* Chicago: City of Chicago, Department of Human Services.

Cleghorn, James Stephen. 1984. "Residents without Residences: A Study of Homelessness in Birmingham, Alabama." In U.S. Congress, Subcommittee on Housing and Community Development, *Homelessness in America, II,* 1104–1233. Washington, D.C.: GPO. Originally written in 1983 as a Master's thesis, University of Alabama.

Clement, Priscilla F. 1984. "The Transformation of the Wandering Poor in Nineteenth-Century Philadelphia." In *Walking to Work,* ed. Eric H. Monkkonen, 56–84. Lincoln: University of Nebraska Press.

Cohen, Carl I., and Jay Sokolovsky. 1989. *Old Men of the Bowery.* New York: Guilford Press.

Crystal, Stephen. 1984. "Homeless Men and Homeless Women: The Gender Gap." *Urban and Social Change Review* 17(1): 2–6.

Crystal, Stephen, and Mervyn Goldstein. 1984. *The Homeless in New York City Shelters.* New York: City of New York Human Resources Administration.

Cuomo, Mario. 1984. "1933/1983—Never Again: A Report to the National Governor's Association Task Force on the Homeless." In U.S. Congress, Subcommittee on Housing and Community Development, *Homelessness in America, II,* 353–443. Washington, D.C.: GPO. Originally published in 1983 by the National Governors' Association.

Giddens, Anthony. 1984. *The Constitution of Society.* Berkeley: University of California Press.

Goffman, Erving. 1986. *Stigma: Notes on the Management of Spoiled Identity.* New York: Touchstone. Originally published in 1963.

Goplerud, Eric. 1987. *Homelessness in Fairfax County.* Fairfax, Va.: Department of Psychology, George Mason University.

Hand, Jennifer. 1976. "Shopping Bag Ladies: A Study in Interstitial Urban Behavior." Paper presented at the Society for the Study of Social Problems annual convention, August.

Harrington, Michael. 1984. *The New American Poverty.* New York: Holt, Rinehart and Winston.

Hoch, Charles, and Robert A. Slayton. 1989. *New Homeless and Old: Community and the Skid Row Hotel.* Philadelphia: Temple University Press.

Hombs, Mary Ellen, and Mitch Snyder. 1983. *Homelessness in America: A Forced March to Nowhere.* Washington, D.C.: Community for Creative Non-Violence.

Hope, Marjorie, and James Young. 1986. *The Faces of Homelessness.* Lexington, Mass.: Lexington Books.

Hopper, Kim, and Jill Hamberg. 1984. *The Making of America's Homeless:*

From Skid Row to New Poor, 1945–1984. New York: Community Services Society.

Jahiel, Rene I. 1987. "The Situation of Homelessness." In *The Homeless in Contemporary Society,* ed. Richard D. Bingham, Roy E. Green, and Sammis B. White, 99–118. Newbury Park, Calif.: Sage Publications.

Joe, Tom, and Cheryl Rogers. 1985. *By the Few for the Few.* Lexington, Mass.: Lexington Books.

Jones, Douglas L. 1984. "The Strolling Poor: Transiency in Eighteenth-Century Massachusetts." In *Walking to Work,* ed. Eric H. Monkkonen, 21–55. Lincoln: University of Nebraska Press. Originally published in 1975.

Katz, Michael. 1989. *The Undeserving Poor.* New York: Pantheon.

Kerr, Peter. 1985. "Suburbs Struggle with Rise in the Homeless." *New York Times,* 22 December, pp. A-1, 30.

King County [Washington] Housing and Community Development Division. 1986. *Homelessness Revisited.* Seattle: King County.

Kozol, Jonathan. 1988. *Rachel and Her Children.* New York: Crown.

Lamb, H. Richard, ed. 1984. *The Homeless Mentally Ill: A Task Force Report of the American Psychiatric Association.* Washington, D.C.: American Psychiatric Association.

Lantz, Sherry A. H. 1986. *Homelessness and Low Income Housing in Chautauqua County, New York.* Dunkirk, N.Y.: Chautauqua County Rural Ministry.

Liebow, Elliot. 1967. *Tally's Corner.* Boston: Little, Brown.

Lovell, Anne M. 1984. "Marginality without Isolation: Social Networks and the New Homeless." Paper presented at the 83rd annual meeting of the American Anthropological Association, Denver, Colo.

Manhattan Borough President's Task Force on Housing for Homeless Families. 1987. *A Shelter Is Not a Home.* New York: Borough of Manhattan.

Melnick, Vijaya L., and Charles S. Williams. 1987. *Homelessness in the District of Columbia.* Washington, D.C.: Center for Applied Research and Urban Policy, University of the District of Columbia.

National Coalition for the Homeless. 1986a. *Malign Neglect: The Homeless Poor of Miami.* New York: National Coalition for the Homeless.

———. 1986b. *National Neglect/National Shame.* Washington, D.C.: National Coalition for the Homeless.

———. 1987a. *Homelessness in the United States: Background and Federal Response.* New York: National Coalition for the Homeless.

———. 1987b. *Out in the Cold: Homelessness in Iowa.* Washington, D.C.: National Coalition for the Homeless.

———. 1987c. *Pushed Out: America's Homeless, Thanksgiving, 1987.* Washington, D.C.: National Coalition for the Homeless.

———. 1987d. *Saving Lives: Emergency Federal Aid Reaches the Streets.* Washington, D.C.: National Coalition for the Homeless.

———. 1989. *American Nightmare: Ending a Decade of Homelessness in the United States.* Washington, D.C.: National Coalition for the Homeless.

———. N.d. *Homelessness in America: A Summary.* Washington, D.C.: National Coalition for the Homeless.

Owen, Greg, Paul, Mattessich, and Judy Williams. 1987. *Results of the Twin City Survey of Emergency Shelter Residents*. St. Paul: Wilder Research Center, Amherst H. Wilder Foundation.

Pearce, Diana, and Harriette McAdoo. 1981. *Women and Children: Alone and in Poverty*. Washington, D.C.: National Advisory Council on Economic Opportunity.

Peterson, W. Jack, and Milton A. Maxwell. 1958. "The Skid Row 'Wino.'" *Social Problems* 5:308–316.

Piliavin, Irving, Michael Sosin, and Herb Westerfelt. 1988. "Conditions contributing to Long-Term Homelessness: An Exploratory Study." Discussion paper no. 853-87. Institute for Research on Poverty, University of Wisconsin—Madison.

Pittman, David J., and C. Wayne Gordon. 1958. *Revolving Door: A Study of the Chronic Police Case Inebriate*. Glencoe, Ill.: Free Press.

Reitman, Ben L. 1937. *Sister of the Road: The Autobiography of Box Car Bertha*. New York: Macaulay.

Research Atlanta. 1984. *The Impact of Homelessness on Atlanta*. Atlanta: Research Atlanta.

Robertson, Marjorie. 1987. "Homeless Veterans: An Emerging Problem." In *The Homeless in Contemporary Society*, ed. Richard D. Bingham, Roy E. Green, and Sammis B. White, 64–81. Newbury Park, Calif.: Sage.

Robinson, Frederic G. 1985. *Homeless People in the Nation's Capital*. Washington, D.C.: Center for Applied Research and Urban Policy, University of the District of Columbia.

Rooney, James F. 1961. "Group Processes among Skid Row Winos: A Reevaluation of the Undersocialization Hypothesis." *Quarterly Journal of Studies on Alcohol* 22(3): 444–460.

Ropers, Richard. 1988. *The Invisible Homeless: An Urban Ecology*. New York: Insight Books.

Rosenthal, Rob. 1989. "Good Cop/Bad Cop: A Social Movement Dynamic." Paper presented at the Society for the Study of Social Problems annual convention, 8 August, Berkeley, Calif.

———. 1991. "Straighter from the Source: Alternative Methods of Researching Homelessness." *Urban Anthropology* 20(2): 109–126.

———. 1993. *Homeless in Paradise*. Philadelphia: Temple University Press.

Rossi, Alice S., and Peter H. Rossi. 1989. *Of Human Bonding: A Life Course Perspective on Parent-Child Relations*. Hawthorne, N.Y.: Aldine de Gruyter.

Rossi, Peter H. 1989. *Down and Out in America*. Chicago: University of Chicago Press.

Rossi, Peter H., James D. Wright, Gene A. Fisher, and Georgianna Willis. 1987. "The Urban Homeless: Estimating Composition and Size." *Science* 235: 1336–1341.

Rousseau, Ann Marie. 1981. *Shopping Bag Ladies*. New York: Pilgrim Press.

Safety Network. 1983–1990. Newsletter of the National Coalition for the Homeless. New York and Washington, D.C.

[Santa Barbara] Single Parent Alliance. 1983. "Background." Leaflet. Santa Barbara, Calif.

———. 1985. Newsletter. Spring issue.

Shulman, Joanne. 1981. "Poor Women and Family Law." *Clearinghouse Review,* February 1981.

Shelby, Barry. 1983. "Assembly Cites the Plight of the Homeless." *Daily Nexus* (University of California, Santa Barbara), 23 February, p. 1.

Shulman, Alix Kates. 1981. "Preface." In Ann Marie Rousseau, *Shopping Bag Ladies,* 10–12. New York: Pilgrim Press.

Sloss, Michael. 1984. "The Crisis of Homelessness: Its Dimensions and Solutions." *Urban and Social Change Review* 17(2): 18–20.

Snow, David, and Leon Anderson. 1987. "Identity Work among the Homeless: The Verbal Construction and Avowal of Personal Identities." *American Journal of Sociology* 92(6): 1336–1371.

Stone, Michael E. 1983. "Housing and the Economic Crisis." In *America's Housing Crisis: What Is to Be Done,* ed. Chester Hartman, 99–150. Boston: Routledge and Kegan Paul.

Stoner, Madeleine R. 1984. "An Analysis of Public and Private Sector Provisions for Homeless People." *Urban and Social Change Review* 17(1): 3–8.

U.S. Bureau of the Census. 1981. *Child Support 1981.* Washington, D.C.: GPO.

U.S. Conference of Mayors. 1982. *Human Services in Fiscal Year 1982: Shrinking Resources in Troubled Times.* Washington, D.C.: U.S. Conference of Mayors.

———. 1984. *Homelessness in America's Cities.* Washington, D.C.: U.S. Conference of Mayors.

———. 1987. *A Status Report on Homeless Families in America's Cities.* Washington, D.C.: U.S. Conference of Mayors.

———. 1989. *Status Report on Hunger and Homelessness in America's Cities, 1989.* Washington, D.C.: U.S. Conference of Mayors.

U.S. Congress, House, Committee on Banking, Finance, and Urban Affairs, Subcommittee on Housing and Community Development. 1984. *Homelessness in America, II.* 98th Cong., 2d sess., ser. 98-64. Washington, D.C.: GPO.

———, Committee on Government Operations. 1985. *The Federal Response to the Homeless Crisis.* 99th Cong., 1t sess., ser. 99-47. Washington, D.C.: GPO.

U.S. Departments of Commerce and Health and Human Services. 1979. *Child Support and Alimony, 1978.* Ser. P-23, no. 106. Washington, D.C.: GPO.

Vexliard, Alexandre. 1956. "The Hobo: Myths and Realities." *Diogenes* 16: 59–67.

Wallace, Samuel. 1965. *Skid Row as a Way of Life.* Totawa, N.J.: Bedminster.

———. 1968. "The Road to Skid Row." *Social Problems* 16(1): 92–105.

Watson, Sophie, with Helen Austerberry. 1986. *Housing and Homelessness.* London: Routledge and Kegan Paul.

Weitzman, Lenore J. 1985. *The Divorce Revolution.* New York: Free Press.

Winograd, Kenneth. 1984. "Street People and Other Homeless: A Pittsburgh Study." In U.S. Congress, Subcommittee on Housing and Community

Development, *Homelessness in America, II,* 1343–1401. Washington, D.C.: GPO.

Wiseman, Jacqueline P. 1970. *Stations of the Lost: The Treatment of Skid Row Alcoholics.* Englewood Cliffs, N.J.: Prentice-Hall.

Woods, William K., and Edward Lee Burdell. 1987. *Homelessness in Cincinnati.* Cincinnati: Applied Information Resources.

Wright, James D. 1989. *Address Unknown.* New York: Aldine de Gruyter.

Wright, James D., and Eleanor Weber. 1987. *Homelessness and Health.* Washington, D.C.: McGraw-Hill.

NEGOTIATING THROUGH CULTURAL DISCOURSES

"NOT JUST THE GIRL SINGER": WOMEN AND VOICE IN ROCK BANDS

Mary Ann Clawson

As a pop genre, rock is founded musically on the valorization of instrument playing, socially on the idealization of the musical group as a collectivity of male peers, a band of brothers, and culturally or ideologically on the conflation of the two. This chapter looks at how women vocalists negotiate their positions within such structures, as women and as vocalists, in rock-oriented, college-level bands. It also looks at how women singers attempt to claim artistic authority for themselves, how they valorize what they do, to themselves and others, and how they negotiate with their fellow musicians. I explore these questions by (1) delineating the gendered social structure of rock music-making and (2) examining contrasting interpretive strategies employed by two women who sing in college bands as they address the problem of marginalization.

Two recent studies of women musicians are among the few to consider women's problematic status in rock music by looking at the experiences of women band members. Groce and Cooper's "Just Me and the Boys? Women in Local-Level Rock and Roll" (1990) finds that women performers suffer from stereotyping and objectification by audiences and discriminatory treatment by male fellow performers in that they are paid less than the men, are pressured to emphasize their sexuality in dress and performance, and above all, are excluded from band decision-making. Bayton's "How Women Become Musicians" (1990) examines the difficulties British women face in learning to play: gaining the technical competence to use electronically amplified instruments and to play without using written scores, learning to listen to pop music analytically, and developing the confidence to claim a musician's identity.

Bayton focuses on impediments that seem internal to women, that is, grounded in their sex role socialization and their identity as women, while Groce and Cooper identify sexist attitudes among male performers and spectators as most central to the experience of women musicians. Both analyses offer much of value: Groce and Cooper document, though they do not theorize, disparities of power between male and female performers. Baynton provides us with a rich and insightful depiction of how women acquire the skills and attitudes which comprise the craft of playing pop and rock music. But despite differences of focus and implicit causation, the articles share a similarity of approach in that each designates problems of attitude and role as central. Each points to, but does not sufficiently delineate, the instructional contexts in which aspiring women musicians must operate.

In contrast, I argue that we cannot understand women's experience without scrutinizing men's as well. The development of the male rock musician is an equally, though differently gendered process. Thus institutional factors that constrain women simultaneously empower men, given that the implicit model of a successful musician is a male musician.

My discussion is based on interviews with musicians who play in college-level bands as well as on earlier ethnographic work on pop music-making (Bennett 1980; Finnegan 1989). In particular I focus on two factors: (1) cultural evaluations of singing, a supposedly "natural" activity, versus instrument playing; and (2) the process of skill acquisition for rock musicians. The relative prestige enjoyed by playing versus singing is implicitly gendered, as is the typical route to instrumental competence. Women vocalists thus find themselves doubly marginalized. In this chapter, I analyze the perceptions and strategies of two women vocalists by placing them in the context of rock and pop music-making as a set of structured, institutionalized, and gendered social practices.

NATURE AND SKILL / THE VOICE AND THE BAND

Vocalists confront cultural interpretations that define singing as a "natural" activity and the voice as the unmediated expression of physical endowment. From this point of view, singing belongs to the realm of the pre- or quasi-social; it is that which almost anyone can do, without instruction, simply by virtue of being human (Bloch and Bloch 1980). In contrast, instrument playing is recognized as a highly developed and painstakingly acquired skill. Moreover, instrument playing is replete with the imagery of an implicitly masculine dominance, as when we speak of someone "mastering" the violin (Dahl 1984: ix–x, 38–39). One does

236

not master the voice, however; it is the self, a given, the expression of the body's own "innate" capacity for music making (Kogan 1987:20).

These assumptions are revealed in my interviews with male band members. Nowhere in their accounts do we find descriptions of musicians striving to develop vocal techniques which in any way parallel the copious descriptions of struggles to develop instrumental skill. In these accounts singing was accorded little or no recognition as a skill that must be conscientiously acquired or developed. Nor was it seen as central to the creative process of music making, even though rock is a song form which demands the participation of a vocalist.

In these bands, singing could emerge as a site of conflict or competition. In some groups, all or most of the band members wanted to sing lead vocals and believed themselves capable of doing so. In others, no one wanted to sing; it was seen as an unpleasant but necessary duty that everyone sought to avoid. While seemingly in conflict, these two approaches actually rest on a similar assumption: that singing is an unproblematic activity, like speaking, which anyone can do. Thus the question of who will sing is often treated as a social or organizational question, a matter of reconciling individual preference with group cohesion, rather than an artistic decision. If anyone can sing, then anyone in the band can sing lead vocals to equivalent effect.

Because it seems so immediate a product of the body, cultural understandings of singing are framed by associations with physicality and feeling and contrasted to rational thought, linked to nature as against culture or skill, and to woman rather than man. The metaphoric linking of man with culture and woman with nature need not be seen as universal in order to be recognized as a recurring theme in post-Enlightenment Euro-American culture (Jordanova 1980; Bloch and Bloch 1980). Thus singing has at least the potential to be gendered female regardless of the actual identity of its practitioner. Male vocalists must sometimes deal with these implicit associations (indeed recognition of singing's gendered character might be an important source of insight into masculine performance styles and modes of self-representation). But for women, the identification of vocalizing with nature is overdetermined. In claiming recognition for what they do, women vocalists must overcome or address a devaluation that derives from two mutually confirming identities: that they are women, and that they sing—"naturally."

In the case of rock-oriented bands, the position of the vocalist is further marginalized by the valorization of instrumental music as symbolized by the public visibility and centrality of the band as the unit of performance. Contemporary pop music, like its predecessors of the forties and early fifties, exhibits a well-articulated division of labor between songwriters, producers/arrangers, studio musicians and musical technicians, and singers. Yet it is the vocalist alone who is the focus of public attention in pop, the only identifiable performer, while instrumental musicians work in the anonymity of the studio or backing band. From Frank Sinatra to Madonna, pop vocalists are not understood to have a fixed artistic or social relationship to the assemblage of musicians who accompany them. Who can name the drummer on a Whitney Houston album? Pop vocalists may be empowered through their visibility to the audience and the special relationship that visibility may facilitate.

In contrast, rock music highlights and values instrument playing in a characteristic way. Rock music posits the band, composed typically of one or more electric guitars, bass, and drums, as its ideal creative and performing unit. In this mode of musical production, the band aspires to be, and is assumed by fans to be, responsible for writing its own songs, playing all instruments, singing vocals, and exercising control over the recording process. It was this ideal, emerging first in the sixties, which symbolically endowed rock music with intentionality and seriousness and legitimated its claims to artistry (Frith 1981:86–88; Lewis 1990:29–33).

Thus musical-genre boundaries include assumptions about the social organization of musical production. In practice these boundaries between pop and rock are often violated, but their importance is confirmed by the efforts which record companies and musicians themselves often make to conform to them, at least publicly. Musically weak band members may be replaced or augmented during the recording process, but this practice is usually denied since it would detract from the notion of the band, the group, as an autonomous creative unit.[1] Moreover, bands often assert collective authorship of songs, even when most of the writing is actually done by one or two members.

Both the ideology of rock artistry and the hegemony of the group or band as the social and artistic subject of rock performance are products of the sixties and early seventies when membership in a band helped define the public identities of that era's most legendary figures. Today the centrality of group identity continues to be symbolized by the fact that rock bands most often carry titles such as Aerosmith, U2, or REM.[2] These names make no reference to the band's personnel and thus designate the collectivity rather than any one individual as the meaningful unit of artistry and focus of audience attention. The lyrics of their songs may center on the heterosexual couple, but the real romance of the band is the romance of its members, as the rock press faithfully chronicles the ups and downs of their stormy relationships: Will Mick and Keith get back together? Will they ever tour again?

As a popular music genre, rock is thus defined and made recognizable by conventions about the gender identity of band members as well as by the centrality of the band as the assumed unit of creativity. Frith (1981:85–86) notes that while "the maleness of the world of rock is reflected in its lyrics, with their assertions of male supremacy . . . for musicians, what is most significant is women's exclusion from the heart of their lives: exclusion from their friendships and work together as comrade craftsmen, in the studio, on the road, in performance." Rock is equated with the band and the band with men, while women vocalists are assumed to operate within the pop model of singer backed by studio musicians.

The experience of Pat Benatar, a popular recording artist of the early eighties, is a case in point. Benatar located her creative identity within a band model, as her career was based on a long-term collaboration with her guitarist and drummer. "But to the record company, she was still a female singer and they promoted her as such," attempting to conceal or downplay the creative contributions of co-workers Neal Geraldo and Myron Grumbacher (Lewis 1990:83). This insistence on portraying Benatar as a pop vocalist rather than a member of a band, as she understood herself, was undoubtedly related to the fact she was a woman. As such, she could be assimilated to the band model, with its masculine connotations, only with difficulty.

But a rock band is, as Pat Benatar maintained, more than a romanticized representation of male camaraderie; it is also a music-making unit. Its collective identity derives from and continues to work as the model for a certain way of learning to play, a route to skill acquisition which is differentially receptive to the participation of men and women, or teenage boys and girls. Because most rock musicians learn to play through the vehicle of the adolescent male peer group, women musicians, including women vocalists, must learn to interpret and negotiate their presence within a social system predicated on and constructed around their absence.

LEARNING TO PLAY: GUYS AND GUITARS

The social definition of rock music as a male activity, through the preponderance of highly visible musicians who are male, presents a powerful symbolic barrier to the development of girls' aspirations, just as it solicits and legitimates the aspirations of boys. Most discussion, however, stops with recognition of this barrier to feminine participation, failing to perceive that gender-differentiated access is also structured by the particular social practices that organize rock music.

Two major aspects of learning to play rock music differentiate it from other forms of musical training. First, rock musicians are largely self-taught in that they learn to play primarily by copying recorded music, although they may learn basic instrumental skills from a teacher, a peer, or an instruction manual. But playing an instrument is the only relevant competence that is learned individually; other requisite skills both contribute to and grow out of the ensemble playing needed to reproduce recorded sounds. Rock musicians may begin learning as individuals, but they must move toward ensemble learning and playing if they are to reproduce what they hear on records and ultimately be able to perform the music they admire.

In consequence, an aspiring rock musician can make only limited progress as an isolated individual. Sooner or later he or she must have access to a group. As Bennett (1980:24–25) writes, "having an instrument represents passing an economic barrier, while having musicians to play with represents passing a more complex *social* barrier." The pool of musicians for more accomplished bands is composed of persons who are already *in* bands or have been in the past. But the formation of the *first* band is necessarily based on the recruitment of individuals who aspire to play in an ensemble but have never done so. They may in fact have never played at all, beyond picking out a few chords. "The aspiring band member," Bennett (1980:25) notes, "finds it necessary to use his or her existing participation in a non-musical grouping to establish a connection with other musicians, and although this could be a church, camp, or club of some kind, the most typical example is the secondary school system."

As a result, skill acquisition is closely linked to friendship groups; the learning process is primarily collective rather than individual. This method has special implications for girls and women, for it means that chief among the resources necessary to become a rock musician is access to a peer group that can function as a pool of like-minded, aspiring musicians from which the first band can be formed. The typical pool for the first band is the friendship group, which is most likely, in early or mid-adolescence, to be a single-sex group.

A substantial body of social scientific research, drawn from developmental psychology and sociology, describes the social lives of boys and girls with an eye to pinpointing the differences between them. The most consistent of these findings is that children's friendships and interactions show extensive gender separation. As Thorne (1989) points out, there are important exceptions to this "two worlds of childhood" model—friendships that cut across gender; instances where group identity coalesces around other points of identification, such as age, race, or ethnicity; and moments of cooperation when gender seems an insignificant factor. Nonetheless, the hegemonic culture of American childhood is organized around a gender separation which serves the social articulation and maintenance of difference (Thorne and Luria 1986; Lever 1976; Eder and Hallinan 1978; Maccoby 1986).

The gender segregation of childhood, which is to a significant degree maintained in early and midadolescence, has obvious implications for those girls who might envision themselves as musicians. As noted earlier, the possibility of realizing musical aspirations rests on the ability of would-be musicians to recruit friends into the enterprise or to be recruited themselves. The idea of a first band tends to emerge tentatively in the context of casual peer-group socializing, and many people become involved not because of driving ambition but because their friends are doing it. As a result, the process of first-band formation is contingent upon social as well as cultural resources, structured by the character of available peer groups. To the extent that a potential musician is excluded from such social networks, his or her opportunities to become part of a rock band will be limited. Since playing rock music is still largely defined as a masculine activity, girls will have disproportionately less access to the relevant peer relationships, which are overwhelmingly male.

In its emphasis on the autonomy of the peer group as the unit of self-education and performance, the rock group stands in distinct contrast to other forms of music performed in the United States. Rock musicians learn largely without adult intervention, supervision, or expertise. Adults have little or no role in teaching skills, certifying excellence, articulating standards, and selecting or directing musicians (Finnegan 1989: 128–129, 139–141; Bennett 1980: 18–19). In the rock band, standards of competence and methods of cooperation, decision making, and conflict resolution are all necessarily generated from within the group and are, at least initially, inseparable from the social life of the group and the interactional skills its members can mobilize on its behalf (Finnegan 1989: 255–272). The model for its organization is grounded in the model of peer-group relations its members have at their disposal.

To the extent that in adolescence peer groups continue to be organized on same-sex lines and extensive mixed-sex but nonsexual interactions remain problematic, girls face significant social as well as cultural obstacles to participation in rock bands. The consequences are as follows: (1) Girls and women are, as we have seen, much less likely to become members of rock groups. (2) When they do participate, they typically bring fewer resources which would allow them authoritative participation: cultural authority, technical expertise, the social and interactional skills which come with years of experience playing in bands. And (3), they continue to be represented disproportionately as vocalists.

TWO WOMEN VOCALISTS: GRANIA AND PAIGE

My analysis here focuses on two women singers, each of whom was a member of a campus-based band at the time of the interview. Grania's band was a pop-oriented group which played covers exclusively.[3] Paige's band performed a combination of rock and rock-inflected traditional music; they played some originals and aspired to develop more of their own material. Both groups may be termed rock-oriented because of their reliance on the traditional electric guitar-bass-drums lineup and their self-identification as *bands* or groups, that is, their adherence to the social model of rock musicianship.

Grania's and Paige's musical backgrounds display marked similarities. Before college, both participated in musical comedy/drama, which represented their major experience in solo musical performance. In addition, each had studied voice formally and sung in school-based choral music groups. In other words, both drew upon similar resources—voice training, experience in public performance—skills acquired through participating in "official" school culture, that is, activities sponsored, sanctioned, and usually supervised, by adults. The adult-sponsored culture of the school seems to be where girls find opportunities for performance, in contrast to the experience of the male band members I interviewed, who had little or no experience with adult-sanctioned and directed performance genres. Neither woman had performed with a rock band prior to college.

What was most striking, in each interview, was a focus, emerging quite spontaneously, on the problematic status of the singer as a "real" musician. For both Grania and Paige, being a vocalist was the most marked factor differentiating them from their bandmates, and it demanded an explanation. This differentiation between singing and playing is revealed, for example, when Paige describes her fellow band members' failure to comment on her efforts as they did each others': "There was *never* really any feedback on *how* I was singing. At first it was like wow you are a great singer, this is so great, but then after that it wasn't really considered an instrument. There would always be comments on people's solos or how people were working in the arrangements, but there was never any feedback on the singer." This comment demonstrates the different understanding of singing and instrument playing held by the band members. Initially they recognized that Paige was a gifted singer; after this, however, her contribution was, in her view, taken as a given, not subject to development and thus not subject to a continuing process of critique and refinement. Their failure to comment on the vocals as they did on the instrumentals may have been caused by an outright devaluing of vocal performance, a view of it as a subsidiary element in the hierarchy of music-making tasks. Alternatively, this silence may have reflected their lack of an available language for discussing and critiquing vocal music. Yet the absence of such a language, among individuals who had been active musicians throughout their adolescence, is itself an indication that singing was not highly valued. Vocal competence was rendered invisible and thus symbolically nonexistent by the lack of critical vocabulary through which it could be recognized and valued.

After an initial period of campus success, the band quickly progressed to off-campus gigs and hopes of a record contract. At this point, Paige did begin to receive comments about her singing as part of a more general response to the higher level of aspirations that now emerged. Yet the nature of these comments was consistent with the earlier silence, for they focused almost exclusively on issues of pitch. Paige commented that

> nobody ever said anything about my vocals and all of a sudden the only thing that's being said is "oh you know you were off tune a little bit the last time we played . . . the intonation on the so and so is not" . . . I've said, "what's the fascination with pitch all of a sudden. . . . It's not so much like I'm taking it personally that I feel like you never listened to me all along. You never gave me any suggestions. I formulated my style of singing."

Here Paige objects to the naturalization of singing which is implicit in the view that pitch is the only thing that can go wrong with someone's singing. The exclusive focus on pitch, a "natural" component of singing (i.e., "she has perfect pitch"), worked to deny that singing involved skill and artistry and maintained its classification as a "natural" activity.

In contrast, both Paige and Grania understand the voice as an instrument. Paige implied this when she castigated her bandmates for excluding singing from the critical process and thus failing to recognize her work as a musician. And Grania was explicit and adamant in her claim for the instrumental status of the voice.

One way she did this was to stress the importance of her vocal training. She had begun to study voice at college, a process which required at least a year of concentration on vocal exercises before she was deemed ready to begin singing songs. For Grania, singing is a physically demanding feat which her vocal training enabled her to undertake:

> People taking singing lessons a lot of times so that they can go in and sing songs and really for the first year you don't do that at all. . . . Singing is such a physical thing that I'm exhausted after I've sung for a couple of hours, or even an hour, if I am really singing out. . . . You can have a beautiful voice and not be able to use it at all because you just can't hold the note or you can't sustain something. You don't have a certain quality that needs more or less air to create it. . . . I think I've made huge, huge strides this year. . . . I think my range and my abilities have just expanded so much.

While she recognizes a beautiful voice as a physical gift, she is insistent that its potential can only be realized by means of rigorous study and practice.

STRATEGIES OF RESISTANCE

How can women vocalists respond to the process of marginalization and devaluation implicit in the naturalizing of vocal performance? What kinds of interpretive options might they pursue in order to reject this implicit subordination and assert artistic authority for themselves? Their comments reveal that both Paige and Grania employed concepts of skill and artistry to understand their contributions and those of fellow band members. But they adopted quite different strategies to negotiate their respective positions and understand the respective character of their contributions.

In accord with her emphasis on the importance of technical training, Grania viewed singing as a more difficult, indeed a riskier activity than the instrumental playing of her fellow band members: "there's a huge difference between the fact that I am my instrument and someone else holds their instrument. For me to hit a high note or to hit a note with a certain quality takes a certain amount of technique or certain knowledge or a certain amount of feeling to get a certain sound. Whereas I think you are hitting a keyboard the sound is going to come out and you just have to be there to do it."

But while arguing that good singing requires *technical* expertise and training, Grania also held singing to be superior by virtue of its greater *artistic* possibilities. She saw a greater identification between singer and sound: "with a voice, I feel like there's sort of more at stake almost because it's you. It's you that's making the sound. The issue of emotion doesn't really come in when you are playing bass." Dedicated instrumentalists would presumably reject these claims; indeed, as we have seen, Grania made them in implicit opposition to the more usual hierarchy of musical authority and creativity. For while she pointed to the emotionality of singing, in contrast to instrument playing, she was careful to emphasize that singing is not a simple or "natural" outpouring of some inner essence of emotion or physicality. Rather, she as singer must constantly engage in the making of artistic choices and face questions about interpretation:

They [instrumentalists] don't have to cultivate a certain attitude or certain something in a song. Whereas in every song I have to have a different goal or different sound or a different emotion when I am singing it. . . .

These guys do their solos, and in that way they are creating and they are really good, but they still have to follow a real basic structure and they still have to be there so I can get my note. But I have much more leeway to change what I am doing than they do, I guess . . . I mean you can get emotion out of a guitar, like when you are making a guitar solo and you can feel it. . . . But I think it's more obvious or more consistently obvious with the singer because they need to project a certain feeling or a certain sound with their voice no matter what note they are singing, no matter what word they are singing.

When pushed, Grania conceded that more accomplished instrumental musicians might reach levels of artistry which parallel those she identified in singing. Yet her strategy is clear: she dealt with the anomalous position of women vocalist by positioning vocal musicianship as, at a minimum, equally skilled and virtuosic, equally expressive, to the musicianship of any instrumental playing. Indeed she went so far as to invert the received hierarchy of value, tending to portray the voice as the superior medium in terms of both skill and artistry.

In contrast, Paige engaged in a more ambivalent set of moves. On the one hand, she, as noted, objected to the band's differential treatment, their failure to recognize the voice as an instrument analogous to theirs. Yet unlike Grania, she viewed her previous years of vocal training as largely irrelevant to her current musical activities.

> MAC: Do you think it's been useful to you what you have done?
> Paige: Only the very basics. Like I know how to breathe and sometimes when I'm in a really tense situation I'll think breathe through your diaphragm—but not really. The music that I learned I'm glad I know but the technique certainly I don't use.

When pressed, Paige also recognized that she had learned stage presence and an ease in performance through her earlier participation in musical comedy and in a high school gospel chorus. Yet her perception of her own musical expertise was structured by the comparisons she drew between her past experiences and those of others in the band. She noted that

> All of them . . . had a lot of training . . . I still don't and didn't then have the vaguest clue how to arrange a song. I didn't know what a stop was and I didn't know what a fill was.
> MAC: And how did they learn those things?
> Paige: They had *all* been in bands.

It seems logical that Paige, like Grania, could have responded by challenging the devaluation of her vocal contributions. She was both aware and resentful of the lack of recognition that band members gave her singing, and particularly their failure to understand that singing was, like playing, a form of skill and a mode of artistic expression. Indeed she emphasized that for the audience, she was indeed the most visible and important member of the band: "I don't think there's a recognition of the fact that I'm very important . . . people will notice if the lead singer isn't there . . . there's no recognition of the dynamic of what that means to an audience at all . . . I was the reason why a lot of people go to see them." Yet even as she argued for the value of her contribution as singer, Paige pursued an alternative strategy: she sought public visibility as a guitarist.

Paige had played acoustic guitar intermittently since her early teens, when she espoused "a flower child personna" and "listened to a lot of Joni Mitchell." In the early life of the band she continued to play acoustic guitar on some songs, while on others she "didn't play . . . and got to dance around and stuff. . . . I was playing acoustic guitar but I really wasn't. . . . I had a pickup and everything but you just *didn't* hear me at all in the band." She was, in her words, "basically a show piece." Eventually she decided that she too would play electric guitar.

At this point in the interview, where Paige explains her decision to play electric, she juxtaposes comments about the band's failure to recognize the importance of her contributions as lead singer, that is, an assertion of the artistic authority of the vocalist, with an alternative view—that in order to become an equal and central part of this group she would have to play: "this fall I decided that it's ridiculous just pretending to play guitar—why don't I either put it down or really start playing and so I decided to switch to electric."

Paige decided to seek musical authority through the guitar: "*I wanted to not be like the traditional girl singer.*" In doing this, she implicitly accepted the dominant ideology that she had previously criticized: the assumption that instrument playing is the highest form of musicianship. Her attempt to appropriate this ideology on her own behalf was not unproblematic.

Although Paige had played acoustic guitar as an accompaniment to her singing, she had never played in a band. Only when she picked up an electric guitar and attempted to play did she begin to develop a concept of ensemble performance: "I didn't know that just strumming along would just muddy up the whole sound . . . I didn't know different techniques that will complement different styles and stuff. You have to *learn* to play parts that will be complimentary to the rest of the band." Years of listening to pop music, singing, and at least dabbling with a solo instrument had not provided Paige with the knowledge that became so obvious to her once she started to play more assertively.

Paige's lack of skill made it "hard for everybody," producing tensions at a time when the band was under pressure to play its best. As a beginning electric guitarist in a group of accomplished musicians, she was given the criticism she had not received as a singer. In part this must be attributed to her lesser skills as a guitarist as well as to the band members' ready language for talking about guitar playing which they lacked for voice. But as a woman, she was also the recipient of somewhat different treatment, as when one of the band members asked another, the individual she had become personally involved with, whether it was "a good idea" for Paige to play.

This unwillingness to confront Paige directly seemed to her a clear indication that, in at least one person's eyes, she was not a "real" member of the band, and moreover, that her participation was most appropriately controlled through negotiation among men rather than through a direct address to her as a peer. In response to such an insinuation, Paige was confrontational, responding that "*I play guitar in the band.*"

Paige had come to believe that she must appropriate the authority of an instrument player in order to gain acceptance and power as a musician. Moreover, she clearly saw her band's willingness to let her play as a key indicator, a test, of their willingness to see her as a "real musician" and a full member of the collectivity. Such a strategy stands in distinct contrast to Grania's calm assertion of singing as the core activity of music making.

Yet Paige, like Grania, invoked the expressivity of her singing as a source of legitimation. She was critical of what she saw as the dominant ethos in the band: "a real disdain for sentimentalism," as typified by one musician's comment that "just because somebody has a microphone doesn't mean I want to hear them *pour* their heart out." Against the dominant band aesthetic of post-punk quirkiness, camp, whimsicality, and abhorence of affect, Paige posed a commitment to meaning and a willingness to express sentiment, if not sentimentality: "I would like to talk about the world and have a song to sing about it, or sing a song that I have a real feeling invested in." Moreover, Paige called on her relationship to the audience to legitimate these claims: "blues tunes that are really soulful that we do, people like it . . . but there's a real split and I don't think Todd and Gregory realize that people have an *emotional attachment* to things we were singing." Here Paige valorizes an idea of performance as a vehicle for emotional expression and a positive view of the power of such expression, grounded in a relationship with an audience. In these strands of her discussion, she comes much closer to Grania's idea of singing as a uniquely personal vehicle of artistry and self-expression.

DILEMMAS OF GENDERED MUSICIANSHIP

What, beyond differences of temperament and self-concept, accounts for the differing strategies chosen by Grania and Paige? What kinds of social resources were the two women able to draw upon to establish their musical identities? And to what extent do their self-accounts and behaviors serve to maintain or disrupt dominant social realities of gendered musicianship?

Grania tends to explain her harmonious relationship with her band, a relationship in which she clearly feels empowered, in terms of their recognition of her strengths in performance. She notes that she is older than they are and that this may affect the feeling of "awe emanating from them." But above all, she notes that they are "sort of impressed," especially when she sings songs that are especially "emotional" or "sexy": "There are a couple of songs that have this sort of emotional thing. And I found that—when I do something new with my voice or when I am being effective at it, they are all—like kind of standing around listening. They tend to sort of come and stand really close to where I am. I don't know. I think there's some crushes happening." Grania sees her band relating to her in part as an audience, in awe of her ability to express emotions and sexuality through song. And although Grania has earlier expressed concern about the sexualization of women in the pop music industry, it is clear she understands her own powers as at least partly contingent on such representations.

It is both logical and likely that Grania is correct in this interpretation. Yet her focus obscures other factors, more structural in character, that may contribute equally to her feelings of power and competence. One of her formative musical experiences was her participation in a campus women's singing group in which voice was the sole instrument. Although singing and performing under college auspices, the group was wholly managed by its members, who were responsible for finding and selecting songs for their repertoire, developing arrangements, and assigning solos. Through her participation, Grania, unlike Paige, had been substantially involved in collective, self-directed music-making with peers. This resource was important, for some part of her confidence undoubtedly derived from past experience in negotiating song selection, arranging, and other group processes.

In addition, Grania's musical aspirations were formed primarily within the pop model of vocalist and anonymous backing band. Grania's early tastes were shaped by her father's involvement with fifties pop and jazz. Moreover, her adolescent interests were centered around Top Forty pop, in contrast to friends who listened to sixties rock such as the Beatles and Stones plus, in Grania's words, more "offbeat stuff" such as Squeeze, Elvis Costello, and the Police. "In high school I always felt like I was a little bit out of it," and this distance may be seen as a demarcation between music produced by musicians working in the rock or guitar band model versus Grania's gravitation toward a pop, voice-oriented style.

Paige, on the other hand, veered during adolescence between an early seventies folk and folk-rock orientation (i.e., another form of voice orientation), which she associated with her best woman friend ("who didn't like anything 'hard' at all"), and a taste for what she describes as "male music," which was invariably encouraged by boyfriends.

I guess guys always introduced me to *male* music. My boyfriend in the beginning of high school our sophomore year was obsessed with Talking Heads. . . . I was hanging out with a bunch of college film majors when I was in high school so that's where I learned about what seemed like weird alternative stuff, like Talking Heads, Brian Eno, stuff like Fred Frith and Robert Fripp. Then when I was going out with somebody a lot older than me in my junior and senior year he gave me a lot of Elvis Costello . . . which now I love.

A hierarchy of taste is at work in Paige's comments, as when she notes that "what's *easiest* for me to listen to is Joan Armatrading—type stuff." She reports having "this reaction against so-called women's music" which she finds "really accessible," and as a result, she "kind of stagnated listening to it."

Because she enjoyed rock, punk, and new wave, genres which identity the band as the unit of creativity, Paige was thrilled to be asked to join a band; it was, for her, a "dream come true." Her history illustrates the problems that young women may have in gaining access to participation in peer-oriented bands, even when they aspire to do so. Asked why she had never been in a band before, given her interest, she responded: "Because I didn't have the initiative to start one. . . . It is a *skill* and I don't, I'm not, unless I wanted to start a *cover* band, I don't write songs, or I didn't then—I'm not a great guitar player. I certainly would have joined any band if I'd been asked but . . ." Paige blames herself, seeing the ability to start a band as a skill she lacks. In fact, like so many others, she was asked to join because of a mutual acquaintance who knew she sang. She exemplifies the ways in which participation is contingent upon access to relevant social networks. As a girl, as a singer, Paige had no sense that she could start a band herself, no sense of having social networks she could or should activate to do so. Yet once in a band, both her musical tastes and her view of music making as a social process involved a desire to be a part of a unit. In contrast, Grania's pop influences lead her to think of musicians more as a backdrop or an accompaniment to singing.

It would be all too easy to identify Grania as a serene heroine, secure in a conception of autonomous womanhood, while marking Paige as a sellout or a dupe, mistakenly trying to conform to male standards and values. This would be incorrect. Each woman engaged in efforts to combat her double marginalization, to subvert dominant understandings of the role of woman vocalist in a band. To affirm difference and to assert similarity are the options which typically present themselves to oppressed and marginalized groups seeking equality. Each strategic move, both the valorization of singing and the appropriation of instrumental power, represents a necessarily problematic choice, each with drawbacks as well as rewards.

In her insistence on playing electric guitar, an activity coded male, Paige seemed to accede to the standards and values of what she herself called "male music." It is arguable that this decision served to ratify the devaluation of vocal music, and with it the denial of a mode of artistic authority which is implicitly feminine. Yet it cannot be seen as a simple act of submission, for it grew from a large schema of resistance and self-assertion. First, Paige was articulate in criticizing fellow band members for their failure to recognize the centrality of her vocal contributions. Second, while she accepted, to a significant degree, the conventions of the rock or band model, she vehemently rejected the role to which such a model would conventionally assign her. Moreover she did this in terms of an explicit gender consciousness, a clearly articulated view that to be "just the girl singer" was to accept a marginalized identity. In her view, if the band was the creative unit of music making, its center of power, she must play to be part of it. Finally, whatever its symbolic implications, her decision necessitated a high degree of resistant behavior. In pursuit of her goal, Paige was willing to be actively disruptive, to provoke and tolerate significant levels of tension, to make herself vulnerable to criticism, in order to assert that she was fully a member of the band. Her resistance was enacted in day-to-day struggles which in and of themselves violated gender conventions and articulated an alternative conception of feminine agency.

Grania's stance seems the more radical. Her resistance took the form of rejecting, indeed overturning, the established hierarchy of musical value by asserting the superiority of vocal musicianship as both craft and interpretive art. Demanding that the voice be recognized as an instrument, and pointing to the training and skill required for its effective use, served to "denaturalize" vocal expression and portray it as a highly and necessarily social activity.

Still, much of Grania's understanding of her artistry rested on her ability to convey emotion and express sexuality, which she felt instrumental music could not easily do. Here one must ask what it means for women to claim artistic authority primarily on the basis of superior expressive gifts and the ability to establish an emotional relationship with an audience. In affirming difference, Grania risked implicating herself in a sexual division of labor which assumes, and thus essentializes, feminine

251

expressivity and masculine rationality. Like Paige, Grania's mode of resistance involved her in contradictory claims.

Finally, it is important to recognize that my focus on individuals here should not be read as a claim that individual acts of resistance are the most meaningful and efficacious. Grania and Paige should be seen rather as figures who delineate available options. The social organization of popular music-making provides, limits, and shapes the choices available to individuals, and such choices are rarely unambiguous. Thus the alternatives confronting Grania and Paige should not be characterized as a stark choice between an autonomous "women's music," if such could exist, and submission to a "masculine" model. It is rather a question of understanding the costs and rewards to women who seek to assert artistic authority in the various genres of mass-marketed, male-dominated popular music. For white women like Grania and Paige, the major options are represented by the male-oriented peer groups of rock music, which operate on a craft model of musicianship which has historically excluded women, versus the pop model, with its more highly articulated division of labor between singers, musicians, and producer-arrangers, a division of labor which has traditionally allowed for women's participation within the context of masculine authority and feminine subordination.

Ultimately, if they continue to perform and find any degree of commercial success, each woman's options will be increasingly defined by the marketing and product-development strategies of a multi-million-dollar music industry. Only rarely does an individual such as Madonna emerge whose creativity and tenacity allow her to turn pop music conventions to the task of subversion. And even Madonna's success, as McClary (1991:150) notes, rests on her ability "to speak intelligibly to the cultural experiences and perceptions of her audience." That Madonna could be read as subversive, that Grania could assert the superiority of vocal music, that Paige could demand as a right to play electric guitar—all these acts of resistance, seemingly individual in character, draw on resources derived, at least in part, from the collective struggles of two decades of feminism. As Susan Bordo writes in the final chapter of this volume, "What this celebration of creative-reading-as-resistance effaces is the arduous and frequently frustrated historical struggle required for the subordinate to articulate and assert the value of their 'difference' in the face of dominant meanings. . . . what Fiske calls 'the power of being different' . . . is won through ongoing political *struggle* rather than through an act of creative interpretation" (see also Clarke 1990:40). Grania's and Paige's stories are meaningful only when placed within this larger framework of structure and contestation.

NOTES

1. Controversies about replacement of band members during recording sessions even include charges that Ringo Starr did not play on early Beatles records. See Weinberg and Santelli 1984:68–70, 187.

2. Laing (1985:41–50) highlights the importance of naming practices in producing expectations about bands and their musical styles.

3. A cover is a song that has already been recorded and popularized by another performer. The existence of a special term to designate songs not originated by the band reveals the rock assumption that bands are, ideally, the creators of their own material.

REFERENCES

Bayton, Mavis. 1990. "How Women Become Musicians." In *On Record: Rock, Pop, and the Written Word*, ed. Simon Frith and Andrew Goodwin. New York: Pantheon.

Becker, Howard S. 1982. *Art Worlds*. Berkeley: University of California Press.

Bennett, H. Stith. 1980. *On Becoming a Rock Musician*. Amherst: University of Massachusetts Press.

Bloch, Maurice, and Jean H. Bloch. 1980. "Women and the Dialectics of Nature in Eighteenth-Century French Thought." In *Nature, Culture and Gender*, ed. Carol MacCormack and Marilyn Strathern. Cambridge: Cambridge University Press.

Clarke, John. 1990. "Pessimism versus Populism: The Problematic Politics of Popular Culture." In *For Fun and Profit: The Transformation of Leisure into Consumption*, ed. Richard Butsch. Philadelphia: Temple University Press.

Dahl, Linda. 1984. *Stormy Weather: The Music and Lives of a Century of Jazzwomen*. New York: Pantheon.

Eder, Donna, and Maureen T. Hallinan. 1978. "Sex Differences in Children's Friendships." *American Sociological Review* 43:237–249.

Fine, Gary Alan. 1980. "The Natural History of Preadolescent Male Friendship Cultures." In Friendship and Social Relations in Children, ed. Hugh C. Foot and Anthony J. Chapman. New York: John Wiley.

Finnegan, Ruth. 1989. *The Hidden Musicians: Music-Making in an English Town*. Cambridge: Cambridge University Press.

Frith, Simon. 1981. *Sound Effects: Youth, Leisure and the Politics of Rock 'n' Roll*. New York: Pantheon.

Groce, Stephen B., and Margaret Cooper. 1990. "Just Me and the Boys? Women in Local-Level Rock and Roll." *Gender and Society* 4(2):220–229.

Jordanova, L. L. 1980. "Natural Facts: A Historical Perspective on Science and Sexuality." In *Nature, Culture and Gender*, ed. Carol MacCormack and Marilyn Strathern. Cambridge: Cambridge University Press.

Kogan, Judith. 1987. *Nothing but the Best: The Struggle for Perfection at the Julliard School*. New York: Random House.

Laing, Dave. 1985. *One Chord Wonders: Power and Meaning in Punk Rock.* Milton Keynes, England: Open University Press.

Lever, Janet. 1976. "Sex Differences in the Games Children Play." *Social Problems* 23:478–487.

Lewis, Lisa A. 1990. *Gender Politics and MTV: Voicing the Difference.* Philadelphia: Temple University Press.

McClary, Susan. 1991. *Feminine Endings: Music, Gender, and Sexuality.* Minneapolis: University of Minnesota Press.

Maccoby, Eleanor E. 1986. "Social Groupings in Childhood: Their Relationship to Prosocial and Antisocial Behavior in Boys and Girls." In *Development of Antisocial and Prosocial Behavior,* ed. Dan Olweuer, Jack Block, and Marian Radke-Yarrow. San Diego: Academic Press.

Ortner, Sherry B. 1974. "Is Woman to Man as Nature Is to Culture?" In *Woman, Culture and Society,* ed. Michelle Z. Rosaldo and Louise Lamphere. Stanford: Stanford University Press.

Thorne, Barrie. 1989. "Girls and Boys Together . . . but Mostly Apart: Gender Arrangements in Elementary Schools." In *Feminist Frontiers II,* ed. Laurel Richardson and Verta Taylor. New York: Random House.

Thorne, Barrie, and Zella Luria. 1986. "Sexuality and Gender in Children's Daily Worlds." *Social Problems* 33:176–190.

Weinberg, Max, and Robert Santelli. 1984. *The Big Beat: Conversations with Rock's Great Drummers.* Chicago: Contemporary Book.

VEILED AGENTS:
FEMININE AGENCY AND
MASQUERADE IN
THE BATTLE OF ALGIERS

Norma Claire Moruzzi

I swear I'm not a hero. The hero is Algeria. As for me, well, I was only one person in a large group. The leader of our group in the Qasbah district of Algiers would assign each of us a job to be done in a certain place at a certain time. And we would do it. My job was to plant bombs. I carried death with me in my hand-bag, death in the shape of time bombs.

—Interview with Jamilah Buhrayd [1]

This chapter, in examining the ways women negotiate their identity at the margins of established and institutionalized powers, deals with this negotiation at two levels, that of form and that of content. While the subject of the essay is an analysis of women's negotiations at the margins of feminine and nationalist identity constructions, as presented in Gillo Pontecorvo's 1966 film *The Battle of Algiers,* the essay itself attempts to negotiate between the often widely separate concerns of nationalist political and psychoanalytic feminist analyses.

Specifically, the essay explores the relationship between women's political agency and their own self-representation as gendered subjects, in a political situation in which the cultural designations of a feminine identity seemingly belie any active political involvement. The Algerian women who participated as guerrillas in the Algerian Revolution used their traditional veils or modern Western clothing interchangeably as a form of feminine masquerade; they styled themselves as subjects whose feminine and national cultural identities would publicly discount any possibility of radical political action, precisely in order to carry out such actions unsuspected. Their agency, through their roles as revolutionary agents, was shrouded in the protective veilings of their feminine masquerade, whether those veilings were the long white robes of traditional Algerian women's clothing or the short skirts of apparent French acculturation.

This combination of feminine masquerade and political agency is well represented in Pontecorvo's *Battle of Algiers*. In order to explicate certain scenes in the film and the historical events those scenes re-create, this essay draws on arguments from political and psychoanalytic theory, especially those of Frantz Fanon and Luce Irigaray. Irigaray's discussion of the role of the feminine as a masquerade, when read alongside Fanon's analysis of the meaning of the veil, or its removal, for the women guerrillas of the Algerian Revolution, extends and deepens the theoretical significance of Pontecorvo's cinematic representations. By considering the film scenes in the context of certain political and psychoanalytic arguments, we can clearly recognize them as illustrations of women achieving political agency through feminine masquerade.

Thus, while the women represented in the film are negotiating at the margins of feminine and national identity, the essay itself is also negotiating at the political margins of feminist, cultural, and film studies material. In this sense, the essay is an attempt not only to make a point about women's political agency and the relationship between their agency and feminine masquerade, but also to write a bridge between political theory and feminist psychoanalytic theory. Individually, neither Fanon nor Irigaray fully covers the gap that so often exists between these two forms of intellectual analysis. (Similarly, the film itself is a cinematic representation of a specific, local national political struggle and does not explicitly develop the theoretical ambiguities it so brilliantly conveys.) By presenting the political and psychoanalytic arguments in conjunction, the essay attempts to bring them both to bear on the film as an illustration of feminine agency and masquerade. To the extent that the film functions as an illustration of the relationship between agency and masquerade, it also functions as a bridge between the separate disciplines of psychoanalytic feminist and political analysis.

Between these two intellectual perspectives lies the problem of women's political agency. Certainly women often participate as active subjects in contemporary political life, but it remains unclear to what degree their participation is still conceptualized as an odd intrusion into what was traditionally defined as a masculine sphere of public action. Often enough it has been assumed that women need to be liberated from the mysterious constructions of the feminine if they are to be fully constituted as active political subjects. Yet the question of essentialism haunts feminism.[2] Although for a long time most have agreed with Simone de Beauvoir that women are made and not born, we still are not sure who or what exactly makes them, especially in those cultural situations in which conflicting definitions of the feminine compete in the same field of reference. How then can women's existence as gendered subjects, or their struggle as political beings, be evaluated if we are not sure what it is that makes them women? The problem of the social construction of the body, of the feminine, of the very notion of woman herself, problematizes issues of cultural analysis and political agency. In addition, despite a variety of emancipatory projects both theoretical and practical, there has been a lurking suspicion that liberation from the category of the feminine may be neither easy nor desirable. Instead, it may be far more useful to explore the ways in which women negotiate versions of the feminine within their experiences of fragmented and often contradictory social identities; this is the position which guides this essay.

Women are made by different discourses that define the gendered female subject, but these discourses can often make the same subject out to be different women. Discourse is not simply a manner of speech or a conversation, but the long genealogy of cultural and political assumptions that align themselves into a contemporary perspective and practice. A set of social practices which one local discourse interprets as the traditional designation of women's oppression may be recognized by another competing discourse as the new characteristic of a radical feminine agency. Thus the behavior of any one woman may tell a very different story, depending on whether the discourse in which her behaviors are codified is primarily defined as religious or secular, ethnic or nationalist, personal or political.

Fragmented though women's experience of feminine subjectivity may be, they maneuver through social, political, and cultural contexts in which their agency places into question any clear distinction between traditional absolutes and modern liberation. Women, whose gendered roles may be understood to be figured by historical and cultural location, by specific geography in a landscape of intersecting loci of traditions and powers, act within that landscape even as their movements shift its constructions. For women, personal identity and agency may as often be manifested through the reappropriation of the traditional designations of the feminine, as through the initiation of some supposedly original, newly emancipated code of behavior. The issue is perhaps not so much the essential content of femininity as the various forms in which women negotiate as feminine subjects with the powers that mark them as such.

THE FILM: THE BASIC STORY

In Pontecorvo's *Battle of Algiers,* the women protagonists, who are closely modeled on the women urban guerrillas of the Algerian Revolution, plant time bombs in three crowded areas in the French section of Algiers: a café, an open-air discothèque, and the Air France terminal. The bombs go off, with devastating effect. To complete their missions the women first must cross from the Casbah into the more modern French city through military checkpoints used by the French to seal off the Arab sector of Algiers. To get through the checkpoints the women in the film, like the women they portray, remove their traditional veils and put on the Western clothing and makeup that enable them to pass as French-Algerian, rather than Arab-Algerian, women. Unveiled, the women are unsuspected. The whole episode, from the women's unveiling through to the bombs' explosions, is one of the central dramas of the film.

These scenes, like much of the rest of the film, are accurate re-creations of actual events. Zohra Drif, Jamilah Buhrayd, and Samia Lakhdari all met with Yacef Saadi, the FLN military commander of Algiers, on 30 September 1956.[3] In retaliation for the French bombing of a civilian house in the Casbah in which seventy people were killed, the young women were to deliver their bombs to civilian targets in French Algiers, and in order to do, they agreed to remove their veils and pretend to be French. In his history of the Algerian Revolution, Alistair Horne (1978:185) describes the incident this way:

> They had been chosen for the job because, with their feminine allure and European looks, they could pass where a male terrorist could not. Noting the shock on their faces, Yacef treated them to a vivid description of the horrors of the Rue de Thèbes outrage, and told them that they were to avenge the Muslim children killed in it. Taking off their veils, the girls tinted their hair and put on the kind of bright, summery dresses and slacks that *pied noir* girls might wear for a day at the beach.[4]

The women remove the veils that identify them as traditional or anti-colonial Arab-Algerian women and put on the clothes and cosmetics that serve to identify them as women who are either Westernized Arabs sympathetic to French colonial rule or French colonial *pied noirs.* In effect, both in life and in the film, the women exchange one set of gendered cultural markers for another. In taking off their veils, they assume a disguise.[5]

FANON: THE DISCOURSE OF POSTCOLONIAL NATIONALISM

Pontecorvo's writing of the film's scenes was informed by Frantz Fanon's extensive analysis of the political use of the veil in the Algerian Revolution (Mellen 1973:60), but Fanon limits his discussion to the specific details of the revolutionary confrontation between colonizer and colonized. In his essay "Algeria Unveiled," Fanon (1965), while respecting the veiled woman as a symbol of Algerian national resistance to the colonial imposition of French cultural norms, equates the beginning of women's overt participation in the Revolution with their removal of their veils.[6] While the veiled woman is capable of symbolic action, her strategic removal of her veil allows her a freer agency, and she herself can take on the role of the (woman) revolutionary.

But Fanon locates the role of the female revolutionary entirely in the Algerian context and sees the veiled women's transfiguration into revolutionaries as complete.[7] He does not address the specific problems of feminine identity and agency, with or without the veil. Rather, the Algerian women's politicization and unveiling as revolutionaries seem to indicate that they are no longer socially constructed as ordinary women. Their appearance, unveiled, and their direct political and military participation in the Revolution would seem to emancipate them from the play of gender itself.

As revolutionaries, these women become authentic political actors, while ordinary women, even politically active women, remain apparently lacking in agency and authenticity. Fanon (1965:50) explicitly rejects any comparison between the unveiled Algerian revolutionaries, whose political activism is inextricable from their feminine transformation, and "women resistance fighters or even secret agents of the specialized services," whose politicization leaves the public presentation of their gendered identity intact. (Fanon seems here to be referring, for instance, to women members of the French Resistance, whose nationalist anti-Nazi partisanship would not have necessitated the reconstruction of their own French feminine identity.) These other women have not solved the problematic lack of agency within the ordinary construction of feminine iden-

259

tity. Their politicization has not totally transformed the demarcations of that identity, the essence of which is its elusive lack, while the Algerian revolutionary has transcended herself and become an authentic original. The Algerian woman who unveils in order to cover her participation in the FLN experiences a political agency that involves the transformation, but not the abdication, of her socially constructed feminine identity. She is no longer a woman made; she has been reborn:

> It is without apprenticeship, without briefing, without fuss, that she goes out into the street with three grenades in her handbag or the activity report of an area in her bodice. She does not have the sensation of playing a role she has read about ever so many times in novels, or seen in motion pictures. There is not that coefficient of play, of imitation, almost always present in this form of action when we are dealing with a Western woman. . . . It is an authentic birth in a pure state, without preliminary instruction. There is no character to imitate. On the contrary, there is an intense dramatization, a continuity between the woman and the revolutionary. (Fanon 1965 : 50)

Yet this birth is achieved through the manifestation of an imitation; these revolutionaries transcend the limitations of the feminine subject by (re)presenting themselves as different women. Whereas Western women revolutionaries may engage in political practice without necessarily putting the social construction of their identity as women on the line, the Algerian woman revolutionary cannot afford that luxury.

This necessity has its compensations, however. For a Western woman the role of the political secret agent may be experienced as a temporary aberration separate from private life, but Fanon insists that the unveiled Algerian revolutionary has had to experience a political commitment that is far more thorough in that it must involve her most private sense of herself as a woman. Her political agency is founded in her self-conscious transformation of her feminine identity. She is not simply a woman who is participating in revolutionary politics; she is herself a revolutionary woman.

These revolutionaries are not just political agents disguised as women. Later in Pontecorvo's film, several of the FLN leaders attempt to move through the streets of the Casbah disguised as women, but they are immediately spotted and chased by a French patrol because they do such a bad job of it.[8] (Their black pants and shoes stick out from under their white robes and give them away.) But the Arab-Algerian women, in unveiling themselves as revolutionaries, are simultaneously successful in their imitation of French-Algerian women. These are women who disguise themselves as women in order to accomplish radical political actions. Nonetheless, despite Fanon's assertions that the unveiled revolutionaries experience an absolute continuity in their role, he acknowledges that they also find they are profoundly alienated from themselves. The unveiled revolutionary assumes a specific political identity, but as an unveiled woman she experiences certain personal difficulties:

> One must have heard the confessions of Algerian women or have analyzed the dream content of certain recently unveiled women to appreciate the importance of the veil for the body of the woman. Without the veil she has an impression of her body being cut up into bits, put adrift; the limbs seem to lengthen indefinitely. . . . The unveiled body seems to escape, to dissolve. . . . She has the anxious feeling that something is unfinished, and along with this a frightful sensation of disintegrating. (Fanon 1965 : 59)[9]

A revolutionary passing as a (Western) woman, she is also a being experiencing a profound sense of bodily and cultural dislocation. She has a political identity, but her identity as a woman is explicitly constructed as a fake. Her embodied feminine identity as a veiled Arab-Algerian woman has had to be dissolved and rejected because it was politically inexpedient in conjunction with her identity as an active revolutionary. Despite Fanon's analysis, the unveiled revolutionary in her feminine disguise is still confronted with the problem of being a woman, or of learning to be one.

If anything, she confronts the problem of feminine identity and agency all the more forcefully, precisely because her experience of political agency is totally dependent on her personification of a feminine identity that is assumed to be lacking in agency. Yet if her political agency is established as real (in that she is active as a revolutionary and a political agent), her feminine (*pied noir*) identity is proven fake, even though she must continue to rely on it in public life. Her authentic political identity (authentic in that she really does carry bombs) is in contradiction to her apparent feminine identity (the passive, *pied noir* feminine identity she must carry off if she is to complete her mission successfully). What, then, is the real nature of this woman's feminine identity? Indeed, is she really real, or only real enough?

IRIGARAY: THE DISCOURSE OF
FEMININE MASQUERADE

Luce Irigaray (1985 : 68–85) develops an account of the feminine whose essence is an imitation. Rather than attempt to escape or transcend the feminine, or bemoan its ubiquitous lack of essence, Irigaray wants to research its shifting location in the discourse that would subordinate it. Although Irigaray's particular project is a genealogy of the feminine and its subordination in the history of philosophy, her analysis is apt: "There is, in an initial phase, perhaps only one 'path,' the one historically assigned to the feminine: that of *mimicry*. One must assume the feminine role deliberately. Which means already to convert a form of subordination into an affirmation, and thus to begin to thwart it" (1985 : 76). Women are not only made, they make themselves up as women by imitating that which is designated as theirs: the feminine. By becoming self-conscious in this imitation which is also their reality, women can begin to displace the set social constructions that supposedly attach to their role. The woman who begins, in all self-consciousness, to play at being a woman, may discover not an escape from domination, but a means of negotiating with the determinations of her subjectivity.

Feminine mimicry, or masquerade, may allow a (female) subject to acknowledge the genealogy of her own victimization and her practical experience of its constraints without becoming immobilized within the identity of the victim. Irigaray (1985 : 76) suggests that women play at womanliness and, through their experience of that play, reconsider the assumed logic of their domination:

> To play with mimesis is thus, for a woman, to try to recover the place of her exploitation by discourse, without allowing herself to be simply reduced to it. It means to resubmit herself—inasmuch as she is on the side of the "perceptible," of "matter"—to "ideas," in particular to ideas about herself, that are elaborated in/by a masculine logic, but so as to make "visible," by an effect of playful repetition, what was supposed to remain invisible: the cover-up of a possible operation of the feminine in language. It also means "to unveil" the fact that, if women are such good mimics, it is because they are not simply resorbed in this function.

In Irigaray's account, the unveiling is neither a revelation of some hidden truth or authenticity nor a liberation into freedom. Rather, this unveiling, like the unveiling in Pontecorvo's film and the unveiling of the Algerian revolutionaries themselves, involves the perpetuation of a feminine masquerade. What is unveiled is not the woman behind the mask, but the fact of the masquerade itself—not truth, but knowledge.

The veil removed is not the feminine agent's veil of artifice, but the veil of ignorance which has covered the eyes of the beholder; unveiled, we as spectators can recognize the operation of a feminine agency, of the feminine agent who remains veiled in her masquerade. The unveiling does not deliver the agent herself into agency, but may allow the spectator to recognize the feminine agent's agency within her veiled or unveiled masquerade. The unveiling is for the benefit of the spectator. The mysterious gauze of artifice has not been removed or become transparent, but now we can recognize and appreciate it for what it is, whatever its manifestation or drapery.

Irigaray explicitly rejects the question of an essence behind the masquerade. Feminine identity is the masquerade and its genealogy; hence Irigaray's own concern with the discourse of the history of philosophy as the field in which to site the feminine masquerade in its various appearances. Those who seek to unravel the mystery of feminine identity should instead attend to the affect of its various dis-guises:

> They should not put it, then, in the form "What is woman?" but rather, repeating/interpreting the way in which, within discourse, the feminine finds itself defined as lack, deficiency, or as imitation and negative image of the subject, they should signify that with respect to this logic a *disruptive excess* is possible on the feminine side. An excess that exceeds common sense only on condition that the feminine not renounce its "style." Which, of course, is not a style at all, according to the traditional way of looking at things. (Irigaray 1985:78)

In this analysis, style is not separable from content. Irigaray poses a feminine style that can be recognized as radical and various in that its negative and elusive essence has always been embodied by a multiplicity of female players. While it may not be possible to define woman, women can continue to experience the essential excess that accompanies their singular lack of centrality. The task of the theorist is not to fill an empty space, reveal a secret truth, or answer an age-old question, but to attend to the disruption that can accompany the apparently ordinary manifestations of embodied feminine style played out through the feminine context. It is precisely in and around the space of the traditional lack of female agency that a politics of the feminine can be identified and found.

Found, but not founded. Irigaray (1985:79) defines the active excess of the feminine as style, a fluidly evanescent dynamic rather than a property or a solid mass. This style, premised on a lack (of the means of fully constituted subjectivity) can accomplish a disruptive excess because it does not establish itself as a respectable subject. Feminine disruptive excess does not constitute itself as a full, fixed identity, just as anticolonial disruptive excess does not constitute itself as a full, fixed identity, because to do so, in either case, would be to accept the masculine/colonizer's appropriation of the standards of subjectivity. The woman, like the anticolonial, has no choice but to participate in a dominant discourse in which she is inherently defined as lacking. If she competes for subjectivity within that discourse, she will always be assimilated into an inferior position.[10] If, however, she actively impersonates the style that defines her lack, she may at least begin to evade the necessary determinations of her own subordination.

For the woman engaged in an anticolonial project, the impersonation is extraordinarily complicated. She is dominated by the discourses of gender and nationality; she masquerades as a woman in a context in which feminine style is (at least) twice configured, in discourses that overlap and mimic each other. She must choose her style of self-representation carefully and with vigilance, and her literal unveiling may itself be an attempt to veil her masquerade.

THE FILM: A CINEMATIC DISCOURSE OF FEMININE AGENCY AND MASQUERADE

Given these discursive limitations, Pontecorvo's *Battle of Algiers* is perhaps a peculiarly appropriate text for studying the nature of feminine identity and the possibility for agency. The film presents some of the incidents about which Fanon was writing, but it does not insist on an unveiled revolutionary identity that is other than a feminine representation. In the film, feminine identity is presented as a varying construction, as an imitation of itself, whether veiled or unveiled. There is no question of authenticity.

Indeed, the film itself plays extensively on the relationship between the authentic and its representation, in that it was made to look and sound like a documentary. Influenced by Rossellini and the Italian neorealists, Pontecorvo employs the classic techniques of neorealist cinema: shooting on location; using nonactors found on the street, in restaurants, and in jail; structuring the plot to avoid melodrama and aim for social significance.[11] *The Battle of Algiers,* however, goes further in that it reproduces a documentary style of such verisimilitude that the credits open with a disclaimer: "This dramatic re-enactment of The Battle of Algiers contains NOT ONE FOOT of Newsreel or Documentary Film." In this film, neorealist style functions as a disturbing double for documentary, the supposedly authentic representation of real events.[12] Like the representations of femininity within the film, *The Battle of Algiers* questions the supposed opposition between authenticity and mere style. In the film the women revolutionaries pass themselves off as ordinary women in order to carry out their political actions. The film itself is art made to look like real life, the better to convey its political message. In both cases, the distinction between the supposedly real and its given representation becomes intentionally blurred.

Pontecorvo decided to make the film look like a different kind of representation because the less artificial look of reportage, even a less artificial look very carefully achieved, would be accepted by the audience as more reliable: "Since the people are used to coming into contact with the black and white reality of the mass media—telephotos, TV newsreels, etc.—an image seems most true to them when it resembles those furnished by the media. . . . So not only did I want to shoot in black and white, I also wanted to use the same lenses which would reproduce images like those of the mass media" (Solinas 1973:167). Pontecorvo's film is carefully styled to look like the less careful, less styled, more authentic reportage of mass media. It appropriates this apparently banal technique, a technique that usually belies any radical political or aesthetic intention precisely in order to cloak those intentions with the immediacy of the familiar and the banal. The audience was provided with a style it had come to associate with the authentic or objective representations of television and the newsreel, in order to present it with consciously politicized art.

The Battle of Algiers looks like a newsreel, which looks like real life. Although the film is obviously a carefully crafted aesthetic project, it also documents, through its own representations that are also repetitions, a revolution's events and actors. The film functions as a kind of double or triple representation: it looks like that which looks like the real. As for the real itself, is it not inevitably only comprehensible when recognizable as its own representation?

265

Within the film, feminine identity is also always a multiple-layered construction, organized in terms of an identifiable politics. But Ponte-corvo, unlike Fanon, does not tie women to a teleological trajectory whose endpoint involves the transcendence of the feminine through revo-lutionary self-enactment, and the removal of their veils. The women in the film do not need to unveil to be revolutionaries; they unveil in order to continue as revolutionaries. But we, the untutored spectators of the film, may need to see them unveiled for us to notice them as individuals and to recognize them as revolutionaries and (political) actors.[13] Veiled, they lack identity for us, even though we have seen them carry weapons and supervise the military initiation of one of the most famous FLN mili-tary commanders.

Very early in the film we see veiled women carrying guns which they deliver to the men who carry out the actual assassinations. Later on, when the unveiled women carry and plant their time bombs, we never see women using guns. (This seems in keeping with the urban guerrilla tactics of the FLN. In the cities, women carried weapons and left bombs, but they did not use guns themselves, while women who joined the rural maquis in the mountains carried arms and seem to have used them.)[14] When Ali la Pointe, one of the few named characters in the film and historically one of the most important FLN leaders in Al-giers, is given his first assignment, he is told that the gun will be passed to him, at the right time, by a (veiled) "young girl" with a basket. He meets the young woman, they trail the police officer who has been des-ignated his target, and at a certain point she passes him the gun. But Ali la Pointe wants to confront the Frenchman, so he moves away from his companion, hissing "Let me go" when she grabs at his arm. Face to face with the officer, Ali shoots, but the pistol isn't loaded, and he has to club the officer with the gun, which he then drops. The veiled woman picks it up and dashes away; Ali follows her and, when they are out of sight, hisses "You betrayed me!" But the woman calmly checks for the police, transfers the gun to the waistband of her skirt underneath her veils, and informs Ali that she is going to take him to meet the man who arranged it all—Djafar (played by Yacef Saadi, who had in fact organized precisely this political initiation for the historical Ali la Pointe) (Horne 1978:187). Notice that the entire initiation has been supervised by a woman.

The first veiled, anonymous woman who carries the gun and knows better than the gunman when is the "right time" to use it is already a fully participating revolutionary, even if she has not been unveiled as such. In a sense, at this point in the film she has not been unveiled in any way: we see neither her face nor her masquerade. The first Arab-Algerian woman whom we see unveiled is not a guerrilla, although she is a revolutionary agent. She is a bride, dressed in Western clothes, whose marriage is clandestinely officiated by an FLN officer; the families' evasion of the French colonial authority, and their choice to register the marriage with the FLN instead, is explicitly called "an act of conscience, and an act of war." Although this wedding is treated as an almost idyllic interlude, the scene does more than show the FLN's consolidation of support within the Arab-Algerian community. It also begins to blur the supposed clear demarcations between heroic and modest action. The young couple glance shyly at each other, while the camera cuts from the men surrounding them to pan up to the women, unveiled but in various versions of traditional dress, who watch from the balconies and the upper stories around the courtyard. Then everyone prays.

This scene begins to confound whatever assumptions about constructions of gender and power we may have brought to the film. We have seen a veiled woman carry a gun; now we have seen an unveiled woman who is a revolutionary bride, a woman whose wedding is itself a radical political act, although she herself seems to assume quite a traditional role in it, despite her short, fitted dress. But it is when the Casbah has been sectioned off from the French city so that any passage between the two is through heavily guarded checkpoints that we observe the first flutter of the veil over the feminine masquerade. The woman with the gun assigned to Ali la Pointe was veiled because that was still considered the appropriate guise for a woman in the FLN; the young bride wears a Western-style dress despite or because of the fact that her marriage is being performed privately and in defiance of French authority. But later in the film, when assassinations are being organized from the Casbah to be carried out in the French city, we see a woman for the first time self-consciously enacting her role as a woman, as a masquerade.

A veiled woman walks through the barbed-wire passageway at a checkpoint out of the Casbah, where soldiers routinely check everyone for identification papers and search for weapons. She is stopped by a soldier who lifts his hands to search her; her veil shifts, and she screams abuse at him. He steps back, she steps by, and his partner, looking annoyed, explains, "You're not supposed to touch their women." The woman continues on to a café, where she approaches a man leaning against a wall. She greets him with a double kiss, while passing him a revolver, and he shoots over her shoulder at a police officer.

The (supposed) Arab hysteric, culturally appalled by the effrontery of the French police officer's attempt to impose order on her body (he complains she has no papers), has accomplished her mission. In order to evade the logic of her domination she has, quite consciously, played the part of the irrational other, that feminine role which is hers by definition in the dominant discourse. This feminine role of the mysteriously cloaked and (appropriately) untouchable Arab woman is premised, for the colonial authorities, on a lack of agency that is presumed so absolute that the veiled woman is allowed to pass. Yet it is by fully enacting this lack, by apparently refusing even to understand that she could be considered a subject and a suspect, in need of proper identification, that the woman gets through to help wreak havoc.

The veil is, of course, a disguise. Only after the colonial authorities have realized that veiled women are possibly not at all lacking in disruptive agency is the cloak of feminine lack transferred to unveiled women. Quite possibly the woman who passes through the checkpoint also removes her veil in the scene soon after: perhaps we recognize her eyebrows. In that scene, however, we recognize her unveiling as her disguise, the full enactment of a masquerade.

When the three women who will carry the bombs remove their veils, they touch their faces and smooth their hair while they watch themselves in the mirror, attempting to secure with their hands the faces which are about to be transformed for the eye. There is a moment of quizzical regret. Then one puts on lipstick; one cuts her hair and dyes it; we see them change their clothes. We see them transform themselves, and we see them watch their own transformation. When Djafar (Saadi) comes in, one of the women asks him, "Ça va, monsieur?" The linguistic shift from Arabic to French is part of her impersonation. Her speaking French indicates that she has shifted discourses; she has reconstructed her feminine signification according to French colonial, rather than Algerian nationalist, definitions, although she has done so in order to maintain her agency as an Algerian nationalist. Previously, the women revolutionaries who wore the traditional white veils did so to signify their nationalist solidarity and anticolonial resistance as well as to secure their own (anonymous) disruptive feminine agency. Their veils were also a masquerade. When the women take off their robes, they incidentally unveil for us, the informed spectators who are privileged to the spectacle of their unveiling, the masquerade that they will continue to perpetuate, in a new guise, on the colonial authorities.

This new, unveiled masquerade, when the women's faces are available to memory and to the camera, is what continues to protect their anonymity, and thus their agency, from those who would identify and control them. This masquerade involves a different construction of their sexuality. Previously, we watched a veiled woman conceal her secret—not her sex but the contradictory fact that she is armed—by representing her response to the threatened violation of that (sexual) secret.[15] Now we watch a woman conceal her secret agency by proffering her sexuality. With dyed hair and a beach bag over her shoulder, she passes through the checkpoint by flirting with the guards. Alistair Horne (1978 : 186) describes the historical scene, which is almost exactly re-created in the film: "On leaving the Casbah Zohra Drif was stopped at a checkpoint by a Zouave who, after examining the forged identity card provided by Yacef, said with a leer: 'I'd like to give you a real going over, but it's not so easy here!' To which she replied coquettishly: 'That could be, perhaps, if you often come to Saint-Eugène beach.'" In the film, her prolonged over-the-shoulder glance guarantees that she remains cloaked in the protective veiling of her successful masquerade. Later we see that same glance, framed from a different angle, in a police surveillance film that is screened within Pontecorvo's film. The film-within-the-film shows civilians passing through a checkpoint a short time before the bombings; the voice-over of the French paratrooper commander states that the guerrillas must be among these Arab men and women. We see a young man dragged off because he doesn't have his identity papers with him, an old peddlar whose box is spilled on the ground, and the tentative, smiling face of the unveiled woman we recognize, moving between the French soldiers. Then the main camera cuts back to the attentive faces of the newly arrived French paratroopers in the audience of the surveillance film. Do we see one, taken in by the pretty face, begin to smile?

This same woman, after she is captured with Djafar, who is conversing in French with the commander of the French paratroopers, interrupts the mutuality between the two (male) leaders by interjecting, in Arabic, that Ali la Pointe is still alive and free in the Casbah. She breaks the momentary bond between the men by reasserting her own Arab-Algerian national and linguistic allegiances. Her choice of language, even more than what she says (and despite her dress), signifies that she is reestablishing her perceived identity as an Arab-Algerian, an identity premised upon a lack of subjective status within the dominant (French colonial) discourse. In rejecting the French language, she rejects whatever privileged status as a token subject her use of that language might have granted her, and explicitly replaces herself within the discursive qualifications of the Arab-Algerian nationalist revolution. At that moment, for the French, she unveils her masquerade.[16]

VEILED AGENTS: WOMEN'S DISCOURSE OF
FEMININE AGENCY AND MASQUERADE

In 1971 Jamilah Buhrayd, who had perhaps been the woman revolutionary most closely associated with Yacef Saadi, was interviewed in French for the Lebanese journal *al-Hawadith* (ᶜAwad 1977).[17] In that interview she very emphatically rejects the glorified political and cultural status the interviewer wanted to ascribe to her and her accomplishments. By doing so, she firmly aligns herself with the collective forces of the revolution rather than claiming for herself the individualized identity of a heroic subject. Instead, she declares herself an ordinary woman participating in a movement that demanded extraordinary commitment from everyone. Like the woman in the film, she denies linguistically any privileged or exceptional status:

> "Oh," said Jamilah, breaking suddenly into Algerian dialect which I could barely understand, "I swear I'm not a hero. Nothing. The hero is Algeria. As for me, well, I was only one person in a large group. The leader of our group in the Casbah district of Algiers would assign each of us a job to be done in a certain place at a certain time. And we would do it. My job was to plant bombs. I carried death with me in my handbag, death in the shape of time bombs. One day I was supposed to put a bomb in a café managed by a Frenchman. I did it. I was unlucky. I fell into their hands. They arrested me. They locked me in a cell. (ᶜAwad 1977:252)

Surprisingly, perhaps, it is precisely her identity as an ordinary woman that Jamilah Buhrayd asserts so emphatically. She does not deny her own political agency, but she is quick to point out that her case was not exceptional; plenty of other women and men were actively involved in the most dangerous aspects of the Algerian Revolution. Instead of a heroic identity, she reveils herself in the most ordinary tropes of the feminine:

> I can't help but smile when I look at that legendary figure called Jamilah. Who is she? Where does she live? What does she think about? I don't know. Perhaps she lives only in books. As for Jamilah whose address is Shakespeare Street, Algiers, and who is married and is the mother of three children, she is really just an ordinary human being. . . . Luckily, the poets didn't spoil that

Jamilah's life and happiness, like they sometimes do to legendary figures. I'm me, Jamilah, the Jamilah that God, not the poets, created. . . . But please don't keep calling me a hero. The word's too big for me. (‹Awad 1977:254)[18]

In her 1929 article "Womanliness as a Masquerade," Joan Riviere (1986:43) concludes her remarkable discussion of feminine masquerade with a return to the old questions: "What is the essential nature of fully developed femininity? What is *das ewig Weibliche?*" Riviere's essay describes her analysis of a married woman professional whose work involved public speaking on political issues. After her speeches, the woman would consistently shift to a markedly coquettish style of behavior and seek the approval of some senior man. Instead of interpreting this behavior as a reversion from professionalism to feminine type, Riviere (1986: 38) explains the woman's behavior as a masquerade:

> Womanliness therefore could be assumed and worn as a mask, both to hide the possession of masculinity and to avert the reprisals expected if she was found to possess it—much as a thief will turn out his pockets and ask to be searched to prove that he has not the stolen goods. The reader may now ask how I define womanliness or where I draw the line between genuine womanliness and the "masquerade." My suggestion is not, however, that there is any such difference; whether radical or superficial, they are the same thing.

Riviere thus asserts the indistinguishability of an essential feminine identity and feminine masquerade. (Her point here is quite like Irigaray's, although it was made much earlier and is more specifically available for application to a political analysis of feminine agency.) If Riviere herself, toward the end of her essay, returns to the question of feminine essentialism, can we not read the gesture as a part of her own feminine masquerade?

Similarly, when Jamilah Buhrayd disclaims her own heroism in favor of an ordinary woman's identity, we must wonder if this is not a strategic gesture. Having experienced life and fame as a revolutionary agent, she also claims the right to more banal feminine pleasures. To what extent, we must ask, is her ability to claim a private life predicated upon her public disavowal of a legendary political identity?

This question remains unanswered. For both Jamilah Buhrayd and Riviere's unnamed analysand, feminine masquerade provided a practical

271

means of negotiating cultural restrictions imposed on women's political agency. Given their insistence on evading the social ramification of their public, political identities on their private, personal lives, it seems clear that both women experienced, or were fearful of experiencing, a disjunction between public and private, political and personal. Their emphatic self-representations as ordinary, feminine women belie their achievements as accomplished political agents, and would seem to indicate a knowledge that the happy virtues of feminine domesticity are premised on gender constructions that tend to preclude political agency.

But both women managed to negotiate this contradiction if not resolve it. By negotiating their feminine identity through the margins of apparently contradictory discourses, they discovered a space in which to enact themselves, a space in which political agency is inextricable from feminine masquerade. By enacting masquerades that made use of the multilayered construction of feminine identity, they engaged aspects of that identity within a practice of feminine agency, a practice itself premised upon a lack of absolute definition. The shifting designations of this masquerade, produced by the lack of fixity inherent in the construction of feminine identity, are deployed as the means whereby feminine agency enables women's political action and private life. These women are not constituted as subjects by a veil of feminine identity or by their removal of that veil. Rather, they can experience a specifically feminine agency through their manipulation of the various veils of feminine identity, veils that are themselves woven as much out of particular discursive requirements as out of individual lengths of cloth.

In this essay, these discursive veils have been associated with the layered construction of individual identities. No essential truth, feminine or otherwise, lies beneath these layers, waiting to be unwrapped. Rather, the intention of this essay has been to display this complex overlap as a particularly rich site for the observation of individual political agency. Just as the women portrayed in Pontecorvo's film skillfully manipulate the various social layers of their feminine Arab/*pied noir* Algerian identity in order to negotiate their own political power with the dominant institutions of authority, this essay has attempted to negotiate among a variety of discourses in order to weave an interpretation of feminine agency that is situated in a larger political context.

In the last scene in *The Battle of Algiers,* a woman, unveiled but in traditional dress, whirls between a crowd and the camera, waving a scarf over her head. The woman is meant to embody Algeria, to signify the upsurge of popular nationalism that occurred even after the urban revolutionary structure in Algiers had been crushed, and to be a mythic feminine symbol of the national collective, as she dances between the mob and the French soldiers' guns. We do not recognize her, except symbolically. To the extent that she represents Algeria, she has no individual identity. To the extent that she is individualized, she enacts a particular kind of feminine political agency—a masquerade.

NOTES

1. Jamilah Buhrayd (her name is also sometimes spelled, in translation, Djamilah Bouhired) was one of the most active women revolutionaries in the FLN (Front de Libération Nationale) during the Algerian Revolution.

2. For a variety of viewpoints on the question of essentialism in feminism, see the issue of the journal *differences* devoted to this problem. In particular, see the interview with Gayatri Spivak (1989: 124–156) in which she further elucidates her own strategic use of essentialism for feminist politics. For an essay that addresses some of the same ideas about strategic essentialism with regard to women's political agency, see Butler 1991. For an essay that addresses this problem specifically with regard to Algerian women, see Lazreg 1988.

3. For specific details about the bombings and the historical organization of the FLN's own battle of Algiers, I relied primarily on Horne 1978: 183–207.

4. *Pied noir* is the accepted term for the French colonists in Algeria, no matter how long an individual has lived there, as opposed to the native Arab (whether Muslim, Jewish, or Christian) population.

5. The significance of the feminine transformation portrayed in the film is discussed by Harlow (1986: ix–xxii), who places the film's scenes in their historical context, particularly noting the reaction of Francophone intellectuals, including Frantz Fanon, Albert Camus, and Simone de Beauvoir, to the war in Algeria and the problematic Western perception of Arab or Arab-Algerian identity. But Harlow evaluates the political and cultural significance of this unveiling only with reference to colonial and postcolonial relations between the West, particularly the French, and Islam, particularly the Arabs; she does not extend her discussion to a consideration of unveiling's possible wider significance.

6. This essay is found in *A Dying Colonialism*, originally published as *L'an cinq, de la révolution algérienne* (Paris: François Maspero, 1959) during the Algerian Revolution. Throughout the book, Fanon treats the traditionally veiled woman as a symbol of Algerian resistance to the imposition of French colonial culture, and as a symbol of the nascent Algerian nation. In this sense, the women's strategic removal of their veils indicates the early emergence of national(ist) identity, but it also reduces the multiple identities of Arab-Algerian women to the Arab-Algerian woman as symbol.

7. Fanon's analysis of this politicized, strategic unveiling is very different from his analysis of unpolitical unveiling, which he seems almost to equate with a form of assimilationist collaboration. In his analysis there is little room for an Algerian woman to configure herself as a feminine subject, apart from the two competing

discourses of nationalist identity (Algerian nationalist and French colonialist). Unfortunately, in this situation a woman's attempt to emancipate herself from traditional (Algerian) gender definitions, without a concurrent Algerian nationalist politicization, inevitably places her at the disposal of the colonialist strategy—one of the major public-legitimation arguments for the colonial presence in Algeria having been that the French were liberating Algerian women from the oppression of Algerian men. See Fanon 1965: 36–43.

This particular train of thought is still all too common among Western observers of non-Western cultures, including feminists. While we may be prepared to complain vociferously about the condition of women in the West, nonetheless it is often taken for granted that improving the condition of women's lives in other cultures is most readily accomplished through their Westernization. While this impulse is one aspect of a wider attitude toward international development, it retains a peculiar urgency when directed toward women. Gayatri Spivak addresses the problem confronting the postcolonial woman who finds herself caught between "white men saving brown women from brown men" and a more traditional, local paternalism that would in turn assert (regarding the Hindu practice of suttee/*sati* or widow immolation) that "The women wanted to die" (see Spivak 1988:271–313). For an analysis of some Egyptian women's seemingly reactionary response to the added pressure their emancipation has placed on them, a response that can be understood as a negotiating of conflicting feminine obligations and opportunities, see Macleod 1991.

8. Historically men were often quite good at disguising themselves as women; Yacef Saadi often moved about the Casbah in veiled disguise in order to elude French surveillance. See Horne 1978:211.

9. Remarkably similar accounts of analysands' descriptions of their bodies escaping definition are found in the writings of the early Gestalt therapist Paul Schilder (1935). See Schilder, as quoted in Martin 1987.

10. Again, note here Fanon's sensitive insight into the almost untenable situation of those Algerian women who unveiled for assimilationist rather than nationalist reasons. These newly unveiled women, who were competing for status as (feminine) subjects on French terms, were then marked as extravagantly available sexual objects by both the French-Algerian and Arab-Algerian communities; their very success at assimilating to the discourse of French femininity placed them at jeopardy both in their own communities and in French colonial circles, where their ability to be just like the French only placed the basic tenets of colonial policy further into contradiction. See Fanon 1965:44, n.8. For another analysis of the problem of the colonial mimic who is "almost the same but not quite"/"almost the same but not white," see Bhabha 1984.

11. In order to represent history on film, Pontecorvo sometimes almost literally re-creates events. The set for the explosion of the house in the rue de Thèbes was built on the site of the building's actual explosion; it was the only open area left in the Casbah that was big enough. With the exception of Jean Martin, a French actor who plays the military commander of the French paratroopers, all the players are nonactors found in Algiers: peasants, a petty thief, tourists, members of the middle class. But Yacef Saadi, the former FLN military commander of

Algiers and the film's Algerian coproducer, plays a slightly fictionalized version of himself—FLN military commander Djafar. And in the scene in which the women unveil themselves, Saadi participates in re-creating a mission he himself had supervised. Thus Pontecorvo shot the film precisely on location, using players who themselves had often been specific actors in the Revolution. The film so well avoids melodrama or sentimentalization of the characters that it was denounced by French and Italian rightists, banned in France and England until 1971, and hailed in the United States as a primer for black urban guerrilla warfare: it was treated as a disruptive revolutionary text. For information about these specific details and conditions of making the film, see Mellen 1973: 16–20 and 72–75.

12. The most striking thing about *The Battle of Algiers*, and the reason for the disclaimer, is not its quality of return or repetition, or its radical politics, but its appearance: the film looks real; it looks like documentary or newsreel footage. Shooting in black and white, with (usually) one hand-held camera, in diffused natural light on very soft stock, Pontecorvo achieved the very grainy, realistic effect of newsreel or television coverage. Scenes were often shot from the angles and with the lenses that reporters would have had to use. In order to create an image of reality, the look of the film was intentionally made less glamorous; the aura was intentionally diminished to allow for a sense of greater recognition and familiarity. For details about the cinematography, see Mellen 1973: 18–19.

13. There is an obvious need to mention here that the experienced cultural participant (whether native or visitor) can easily recognize one veiled woman from another. Height, posture, carriage, and the manner of the wearer all contribute to her individuation in the eye of the beholder trained to notice such differences. To assume that all veiled women look alike is somewhat equivalent to the notorious claim that all members of any (other or minority) race look alike. Nonetheless, Pontecorvo does not allow us, as spectators of the film, to become well enough acquainted with the veiled revolutionaries, in our brief glimpses of them, to recognize or specifically individualize them until they unveil and we can see their faces.

For theorizations of both the female spectator's relationship with film and the role of the (translucent or Western) veil in the filmic presentation of desire (especially the spectator's desire to see the face), see Doane 1982 and 1989.

14. See Fanon's discussion of the military role of women and the difficulty the men had making the decision to allow women to participate in the explicitly military aspects of the Revolution (Fanon 1965: 48–54). Note especially Fanon's description of the men's soul-searching over allowing women to participate actively (implying that it would be a nobler thing for the men to allow/demand that the women passively receive the outcome of a nationalist revolution in which they had no active part except suffering). Note also the way women, as they become more active as revolutionaries, are linguistically masculinized, while the revolution is feminized. For instance: "With this phase, the Algerian woman penetrates a little further into the flesh of the Revolution" (Fanon 1965:54).

15. That the gun functions symbolically as the phallus, and that therefore these armed women conceal, under their robes, the secret that they do indeed have the phallus, is too obvious a point to belabor. Its relevance to the film, and the mas-

querade of the historical Algerian women revolutionaries, lies in the observation that the women dressed themselves in precisely the feminine disguise that they knew would signify to the French that they were women without the phallus: they were able to have the gun/the phallus by representing themselves as that which was defined as lacking it.

16. Interestingly, the women in the film are not named. While this may seem insensitive of Pontecorvo, since the main male characters all have names and are consistently identified, this lack of names is in keeping with the self-representation of the women revolutionaries themselves. Only the young bride is identified as Fathia during her wedding, and at the end of the film the unveiled revolutionary, who we know is about to die with the last of the active FLN guerrillas in Algiers—the young husband, a little boy called Le Petit Omar, and Ali la Pointe—is identified as Hassiba. In the film credits, these two are the only women mentioned, but even here their identities are difficult to establish. In the various credits published with the film, the screenplay, and the film guide, the women are listed with slightly different names and different spellings. Although the different spellings can be ascribed to the various transliterations from Arabic, and occur with other characters' names in the film, and with other individuals involved in the Revolution (the previously mentioned Jamilah Buhrayd and Djamilah Bouhired, for instance), the slight variations in the names themselves are harder to explain. Thus the film lists Fusia El Kader and Samia Kerbash, without character identification; Solinas in the screenplay lists Fawzia El-Kader as playing Halima and Samia Kerbash as playing Fathia; Mellen in the film guide lists Fawzia El Kader as playing Hassiba and Michele Kerbash as playing Fathia. See Solinas 1973:xv; Mellen 1973:1.

17. Note that the Lebanese (male) interviewer and the Algerian (female) subject of the interview conduct their conversation, for the most part, in their shared colonial language (French), since Lebanese and Algerians speak forms of Arabic that are not necessarily mutually intelligible.

18. At the beginning of the interview, the male interviewer describes Jamilah Buhrayd as she appears to him, a male spectator, noting her good figure, glossy hair, clear complexion, Western clothes, and the gold Islamic symbol she wears around her neck, the signifier that despite her clothing (and her marriage to the Christian lawyer who conducted her legal defense), she is religious. See ʿAwad 1977:252.

REFERENCES

ʿAwad, Walid. 1977. "Interview with Jamilah Buhrayd, Legendary Algerian Hero." Trans. Elizabeth Warnock Fernea and Basima Quattan Bezirgan. In *Middle Eastern Muslim Women Speak*, ed. Elizabeth Warnock Fernea and Basima Quattan Bezirgan, 249–262. Austin: University of Texas Press.

Bhabha, Homi. 1984. "Of Mimicry and Man: The Ambivalence of Colonial Discourse." *October* 28 (Spring): 125–133.

Butler, Judith. 1991. "Contingent Foundations: Feminism and the Question of 'Postmodernism.'" *Praxis International* 11 (2): 150–165.

Doane, Mary Ann. 1982. "Film and the Masquerade: Theorising the Female Spectator." *Screen* 23 (3–4): 74–87.

———. 1989. "Veiling over Desire: Close-ups of the Woman." In *Feminism and Psychoanalysis,* ed. Richard Feldstein and Judith Roof, 105–141. Ithaca, N.Y.: Cornell University Press.

Fanon, Frantz. 1965. *A Dying Colonialism.* Trans. Haakon Chevalier. New York: Grove Press.

Harlow, Barbara. 1986. "Introduction." In Malek Alloula, *The Colonial Harem.* Trans. Myrna Godzich and Wlad Godzich. Minneapolis: University of Minnesota Press.

Horne, Alistair. 1978. *A Savage War of Peace: Algeria, 1954–1962.* New York: Viking Press.

Irigaray, Luce. 1985. "The Power of Discourse and the Subordination of the Feminine." In *This Sex Which Is Not One,* 68–85. Trans. Catherine Porter with Carolyn Burke. Ithaca, N.Y.: Cornell University Press.

Lazreg, Marnia. 1988. "Feminism and Difference: The Perils of Writing as a Woman on Women in Algeria." *Feminist Studies* 14 (1): 81–107.

Macleod, Arlene Elowe. 1991. *Accommodating Protest: Working Women, the New Veiling, and Change in Cairo.* New York: Columbia University Press.

Martin, Emily. 1987. *The Woman in the Body.* Boston: Beacon Press.

Mellen, Joan. 1973. *Filmguide to "The Battle of Algiers."* Bloomington: University of Indiana Press.

Riviere, Joan. 1986. "Womanliness as a Masquerade." In *Formations of Fantasy,* ed. Victor Burgin, James Donald, and Cora Kaplan. New York: Methuen.

Schilder, Paul. 1935. *The Image and Appearance of the Human Body.* Psyche Monographs No. 4. London: Kegan Paul, Trench, Trubner.

Solinas, PierNico, ed. 1973. *Gillo Pontecorvo's "The Battle of Algiers": A Film Written by Franco Solinas.* New York: Charles Scribner's Sons.

Spivak, Gayatri Chakravorty. 1988. "Can the Subaltern Speak?" In *Marxism and the Interpretation of Culture,* ed. Cary Nelson and Lawrence Grossberg. Urbana: University of Illinois Press.

Spivak, Gayatri, with Ellen Rooney. 1989. "In a Word." *differences* 1 (2): 124–156.

CHOOSING CHOICE: IMAGES OF SEXUALITY AND "CHOICEOISIE" IN POPULAR CULTURE

Elspeth Probyn

I have a button emblazoned with the words "Redheads for choice." As with many political badges, it is both succinct and ambiguous, and when I found it in the basket of buttons at my local feminist, gay, and lesbian bookstore I was unsure of its semiotic play. While the idea is cute ("blonds," "brunettes," and "gray-haired women" all for choice), the choice on offer was limited. For a start, the phrase "gray-haired women" does not have the same semantic cachet as the others do, and more problematic is the way in which women of color are excluded from this choice. Furthermore, I am wary of the discursive inflation of "choice," and I wondered what articulation of choice I had bought into. Of late, choice seems to be coming at us from all sides; it can be found just as easily on the Left as on the Right. On the one hand, choice is perfectly at home within a liberal feminist platform where women's equality, placed outside of the material dictates of class, race, age, and sexuality, can be presented in terms of good will and choice. On the other hand, choice can also be used to articulate various antifeminist stances: for example, the notion that being married and with children is naturally every woman's choice. In a more vindictive move, choice can be used to argue that affirmative action takes away the God-given right to choose the best person disregarding gender or race. It is, of course, well known that white men have neither a gender nor a color. However, perhaps the most compelling use of choice is when it is used to sum up a certain articulation of agency. In this vein we are supposed to feel that because there is no one solution to the world's problems, individuals just have to go on their own choices. In part this seems to be the logic of a recent promotional campaign which attempts to re-sell *Good Housekeeping* magazine to another

278

generation of women. As one of the early examples of new traditionalism, the television and magazine advertisements show well-dressed, middle-class women in their thirties at home with equally well-dressed children. It is a picture of calm, reflecting that in the face of chaos, the right choices have been made. As the advertising executives stated: "It was never an issue except among feminists who felt that we were telling women to stay home and have babies. We're saying that's okay. But that's not all we're saying. We're saying they have a choice. It's a tough world out there" (quoted in Savan 1989: 49). Call it a postmodern refusal of metanarratives or merely the commercial appropriation of a changing political world scene, but this use of choice deftly conjures up a postfeminist view of women. The strategy here is both to congratulate women for having the ability to choose what is right and to commiserate with us about how hard it is to be a woman right now.

While part of the appeal of a slogan such as "Redheads for choice" is its polysemic play, its capacity to allow for the creative intermingling of meanings, it is also and always weighed down by other cultural slogans and past choices made by others. On a seemingly frivolous level the equation of hair color and choice recalls those deeply invasionary sayings embedded in popular culture: "Only your hairdresser knows for sure"; "Blonds have more fun," and so forth. In more serious matters, "prochoice" signifies the right to abortion. However, even here, where its work has been vitally important, we have to recognize that the choice in prochoice opens up a semiotic space now occupied by antiabortionists. Thus the discourse of choice is redirected and comes to mean that fetuses have the right to choose. Similarly the decision to have an abortion is represented as just one choice among many: that the decision to have an abortion is an easy matter—that women simply choose it as they might their hair color. Here the primacy of choice blurs the fact that abortion is for most women an extremely painful emotional and physical experience, that it is for many the last choice.

Just as the rules of grammar force one to choose *something* (*to choose* is a transitive verb requiring an object in order to complete its meaning), at a pragmatic level, political statements need some sort of closure in order to be effective. I therefore added an antihomophobia button, thereby hoping to clarify the type of choice I want. I could have also added an "Every child, a chosen child" button or an antiracism one, thus signifying the type of world I would choose to live in as opposed to the one I inhabit. As a political gesture this semiotic game is inscribed within what Rosi Braidotti (1989) has called, after Irigaray, a politics of "as if." As such these buttons point to the fact that, as feminists, we must

279

continue to work within a future anterior tense in the hopes of rendering an "as if" into an "is." The "as if," for me, is a way of conceptualizing modes of analysis that insist on what Jean-François Lyotard (1986) has defined as the "post/modo": "ce qui aura été fait" (what will have been done). And it is clear that as a political strategy, the wearing of these buttons is one way of rendering concrete the type of "as ifs" we want to make real. However, at a theoretical level, it obviously has its limits. I am not advocating, as an analytic choice, Woman as textual landscape. Perhaps I'm just getting old(fashioned), but the sartorial move to use the body as political billboard no longer holds as much appeal as it once did. While I do not want to denigrate the imaginative and political play that can be initiated by them, there are only so many political T-shirts and slogans one can, at any one time, put on. (I do have a great T-shirt that combines "In Bed with Madonna," a photograph of Madonna herself, and "Queer Pride 1991" that I have yet to find the guts to wear teaching.) Without writing off the import of wearing your choice or minimizing the courage that it sometimes takes to do so, I think that in the face of the mounting articulations of choice we need to theorize what we want "choice" to do for us.

CHARTING CHOICE

In this chapter I map some of the current configurations of choice emerging on the (mainly) North American popular cultural scene. As a feminist theorist and woman facing my own difficult choices, I consider ways in which we might be able to rearticulate the types of choices on offer to us. My particular concern is with the question of sexuality and how we may be able to rearticulate the welter of choices on hand in order to formulate a way of putting forth choice on our own terms. The type of choices that I want can be seen as both personal aspirations and a necessary part of a political agenda of feminist cultural analysis. In order to realize these choices, we need to elevate to a theoretical level the question of what choice means to feminists as well as what we want it to mean within feminism in the 1990s. While choice is a pragmatic matter facing women in their everyday lives, it must also be seen as a major problematic for feminism. As an immediate issue we need to recognize that the public representations of choice are rearticulating the social landscape in which feminism needs to intervene, meaning that we have to rethink the semiotic effects of how choice is used in feminist discourse. At another level, one which is also crucial but more abstract, representations of choice raise epistemological questions about the status of public images and their relation to the material world.

In simple terms this involves reconceptualizing how as women w live with these discourses. For me and for other feminist theorists, th questions raised by this seemingly evident problematic are deeply intertwined with issues of how we portray the lived as well as of how women experience their quotidian situations. While the recent past of cultural studies have been littered with pronouncements about women "resisting" various media forms, the vocabulary of resistance and negotiation leaves much to be desired.[1] To put it bluntly, the good intentions of these theoretical attempts to rescue women from cultural dupedom are often at the expense of elaborating more difficult questions about how as women we experience the social and affective processes imbricated in the representation of gender.

As part of an ongoing project I have been analyzing the emergence and the articulation of the discourses of postfeminism and new traditionalism in prime-time Québécois and American television. I was in part drawn to these instances because of the prominence of choice within their distinct forms and contents. In general these discourses actively represent women as re-positioned in the home, as they re-articulate different forms of family (single parent, corporate, "traditional," etc.). The aim of my project is twofold: first, to identify the discursive logic of the representation of women and the home and/or the family; and second, to reconceptualize these discourses as technologies of the self (Foucault 1988), producing alternative constructions of the materiality of women's sexuality. The accent here is not on resistance, which to my mind is overly laden with connotations of a single brave soul or class battling against a vast entity, or on negotiation, which strikes me as a rather calm and even type of action taking place between two equal parties. Rather what I am interested in is the "work" of images, both as they circulate in our lives and how, as individuals and theorists, we can put images to work in such a way as to materialize other options, thoughts, and modes of existence. In short, I want to realize the imaginary.

To my mind the term *choiceoisie* captures a logic of discursivity (how discourses emerge and move) as well as the possibility of making the materiality of other choices evident. I argue that *choiceoisie* can be seen as a discursive configuration that articulates both the cultural texts of the moment as well as the social experiences which these public representations seek to delineate. The work of the feminist critic is to bend these discourses upon themselves, revealing in their very interstices ways of thinking the social differently: as Teresa de Lauretis (1987: 137) so

281

eloquently puts it, to "see 'difference differently,' to look at women with eyes I've never had before and yet my own."

Another way of looking at the doubled move of this articulation is to conceptualize it as what Raymond Williams calls a "structure of feeling"[2] in emergence. As Lawrence Grossberg (1984: 400) argues, "For Williams, the crucial mediation by which cultural text and social reality are linked is defined by the notion of the 'structure of feeling.'" As a structure of feeling, choiceoisie marks the marshaling together of a number of discursive and nondiscursive factors. On the one hand, choiceoisie can be seen at work in the emergence of popular representations of women as happily choosing to be at home. This type of image can be found across a number of sites, including recent television shows (what is now called female-centred television) and, of course, numerous advertising campaigns. On the other hand, the image of choice is also present in the current dismantling of legislative "rights" for women. In a particularly telling instance the Supreme Court of Canada recently struck down the rape shield law, which prevented use of a rape victim's past sexual activities as evidence at trial. In theory it now stands that a woman's earlier choice to participate in a sexual act can be used as evidence against her—that when she says no she means yes because perhaps once in her life she had chosen to say yes. This logic is bewildering to say the least; it is also oblivious to the conjunctural nature of any act involving choice. Choice is not a simple matter: its discursive effects can be welcome (I happen to like most of the female-centred television on offer), or it can entail devastating effects. Given the diversity of significations that choice allows, it is imperative to analyze its conditions of possibility: the discourses that allow for the emergence of choiceoisie as well as the positivity of choiceoisie—as a discourse what it allows or disavows, and what we can do with it.

If for North American women choice seems to loom large, beckoning us from all sides, as an object of inquiry it remains elusive. Of course one could rightly argue that at a material level the great majority of women still have very little to choose from and that all these representations that fill the air with alluring options are but ideological manifestations. There is no doubt that these discourses do indeed work ideologically: choiceoisie fulfills its mandate as ideological by precisely offering women a position in an imaginary relation to their material lives. Ideological as these discursive positions may be, we cannot afford to dismiss them as so many chimeras. In other words, discourses of choice construct positions for women—they place us in relation to other discourses and in relation to our everyday lives. For instance, when I watch a television program like

Murphy Brown and see Murphy, a successful television journalist, choosing to have a child by herself, I am offered a place in a discourse. This position may be quite comfortable, and it allows me to view other discourses: those that construct an image of successful career women or that proffer the possibility of having a child later in life (the character of Murphy Brown, played by Candice Bergen, is said to be forty-two years old). This representation of "baby without man" can then allow me as I watch to think, or to represent myself, in a number of possible positions: it may allow me to place myself outside the normalized vision of the institution of the family, or it may reaffirm the discursive strength of that institution. While the representation of Murphy's choice probably does not match up with the structures of most women's lives as they are lived, it nonetheless potentially has the power to effect changes in the "feeling" of the lived. This may be expressed in very small ways (from "how will she get by without a husband/father" to "if she can do it, maybe I can too").

However minuscule and undecided these reactions may be, they attest to the possibility of an altered affectivity. Representations of choice can translate into a feeling of possibility. The pull of the possible that may accompany images of choice has the power to rearrange the affectivity of my material circumstances: it cannot perhaps change them substantively, but it certainly can (for better or worse) make them feel differently. In turn this discursive upheaval, this rearrangement of the feel of the material, must be recognized as constituting an important element in the materiality of women lives. To be very prosaic about it, rearranging the furniture in a room changes the material feeling of the space of the room just as much if not more so than would the addition of a new piece of furniture. It should be clear that I am not suggesting a causal relationship between representations and their reception. However, I want to emphasize the necessity of analyzing the affective implications of the images of choice as they circulate within the material structures of our lives.

What I want to begin to elaborate here is a conjunctural analysis of choiceoisie as it is articulated across the discourses of postfeminism and new traditionalism. In proposing to interrogate their conjuncture, I hope to avoid a bifurcation of the material and the discursive. The positivity of the conjunctural allows us to study, in a Foucauldian sense, the arrangement of an established discursive terrain as well as what that ground then allows as materially experienced social moments. In arguing that the discursive presence of choice is an important conjunctural problematic for feminists and for feminism, I draw attention to the ways in which, following Althusser, a problematic is always constituted in the presence and absence of problems and concepts. I want to emphasize the continually shifting nature of the articulations among these discourses, remembering that the conjuncture is made of "the backwardnesses, forwardnesses, survivals and unevennesses of development which *co-exist* in the structure of the historical present" (Althusser 1975: 106). Thus while some of the choices on offer may seem frivolous, they are bound up with larger questions that directly effect the lives of women. And while some of the choices may seem reprehensible, they are also up for grabs, open to feminist reformulation.

Indeed feminism itself is bound up in the discourse of choice; it is one of the factors involved in the contemporary discursive positivity. In other words, the logic of choice could not exist in its specific forms if feminism did not constitute part of the historical present of North American popular culture. As Judith Mayne (1988: 30) argues, "feminism has been appropriated and assumed by, or otherwise grafted onto, mass cultural forms." That for the most part it is a repressed and abject strata (what Mayne calls "prime-time feminism" as opposed to "authentic" feminism) does not lessen its circulation through and across various popular discourses and images. The task at hand is the rearticulation of these discourses in order to remake the image of choice in the light of feminist goals. This is then to work toward subverting the order of the choices on offer, to find in the images of choiceoisie a way of folding the discourse of choice back onto itself.

The French philosopher Michèle Le Doeuff has argued that if we look closely enough at a text (in her case, philosophical discourses and systems) we will probably find a troubling image or images. For example, in her analysis of the seventeenth-century philosopher Pierre Roussel she finds a strange image of women's bodies: "Roussel genitalizes the whole body, but degenitalizes sex." (1981–82: 45). Le Doeuff uses the rhetorical term "chiasmas" to explain the functioning of this logic: "the denial of a quality 'x' to an object or place which common sense holds it actually to possess, with the compensating attribution of that same quality to everything but that object or place" (40). Roussel's image has "sex" in all parts of a woman's body except where one often (also) finds it. This type of argument then produces "Silence as to the literal meaning, a void at the centre; metonymic proliferation everywhere else" (40–41). It should be clear that Roussel was not an early advocate of "finding your erotogenic zones," but rather used this image to construct a system of knowledge which could effectively exclude women from being a subject of knowledge. In other words, this image of pan-genitalized woman further renders her an object to be known by others. With regard to "choice" and women's lives, we can argue that the quality of being able to choose something over something else is also displaced from where it ought to be. Rather than in the hands of the woman choosing, choice in some situations is represented as already having been made, always and already chosen. In other words, the active quality of choosing is replaced by a plethora of nouns, of choices made.

While Le Doeuff is talking about a mode of argumentation within philosophy, we can see a similar move in the arrangement of discourses elsewhere. Returning to *Good Housekeeping*'s advertising campaign, we find a rather silent and still discursive image in the midst of the representation of women now choosing "kids or not." The text for the television advertisement for *Good Housekeeping* reads: "Mothers haven't changed. Kids haven't changed. Families haven't changed. Love hasn't changed. What is fundamental to our lives, what really matters . . . hasn't changed" (quoted in Savan 1989: 49). Thus the quality of actively choosing, which in common sense seems necessarily to apply to questions about family, kids, love, or reproducing, is silenced. Choice here is displaced by an image of something "fundamental." In Le Doeuff's terms, we can say that this is a "winking" image, that the image indicates the text is up to something. As Meaghan Morris (1988b: 85) explains, "The procedure of tacitly quoting an image already invested by a previous philosophy is what Le Doeuff calls 'winking.'"

Taking up this rather lovely metaphor, I argue that within the discourse of choice we are confronted with images that wink at us, saying, you think you're choosing this (nod, nod—nudge, nudge—wink, wink), but actually we know the choice is already made—"what's fundamental hasn't changed." These winking images are thus invested with knowledges other than those they profess to offer. As choice blinks at us, we catch other images of women: those that show us women as either unable to choose or having nothing to choose from. In other words, images of choiceoisie conjure up, cite, and refer to other deeply ingrained images of women in popular culture—of women speechless in front of door number one, two, or three. They also, of necessity, refer us back to images of the "old" traditionalism, where women simply were (ontologically) lodged in the home. In fact they cite an image of home organized around the figure of woman. What I want to argue is that when images wink within the discourses of choice, they are nodding to other popular knowledges. In this movement of citing, nodding, nudging, and winking, they tell us that the text is up to something, that something is bothering it. As we follow the references mobilized by these winking images, we begin to find ways of troubling their discursive stability. We can disturb the construction of the "fundamental" by analyzing the type of choices that are articulated as its ground.

Getting back to basics, however, I should attempt a rough definition of the type of choice postfeminism and new traditionalism put on offer. As many of us have already found out, the question of what constitutes postfeminism is not an evident one. My pairing of it with the discourse of new traditionalism is one way of specifying its reach. Indeed, one could say that new traditionalism is but another way of saying postfeminism: "a polite code word of postfeminism, meaning 'Let's not talk any more about women'" (Showalter 1986: 222). While this definition does not get us very far in describing what these discourses actually do want to talk about, for heuristic reasons if not scientific protocol I use my experiences and memories as markers of their appearances. Rather like the term postmodernism, the exact scope, meaning, and time of arrival of these two notions upon the cultural scene are vague and hard to pin down. As a rough time frame we are talking about the mid- to late eighties, a period which witnessed, according to *Newsweek,* an unprecedented rise in the number of what they called female-centered television shows on prime time. The cover story back in March 1989, "How Women Are Changing TV," made it clear that "the feminization of television has surprisingly little to do with feminism" (48). Reading between the lines we can see the winking image here: you thought all those women on television were the result of decades of feminist work, but guess what, they have *surprisingly* little to do with feminism.

At the outset we can say that postfeminism seeks to define a new generation of women who have "little to do with feminism." However, it also seeks to portray a generation of women who have been through feminism and now want a break from the rigors of being "politically correct." It is not altogether surprising that along with the rise of postfeminism we should find vehement attacks against the Left and the mobilization of "pc" as an image of nasty, coercive thought-policing. As B. Ruby Rich said in the *Village Voice* (10 August 1991, p. 31) of the queen of anti-pc, Camille Paglia, "Paglia is symptomatic: she reflects the alienation of many women from the ideological excesses of feminism in its 70s phase." Rich also deftly defuses Paglia's claims while she warns against dismissing her lightly. In a similar vein, the articulation of new traditionalism and postfeminism is attractive and tenacious: in part its appeal lies in the way it holds out the idea of a bit of comfort after a long hard fight. Like the famous advertising slogan for Virginia Slims cigarettes, "You've come a long way baby," it is a complicitous discourse. It says, we know you are a feminist but, hey, chill out and have a smoke;

conversely, it may also wink at us by merely removing the sting from feminist statements. The image here is one of a businesswoman (perhaps still wearing sneakers with her suit) who at the end of the day just wants to go home and put her feet up. As Madonna put it in "Like a Prayer," "Life is a mystery/Everyone must stand alone/I hear you call my name and it sounds like home."

Like Madonna, another postfeminist image is that of the (ex)feminist who wants to have a little fun. In the Canadian film *A Winter Tan* (1988), the protagonist Maryse Holder says she is taking a vacation from feminism. Based on the true story of a feminist academic who left her college to wander around Mexico, this tale is quite literally post feminism (or at least what can come after teaching feminist literary theory). As she drinks tequila, smokes dope, swims, and pleases herself with young Mexican boys, Maryse remarks that "there is feminism and then there's fucking" (quoted in Weinstock 1989: 138). Maryse is shown as out of control, and in a heavy moralistic ending she is killed by one of her young lovers. One of the more memorable lines in the film has Maryse saying, "it must have been to curb my natural sluttishness that I became a feminist in the first place" (quoted in Weinstock 1989: 138). In other words, "You thought I was a feminist but (wink, wink) I really just wanted to fuck men." Deeper down there is a more menacing wink: feminism is a way for women to escape the rigors of the "real" world, of being a "real" woman.

In other postfeminist representations of choice the emphasis is on responsibility and individual agency. A recent advertising campaign for Nike athletic shoes plays up the individualism of choice while at the same time winking at us outrageously. The eight-page magazine advertisement (*Vanity Fair,* April 1991) opens with the image of a young girl against a sort of midwestern sky, and the text reads: "You were born a daughter. You looked up to your mother. You looked up to your father. You looked up to everyone. You wanted to be a princess. You thought you were a princess." The message of the ad is one of choice, but the images are nearly all of women's inability to choose. Each page brings us a different photograph of a woman working out and another of the appropriate shoe, as the text reminds us how indecisive "you" were: "You wanted to own a horse. You wanted to be a horse"; "You wanted to be good in algebra. You hid during algebra. You wanted the boys to notice you. You were afraid the boys would notice you." The text goes on to recount what "you" wanted, building an image of a perfect dizzy broad until, on the penultimate page, the single line appears: "You became significant to yourself." The final page has a smiling woman who is thirtysomething, again against the prairie sunset (or in keeping with the moral tenor, it's probably a sunrise), as the text tells us among other things that "Sooner or later, you start taking yourself seriously. You know when to take a break . . . Because you know it's never too late to have a life. And never too late to change one." Then comes the final crunch as the weight of Nike instructs us: "Just do it."

The discourse here is constructed around the winking images of "us" as we used to be before we chose "to start taking ourselves seriously." Interestingly enough, although the images are posed in such a way as to present "us" (a collective body of American girls/women) as endearingly flighty, the onus is put squarely on the individual to "do something that makes you stronger, faster, more complete." In other words, the text plays on the ideal of female teenagers as a unified discourse, while it pulls for individuality ("You were picked last for the team. You were the best on the team. You refused to be on the team."). In the terms of choiceoisie, individuality also becomes ambiguous—it can be read as a politically correct refusal of collegiate ideology, just as it can also read as rugged individualism (every girl for herself). At the same time that "we" are presented as historically unable (as a group) to make up our minds, choice is presented as a straightforward matter: any woman can make up her mind to have, or change, a life. Thus young girls are portrayed as having a number of choices to make: from career choices ("You wanted to be a veterinarian. You wanted to be president. You wanted to be the president's veterinarian.") to choices about love and friendship ("You fell in love. You fell in love. You fell in love. You lost your best friend. You lost your other best friend. You really fell in love. You became a steady girlfriend. You became a significant other.").

Choices abound, but "we" are shown as incapable of choosing, or if we do we make the wrong one ("You didn't go to the prom. You went with the wrong person."). While some presumably serious choices like career selection are presented in a frivolous manner, others are shown as not real choices. Whether or not to choose your best friend over your boyfriend is presented as already decided ("You *became* a steady girl-friend"). In other words, there seems to be little active choosing going on where one would think it would be most present. I still vividly recall my best friend and I having long conversations about choosing not to drop each other when or if "the boys" called. In the popular culture of women, as it is both practiced and publicly represented, it is commonly agreed that the question of allegiance to the best friend or to the boyfriend is a difficult one. However, the image that winks at us here is that it's not a real choice, that we know in advance which one is chosen. Thus in this scenario the quality of choice (i.e., the act of choosing something) is displaced from the question of careers, friendship, and romance. In the end the only place one finds choice is in oneself. However, if we *become* all manner of things (a girlfriend, a significant other, significant to ourselves. etc.), how do we finally choose ourselves?

THE ANATOMY OF A KISS

The question of being, becoming, or choosing was central to the spring 1991 television season's most interesting case of choice featuring the infamous kiss between C. J. Lamb and Abby Perkins on *L.A. Law*. While a kiss definitely occurred, that is, two pairs of lips touched, it also constitutes a winking image par excellence: when is a kiss not a kiss? This image is particularly (and wonderfully) troubling because it openly nodded to the possibility that the women might be choosing each other as lovers. It was a nod that was quickly picked up: according to *Newsday*, NBC "does not acknowledge that what happened was a lesbian kiss" (*Montréal Gazette*, 6 March 1991). The cover photograph for an article in the *New York Times* titled "Gay Images: TV's Mixed Signals" (19 April 1991) had C.J. and Abby smiling at each other but definitely not kissing. According to the *Village Voice* (4 May 1991), the assistant managing editor of the *Times* Allan Siegal ordered the photo of the two kissing to be pulled because "I didn't like the picture." NBC and Siegal aside, many viewers, myself included, did like the image and chose to read it as the door swinging open. And as a winking image, it occasioned other nods toward the deliciously ambiguous C.J. Obviously it was not a representation of out lesbian sexuality, but in its fumbling way it can be analyzed as constituting a new pivot point in the rearticulation of prime-time choice.

Before we get into the kiss, let me set the scene. As Mayne argues (1988),[3] *L.A. Law* is shot through with nods to feminism. Over the years it has also articulated a certain postfeminist, new traditionalist gloss, perhaps best seen in the development of Anne and Stuart's quest for a child. The firm itself is represented as a family, complete with papa (Leyland), evil stepmother (Rosalind), and rebellious teenagers (the young generation). It has featured such politically correct story lines as a lawyer who is a dwarf, a love affair between two mentally disadvantaged adults, a gay lawyer who subsequently is represented as having AIDS, and a woman who rebuffs the sleazy Arnold Becker and comes out as a lesbian. Its main characters also include a "buppy" who gets radical (Jonathan) and an interracial couple (Gracie and Victor). Of the two participants in the kiss, Abby has gone from being portrayed as a mousy victim fighting for custody of her child to her recent glamorized persona. C.J. has evolved from a marginal character to one who often saves the firm's financial bacon.

The kiss brings together (quite literally) two feminist characters as it also articulates a postfeminist female camaraderie. Thus C.J. has been giving Abby advice on how to make more money, and they both have been "doing dinner" when C.J. kisses Abby on the lips and she responds in kind. The next day Abby comes into C.J.'s office to tell her that "she likes men," to which C.J. responds that she does too. After that the kiss is suspended, resurfacing occasionally in a few ambiguous meetings over the photocopy machine. However, in the May 2d episode, Abby invites herself to dinner chez C.J., where the tension, at least for her, continues to grow. But rather than finding consummation, Abby gets ditched. C.J.'s blistering line is: "You're not honest enough to be a friend, let alone anything else. Consider yourself dumped." Now given the lack of honesty on the part of most of the characters, this turn of events is intriguing. Consider, for example, the subplots that have accompanied the development of the C.J./Abby kiss: Anne, Leyland, and Rosalind perform an elaborate lie; Rosalind falls down an elevator shaft and is killed; the younger partners scheme against the father; Arnold (again) cheats on his wife, and so forth. In a twist that would make Foucault happy, honesty only becomes an issue in relation to the representation of sex and sexuality, and more particularly, sexual choice.

Enough of the foreplay. Let's analyze what the image of the kiss is nodding to. There is of course the distinct possibility that once again we have a straight representation of the titillation of lesbianism or a convenient way to kill off the development of a potential lesbian couple on the show. However, the image of the kiss is also deeply invested with other knowledges. A new traditionalist reading reveals the (nasty) nod about career women in general and female lawyers in particular: this draws its meaning from representations that would have shown them as sublimating their maternal (new traditionalist) choices in their work. Here we have hard women, phallic postfeminists, who wield power in the boardroom instead of in the bedroom. The nudge, nudge—wink, wink is along the lines of "they can't get a man, so they resort to women."

As such the image does not overly bother the smooth running of dominant discourses. However, when we consider the kiss's relation to honesty, things get more interesting. C.J.'s line to Abby about not being honest enough to be a friend let alone anything else reinvests the image with other knowledges. For a start, in this context the image of honesty brings with it images of secrecy and coming out. Here an intertextual nod is given to a previous story line about the politics of "outing." However, honesty is also deeply connected to the discourse of new traditionalism as the return of fundamental values to America. The nod here is to the image of George Washington being unable to tell a lie or to the revamped image of George Bush saying "read my lips." While non-Americans may be amazed at the widespread dishonesty that is a part of American popular culture (from Watergate and Irangate to the way *Dallas* wrote off an entire season as just "a dream"), being straightforward is a truly American image. (Where else could one find images such as the slogan for Missouri—"The Show-me State"?)

Honesty is therefore nothing new within American discourses on America; it is, however, novel when it becomes the key issue in the depiction of sexual attraction between two women. One reading of the winking image of honesty is that C.J. wants Abby to choose to come out. Against the depiction of Abby desperately drinking wine in order to get ready for the continuation and consummation of the kiss, C.J. wants an honest choice. This in turn nods to that most troublesome knowledge—you can *choose* to be lesbian or bisexual. Overriding previous images of gays and lesbians as "being" homosexual, this image is invested with the fact that homosexuality can and is chosen; it is a "fundamental" choice. And as Nike says so well, just do it.

Needless to say, this image of choosing to be with a woman is deeply bothersome to the dominant discourses of heterosexuality. As Eve Kosofsky Sedgewick (1990: 71) argues,

> a lot of the energy of attention and demarcation that has swirled around issues of homosexuality since the end of the nineteenth century, in Europe and the United States, has been impelled by the distinctively indicative relation of homosexuality to wider mappings of secrecy and disclosure, and of the private and the public, that were and are critically problematical for the gender, sexual, and economic structures of the heterosexist culture at large.

The kiss, and what follows, articulates the openness of choice and causes energies to swirl. Set in the corporate family, this image puts into motion questions about the hegemony of heterosexuality: it disturbs the discursive logic whereby one is always already straight or gay. While I make no pretense that this image alone can topple heterosexist rule, what is interesting is the way in which this kiss colludes with the dominant interpretations of choiceoisie as it ever so slightly disrupts and discomforts them. After all, in a postfeminist economy no one questions the right of women to choose whether to work or not. The choice of whom one sleeps with is now also firmly embedded within popular knowledges and representations. It seems to me that as choice builds upon choice, the question of sexual choice is only a wink away.

CHOOSING OUR OWN CHOICES

Of course my reading of the choices on offer may only be wishful thinking. However, there is a logic in my analysis that precisely wants to turn on a mode of thinking that can realize wishes. In conclusion I want to restate the problematic that choiceoisie constitutes for feminist analysis. As a structure of feeling, choiceoisie can be said to be rearticulating the way in which our material choices (or lack of them) feel. It can be argued that postfeminism holds out a brave new world for women where they will no longer need feminism. As such it constitutes both reactionary and utopic sets of discourses. Many of the images that currently surround us try to articulate the reactionary with the utopic by offering women an image of what is already chosen, by offering choice within a paradigm of the "fundamental." One feminist reaction to this scenario would be to forcefully point out that women (as a class) cannot buy into these choices, that quite simply, choiceoisie is but the updating of an entrenched bourgeois ideology. In many ways this analysis is correct; the choices on offer are not for most of us, and furthermore they are clearly articulated in a rampant individualism. However, what I have been arguing is that images can rearrange the affective knowledge of the material: they can be made to change the ways in which our lives feel to us.

The feminist analysis I have been proposing focuses on how we can put the discourses and images of choice to work for us. In reversing the logic of the chiasmas which operates in choiceoisie, by displacing the quality of choosing something actively back onto the choices we want and need to make, we can begin to put the choice back into prochoice. For a start this means confronting choiceoisie by analyzing the way its images wink at other social knowledges. In taking up the polysemic nature of these images, a feminist analysis can then turn the image in other directions and trace out alternative lines of articulation. Thus, for example, the *L.A. Law* kiss becomes more than the sum of four lips; reworked, it has the potential to raise the question of coming out and being honest about one's feelings for women. At the very least it shows a postfeminist woman who can say that she likes women; it also shows, in the image of Abby, how difficult it is in our culture for women to choose women. This may be as far as the televisual image goes; it is not, however, the extent of how it may feel at home. Furthermore, it cannot be the end point of feminist analyses.

The feminist choice that I make in the spirit of the "as if" is to read this image of a kiss between women as the start of something more. I choose to take it seriously, as a sign of passion between two women. I also choose to articulate it as a challenge on both a personal and theoretical level. From ACT UP's "kiss-ins" to Gran Fury's poster of same-sex couples of various colors kissing, we know that kisses do make a difference. The point then is to take the choices on offer and to remake them as feminist images—ones that wink and nod and nudge their ways into our lives. In so doing, in folding and bending the discourses of choice, we can put forward other choices that are hidden in the logics of postfeminism and new traditionalism. In the final analysis, this redhead is for all the choices she can get.

NOTES

1. Morris (1988a) forcefully raises the very limited theoretical vocabulary of some cultural studies' practitioners. Her argument inspired my article, Probyn 1990, wherein I critique John Fiske's construction of the feminine as an ontological category of resistance. I should also mention that the term *choiceoisie* is originally Leslie Savan's (1989).

2. "Structure of feeling" is one of Raymond Williams's key terms, which he variously defines. One of my favorite definitions is the following: "It is as firm and definite as 'structure' suggests, yet it operates in the most delicate and tangible parts of our activity. In one sense, this structure of feeling is the culture of a period: it is the particular living result of all the elements in the general organisation" (1954: 48). Unfortunately there is not the time to enter into a full discussion of the use of this term in Williams's analysis. However, for some of the debates raised by his concept of "structure of feeling," see the interviews that *New Left Review* conducted with Williams (in Williams 1979). I discuss the ways in which Williams can be of use and inspiration to feminist cultural analysis in Probyn 1933.

3. After I completed this chapter I had the pleasure of listening to Mayne's "*L.A. Law* and Prime-Time Lesbianism" at the "Console-ing Passions: Television, Video, and Feminism" Conference, University of Iowa, April 1992. Among many important points, Mayne raised the theoretical necessity of acknowledging the informal lesbian gossip phone trees in relation to lesbian representations on television.

REFERENCES

Althusser, Louis. 1975. "The Object of Capital." In Louis Althusser and Etienne Balibar, *Reading Capital*. Trans. Ben Brewster. London: New Left Books.

Braidotti, Rosi. 1989. "The Politics of Ontological Difference." In *Between Feminism and Psychoanalysis*, ed. Teresa Brennan. London: Routledge.

de Lauretis, Teresa. 1987. *Technologies of Gender*. Bloomington: Indiana University Press.

Le Doeuff, Michèle. 1981–1982. "Pierre Roussel's Chiasmas." *I&C*, no. 9, pp. 39–70.

Grossberg, Lawrence. 1984. "Strategies of Marxist Cultural Interpretation." *Critical Studies in Mass Communication* 1: 392–421.

Foucault, Michel. 1988. *Technologies of the Self*. Ed. Luther H. Martin, Huck Gutman, and Patrick H. Hutton. Amherst: University of Massachusetts Press.

Lyotard, Jean-François. 1986. *Le postmoderne expliqué qux enfants*. Paris: Galilée.

Mayne, Judith. 1988. "*LA Law* and Prime-Time Television." *Discourse* 10(2): 30–47.

Morris, Meaghan. 1988a. "Banality in Cultural Studies." *Discourse* 10(2): 3–29.

———. 1988b. "Operative Reasoning: Reaching Michèle Le Doeuff." In *The Pirate's Fiancée: Feminism, Reading, Postmodernism*. London: Verso.

Probyn, Elspeth. 1990. "New Traditionalism and Post-Feminism: TV Does the Home." *Screen* 31(2): 147–159.

———. 1993. *Sexing the Self: Gendered Positions in Cultural Studies*. London: Routledge.

Savan, Leslie. 1989. "Op Ad." *Village Voice*, 7 March.

Sedgewick, Eve Kosofsky. 1990. *Epistemology of the Closet*. Berkeley: University of California Press.

Showalter, Elaine. 1986. "Shooting the Rapids." *Oxford Literary Review*, 218–224.

Weinstock, Jane. 1989. "Out of Her Mind: Fantasies of the 26th New York Film Festival." *Camera Obscura* 19: 138–140.

Williams, Raymond. 1979. *Politics and Letters*. London: Verso.

Williams, Raymond, with Michael Orrom. 1954. *Preface to Film*. London: Film Drama.

"MATERIAL GIRL": THE EFFACEMENTS OF POSTMODERN CULTURE

Susan Bordo

PLASTICITY AS POSTMODERN PARADIGM

In a culture in which organ transplants, life-extension machinery, micro-surgery, and artificial organs have entered everyday medicine, we seem on the verge of practical realization of the seventeenth-century imagination of body as machine. But if we have technically and technologically realized that conception, it can also be argued that metaphysically we have deconstructed it. In the early modern era, machine imagery helped to articulate a totally determined human body whose basic functionings the human being was helpless to alter. The then dominant metaphors for this body—clocks, watches, collections of springs—imagined a system that is set, wound up, whether by nature or God the watchmaker, ticking away in predictable, orderly manner, regulated by laws over which the human being has no control. Understanding the system, we can help it to perform efficiently, and intervene when it malfunctions. But we cannot radically alter the configuration of things.

Pursuing this modern, determinist fantasy to its limits, fed by the currents of consumer capitalism, modern ideologies of the self, and their crystallization in the dominance of "American" mass culture, Western science and technology have now arrived, paradoxically but predictably (for it was a submerged, illicit element in the mechanist conception all along), at a new, "postmodern" imagination of human freedom from bodily determination. Gradually and surely, a technology that was first aimed at the replacement of malfunctioning parts has generated an industry and an ideology fueled by fantasies of rearranging, transforming, and correcting, an ideology of limitless improvement and change, defying the historicity, the mortality, and indeed the very materiality of the body. In place of that materiality, we now have what I call "cultural plastic." In place of God the watchmaker, we now have ourselves, the master sculptors of that plastic. This disdain for material limits, and intoxication with freedom, change, and self-determination, is enacted not only on the level of the contemporary technology of the body but in a wide range of contexts, including much of contemporary discourse on the body, both casual and theoretical, popular and academic. In this chapter, looking at a variety of these discursive contexts, I attempt to describe key elements of this paradigm of plasticity and expose some of its effacements—the material and social realities that it denies or renders invisible.

PLASTIC BODIES

"Create a masterpiece, sculpt your body into a work of art," urges *Fit* magazine. "You visualize what you want to look like, and then you create that form." "The challenge presents itself: to rearrange things." "It's up to you to do the chiseling. You become the master sculptress" (quoted in Rosen 1983: 72, 61). The precision technology of body sculpting, once the secret of the Arnold Schwarzeneggers and Rachel McLishes of the professional bodybuilding world, has now become available to anyone who can afford the price of membership in a gym. "I now look at bodies," says John Travolta, after training for the movie *Staying Alive,* "almost like pieces of clay that can be molded" (*Syracuse Herald,* 13 January 1985). On the medical front, plastic surgery, whose repeated and purely cosmetic employment has been legitimated by Michael Jackson, Cher, and others, has become a fabulously expanding industry, extending its domain from nose jobs, face lifts, tummy tucks, and breast augmentations to collagen-plumped lips and liposuction-shaped ankles, calves, and buttocks. In 1989, 681,000 procedures were done, up 80 percent over 1981; over half of these were performed on patients between the ages of eighteen and thirty-five (*Cosmopolitan,* May 1990, p. 96). Trendy *Details* magazine describes "surgical stretching, tucking and sucking [as] another fabulous [fashion] accessory" and invites readers to share their cosmetic surgery experiences in the monthly column "Knifestyles of the Rich and Famous." In that column, the transportation of fat from one part of the body to another is described as breezily as changing hats:

> Dr. Brown is an artist. He doesn't just pull and tuck and forget about you. . . . He did liposuction on my neck, did the nose job

and tightened up my forehead to give it a better line. Then he took some fat from the side of my waist and injected it into my hands. It goes in as a lump, and then he smoothes it out with his hands to where it looks good. I'll tell you something, the nose and neck made a big change, but nothing in comparison to how fabulous my hands look. The fat just smoothed out all the lines, the veins don't stick up anymore, the skin actually looks soft and great. [But] you have to be careful not to bang your hands. (Lizardi and Frankel 1990: 38)

Popular culture applies no brakes to these fantasies of rearrangement and self-transformation. Rather, we are constantly told that we can "choose" our own bodies. "The proper diet, the right amount of exercise and you can have, pretty much, any body you desire," claims Evian. Of course the rhetoric of choice and self-determination and the breezy analogies comparing cosmetic surgery to fashion accesorizing are deeply mystifying. They efface not only the inequalities of privilege, money, and time that prohibit most people from indulging in these practices, but the desperation that characterizes the lives of those who do. "I will do anything, *anything*, to make myself look and feel better," says Tina Lizardi (whose "Knifestyles" experience I quoted above). Medical science has now designated a new category of "polysurgical addicts" (or, as more casually referred to, "scalpel slaves") who return for operation after operation, in perpetual quest of the elusive yet ruthlessly normalizing goal, the "perfect" body (Conant, Gordon, and Donovan 1988: 58–59). The dark underside of the practices of body transformation and rearrangement reveals botched and sometimes fatal operations, exercise addictions, and eating disorders. And of course despite the claims of the Evian ad, one cannot have *any* body one wants—for not every body will *do*. The very advertisements whose copy speaks of choice and self-determination visually legislate the effacement of individual and cultural difference and circumscribe our choices; all the bodies—male and female—exhibit the same lean, muscled profile.

That we are surrounded by homogenizing and normalizing images—images whose content is far from arbitrary, but instead suffused with the dominance of gendered, racial, class, and other cultural iconography—seems so obvious as to be almost embarrassing to be arguing here. Yet contemporary understandings of the behaviors I have been describing not only construct the situation very differently, but in terms that preempt precisely such a critique of cultural imagery. Moreover, they reproduce, on the level of discourse and interpretation, the same conditions that postmodern bodies enact on the level of cultural practice: a construction of life as plastic possibility and weightless choice, undetermined by history, social location, or even individual biography. A 1988 *Donahue* show offers my first illustration.

The show's focus was a series of television commercials for DuraSoft colored contact lenses. In these commercials (as they were originally aired), a woman was shown in a dreamlike, romantic fantasy—for example, parachuting slowly and gracefully from the heavens. The male voiceover then described the woman in soft, lush terms: "If I believed in angels, I'd say that's what she was—an angel, dropped from the sky like an answer to a prayer, with eyes as brown as bark (significant pause). No, I *don't think so*." At this point the tape is rewound to return us to, "With eyes as violet as the colors of a child's imagination." The commercial concludes: "DuraSoft colored contact lenses. Get brown eyes a second look."

The question posed by Donahue: Is this ad racist? Donahue clearly thought there was controversy to be stirred up here, for he stocked his audience full of women of color and white women to discuss the implications of the ad. But Donahue apparently was living in a different decade than most of his audience, who found nothing "wrong" with the ad and everything "wrong" with any inclinations to "make it a political question." Here are some comments taken from the transcript of the show:

Why does it have to be a political question? I mean, people perm their hair. It's just because they like the way it looks. It's not something sociological. Maybe black women like the way they look with green contacts. It's to be more attractive. It's not something that makes them—I mean, why do punk rockers have purple hair? Because they feel it makes them feel better. (White woman)

What's the fuss? When I put on my blue lenses, it makes me feel good. It makes me feel sexy, different, the other woman, so to speak, which is like fun. (Black woman)

I perm my hair, you're wearing makeup, what's the difference? (White woman)

I want to be versatile . . . having different looks, being able to change from one look to the other. (Black woman model)

We all do the same thing, when we're feeling good we wear new makeup, hairstyles, we buy new clothes. So now it's contact lenses. What difference does it make? (White woman)

It goes both ways . . . Bo Derek puts her hair in cornstalks, or corn . . . or whatever that thing is called. White women try to get tan. (White woman)

She's not trying to be white, she's trying to be different. (About a black woman with blue contact lenses)

It's fashion, women are never happy with themselves.

I put them in as toys, just for fun, change. Nothing too serious, and I really enjoy them. (Black woman; all quotations from Donahue transcript #05257)

Some things to note here: First, making up, fixing one's hair, and so forth are conceived only as free *play*, fun, a matter of creative expression. The one comment that hints at women's (by now depressingly well documented) dissatisfaction with their appearance trivializes that dissatisfaction and puts it beyond the pale of cultural critique: "It's fashion." What she means is: "It's *only* fashion," whose whimsical and politically neutral vicissitudes supply endless amusement for women's eternally superficial values. ("Women are never happy with themselves.") If we are never happy with ourselves, it is implied, that is due to our female nature; this unhappiness is not to be taken too seriously or made into a "political question." Second, the "contents" of fashion, the specific ideals that women are drawn to embody (ideals that vary historically, racially, and along class and other lines), are seen as arbitrary, without meaning; interpretation is neither required nor even appropriate. Rather, all motivation and value come from the interest and allure—the "sexiness"—of change and difference itself. Blue contact lenses for black women, it is admitted, make one "other" ("the other woman"). But that "other" is not a racial or cultural "other"; she is sexy because of the piquancy, the novelty, the erotics of putting on a different self. *Any* different self would do, it is implied. Closely connected to this is the construction of *all* cosmetic changes as the same: perms for the white women, corn rows on Bo Derek, tanning, makeup, changing hairstyles, blue contacts for black women—all are seen as having equal political valance (which is to say *no* political valance) and the same cultural meaning (which is to say *no* cultural meaning) in the heterogeneous yet undifferentiated context of "the things women do" "to look better, be more attractive." The one woman in the audience who offered a different construction of things, who insisted that the styles we aspire to do not simply reflect the free play of fashion or female nature—who indeed went as far as claiming that we "are brainwashed to think blond hair and blue eyes is the most beautiful of all," was regarded with hostile silence. Then, a few moments later, someone challenged: "Is there anything *wrong* with blue eyes and blond hair?" The audience enthusiastically applauded this defender of democratic values.

This "conversation"—a paradigmatically postmodern conversation, as I argue shortly—effaces the same general elements as the rhetoric of body transformation discussed earlier. First, it effaces the inequalities of social position and the historical origins which, for example, render Bo Derek's corn rows and black women's hair straightening utterly noncommensurate. On the other hand we have Bo Derek's privilege, not only as so unimpeachably white as to permit an exotic touch of "otherness" with no danger of racial contamination, but as a trend-setting famous movie star. In contrast, and mediating a black woman's "choice" to straighten her hair, is a cultural history of racist body-discriminations such as the nineteenth-century comb test, which allowed admission to churches and clubs only to those blacks who could pass through their hair without snagging it a fine-tooth comb hanging outside the door. (A variety of comparable tests—the pine-slab test, the brown bag test—determined whether one's skin was adequately light to pass muster [Glanton 1989]).

Second, and following from these historical practices, there is a "disciplinary" reality that is effaced in the construction of all self-transformation as equally arbitrary, all variants of the same trivial game, without differing cultural valance. I use the term *disciplinary* here in the Foucauldian sense, as pointing to practices which do not merely transform but *normalize* the subject. That is, and to repeat a point made earlier, not every body will do. A 1989 poll of *Essence* magazine readers revealed that 68 percent of those who responded wear their hair straightened chemically or by hot comb (*Essence,* June 1989, p. 71). "Just for fun?" The kick of being "different"? When we look at the pursuit of beauty as a normalizing discipline, it becomes clear that not all body transformations are "the same." The general tyranny of fashion—perpetual, elusive, and instructing the female body in a pedagogy of personal inadequacy and lack—is a powerful discipline for the normalization of *all* women in this culture. But even as we are all normalized to the requirements of appropriate feminine insecurity and preoccupation with appearance, more specific requirements emerge in different cultural and historical contexts, and for different groups. When Bo Derek put her hair in corn rows, she was engaging in normalizing feminine practice. But when Oprah Winfrey admitted on her show that all her life she has desperately longed to have "hair that swings from side to side" when she shakes her head, she revealed the power of racial as well as gender normalization, normalization not only to "femininity," but to the Anglo-Saxon standards of beauty that still dominate on television, in movies, in popular magazines. Neither Oprah nor the *Essence* readers (nor the many Jewish women—myself included—who ironed their hair in the 1960s) have creatively or playfully invented themselves here.

DuraSoft knows this, even if Donahue's audience does not. Since the campaign first began, the company has replaced the original, upfront magazine advertisement with a more euphemistic variant from which the word *brown* has been tastefully effaced. (In case it had become too subtle for the average reader, the model now is black—although it should be noted that DuroSoft's failure to appreciate brown eyes renders the eyes of the majority of the world's people not worth "a second look.") In the television commercial, a comparable "brownwash" was effected; here "eyes as brown as . . ." was retained, but the derogatory nouns—"brown as boots," "brown as bark"—were eliminated. The announcer simply was left speechless: "eyes as brown as . . . brown as . . . ," and then, presumably unable to come up with an enticing simile, he shifted to "violet." As in the expurgated magazine ad, the television commercial ended: "Get *your* eyes a second look."

When I showed my students these ads, many of them were as dismissive as the Donahue audience, convinced that I was once again turning innocent images and practices into "political issues." I persisted: if racial standards of beauty are not at work here, then why no brown contacts for blue-eyed people? A month later, two of my students triumphantly produced a DuraSoft ad for brown contacts, appearing in *Essence* magazine, and with an advertising campaign directed at black consumers, offering the promise *not* of "getting blues eyes a second look" by becoming excitingly darker, but of "subtly enhancing" already dark eyes, by making them *lighter* brown. The creators of the DuraSoft campaign clearly know that not all "differences" are the same in our culture, and they continue, albeit in ever more mystified form, to exploit and perpetuate that fact.

PLASTIC DISCOURSE

The Donahue DuraSoft show (and indeed, any talk show one might happen to tune to) provides a perfect example of what we might call a postmodern conversation. All sense of history and all ability (or inclination) to sustain cultural criticism, to make the distinctions and discriminations that would permit such criticism, have disappeared. Rather, in this conversation, "anything goes"—and any positioned social critique (for example, the woman who, speaking clearly from consciousness of racial oppression, insisted that the attraction of blond hair and blue eyes has a cultural meaning significantly different from that of purple hair) is immediately destabilized. Instead of distinctions, endless *differences* reign— an undifferentiated pastiche of differences, a grab bag in which no items are assigned any more importance or centrality than any others. Television is, of course, the great teacher here, our prime modeler of plastic pluralism: if one Donahue show features a feminist talking about battered wives, the next day a show features mistreated husbands. Incest, exercise addiction, women who love too much, the sex habits of priests, disturbed children of psychiatrists, male strippers—all have their day, all are given equal weight by the great leveler: the frame of the television screen.

This spectacle of difference defeats the ability to sustain coherent political critique. Everything is the same in its unvalanced difference. ("I perm my hair. You're wearing makeup. What's the difference?") Particulars reign, and generality—which collects, organizes, and prioritizes, suspending attention to particularity in the interests of connection, emphasis, and criticism—is suspect. So whenever some critically charged generalization was suggested on the Donahue Durasoft show, someone else would invariably offer a counterexample—for example, "I have blue eyes, and I'm a black woman," "Bo Derek wears corn rows"—to fragment the critique. What is remarkable is that people accept these examples *as* refutations of social critique. They almost invariably back down, utterly confused as to how to maintain their critical generalization in the face of the destabilizing example. Sometimes they qualify, claiming they meant "some" people, not all. But of course they meant neither all nor some. They meant *most*—that is, they were trying to make a claim about social or cultural *patterns*—and that is a stance that is increasingly difficult to sustain in a postmodern context, where we are surrounded by endlessly displaced images and no orienting context to make discriminations.

Those who insist on an orienting context (and who therefore do not permit particulars to reign in all their absolute "difference") are seen as "totalizing," that is, as constructing a falsely coherent and morally coercive universe that marginalizes and effaces the experiences and values of others. ("What's *wrong* with blond hair and blue eyes?") As someone who is frequently interviewed by local television and newspaper reporters, I have often found my feminist arguments framed in this way, as they were in a recent article on breast augmentation surgery. After several pages of "expert" recommendations from plastic surgeons, my cautions about the politics of female body transformation (none of them critical of individuals contemplating plastic surgery, all of them of a "cultural" nature) were briefly quoted by the reporter, who then went on to end the piece with a comment on *my* critique—from the director of communications for the American Society of Plastic and Reconstructive Surgery:

> Those not considering plastic surgery shouldn't be too critical of those who do. It's the hardest thing for people to understand. What's important is if it's a problem to that person. We're all different, but we all want to look better. We're just different in what extent we'll go to. But none of us can say we don't want to look the best we can. (Bien 1990)

With this tolerant, egalitarian stroke, the media liaison of the most powerful plastic surgery lobby in the country presents herself as the protector of "difference" against the homogenizing and stifling regime of the feminist dictator.

Academics do not usually like to think of themselves as embodying the values and preoccupations of popular culture on the plane of high theory or intellectual discourse. We prefer to see ourselves as the demystifyers of popular discourse, bringers-to-consciousness-and-clarity rather than unconscious reproducers of culture. Despite what we would *like* to believe of ourselves, however, we are always within the society that we criticize, and never so strikingly as at the present postmodern moment. All the elements of what I have here called "postmodern conversation"—intoxication with individual choice and creative *jouissance*, delight with the piquancy of particularity and mistrust of pattern and seeming coherence, celebration of "difference" along with an absence of critical perspective differentiating and weighing "differences," suspicion of the totalitarian nature of generalization along with a rush to protect difference from its homogenizing abuses—all have become recognizable and familiar elements of much of contemporary intellectual discourse. Within this theoretically self-conscious universe, moreover, these elements are not merely embodied (as in the Donahue/DuraSoft conversation), but are explicitly thematized and *celebrated*—as inaugurating new constructions of the self, no longer caught in the mythology of the unified subject, embracing of multiplicity, challenging the dreary and moralizing generalizations about gender, race, and so forth that have no preoccupied liberal and left humanism.

For this celebratory, academic postmodernism, it has become highly unfashionable—and "totalizing"—to talk about the grip of culture on the body. Such perspective, it is argued, casts active and creative subjects as "cultural dopes," "passive dupes" of ideology; it gives too much to dominant ideology, imagining it as seamless and univocal, overlooking both the gaps which are continually allowing for the eruption of "difference" and the polysemous, unstable, open nature of all cultural texts. To talk about the grip of culture on the body (as, for example, in "old" feminist discourse about the objectification and sexualization of the female body) is to fail to acknowledge, as theorist Janice Radway put it, "the cultural work by which nomadic, fragmented, active subjects confound dominant discourse" (Duke University, spring 1989).

So, for example, contemporary culture critic John Fiske (1987b: 19) is harshly critical of what he describes as the view of television as a "dominating monster" with "homogenizing power" over the perceptions of viewers. Such a view, he argues, imagines the audience as "powerless and undiscriminating," and overlooks the fact that

> Pleasure results from a particular relationship between meanings and power. . . . There is no pleasure in being a "cultural dope." . . . Pleasure results from the production of meanings of the world and of self that are felt to serve the interests of the reader rather than those of the dominant. The subordinate may be disempowered, but they are not powerless. There is a power in resisting power, there is a power in maintaining one's social identity in opposition to that proposed by the dominant ideology, there is a power in asserting one's own subcultural values against the dominant ones. There is, in short, a power in being different.

Fiske then goes on to produce numerous examples of how *Dallas, Hart to Hart,* and other television shows have been read (or so he argues) by various subcultures to make their own "socially pertinent" and empowering meanings out of "the semiotic resources provided by television."

Note, in Fiske's insistent, repetitive invocation of the category of "power," a characteristically postmodern flattening of the terrain of power relations, a lack of differentiation between, for example, the power involved in creative *reading* in the isolation of one's own home and the power held by those who control the material production of television shows, or the power involved in public protest and action against the conditions of that production, or the dominant meanings—for example, racist and sexist images and messages—therein produced. For Fiske, of course, there are no such dominant meanings, that is, no elements whose ability to grip the imagination of the viewer is greater than the viewer's ability to "just say no," through resistant reading of the text. That ethnic and subcultural meaning *may* be wrested from *Dallas* and *Hart to Hart* becomes for Fiske proof that dominating images and messages are only in the minds of those totalitarian critics who would condescendingly "rescue" the disempowered from those forces that are in fact the very medium of their creative freedom and resistance ("the semiotic resources of television").

Fiske's conception of power—a terrain without hill and valleys, where all "forces" have become "resources"—reflects a common post-modern misappropriation of Foucault. Fiske conceives of power as the *possession* of individuals or groups, something they "have"—a conception Foucault takes great pains to criticize—rather than (as in Foucault's reconstruction) a dynamic of noncentralized forces, its dominant historical forms attaining their hegemony not from magisterial design or decree, but through multiple "processes, of different origin and scattered location," regulating and normalizing the most intimate and minute elements of the construction of time, space, desire, embodiment (Foucault 1979: 138). This conception of power does *not* entail that there are no dominant positions, social structures, or ideologies emerging from the play of forces; the fact that power is not held by any *one* does not mean that it is equally held by *all*. It is "held" by no one; rather, people and groups are positioned differentially within it. This model is particularly useful to the analysis of male dominance and female subordination, so much of which is reproduced "voluntarily," through our self-normalization to everyday habits of masculinity and femininity. (This is what Fiske calls being a "cultural dope.") Within such a model, one can acknowledge that women may indeed contribute to the perpetuation of female subordination (for example, by embracing, taking pleasure in, and even feeling empowered by the cultural objectification and sexualization of the female body) without this entailing that they have "power" in the production and reproduction of sexist culture.

Foucault does insist on the *instability* of modern power relations, that is, that resistance is perpetual and unpredictable, and hegemony precarious. This notion is transformed by Fiske (perhaps under the influence of a more deconstructionist brand of postmodernism) into a notion of resistance as *jouissance,* a creative and pleasurable eruption of cultural "difference" through the "seams" of the text. What this celebration of creative-reading-as-resistance effaces is the arduous and frequently frustrated historical struggle required for the subordinated to articulate and assert the value of their "difference" in the face of dominant meanings—meanings that often offer a pedagogy directed at the reinforcement of feelings of inferiority, marginality, ugliness. During the early 1950s, when *Brown v. the Board of Education* was wending its way through the courts, as a demonstration of the destructive psychological effects of segregation, black children were asked to look at two baby dolls, identical in all respects except color. The children were asked a series of questions: Which is the nice doll? Which is the bad doll? Which doll would you like to play with? The majority of black children, Kenneth Clark reports, attributed the positive characteristics to the white doll and the negative characteristics to the black. When Clark asked one final question— "Which doll is like you?"—they looked at him, as he says, "as though he were the devil himself" for putting them in that predicament, for forcing them to face the inexorable and hideous logical implications of their situation. Northern children often ran out of the room; southern children tended to answer the question in shamed embarrassment. Clark recalls one little boy who laughed, "Who am I like? That doll! It's a nigger and I'm a nigger!" (related by Clark in Bill Moyers, "A Walk through the Twentieth Century: The Second American Revolution," PBS Boston).

Not acknowledging the hegemonic power of normalizing imagery can be just as effacing of people's experiences of racial oppression as lack of attentiveness to cultural and ethnic differences, and just as implicated in racial bias—as postmodern critics sometimes seem to forget. A recent article in *Essence* described the experience of a young black woman who had struggled with compulsive overeating and dieting for years and who had finally sought advice from her high-school guidance counselor, only to be told that she didn't have to worry about managing her weight because "black women can go beyond the stereotype of woman as sex object" and "fat is more acceptable in the black community." Saddled with the white woman's projection onto her of the stereotype of the asexual, maternal Mammy, the young woman was left to struggle with an eating disorder that she wasn't "supposed" to have (Powers 1989).

None of this is to *deny* what Fiske calls "the power of being different," but rather to insist that it is won through ongoing political *struggle* rather than through an act of creative interpretation. Here, once again, although many postmodern academics may claim Foucault as their guiding light, they differ from him in significant and revealing ways. For Foucault, the metaphorical terrain of resistance is explicitly that of the "battle"; the "points of confrontation" may be "innumerable" and "instable," but they involve a serious, often deadly struggle of embodied (that is, historically situated and shaped) forces (Foucault 1979: 26–27). The Foucauldian metaphor of the body as battleground (rather than postmodern playground) more adequately captures, as well, the *practical* difficulties involved in the political struggle to empower "differences." *Essence* magazine consciously and strenuously has tried to promote diverse images of black strength, beauty, and self-acceptance. Beauty features celebrate the glory of black skin and lush lips; other departments feature interviews with accomplished black women writers, activists, and teachers, many of whom model styles of body and dress that challenge the hegemony of white Anglo-Saxon standards. The magazine's advertisers, however, continually play upon and perpetuate consumers' feelings of inadequacy and insecurity over the racial characteristics of their bodies. Advertisers insist (albeit in more mystified form than in the 1950s, when products were labeled "straightener" and "bleach cream") that hair must be "relaxed" and skin "faded" in order to be beautiful; they almost always employ models with fair skin, Anglo-Saxon features, and (as one ad describes it) "hair that moves," ensuring association of their products with fantasies of becoming what the white culture most prizes and rewards. In every issue, *Essence* thus fights an ongoing battle over the black woman's body and the power of its "differences" ("differences" which actual black women embody to widely varying degrees, of course), struggling to keep its message of African-American self-acceptance clear and dominant, while submitting to economic necessities on which its survival depends. Let me make it clear here that such self-acceptance, not the reverse tyranny that constructs light-skinned and Anglo-featured African-Americans as "not black enough," is the message *Essence* is trying to convey, against a culture which has declared for centuries that to be black is already to be "too black." This terrain, clearly, is not a playground, but a minefield that threatens to deconstruct "difference" *literally* (and not merely literarily) at every turn.

307

"MATERIAL GIRL": MADONNA
AS POSTMODERN HEROINE

John Fiske's conception of "difference," in the section quoted above, at least imagines resistance as challenging specifiable historical forms of dominance. Women, he argues, connect with subversive "feminine" values leaking through the patriarchal plot of soap operas; blacks laugh to themselves at the glossy, materialist-cowboy culture of "Dallas." Such examples suggest a resistance directed against *particular* historical forms of power and subjectivity. For some postmodern theorists, however, resistance is imagined as the refusal to embody *any* positioned subjectivity at all; what is celebrated is continual creative escape from location, containment, and definition. So, as Susan Rubin Suleiman (1986: 24) advises, we must move beyond the valorization of historically suppressed values (for example, those values that have been culturally constructed as belonging to an inferior, female domain and generally expunged from Western science, philosophy, and religion) and toward "endless complication" and a "dizzying accumulation of narratives." She appreciatively (and perhaps misleadingly) invokes Derrida's metaphor of "incalculable choreographies" to capture the dancing, elusive, continually changing subjectivity that she envisions, a subjectivity without gender, without history, without location. From this perspective, the truly resistant female body is not the body that wages war against feminine sexualization and objectification, but the body that, as Cathy Schwichtenberg (1990) has put it, "uses simulation strategically in ways that challenge the stable notion of gender as the edifice of sexual difference . . . [in] an erotic politics in which the female body can be refashioned in the flux of identities that speak in plural styles." For this erotic politics, the new postmodern heroine is Madonna.

This celebration of Madonna as postmodern heroine is not the first time she has been portrayed as a subversive culture-figure. Until recently, however, Madonna's resistance has been seen along "body as battleground" lines, as deriving from her refusal to allow herself to be constructed as a passive object of patriarchal desire. John Fiske, for example, argues that this was a large part of Madonna's original appeal to her "wanna-bes"—those hoards of largely white, middle-class preteens who mimicked Madonna's moves and costumes. For the "wanna-bes," Madonna demonstrated the possibility of a female heterosexuality independent of patriarchal control, a sexuality that defied rather than rejected the male gaze, teasing it with her *own* gaze, deliberately trashy and vulgar, challenging anyone to call her a whore and ultimately not giving a damn what judgments might be made of her. Madonna's rebellious sexuality, in this reading, offered itself not as coming into being through the look of the Other, but as self-defining and in love with, happy with itself—something rather difficult for women to achieve in this culture—and which helps explain, as Fiske (1987a) argues, her enormous appeal to teenage girls. "I like the way she handles herself, sort of take it or leave it; she's sexy but she doesn't need men . . . she's kind of there all by herself," says one. "She gives us ideas. It's really women's lib, not being afraid of what guys think," says another (quoted in Skow 1985: 77).

Madonna herself, significantly and unlike most sex symbols, has never advertised herself as disdainful of feminism or constructed feminists as man-haters. Rather, in a 1985 *Time* interview, she suggests that her lack of inhibition in "being herself," and her "luxuriant" expression of "strong" sexuality, is her *own* brand of feminist celebration (Skow 1985: 81). Some feminist theorists would agree. Molly Hite (1988: 121–122), for example, argues that "asserting female desire in a culture in which female sexuality is viewed as so inextricably conjoined with passivity" is "transgressive":

> Implied in this strategy is the old paradox of the speaking statue, the created thing that magically begins to create, for when a woman writes—self-consciously from her muted position as a woman and not as an honorary man—about female desire, female sexuality, female sensuous experience generally, her performance has the effect of giving voice to pure corporeality, of turning a product of the dominant meaning-system into a producer of meanings. A woman, conventionally identified with her body, writes about that identification, and as a consequence, femininity—silent and inert by definition—erupts into patriarchy as an impossible discourse.

Not all feminists would agree with this statement, of course. For the sake of the contrast I want to draw here, however, let us grant it and note as well that an argument similar to Fiske's can be made concerning Madonna's refusal to be obedient to dominant and normalizing standards of female *beauty*. I'm now talking, of course, about Madonna in her more fleshy days. In those days, Madonna saw herself as willfully out of step with the times. "Back in the fifties," she says in the *Time* interview, "women weren't ashamed of their bodies." (The fact that she is dead wrong is not relevant here.) Identifying herself with that time and what she calls its lack of "suppression" of femininity, she looks down her nose at the "androgynous" clothes of our time and speaks warmly of her own stomach, "not really flat" but "round and the skin is smooth and I like it." Contrasting herself to anorectics, whom she sees as self-denying and self-hating, completely in the thrall of externally imposed standards of worthiness, Madonna (as she saw herself) stood for self-definition through the assertion of her own (traditionally "female" and now anachronistic) body type.

Of course this is no longer Madonna's body type. Shortly after her 1987 marriage to Sean Penn she began a strenuous reducing and exercise program, now runs several miles a day, lifts weights, and has developed, in obedience to dominant contemporary norms, a tight, slender, muscular body. Why did she decide to shape up? "I didn't have a flat stomach anymore," she has said. "I had become well-rounded." Please note the sharp about-face here, from pride to embarrassment. My point, however, is not to suggest that Madonna's formerly voluptuous body was a nonalienated, freely expressive body, a "natural" body. While the slender body is the current cultural ideal, the voluptuous female body is a cultural form too (as are all bodies) and was a coercive ideal in the 1950s. My point is that in terms of Madonna's *own* former lexicon of meanings—within which feminine voluptuousness and the choice to be round in a culture of the lean were clearly connected to spontaneity, self-definition, and defiance of the cultural gaze—the terms set by that gaze have now triumphed. Madonna has been normalized; more precisely, she has self-normalized. Her "wanna-bes" are following suit. Studies suggest that as many as 80 percent of nine-year-old suburban girls (the majority of whom are far from overweight) are making rigorous dieting and exercise the organizing discipline of their lives (*Wall Street Journal*, 11 February 1986). They don't require Madonna's example, of course, to believe that they must be thin to be acceptable. But Madonna clearly no longer provides a model of resistance or "difference" for them.

None of this "materiality"—that is, the obsessive body-praxis that regulates and disciplines Madonna's life and the lives of the young (and not so young) women who emulate her—makes its way into the representation of Madonna as postmodern heroine. In the terms of this representation (in both its popular and scholarly instantiations), Madonna is "in control of her image, not trapped by it"; the proof is her ironic and chameleonlike approach to the construction of her identity, her ability to "slip in and out of character at will," (Texier 1990) to defy definition, to keep them guessing. In this coding of things, as in the fantasies of the polysurgical addict (and, as I have argued elsewhere, the eating-disordered woman [Bordo 1985], *control* and *power*—words that are

310

invoked over and over in discussions of Madonna—have become equivalent to *self-creating*. Madonna's new body has no material history: it conceals its continued struggle to maintain itself; it does not reveal its pain. (Significantly, Madonna's "self-exposé," the documentary *Truth or Dare*, does not include any scenes of her daily workouts.) It is merely another creative transformation of an ever-elusive subjectivity. "More Dazzling and Determined Not to Stop Changing," *Cosmopolitan* (July 1987) describes Madonna: "whether in looks or career, this multitalented dazzler will never be trapped in *any* mold!" The plasticity of Madonna's subjectivity is emphasized again and again in the popular press, particularly by Madonna herself. It is how she tells the story of her "power" in the industry. "In pop music, generally, people have one image. You get pigeonholed. I'm lucky enough to be able to change and still be accepted . . . play a part, change characters, looks, attitudes" (Ansen 1990: 311).

Madonna claims that her creative work too is meant to escape definition. "Everything I do is meant to have several meanings, to be ambiguous," she says. She resists, however (and in true postmodern fashion), the attribution of serious artistic intent; rather (as she recently told *Cosmo*) she favors irony and ambiguity "to entertain myself" and (as she told *Vanity Fair*) out of "rebelliousness and a desire to fuck with people" (Sessums 1990: 208). It is the postmodern nature of her music and videos that has most entranced academic critics, whose accolades reproduce in highly theoretical language the same notions emphasized in the popular press. Susan McClary (1990: 2) writes:

> Madonna's art itself repeatedly deconstructs the traditional notion of the unified subject with finite ego boundaries. Her pieces explore . . . various ways of constituting identities that refuse stability, that remain fluid, that resist definition. This tendency in her work has become increasingly pronounced; for instance, in her recent controversial video "Express Yourself" . . . she slips in and out of every subject position offered within the video's narrative context . . . refusing more than ever to deliver the security of a clear, unambiguous message or an "authentic" self.

Later in the same piece, McClary describes "Open Your Heart to Me," which features Madonna as a porn star in a peep show, as creating "an image of open-ended *jouissance*—an erotic energy that continually escapes containment" (1990: 12). Now to many feminist viewers, this particular video may be quite disturbing for a number of reasons. First, unlike many of Madonna's older videos, and like most of her more recent ones, "Open Your Heart" does not visually emphasize Madonna's subjectivity or desire—through, for example, frequent shots of Madonna's face and eyes, flirting with and controlling the reactions of the viewer. Rather, it places the viewer in the position of the voyeur by presenting Madonna's body-as-object, now perfectly, plasticity taut and tightly managed, for display. To be sure we do not identify with the slimy men depicted *in* the video, drooling over Madonna's performance; but, as E. Ann Kaplan (1983) has pointed out, the way men view women *in* the filmic world is only one species of objectifying "gaze." There is also *our* (that is, the viewer's) gaze, which may be encouraged by the director to be either more or less objectifying. In "Open Your Heart," as in virtually all rock videos, the female body is offered to the viewer purely as a spectacle, an object of sight, a visual commodity to be consumed. Madonna's weight loss and dazzling shaping-up job make the spectacle of her body all the more compelling; we are riveted to her body, fascinated by it. Many men and women may experience the primary reality of the video as the elicitation of desire *for* that perfect body; women, however, may also be gripped by the desire (and likely impossibility) of *becoming* that perfect body.

These elements can be effaced, of course, by a deliberate abstraction of the video from the cultural context in which it is historically embedded (the continuing containment, sexualization, and objectification of the female body) and in which the viewer is implicated as well, and by treating the video as a purely formal "text." Taken as such, "Open Your Heart" presents itself as what Kaplan (1987: 63) calls a "postmodern video": it refuses to "take a clear position *vis à vis* its images" and similarly refuses a "clear position for the spectator within the filmic world . . . leaving him/her decentered, confused." McClary's reading of "Open Your Heart" emphasizes precisely these postmodern elements, insisting on the ambiguous and unstable nature of the relationships depicted in the narrative of the video and the frequent elements of parody and play. "The usual power relationship between the voyeuristic male gaze and object" is "destabilized," she claims, by the portrayal of the male patrons of the porno house as leering and pathetic. At the same time, the portrayal of Madonna as porno-queen-object is deconstructed, McClary argues, by the end of the video, which has Madonna changing her clothes to those of a little boy and tripping off playfully, leaving the manager of the house sputtering behind her. McClary reads this as "escape to androgyny," which "refuses essentialist gender categories and turns sexual identity into a kind of play." As to the gaze of the viewer, she admits that it is "risky" to "invoke the image of porn queen in order to perform its deconstruction," but concludes that the deconstruction is successful: "In this video, Madonna confronts the most pernicious of her stereotypes and attempts to channel it into a very different realm: a realm where the feminine object need not be the object of the patriarchal gaze, where its energy can motivate play and nonsexual pleasure" (McClary 1990: 13).

I would argue, however, that despite the video's evasions of clear or fixed meaning, there *is* a dominant position in this video, and it is that of the objectifying gaze. One is not *really* decentered and confused by this video, despite the "ambiguities" it formally contains. Indeed, the video's postmodern conceits, I would suggest, facilitate rather than deconstruct the presentation of Madonna's body as an object on display. For in the absence of a coherent critical position *on* the images, the individual images themselves become preeminent, hypnotic, fixating. Indeed, I would say that ultimately this video is entirely about Madonna's body, the narrative context virtually irrelevant, an excuse to showcase the physical achievements of the star, a video centerfold. On this level, any parodic or destabilizing element appears as utterly, cynically, mechanically tacked on, in bad faith, a way of claiming trendy status for what is really just cheesecake—or, perhaps, soft-core pornography.

Indeed, it may be worse than that. If the playful "tag" ending of "Open Your Heart" is successful in deconstructing the notion that the objectification, the sexualization of women's bodies is a serious business, then Madonna's *jouissance* may be "fucking with" her youthful viewer's perceptions in a dangerous way. Judging from the proliferation of rock lyrics celebrating the rape, abuse, and humiliation of women, the message—not Madonna's responsibility alone, of course, but hers among others, surely—is getting through. The artists who perform these misogynist songs also claim to be speaking playfully, tongue-in-cheek, and to be daring and resistant transgressors of cultural structures that contain and define. Ice T, whose rap lyrics gleefully describe the gang rape of a woman—with a flashlight, to "make her tits light up"—claims that he is only "telling it like it is" among black street youth (he compares himself to Richard Wright) and scoffs at feminist humorlessness, implying as well that it is racist and repressive for white feminists to try to deny him his indigenous "style." The fact that Richard Wright embedded his depiction of Bigger Thomas within a critique of the racist culture that shaped him, and that *Native Son* is meant to be a *tragedy,* was not, apparently, noticed in Ice T's "postmodern" reading of the book, whose critical point of view he utterly ignores. Nor does he seem concerned about what appears to be a growing fad—not only among street gangs, but in fraternity houses as well—for gang rape, often with an unconscious woman and surrounded by male spectators. (Some of the terms popularly used to describe these rapes include "beaching"—the woman being likened to a "beached whale"—and "spectoring," to emphasize how integral a role the onlookers play.)

As for Madonna and the liberating postmodern subjectivity that McClary and others claim she is offering, the notion that one can play a porno house by night and regain one's androgynous innocence by day does not seem to me to be a refusal of essentialist categories about gender, but rather a new inscription of mind/body dualism. What the body does is immaterial, so long as the imagination is free. This abstract, unsituated, disembodied freedom, I have argued in this essay, celebrates itself only through the effacement of the material praxis of people's lives, the normalizing power of cultural images, and the continuing social realities of dominance and subordination.

NOTE

This article originally appeared in *Michigan Quarterly Review*, Fall 1990. It is here reprinted with minor revisions and without the illustrations that accompanied the original version. An illustrated version also appears in my book *Unbearable Weight: Feminism, Western Culture and the Body*, University of California Press, 1993.

REFERENCES

Ansen, David. 1990. "Magnificent Maverick." *Cosmopolitan*, May, p. 311.
Bien, Linda. 1990. "Building a Better Bust." *Syracuse Herald*, 4 March.
Bordo, Susan. 1985. "Anorexia Nervosa: Psychopathology as the Crystallization of Culture." *Philosophical Forum* 17(2): 73–103.
Conant, Jennet, Jeanne Gordon, and Jennifer Donovan. 1988. "Scalpel Slaves Just Can't Quit." *Newsweek*, 11 January, pp. 58–59.
Fiske, John. 1987a. "British Cultural Studies and Television." In *Channels of Discourse*, ed. Robert C. Allen, 254–290. Chapel Hill: University of North Carolina Press.
———. 1986b. *Television Culture*. New York: Methuen.
Foucault, Michel. 1979. *Discipline and Punishment*. New York: Vintage.
Glanton, Dahleen. 1989. "Racism within a Race." *Syracuse Herald American*, 19 September.
Hite, Molly. 1988. "Writing—and Reading—the Body: Female Sexuality and Recent Feminist Fiction." *Feminist Studies* 14(1): 121–142.

Kaplan, E. Ann. 1983. "Is the Gaze Male?" In *Powers of Desire*, ed. Ann Snitow, Christine Stansell, and Sharon Thompson, 309–327. New York: Monthly Review Press.

———. 1987. *Rocking around the Clock: Music, Television, Postmodernism and Consumer Culture*. New York: Methuen.

Lizardi, Tina, and Martha Frankel. 1990. "Hand Job." *Details*, February, p. 38.

McClary, Susan. 1990. "Living to Tell: Madonna's Resurrection of the Fleshly." *Genders*, no. 7, pp. 1–22.

Powers, Retha. 1989. "Fat Is a Black Woman's Issue." *Essence*, October.

Rosen, Trix. 1983. *Strong and Sexy*. New York: Putnum.

Schwichtenberg, Cathy. 1990. "Postmodern Feminism and Madonna: Toward an Erotic Politics of the Female Body." Paper presented at the University of Utah Humanities Center, National Conference on "Rewriting the (Post)Modern: (Post)Colonialism/Feminism/Late Capitalism," 30–31 March.

Sessums, Kevin. 1990. "White Heat." *Vanity Fair*, April, p. 208.

Skow, John. 1985. "Madonna Rocks the Land." *Time*, 27 May, pp. 77, 81.

Suleiman, Susan Rubin. 1986. "(Re)Writing the Body: The Politics and Poetics of Female Eroticism." In *The Female Body in Western Culture*, ed. Susan Rubin Suleiman. Cambridge: Harvard University Press.

Texier, Catherine. 1990. "Have Women Surrendered in MTV's Battle of the Sexes?" *New York Times*, 22 April.

315

NOTES ON CONTRIBUTORS

Susan Bordo is a professor of philosophy and holds the Joseph C. Georg Chair at Le Moyne College. She is the author of *The Flight to Objectivity: Essays on Cartesianism and Culture* (SUNY Press, 1987) and the coeditor (with Alison Jaggar) of *Gender/Body/Knowledge: Feminist Reconstructions of Being and Knowing* (Rutgers University Press, 1989). Her latest book, *Unbearable Weight: Feminism, Western Culture, and the Body,* was published by the University of California Press in fall 1992.

Linda Boynton Arthur did her graduate work in sociology at the University of California, Davis. She has done extensive work analyzing the symbolic meaning of clothing among the Amish and Mennonites as well as university sororities. She has published one book and eighteen articles.

Mary Ann Clawson teaches sociology at Wesleyan University. Her book *Constructing Brotherhood: Class, Gender, and Fraternalism in Nineteenth-Century America* looked at the interaction of masculinity and class identity in all-male fraternal orders. Current work on gender and rock music extends her interest in varieties of masculine social organization.

Kathy Davis is an associate professor in women's studies at the Faculty of Social Sciences, University of Utrecht, in the Netherlands. She has studied and taught at various European universities since leaving the United States on a scholarship in 1971. Her publications are in the fields of feminist theory, medical sociology, and discourse analysis and include two books, *Power under the Microscope* (Foris Publications, Dordrecht,

1988) and *The Gender of Power* (with M. Leijenaar and J. Oldersma; Sage, 1991). She is currently working on a book about femininity and cosmetic surgery called *Re-shaping the Female Body,* to be published by Routledge.

SUE FISHER is an associate professor at Wesleyan University where she teaches in both the sociology department and the women's studies program. She is the author of *In the Patient's Best Interest: Women and the Politics of Medical Decision-Making* (Rutgers University Press, 1988), *Gender and Discourse: The Power of Talk* (with A. D. Todd; Ablex Publishing, 1988), *Discourse and Institutional Authority: Medicine, Education and Law* (with A. D. Todd; Ablex Publishing, 1986), and *The Social Organization of Doctor-Patient Communication* (with A. D. Todd; Center for Applied Linguistics, 1983; 2d ed., Ablex Publishing, 1992). Her chapter in this book is influenced by a book she is currently writing, *Caring Gone Public: The Negotiation of Identity in Provider-Patient Encounters* (Rutgers University Press, forthcoming).

LINDA GORDON is the Florence Kelley Professor of History at the University of Wisconsin–Madison. She received her Ph.D. from Yale in Russian history. She is author of *Woman's Body, Woman's Right: A History of Birth Control in America* (1976; 2d ed., 1990), *Heroes of Their Own Lives: The Politics and History of Family Violence* (1988), *Cossack Rebellions: Social Turmoil in the 16th Century Ukraine* (1983), and editor of *America's Working Women: A Documentary History* (1976) and *Women, the State, and Welfare* (1990). Her chapter in this volume is part of a larger project on the history of welfare in the United States; it is also influenced by a book she is writing with philosopher Nancy Fraser on contemporary welfare discourse.

NINA GREGG teaches communication and feminist theory in the Department of Communication at the University of Pittsburgh. She received a Ph.D. in communication from McGill University and was cochair (1990–1992) of the Feminist Scholarship Interest Group of the International Communication Association. Her current research project on blue-collar women's activism in response to loss of their jobs reflects her continuing interest in the politics of location and women's generation of meaning.

NORMA CLAIRE MORUZZI received her Ph.D. in political science from Johns Hopkins University in 1990. Her dissertation focused on the construction of the body in Hannah Arendt's political theory, and her sub-sequent work has been an exploration of the multiple layers of political identity connected with the politicization of Islamic women's veiling. She has taught at Towson State University and at the University of California at San Diego, and is currently an assistant professor in women's studies and political science at the University of Illinois at Chicago.

ELSPETH PROBYN teaches sociology of culture at the Université de Mon-tréal. She has published numerous articles on feminism, media analysis, postmodernism, the body, and the self in various journals and anthol-ogies, including *Cultural Studies, Communications, Hypatia, Feminism/ Postmodernism,* and *Body Invaders.* She is author of *Sexing the Self: Positions in Feminist Discourse* (Routledge, 1992) and editor of a special issue of *Sociologies et Sociétés* titled "Entre le corps et le soi: Une sociol-ogie de la subjectivation." She is currently preparing an anthology, *The Body in Question,* as well as a book, *Sexual Choiceoisie: Mapping Post-Feminism and New Traditionalism.*

ROB ROSENTHAL received his Ph.D. from the University of California at Santa Barbara in 1987. He is currently an assistant professor of sociology at Wesleyan University, specializing in urban and housing courses, and the director of Fuse Music. He has written frequently on homelessness, including *Homeless in Paradise: A Map of the Terrain* (Temple University Press, 1992).

ANN-LOUISE SHAPIRO is an associate professor of history at Wesleyan University where she teaches European history and women's studies. She has published *Housing the Poor of Paris, 1850–1902* and numerous ar-ticles on the meaning of female criminality in fin-de-siècle Paris. She is currently completing *Breaking the Codes: Interpretations of Female Criminality in Fin-de-Siècle Paris* and has edited a special issue of *History and Theory* on feminist theory and history.

ELIZABETH WILSON is the author of a number of books, including *Adorned in Dreams: Fashion and Modernity, The Sphinx in the City,* and *Prisons of Glass,* a novel. A second novel, a thriller, *The Lost Time Café,* will be published in 1993. She is a professor in the Faculty of En-vironmental and Social Studies at the University of North London, and lives in London with her partner and their daughter.